# Sensations, Th

MW01675456

Brian Loar (1939–2014) was an eminent and highly respected philosopher of mind and language. He was at the forefront of several different field-defining debates between the 1970s and the 2000s—from his earliest work on reducing semantics to psychology, through debates about reference, functionalism, externalism, and the nature of intentionality, to his most enduringly influential work on the explanatory gap between consciousness and neurons. Loar is widely credited with having developed the most comprehensive functionalist account of certain aspects of the mind, and his "phenomenal concept strategy" is arguably one of the most significant developments on the ancient mind/body problem.

This volume of essays honours the entirety of Loar's wide-ranging philosophical career. It features fifteen original essays from influential figures in the fields of philosophy of language and philosophy of mind, including those who worked with and were taught by Loar. The essays are divided into three thematic sections covering Loar's work in philosophy of language, especially the relations between semantics and psychology (1970s-80s), on content in the philosophy of mind (1980s-90s), and on the metaphysics of intentionality and consciousness (1990s and beyond). Taken together, this book is a fitting tribute to one of the leading minds of the latter-20th century, and a timely reflection on Loar's enduring influence on the philosophy of mind and language.

**Arthur Sullivan** is Associate Professor at Memorial University of Newfoundland, Canada. He works primarily in the Philosophy of Language, and in overlapping parts of Metaphysics, Epistemology, and Cognitive Science. He is the author of *Reference and Structure* (Routledge, 2013), *The Constitutive A Priori* (2018), and dozens of published articles.

## Routledge Festschrifts in Philosophy

**Mind, Language and Morality**
Essays in Honor of Mark Platts
*Edited by Gustavo Ortiz Millán and Juan Antonio Cruz Parcero*

**Sensations, Thoughts, Language**
Essays in Honor of Brian Loar
*Edited by Arthur Sullivan*

For more information about this series, please visit: www.routledge.com/Routledge-Festschrifts-in-Philosophy/book-series/RFSP

# Sensations, Thoughts, Language

## Essays in Honor of Brian Loar

Edited by Arthur Sullivan

Routledge
Taylor & Francis Group
LONDON AND NEW YORK

First published 2020 by Routledge

2 Park Square, Milton Park, Abingdon, Oxon OX14 4RN
605 Third Avenue, New York, NY 10017

*Routledge is an imprint of the Taylor & Francis Group, an informa business*

First issued in paperback 2022



Publisher's Note

The publisher has gone to great lengths to ensure the quality of this reprint but points out that some imperfections in the original copies may be apparent.

*Library of Congress Cataloging in Publication Data*
A catalog record for this book has been requested

ISBN: 978-1-138-49797-9 (hbk)
ISBN: 978-1-03-233790-6 (pbk)
DOI: 10.4324/9781351017435

Typeset in Sabon
by Apex CoVantage, LLC

# Contents

# Acknowledgements

Many people have helped with various aspects of this project, in lots of different little ways, over the past few years. In many cases, it was just genuine enthusiasm about the driving idea, which of course is ultimately attributed to Brian, but which definitely helped to steer this project through to completion. Thank you.

I am grateful to Biplab Halder, a graduate student research assistant at Memorial University, who did a lot of work on the production of this volume—always well done and on time. Most of all, huge thanks to Stephanie Beardman and Stephen Schiffer, for too many things to try to summarize.

# Introduction

*Arthur Sullivan*

Brian Loar (1939–2014) was an eminent and highly respected philosopher of mind and language. He was at the forefront of several different field-defining debates between the 1970s and the 2000s—from his earliest work within the Gricean program of reducing semantics to psychology, through debates about reference, functionalism, externalism, and the nature of intentionality, on into his most enduringly influential work on what has become known as "the phenomenal concept strategy" for understanding the explanatory gap between consciousness and neurophysiology. This volume of essays honours the entirety of Brian's wide-ranging philosophical career. It features 15 original essays from influential figures in the fields of philosophy of language and philosophy of mind, including some who were fellow students with Brian, some who worked alongside him, and some who were his students.[1]

Brian was born in Brooklyn and raised in Morristown, New Jersey. He received his B.Phil from Oxford in 1965, and then went on to write a D.Phil dissertation on "Sentence Meaning" at Magdalen College. His B.Phil supervisor was A.J. Ayer, though Brian has remarked that regular conversations with Peter Geach were the most valuable to him in his undergraduate years. The D.Phil thesis grew out of conversations with Paul Grice and Stephen Schiffer (both of whom remained lifelong friends). The "Acknowledgements" page on Brian's D.Phil dissertation also registers thanks to Peter Strawson, among others. So, Brian was at the center of the Oxford 1960s Philosophy scene, and it shaped his conception of the substance and methods of the discipline in a deep, enduring way. Brian established many important philosophical friendships there.

After Oxford, Brian taught briefly at the Universities of Calgary and Michigan, before moving to the University of Southern California in 1976. There he was a sustained, influential force in the rising fortunes of the department. Students and junior colleagues at USC remember Brian for being patient and encouraging, despite his well-earned reputation as a forceful debater. In 1994, Brian moved on to Rutgers University, where he was at the center of Rutgers' rise to the highest echelon of the philosophical world, and where he remained until his retirement. Adding to the wonderful ranks of the philosophers of mind already at Rutgers—Jerry Fodor, Stephen Stich, Francis Egan, Colin McGinn, Brian McLaughlin, among others—Brian Loar cemented Rutgers' place at the forefront of the field. It was a very special place to be, when I had the enormous good fortune to be a Visiting PhD student there in 1996 and 1997, under Brian's supervision.

Brian was universally respected and admired within the discipline. Across the years and across continents, many times I have gotten the awed reaction: "Wow! You studied with *Brian Loar*!" I have heard him characterized, several times by world-class experts, as among the very few, very best philosophical minds of the latter-20th century. In a way that is hard to put your finger on, exactly, Brian just seemed to do philosophy differently than others—"at another level" is an expression I have often heard used in attempts to describe what is unique about his work. He was a powerful and original thinker, who left a marked impression on those who saw him at work. To cite a few illustrative career highlights:

- Even though Brian is most widely known today for his work in the philosophy of mind, his body of work within the philosophy of language published in the 1970s is really quite scarcely paralleled—an even more impressive achievement, when we consider that the 1970s stands out, in the recent history of the discipline, for remarkable accomplishments in the philosophy of language. Recanati (Chapter 3) argues that (1972) "Reference and Propositional Attitudes" was underappreciated because it was ahead of its time; and Perry (Chapter 2) makes a similar case about (1976) "Semantics of Singular Terms". (1976) "Two Theories of Meaning" has also stood the test of time rather well. Schiffer (Chapter 4) calls it Brian's best paper in the philosophy of language—and in his above-mentioned Introduction to Loar (2017), Schiffer describes its "devastating objections" to Davidson's program, its "subtle marriage of Grice and Chomsky", and its attaining "as good an account of sentence meaning as a Gricean can hope to achieve".[2]
- (1981) *Mind & Meaning* (Cambridge University Press), a notoriously daunting and densely-packed book, is widely credited as having developed the most thorough and comprehensive functionalist account of the mind, ever.
- (1988) "Social Content and Psychological Content" is justly one of the most influential and widely cited papers from the semantic externalism debates of the late 20th century, for Brian's distinctive surgical assessment of exactly what should trouble a Fregean, from the arguments of Kripke, Putnam, and Burge.[3]
- Brian was among the first to explicitly bring the notion of "phenomenal intentionality" (i.e., a kind of intentionality that arises from the subjective, phenomenal content of conscious experience) to bear on certain late-20th century debates in the philosophy of mind; and the

program of building a general theory of intentionality upon this base has since gone viral. (Chapters 6, 7, 8, and 15 are all focused on Brian's work on this notion. Kriegel (Chapter 7) says that the basic idea occurs in (1987) "Subjective Intentionality", predating Brian's explicit coinage of the term by over a decade.)[4]

- Brian's "phenomenal concept strategy", developed throughout a series of papers beginning in 1990, is among the most significant recent developments on understanding the ancient mind/body problem. This original work of Brian's changed the philosophy of mind, and its legacy endures, as is attested by its impact on Chalmers' (2003) influential taxonomy of materialisms, as well as many of the papers collected below—especially Chapters 6, 12, 13, and 14, in which this strategy plays a central role.[5]

I only knew a small part of Brian, for a relatively short time. I can say, though, that it was truly an amazing experience to work through a philosophical problem with him, one on one. *What a mind!* In our personal dealings, he was unfailingly kind and generous, gracious and urbane. He remained a dependable, helpful mentor to me for years. I am very happy to be able to play a role in this tribute to such a wonderful person and important philosopher.

[§]

The papers are divided into three thematic sections, although a considerable degree of overlap is unavoidable. Part I is focused on Brian Loar's work in philosophy of language, and on the relations between semantics and psychology (1960s-80s), Part II on content in the philosophy of mind (1970s-90s), and Part III on the metaphysics of intentionality and consciousness (1980s and beyond). Taken together, this book is a fitting tribute to one of the leading minds of the latter-20th century, and a timely reflection on Brian Loar's enduring influence on the philosophy of language and mind.

The title is meant to span the range of Brian's core interests, sprawling from Oxford 1960s philosophy of language, through 1980s West Coast expeditions—from functionalism and externalism to subjective intentionality and phenomenal concepts—and on to Rutgers 1990s metaphysics of mind. It is also meant to evoke a constitutive (Gricean, physicalist) progression, from sensation to thought to language, which held constant, underlying these changes of focus from decade to decade. The title was suggested by Stephen Schiffer, and it thankfully replaced several earlier, fumbling variants on "Meaning and/or Mind and/or Consciousness".

[§]

**Part I** *Chapter 1, Daniel Harris, "Intention Recognition as the Mechanism of Human Communication":* This paper is a contemporary assessment of the Gricean "intentionalist program" of reducing semantic facts to psychological terms, to which Loar was one of the most important early contributors (along with Stephen Schiffer, David Lewis, and others). Harris reconsiders this program in light of significant developments within cognitive science and the philosophy of psychology. According to Harris, intentionalism should be taken not as a 20th-century style explication of "meaning", but rather to guide a current conception of the psychological mechanisms underlying linguistic communication. In this way, many valuable insights of these earlier intentionalists still have urgent relevance for the ongoing project of discerning the contours of the cognitive architecture underlying our capacity to communicate.

*Chapter 2, John Perry, "Loar, Donnellan, and Frege on Descriptions":* This paper is focused on the theory of reference developed in Loar's (1976) paper "The Semantics of Singular Terms". Loar's view is "Fregean" in that "the function of a singular term is to introduce an *individual concept* into what is meant or expressed on its particular uses". One of Loar's goals is to show how such a view can accommodate Donnellan's (1966) "referential"/ "attributive" distinction. Perry is generally sympathetic to Fregeanism, and is impressed and influenced by Loar's skillful treatment of some potential pitfalls. From that base, Perry explores two departures from Loar. One is an exegetical point of Frege scholarship, going back to the *Begriffsschrift* to motivate a different Fregean theory of reference. The second is methodological, urging a reorienting of semantics as focused on the notion of convention, as opposed to meaning.

*Chapter 3, François Recanati, "Modes of Presentation in Attitude Reports":* The point of departure for this paper is Loar's earliest published paper, (1972) "Reference and Propositional Attitudes". There Loar detects a conflation which befalls Quine's seminal (1956) work "Quantifiers and Propositional Attitudes"—namely, the distinction between *de re*/ *de dicto* attitudes does not exactly match up with the distinction between *de re*/ *de dicto* attitude reports (notwithstanding the significance of both distinctions, and despite their broad overlap over paradigm cases). Recanati explores, develops, and supports Loar's more discriminating alternative picture. He then goes on to argue that Loar's picture is not comprehensive enough, and to defend his own more refined alternative.

*Chapter 4, Stephen Schiffer, "Expression-Meaning and Vagueness":* This paper takes off from Loar's account of "expression-meaning", developed in his dissertation, and published in his (1976) paper "Two Theories of Meaning". In Schiffer's opinion, this account "is probably as good an account of expression-meaning as . . . can be achieved" within the intentionalist program. However, it was (understandably) an idealization which ignored vagueness, and vagueness has been extensively studied in the interim (by Schiffer among many others). Schiffer's guiding question is: can Loar's account of expression-meaning be revised to accommodate vagueness? What results is a discussion of vagueness, intention, context, and content, and the entire enterprise of compositional semantics itself, culminating in an edified pessimism on that guiding question.

*Chapter 5, Arthur Sullivan, "Limning the External Dimensions of Meaning":* This paper explores some characteristic distinctions in Loar's work between certain externalist theses about reference and truth conditions on the one hand, and on the other hand certain internalist theses about meaning and content. As Joe Levine points out in his review of Loar (2017) (in the online *Notre Dame Philosophical Reviews*) one of the threads running throughout Loar's career is the conviction that Frege's basic insight about content is compatible with a compelling insight underlying Kripke's, Putnam's, and Burge's externalism. This paper aims to explain how this all adds up, given, first, a distinction between externalism about reference and anti-individualism about content, and, second, some due caution with respect to how those notions relate differentially to different sub-categories of terms or concepts.

**Part II** *Chapter 6, David Bourget, "Relational vs. Adverbial Conceptions of Phenomenal Intentionality":* This is the first of three consecutive chapters dedicated to exploring and extending the "phenomenal intentionality" tradition, in which Loar's work plays a seminal role. Bourget's guiding question is whether phenomenal intentionality, contra Loar's own view, should be seen to have a relational structure of the sort envisaged in Russell's theory of acquaintance. Bourget gives three arguments in favor of a relational view, and defends it from a variety of objections. He also argues that this relational view is compatible with Loar's "phenomenal concept strategy".

*Chapter 7, Uriah Kriegel, "Phenomenal Intentionality and the Perception/Cognition Divide":* Proponents of phenomenal intentionality typically also endorse the idea of "cognitive phenomenology" (i.e., the phenomenal character of cognitive states such as thoughts and judgments grounds their intentionality). This combination creates a challenge, though: namely, how to account for the manifest phenomenological difference between perception and cognition. Kriegel's paper argues that there is no obvious account of this difference, articulating three plausible options and showing why none of them work. Kriegel concludes by considering the phenomenal-intentionalist's options moving forward.

*Chapter 8, Michelle Montague, "Cognitive Phenomenology, Sensory Phenomenology, and Rationality":* This paper is similarly focused on "cognitive phenomenology", and explores how that aspect of conscious thoughts relate to what Montague calls their "sensory-phenomenological" and their "rational" properties. Building on work from Loar's later papers, and contra arguments by Pautz (2013), Goff (2018), and others, Montague defends the thesis that while the sensory-phenomenological properties of conscious thoughts can float free from their intentional content, both their cognitive-phenomenological and rational properties are essentially connected to their intentional content.

*Chapter 9, David Pitt, "Loar's Compromised Internalism":* Turning from specific work on phenomenal intentionality to a more general assessment of a broader phase of Loar's later career, Pitt argues that Loar's internalism is not internalist enough. According to Pitt, if we take seriously the content and implications of Loar's insightful work on intentionality, phenomenology, and their constitutive interrelations, then the proper response to Burge's externalist arguments is not to accommodate them, as Loar sought to, but rather to show why they need not be accommodated. Pitt motivates the claim that Loar's theory of intentionality is ultimately compromised by an overly narrow view of the scope of phenomenology.

*Chapter 10, Mark Sainsbury, "Loar on Lemons: The Particularity of Perception and Singular Perceptual Content":* Sainsbury's paper is focused on questions about exactly what it is for perceptions to manifest particularity, and he defends the thesis that they do so in virtue of their having correctness conditions that stem from the causal relation that constitutes perceiving. This requires extensive exploration of relations between perceptual resources and discriminative (and other) abilities (and capacities). Loar's "rich and suggestive" discussion of the "lemons" cases in his (2003) "Phenomenal Intentionality as the Basis of Mental Content" plays a central role throughout this paper, though Sainsbury ends up in disagreement with Loar on some key issues pertaining to interrelations between intentionality and content.

*Chapter 11, Michael Tye, "The Sense of 'Looks'":* A tribute to Loar's work on the nature of phenomenal states within a physicalist metaphysics of mind, Tye's paper is focused on the questions: does the term "looks", as used perceptually, have multiple senses or a single one? What is its sense or senses? In some classic literature, both Chisholm (1957) and Jackson (1977) argue that there are three distinct senses of the term, though they disagree as to exactly how they should be characterized. Tye works through the interim literature on these questions. He ultimately defends the view that there is only one such sense, and draws out some pertinent consequences for certain aspects of the philosophy of mind.

**Part III** *Chapter 12, Katalin Balog, "Hard, Harder, Hardest":* Moving on to Loar's latest work on the metaphysics of consciousness, Balog's paper is a development and defense of the phenomenal concept strategy. Chalmers (1996) famously coined "the hard problem" of consciousness; Block (2002) goes on to distinguish "the harder problem" from that one. Balog adds a third progression in that series, and argues that the best available materials for a solution to all three can be found in the later works of Brian Loar. The paper is an ambitious, challenging discussion of the sense and the reference of phenomenal concepts, and of what their interrelations show about the explanatory gap.

*Chapter 13, Janet Levin, "'Phenomenal States' and the Scope of the Phenomenal Concepts Strategy":* This paper is addressed to evaluating how successful Loar's "phenomenal concept strategy" is, if framed as an attempt to genuinely accommodate some driving motivations for dualism, within an austere physicalist metaphysics. Levin argues that, by and large, and despite some residual protesting from dualists, the strategy does succeed. However, she goes on to argue that the strategy is more limited in scope than some might try to take it. In particular, she argues that the strategy is not really much help for certain questions about intentionality and reference.

*Chapter 14, Joseph Levine, "Phenomenal Concepts and the First-Person Perspective":* This paper is about potential tensions between some longstanding, core commitments in Loar's thought, namely: "physicalism about the mental; the existence of a first-person, narrow form of intentional content; and the absence of an a priori connection between descriptions of physical phenomena and mental phenomena". Loar's entire oeuvre may be seen as a subtle and rarified attempt to implement this difficult maneuver (i.e., first we make peace between Frege and Burge; then we delve into subjective intentionality and cognitive phenomenology; next we develop the phenomenal concepts strategy; and so on). Levine argues that, while the attempt is monumental, in the end, it doesn't ultimately work.

*Chapter 15, Georges Rey, "The Non-Primacy of Subjective Intentionality":* The final paper is focused on the legitimacy of Loar's conception of subjective intentionality, within a naturalistic philosophy of mind. While finding Loar's work on this notion subtle and imaginative, Rey is skeptical that the notion will serve the important explanatory role of intentionality in psychology, because it needs more objective bases. Rey suspects Loar felt driven to a subjective notion by his despair about any objective "reduction" of intentionality, but argues that such despair was premature, especially given the resources of functional definitions in an ultimate theoretical psychology, along lines that Loar himself had set out so well in his (1981) *Mind and Meaning*. The paper is a penetrating discussion of the metaphysical status of the first-person perspective, and of reductionism in the philosophy of mind.

## Notes

1. Thanks to Stephanie Beardman, Janet Levin, and Stephen Schiffer for help with this Introduction. I highly recommend Schiffer's "Introduction to Part I" from the posthumous collection of Brian's essays *Consciousness and Meaning: Selected Essays*. Oxford University Press, 2017, Balog & Beardman (Eds). It is a philosophical biography of the first few decades of Brian's career that could only have been written by such a lifelong good friend and fellow traveller through the debates.
2. (1972) "Reference and Propositional Attitudes". *Philosophical Review* (81): 43–62.

   (1976) "The Semantics of Singular Terms". *Philosophical Studies* (30): 353–377.

(1976) "Two Theories of Meaning". In Evans & McDowell (Eds.), *Truth and Meaning*, Oxford: Oxford University Press.

3. (1988) "Social Content and Psychological Content". In Grimm & Merrill (Eds.), *Contents of Thought*, University of Arizona Press.
4. (1987) "Subjective Intentionality". *Philosophical Topics* (15): 89–124.

(2003) "Phenomenal Intentionality as the Basis of Mental Content". In Hahn & Ramberg (Eds.), *Essays on the Philosophy of Tyler Burge*, Cambridge, MA: MIT Press.

5. (1990) "Phenomenal States". *Philosophical Perspectives* (4): 81–108.

Chalmers, D. (2003) "Consciousness and Its Place in Nature". In Stich & Warfield (Eds.), *Blackwell Guide to the Philosophy of Mind*.

# Part I

# Philosophy of Language, and Relations Between Semantics and Psychology

# 1 Intention Recognition as the Mechanism of Human Communication

*Daniel W. Harris*

## 1. The Intentionalist Program

My topic is a research program variously called "intentionalism", "Griceanism", and "intention-based semantics". Following Grice (1957, 1968, 1969), contributors to this program have sought to show how facts about meaning and communication boil down to facts about our psychology, with a special emphasis on our capacity for revealing and recognizing intentions.

The central claim of intentionalism is that what someone means when speaking or otherwise attempting to communicate is a matter of what they communicatively intend. An agent communicatively intends something when they make an utterance with the intention of having a certain effect on their addressee's mind, partly by way of revealing to them the intention to do so. Communication happens when the addressee recognizes what kind of effect the agent intends to have on them. An "utterance", in the sense at issue here, can be any overt behavior that serves as evidence of the agent's intentions, and needn't be verbal or linguistic. In the right circumstances, one can communicate via an idiosyncratic gesture, by making a U-Turn on one's scooter, or by any other observable action. What language adds to this picture is a powerful way of offering rich and systematic evidence of what one means.

In the work of Brian Loar and Stephen Schiffer, intentionalism became part of a research program whose explicit aim is to show how meaning fits into the natural order.[1] One thing that makes this a pressing issue is that the kind of communicating that we do—particularly, but not only, with language—is hard to come by elsewhere in nature. A few other species of animals are capable of formulaic noises, gestures, or dances that prompt their conspecifics to avoid threats and seize opportunities in their immediate environments. But their simple signaling systems are so much less powerful and flexible than the distinctively human variety that the latter almost certainly demands a *sui generis* explanation.

The quest to naturalize meaning would have seemed particularly pressing in the mid-20th century, when philosophy still suffered from the hangovers of behaviorism and positivism and when semantic vocabulary was met with distrust. Loar, Schiffer, and others conceived of intentionalism as part of a larger reductionist project: first use a broadly Gricean strategy to reduce facts about what words and sentences mean to facts about what speakers mean by them, then reduce facts about what speakers mean to facts about their psychological states, and then find some way to further reduce the needed parts of psychology to more basic domains—ultimately to physics.

My focus here will be on the part of this project that belongs to the philosophy of language. What are the prospects for a reductive explanation of the facts about human communication, including linguistic communication, in terms of intention recognition and related psychological capacities? In particular, how should this research program be updated in light of the theoretical and empirical resources now available?

## 2. Intentionalism and Explication

Understood as a reductive program, intentionalism seeks to explain higher-level phenomena to do with meaning in terms of lower-level phenomena to do with psychology and ultimately physics. How is this talk of "levels" and "explanation" to be understood?

Beginning with Grice, the central hypotheses of intentionalists have often taken the form of explications such as (1).

1. "*U* meant something by uttering *x*" is true iff, for some audience *A*, *U* uttered *x* intending

    (i) *A* to produce a particular response *r*
    (ii) *A* to think (recognize) that *U* intends (i)
    (iii) *A* to fulfill (i) on the basis of his fulfilment of (ii).

(Grice 1969, 151)

Although these explications are often stated with symmetric connectives like "iff" or "$=_{df}$", it is clear that something asymmetric is always intended. The schematic statements on the left are there to have light shed on them, and those to the right are there to do the shedding. The right is the *explicans* to the left's *explicandum*. The left is a high-level description of the same phenomenon that the right describes at a lower level.

What is the point of explication? One traditional answer is that explications offer analyses of concepts. On this view, (1) is an attempt to articulate what is already there in one of our ordinary concepts of meaning. It is an attempt to unpack the concept's underlying structure in terms of more fundamental concepts.

Some work in the intentionalist program—particularly most early work—makes sense only if we think of explication as something like conceptual analysis. Grice begins "Meaning" (1957) by distinguishing natural and non-natural meaning before subdividing the latter into timeless meaning and utterer's meaning. His method is to attend to subtle cues about our ordinary usage of "means" and its cognates. "I cannot say 'those spots meant measles, but he hadn't got measles'", Grice tells us, but one *can* say, "'Those three rings on the bell . . . mean that the bus is full' . . . and go on to say, 'but it isn't in fact full—the conductor has made a mistake'" (Grice 1957, 377–378). The "can" here is that of felicitous usage. As competent users of the English verb(s), "to mean", we are intended to knowingly agree. Grice goes on to offer a tentative explication for each kind of non-natural meaning. In later work, Grice and others would painstakingly hone these explications by means of the method of cases. Particularly when it came to utterer's meaning (a.k.a. "speaker meaning"), an enormous number of explications have been proposed, and each has been met with intuitive counterexamples.[2] These counterexamples take a standard form. A situation is presented in which someone meets the proposed criteria for utterer's meaning but intuitively fails to instantiate the concept under investigation (or vice versa). As Grice (1969, 155) puts one such *coup de grace*, "I do not think that one would want to say that *U* had meant something by throwing the banknote out of the window". Again, we are meant to nod along: the key premises of these arguments are judgments about how we, ordinary speakers, would use the word "mean". Given this methodology, in which an explication's success hangs on its accordance with ordinary usage, the aim of explication can only be to analyze our concepts or to spell out the meanings of our words.

This project is methodologically ill conceived. One reason for pessimism is inductive. Since Plato, philosophers have been trying very hard to give necessary-and-sufficient conditions for some concepts in terms of others in a way that stands up to intuitive scrutiny. So far, we have succeeded approximately zero times. This is not conclusive proof that the job can't be done, any more than the failures of alchemists prove that lead can't be made into gold. But it should not inspire confidence.[3] Another reason for pessimism arises from the broader goals of intentionalism. We seek to boil meaning down to psychology and ultimately to physics. But psychologists and physicists discover new things all the time, and they sometimes even engineer new concepts in which to frame these new things. Most of us therefore lack some of the concepts (and most of the truths) in terms of which statements about meaning would have to make their way down the conceptual hierarchy. Our intuitions about counterexamples cannot bear the epistemic load of this procedure.

By the early 1980s, we find Loar and Schiffer explicitly distancing themselves from conceptual analysis. Loar (1981, 41–43) tells us that "philosophical explication does not have to be seen as Moorean analysis", argues that it needn't "depend on any non-natural analyticity", and gestures at explication as a naturalistically respectable practice in the philosophy of science. According to Loar, the aim of an explication is to conservatively replace ordinary concepts with concepts capable of doing serious theoretical work.

Schiffer (1982, 120) is even more explicit about his methodological aims:

> Certain intention theoretical writings have, unwittingly, tended to foster the misleading impression that the program was an exercise in conceptual analysis, the aim and the end of which was the definition of various ordinary language semantical idioms in terms of certain complexes of propositional attitudes. . . . In fact, the program need have no truck with conceptual analysis. . . . The intention theorist seeks to reduce the having of content of marks and sounds to the having of content of psychological states.

How, then, to proceed? Schiffer retains his own earlier explications, but adorns the central terms of his explicanda with asterisks—"meaning*" instead of "meaning", and so on—in order to mark them out as technical terms rather than items from our ordinary vocabulary. We should understand the explications as "stipulative definitions" which "may not be realized" (1982, 123). Once thereby linked to lower-level claims, the top-level claims serve as empirical hypotheses about what people are doing when they speak. We all know that speakers mean things by their words. But do they also mean* things by their words, with all that that (stipulatively) entails? Schiffer's claim—an empirical hypothesis—is that they do.

This methodology is a clear improvement over the idea that intentionalism is a project in conceptual analysis. It allows us to be in the business of discovering the hidden underlying nature of meaning and communication, rather than merely reformulating what is supposedly already implicit in our conceptual schemes. It gives sense to the idea that our reductive project ultimately aims to recruit parts of science that most of us don't know much about. And it relieves us of the misguided task of testing explications against our intuitive judgments about cases.

Or, at least, it should. The Schiffer of the 1980s still appeals to our judgments about cases—for example, when arguing that Grice's explication of utterer's meaning works better as an explication of "telling" (Schiffer 1982, 121). There is also something fishy about the fact that his explications, presented in this new methodological context, are the very same explications that he'd painstakingly arrived at a decade earlier via the method of cases. Given our rejection of conceptual analysis and, with it, the central methodological role played by intuitive counterexamples, aren't these explications ill-gotten gains? Shouldn't we have to begin from scratch with careful, empirically-grounded theorizing about what kind of psychological states and processes explain our communicative capacities?

## 3. Intentionalism and Mechanistic Explanation

Latter-day intentionalists have mostly eschewed the explication-centric methodology of Grice, Loar, and Schiffer. In part, this is because the intentionalist program has migrated from philosophy into cognitive science. Some have focused on developing models of the cognitive processes by means of which humans recognize communicative intentions.[4] Some have investigated the processes by which we design our utterances to affect particular addressees' mental states.[5] Others have focused on the interrelated development of intention-recognition, communication, and language in children.[6] Still others have investigated the role of intention-recognition in the evolution of language and communication, in part through comparative study of human and non-human communication.[7] This work belongs to the intentionalist program. But its methodology differs from earlier work. One finds few explications in the style of (1), and even fewer intuition-driven counterexamples. In their place is a wide range of empirical considerations, all bearing on the extent to which our communicative capacities can be explained in terms of our underlying capacity for intention recognition. Although we are still dealing with a kind of reductive explanation, it is not of the kind pursued by Loar and Schiffer.

I think that we can make sense of this shift in the methodology of intentionalists by considering some recent work by philosophers of science on the nature of reductive explanation in the special sciences more generally.

Consider the model of inter-theoretic reduction that was, until recently, dominant in the philosophy of science. Suppose we have a high-level theory that is framed in a proprietary stock of predicates and we want to reduce it to a lower-level theory with its own predicates. To do this, we formulate *bridge principles* that, together with the laws of the low-level theory, entail the laws of the high-level theory (Nagel 1961, ch.11). These bridge principles take the form of biconditionals that connect the two theories' vocabularies. By thus reducing the high-level theory to the low-level theory, we explain the truth of the former in terms of the more fundamental and better-established truth of the latter.

A lesson of recent work in the philosophy of science is that although this sort of account may make sense of reductive explanations in physics—for example, the reduction of thermodynamics to statistical mechanics (Nagel 1961, 338–44)—it mischaracterizes the kinds of successful reductive explanations that one finds in biology, neuroscience, psychology, and other high-level special sciences. One big problem with the traditional model is that formulating predictive laws isn't among the central activities of these sciences, and so it is not possible to show how such laws stand in entailment relations to laws at higher or lower levels.

A wave of recent work has argued that the dominant form of reductive explanation in biology and related special sciences involves showing how processes at one level are explained by the activities of underlying *mechanisms* at lower levels.[8] Godfrey-Smith (2008, 54) summarizes recent thinking about this style of explanation as follows:

> When we look at successful reductionist research programs in areas like biology, we do see an accumulation of information about how various biologically important processes occur. We now have a good understanding of processes like photosynthesis, respiration, protein synthesis, the transmission of signals in the brain, the action of muscles, the immune response, and so on. This sort of work can reasonably be, and often is, described as reductionist. We are taking a high-level process or capacity, and explaining how it works in terms of lower-level mechanisms and entities.

In mechanistic explanations, relations between levels of explanation are part-whole relations rather than entailment relations. In molecular biology, for example, reductive explanation usually amounts to identifying the distinct physical parts of a larger system and showing how their chemical and mechanical activities add up to the activities and the system as a whole. To explain the transmission of chemical energy through synapses, for example, we identify the parts of neurons that contribute to this process and show how their activities contribute to the larger process in which they play a role (Machamer, Darden, and Craver 2000, 8–13).

More recently, the idea of mechanistic explanation has been extended to characterize reductive explanation in cognitive science.[9] In this context, the mechanisms in question may be subsystems that are individuated in terms of their information-processing roles within a larger system, rather than as physical parts of an entity (Bechtel 2008, ch.1). Still, it makes sense to explain the activities and capacities of a system in terms of the capacities, activities, and interactions of its subsystems. This is just the project of investigating human cognitive architecture, which has been a central task in cognitive science for decades.

My point in summarizing these methodological ideas is that I think that they should be self-consciously absorbed by the intentionalist program. Like the domains that have interested the new mechanists, our explananda are not well understood in terms of scientific laws or even well-organized theories. There are no laws of speaker meaning or communication. It is a bit strange even to say that we have a theory of these things that we are seeking to reduce. Even semantics, which is now a mature scientific research program, does not produce laws but a body of lexical semantic values and composition rules, mental representations of which are thought to play a causal role in language processing.

What intentionalism seeks to explain is the human capacity to communicate. Our method for doing this should be to study the systems and subsystems of the mind that are at work when we mean things by our utterances and work out the meanings of others' utterances. We should study how these systems work, how they collaborate, why they sometimes fail, how they evolved in our ancestors, and how they come online in children. In other words: we should study the nature and origins of the cognitive architecture underlying human communication.

This methodology is already embodied, if not explicitly avowed, in some of the cognitive-scientific contributions to intentionalism that I mentioned at the start of this section. There are even glimmers of it in some work of Grice, Loar, and Schiffer. I will point to some of these glimmers in §7, but I will also argue that they have tended to go undeveloped, in part because of an excessive and sometimes competing focus on explication. Although we needn't eschew explications entirely, I think that we should give them a secondary role in our theorizing.

Here is what I propose to do in the rest of this paper. First, in §4, I will outline an intentionalist answer to the question of what goes into our capacity to communicate. In §5, I will sketch a partial theory of the cognitive architecture underlying communication. In later sections, I will put these ideas to work, both by showing how they settle issues within the intentionalist program (§§6–7) and by showing how they dissolve certain objections to it (§8).

## 4. What Makes Up Our Capacity to Communicate?

What about us makes human communication so much more flexible and powerful than communication in other species? I will focus on three psychological capacities that together go a long way toward explaining what is unique about us. These are *mindreading*, *planning*, and *language*.

To mindread is to treat a part of the world as an agent and predict or infer its mental states. Humans have a uniquely powerful capacity and compulsion to mindread. We continually track the thoughts and motives of the people around us, and our go-to strategy for understanding their behavior is by reasoning about their states of mind. Mindreading has been one of the most intensively researched topics in cognitive science since the 1980s, spanning developmental and cognitive psychology, cognitive ethology, and the philosophy of psychology.

To identify a communicative intention is to engage in an advanced form of mindreading. It is to infer the intention as the best explanation of an utterer's behavior, in light of the utterance they've produced and whatever other background information may be available and relevant. Mindreading also plays a crucial role in the performance of communicative acts, since designing an effective utterance means predicting how it will impact the mind of one's addressee.

By planning, I mean the process of forming intentions and reasoning from those intentions together with one's beliefs to further intentions, all for the purposes of coordinating one's actions.[10] Planning has been a central topic in the philosophy of action since the seminal work of Bratman (1987), who emphasized that serving as the premises and conclusions of practical reasoning is central to the functional role of intentions.

One part of planning is conceiving of options and choosing between them by weighing preferences and emotional reactions. This is a process that decision theorists, psychologists, and neuroscientists have long studied. One of Bratman's central insights was to recognize that a theory of choice would capture only one narrow step in the planning process. This is because the way that an agent makes any given choice is constrained by the intentions they have formed as a result of prior practical reasoning. To choose is normally to select a subplan of one's prior plan, a way of implementing intentions that one already has. Intentions are relatively stable commitments that play a dual role of controlling action and constraining the options that must be considered in further practical reasoning. Planning is a way of overcoming our cognitive limitations by letting prior decisions lessen the burden of making further choices.

Our capacity for planning is part of our capacity for communication because communicative intentions function in the usual way as both the premises and conclusions of practical reasoning. Each communicative intention is itself a subplan of our other prior intentions, the result of practical reasoning about the proper means to our broader ends. If what I communicatively intend when I say "buy me a drink" is for you to form an intention to buy me a drink, I do so not for no reason, but presumably as a means to the end of getting a drink. Each communicative intention itself has the structure of a complex plan: my intention for you to recognize what kind of effect I intend to have on you is intended to be a partial means to the end of having that very effect. This is what sets communicative intentions apart from less cooperative ways of getting people to change what they believe and intend, and it is what allows us to use utterances that give evidence of our intentions as a means of realizing those very intentions.

Once a communicative intention is formed, it must serve as a premise in further reasoning about what kind of utterance to make. If you and I have a habit of buying each other drinks, I may be able to get my point across by simply pointing to the bar and miming the action of tilting a glass toward my lips. If I can't rely on this background, I might have to be more explicit: "How about if you get me an IPA for this round and I'll get the next?". Choosing between these and the many other possible ways of getting you to recognize my intended effect depends on fast and intelligent practical reasoning that draws on both my prior plans and what I know about you, including what I am able to infer about your actual and potential mental states.

What I have said so far applies to nonlinguistic as well as linguistic communication, which are both, at their core, driven by planning and mindreading. What distinguishes the two is that linguistic utterances are the product of a capacity that allows us to encode and decode powerful and highly structured evidence of our intentions. (I will say more about this in §5.)

The distinctive claim of intentionalism, as I conceive of it, is that intention recognition is the process at the core of distinctively human communication, and that language plays a subservient role when it is involved at all. The most explicit articulations of this claim in the literature have been due to Sperber and Wilson (1995, ch.1) and Scott-Phillips (2014, ch.1), who make the point by distinguishing two models of communication. In the "code model", a sender encodes some informational content in a signal and sends it through a transmission channel to a receiver, who decodes the signal to access the content. In the "ostensive-inferential" model, communication is a process in which the receiver must combine the evidence gleaned from the sender's utterance with other information at their disposal in order to infer the sender's intention. The two models may be combined when an encoding—decoding process subserves intention recognition. Following Sperber and Wilson, I claim that this is what is going on when we communicate with language: a speaker encodes evidence of what they communicatively intend in a linguistic utterance, but merely decoding this utterance is never sufficient on its own for successful communication; further inference is always required to identify the speaker's intention.

Intentionalism is usually associated with the idea that speaker meaning—and so, intention recognition—takes explanatory priority over linguistic meaning. There is a clear sense in which I agree with this claim: I think that linguistic processing always subserves intention recognition in human communication. This is a claim about the priority of one process over another in actual episodes of communication.

There are other priority claims that might interest us as well. Some have argued that language evolved to subserve communication by intention recognition, or that the biological function of language is to play this role.[11] Similarly, some have argued that mindreading plays a central role in certain aspects of language acquisition—a view on which at least some of the mechanisms underlying intention recognition are developmentally prior to the capacity for language.[12]

These are interesting claims, and if they turn out to be true, then they lend strong support to intentionalism. But I want to stress that intentionalism, as I have articulated it, does not entail these evolutionary or developmental claims, and can be true even if they are false. It could be that our language mechanism(s) evolved to play some non-communicative role but were later repurposed for communication. Likewise, it might be that the biological function of the mechanisms underlying our language capacity is not, or is not *only* to subserve communication, but that we routinely use it to communicate anyway. (By analogy, typing on a keyboard would not be the biological function of human fingers even in a near-future dystopia in which that's all we use them for.) Similarly, it could be that language acquisition is accomplished almost entirely by domain-specific mechanisms and does not recruit the mechanisms underlying intention-recognition. But this independence in acquisition is compatible with my claim that language subserves intention recognition in communication. So, although intentionalism has often been presented as having evolutionary and developmental components, and although I find those ideas to be interesting and worth pursuing, I wish to separate my central claim from them here.

## 5. Communication and Cognitive Architecture

How are our capacities for mindreading, planning, and language realized in our cognitive architecture? In previous work, I have defended a partial answer to this question that draws on a model of the mind originally developed by Fodor (1983). On Fodor's view, the mind is divided into one or more central-cognitive systems and an array of peripheral input-output systems that mediate between central cognition and our sensory systems (in perception) and motor systems (in action). These input-output systems, or modules, are set apart by a cluster of features: they are fast, automatic, domain-specific, functionally dissociable from other systems, and in some cases associated with specific brain areas or evolutionary origins. The trait that Fodor has most emphasized is that modules are informationally isolated from each other and from central cognition. Although they send outputs to and/or take inputs from central cognition, their internal processes are insensitive to beliefs and memories to which central-cognition has access. Instead, they draw on proprietary databases of information to which central-cognition in turn lacks access. This allows them to perform their tasks quickly and in a way that generally isn't under voluntary control. Because their informational resources are circumscribed, modular systems are amenable to computational modeling in a way that abstracts from other cognitive resources. This sort of computational modeling tends to be less effective when it comes to what Fodor thought of as central-cognitive systems, which are less restricted in the information on which they can draw.

One of Fodor's main examples of a modular input-output system is the language system. On Fodor's view, linguistic theory is the study of the databases on which linguistic processing draws, and psycholinguistics is the study of how these databases develop and are deployed in the perception and production of speech. In recent work, I have argued that the language system includes a semantic subsystem, and that our best current semantic theories should be understood as models of this subsystem's proprietary database of information, on which it draws in order to bridge the gap between syntactic representations to semantic representations in both the perception and production of utterances (Harris 2017, forthcoming).

In language perception, the inputs to semantic processing are LFs, which are the outputs of syntactic processing. The outputs of semantic processing, I claim, are incomplete representations of the communicatively intended effect associated with the sentence being perceived. When I hear someone utter "he lives in Montana", my semantic system outputs a representation of a property shared by beliefs that predicate living in Montana of some male individual. This representation is passed to the central-cognitive system responsible for mindreading, where it serves as partial and defeasible evidence of the kind of mental state that the speaker intended to put me in. In this case, my mindreading system would have to infer which male is being referred to, whether the speaker is being wholly literal, and, if not, what else they might mean.

In language production, the system responsible for planning sends instructions to the language system, which transforms these instructions into phonological representations of an utterance, which are then turned into motor instructions for the relevant articulatory system. I will refer to the instruction that the planning system sends to the language system as an *utterance plan*. I assume that utterance plans are themselves intentions. When one produces an utterance in order to communicate, one's utterance plan is itself a subplan of one's communicative intention. Language production has been much less studied than language perception, and there are difficult questions about how each step in this process works. I will bracket most of these questions here. In particular, it is unclear just what information is included in utterance plans.[13] Suffice it to say that utterance plans must include some information about the mental attitude and content of a mental state to be produced, as well as some other crucial information about an addressee and a context. For example, if the content to be communicated is about the addressee, then the language system will need this information so that it can select a second-person pronoun rather than a third-person pronoun in the appropriate position.

In brief, my argument for the modularity of semantics rests on explanatory inferences from four empirical premises.[14] First, contemporary semantics has had to painstakingly reverse engineer all that we know about expressions' semantic values and the principles by which they compose. The best explanation is that this information is inaccessible to central cognition, and so unsusceptible to introspection. Second, semanticists have had a lot of success with this project, and have been able to generate precise empirical predictions about sentence meanings from concise semantic theories. By contrast, we have no predictive theory of the processes underlying mindreading. The best explanation for this is that semantic processing, unlike central cognition, depends on an encapsulated body of information that can be concisely modeled. Third, our beliefs, desires, and intentions seem to have little impact on how we compose the meanings of the sentences we perceive. For example, strongly held false beliefs about semantics do nothing to interfere with one's semantic processing ability. The best explanation is that the information drawn on by semantic processing is largely sequestered from our beliefs and other central-cognitive states. Fourth, contemporary semantics tells us that the principles that guide semantic processing are framed in terms of concepts like *semantic type*, *numerical index*, and *assignment function*, but most competent speakers lack the ability to form beliefs and other central-cognitive representations in terms of these concepts. The best explanation of this is that the semantic module has its own proprietary conceptual repertoire, which only partially overlaps the conceptual repertoire of central cognition. These arguments give us a compelling reason to think that the body of information that underlies a speaker's semantic competence is cut off from their beliefs, intentions, and other central-cognitive representations, and that it is this body of information of which semantics is the study.

My position that semantic processing is subserved by a subsystem of a modular language system leaves open a range of positions about the cognitive architecture underlying mindreading and planning.

One possibility is that mindreading and planning are not the products of distinct subsystems at all, but are both grounded in a general-purpose central-cognitive system. Some have read this view into Fodor (1983), who points out that there seem to be no principled limits to the kinds of beliefs, intentions, or other central-cognitive representations that may, on occasion, factor into mindreading and planning. Some psychologists have likewise argued, mostly on developmental grounds, that mindreading is an application of our general-purpose cognitive capacity for theorizing about the world.[15]

On the other hand, some have found reasons other than informational isolation to posit specialized mindreading and planning systems. Unlike various other kinds of theoretical knowledge, mindreading is universal to cognitively unimpaired humans, develops on a relatively fixed and predictable schedule, and is selectively impaired in people with autism (Baron-Cohen, Leslie, and Frith 1985; Baron Cohen 1997) and in people with damage to certain brain areas (Rowe et al. 2001; Frith and Frith 1999). These considerations have led some to posit one or more innate, domain-specific mechanisms and/or bodies of knowledge underlying the mindreading capacity.[16] Some have argued on similar grounds that planning is the product of one or more dedicated cognitive mechanisms[17] And some have argued that the systems underlying planning and mindreading are deeply intertwined, on the grounds that mindreading recruits the planning system in order to simulate others' planning processes.[18]

Although I find some of the arguments for discrete systems underlying mindreading and planning persuasive, I won't take a stand on these issues here. I will sometimes speak of "the planning system" or "the mindreading system", but these phrases should be understood to be compatible with the possibility that mindreading and planning are performed by the same system, or by some perhaps-overlapping constellation of systems.

## 6. Semantics Doesn't Reduce to Propositional Attitudes

My position on the informational isolation of semantics is incompatible with the view that the semantic facts about natural language can be wholly explained by speakers' propositional attitudes—a view that has often been endorsed by intentionalists. This view is suggested, for example, by Grice's (1957, 385) original, albeit thoroughly hedged explication of utterance-type meaning:

> "$x$ means$_{NN}$ (timeless) that so-and-so" might as a first shot be equated with some statement or disjunction of statements about what "people" (vague) intend (with qualifications about "recognition") to effect by $x$.

Loar and Schiffer attempted to concretize Grice's proposal by combining it with Lewis's (1975, 1969) theory of linguistic convention, which itself explicates conventions in terms of participants' common knowledge about their regularities of belief and behavior. As a result, we find Loar and Schiffer saying things like this:[19]

> If we knew all the communicative intentions and other propositional attitudes of members of *P*, as well as their correlations with utterances of sentences of *L* within *P*, and if we had time enough and computational power for ideal reflection, we could then directly infer a priori that *L* is the language of *P*.
>
> (Loar (2001); reprinted in Loar [2017, 127])

> once we have decided on a scheme of attributing propositional attitudes to a population—and that is presupposed, in Lewis's theory and in mine, in assigning a language to a population—then there is a non-arbitrary way of selecting one grammar.
>
> (Loar 1976, 160)

Loar follows Lewis in taking a language to be a pairing of sentences with meanings and a grammar to be a finite specification of a language. If population members' propositional attitudes determine the language they use, then they also determine the meanings of all of the sentences of their language. And if their propositional attitudes determine the grammar that we should attribute to them, then all of the semantic properties of their language are thereby determined. But if semantics is the study of a semantic module, as I have claimed, then this is incorrect. The body of information that determines the semantic properties of the language I speak is not what I believe or know, but rather the proprietary database of a mechanism that plays a causal role in the interpretation and production of meaningful speech.

## 7. Explication Versus Explanation

Intentionalists have sometimes shown recognition of the phenomena that have led me to posit the modularity of semantics. Near the end of *Mind and Meaning*, Loar (1981, 259) argues that "the Chomskyan idea of the internalization of the generative procedures of a grammar has got to be invoked to make sense of the entrenchment of a grammar, and therefore to make sense of literal meaning" and goes on to say that "the exact force of this can't be spelled out antecedently to a detailed psycholinguistic theory". In saying these things, Loar stands at the edge of an empirically informed inquiry into the actual psychological underpinnings of our linguistic competence.

But he turns back. His top priority is to give necessary-and-sufficient conditions for the meaningfulness of expressions. And although what actually explains our semantic competence with a language may be certain contingent features of our psychological makeup, Loar judges that these aren't essential features of users of a language like ours. Two users of the same language could have different psychological makeups, he reasons. He therefore goes on to say that his view ultimately does not depend on "whether a psycholinguistic theory of such an adventurous kind is true" (Loar 1981, 260).

Elsewhere, Loar (1976, 158) spells out this line of thought more explicitly:

> There may be a Chomsky sense of knowledge—having an internal representation—in which a speaker knows the rules of his language, but that is a psychological hypothesis and, however reasonable it is, we do not want to build it into an *explication* of what it is for *L* to be the language of *P* Better that it should be offered, at a later stage, as an *explanation* of how it is possible for a complex entity like English to be the language of the population of English speakers.

I think that this passage helps us to see the downside of the traditional, explication-driven methodology. In the quest to give necessary-and-sufficient conditions that apply to all actual and possible users of a language, we are driven to prescind from more and more of the actual psychological details of how humans use language to communicate, since there *could* be creatures who outwardly use language like us but whose psychological inner-workings are different.[20] Explication and explanation become competing goals in a situation of this kind; achieving the former forces us to postpone the latter.

Indeed, Loar and (early) Schiffer don't prescind far enough. Their propositional-attitude-laden explications aren't even true of humans—or so I have argued. Something that abstracts even more from psychological detail is needed. Schiffer (2003, ch.3, 2006) addresses this problem in more recent work, where he argues that semantic competence is a matter of having *some* "information-processing state" that plays the "knowledge-of-meaning role". To play this role, a state must causally mediate between perception of an utterance and a belief that the speaker thereby performed a speech act with a certain kind of content and a certain kind of force. This is a role that could be played by propositional attitudes or, as I have argued, by an information-processing mechanism that is isolated from cognition. Grice (1968) formulates a similar proposal, on which the meaning of an utterance-type is explicated in terms of the "procedures" that language users have "in their repertoires" to use the expression with certain intentions. Grice does not say what it is to have this kind of procedure in one's repertoire, though nothing that he says rules out either a theory involving propositional attitudes or one involving an informationally isolated language system.

Here Schiffer and Grice prescind almost completely from psychological mechanisms. In so doing, they almost completely forsake explanation in favor of explication. In response to the question of how we comprehend speech, the accounts of Schiffer and Grice can tell us only that we possess *some* information-processing state or procedure for doing so.

In the traditional, Nagelian model of inter-theoretic reduction, explication (via bridge principles) is supposed to *yield* explanation by showing us how to reduce a less-established, high-level theory to a better-established, low-level theory. But because they take our linguistic capacities to be multiply realizable, Loar and Schiffer's quest for explication instead leads them away from explanation.

A common response to this kind of dilemma is to abandon the search for necessary-and-sufficient conditions and to settle for sufficient conditions instead. In place of explication-driven reduction, we could seek supervenience relations, grounding relations, or some other asymmetric dependence relation that holds between the semantic facts and the psychological facts that underlie them—in actual humans if not in some hypothetical behaviorally similar beings. In his last work on intentionalism, Loar (2001) makes this move, articulating a "minimal Gricean thesis" as follows: "Facts about speakers' intentions together with certain other psychological factors asymmetrically determine social meaning; the latter conceptually supervenes, asymmetrically, on the former" (Loar (2001); reprinted in (2017, 127)). Given my approach to intentionalism, I take it to be true that the semantic facts supervene on (and are grounded in) facts about human psychology. The interesting question is: *which* facts about human psychology? The best way to answer this question is to engage in the project of mechanistic explanation that I advocated in §3. The right supervenience (or grounding) claims will be little more than summaries of the results of this project.

## 8. Non-Communicative Language Use

I want to show how the methodology that I have recommended can help the intentionalist program to make some progress. To do this, I will consider the perennial objection that intentionalism fails to make sense of non-communicative uses of language.[21]

The objection usually takes the following form. Intentionalists tell us that to mean something by an utterance one must intend to change the mental state of an addressee. But we often use language—meaningfully, it seems—in ways that aren't naturally described in these terms. Wilson and Sperber (1988, 213) imagine someone saying, "please don't rain" while looking up at a cloudy sky, or muttering "start, damn you!" at their car. We often talk to our pets and babies, we practice speeches out loud, and we write in diaries. We speak or write with the aim of better articulating inchoate ideas rather than communicating them to others. We seem to engage in inner speech—a kind of thought that happens in the medium of natural language. These all look like non-communicative uses of language. In particular, these seem to be meaningful uses of language in the absence of communicative intentions.

The traditional intentionalist has a few options for how to respond, and needn't apply any one strategy to all cases.

We should sometimes say that the speaker *does* have the communicative intentions in question. When writing a diary, a speaker may intend to communicate with their future self. Confronted with someone who is talking to a cat or muttering at their car, it might be best to say that they are suffering from a momentary lapse of rationality: they are acting in ways that don't make sense given what they believe, as they would likely admit if pressed.[22]

In other cases, we should deny that the speaker really means anything. When practicing a speech one engages in pretense, which must be distinguished from genuine speaker meaning, just as practicing the footwork for a dance routine should be distinguished from dancing (cf. Grice (1969, 174)). When I am writing in order to clarify my thoughts or engaging in inner speech, I am engaged in a different-enough activity than when I am speaking to another person that it is unhelpful to group them together for theoretical purposes.

We should not be surprised if these defensive strategies don't satisfy all skeptics. They can seem ad hoc. For the skeptic who is still wedded to the method of cases, they may in some cases seem question-begging, since they deny intuitions that the skeptic brings to us as evidence. More importantly, these responses can be accused of missing the real force of some of the purported counterexamples. Traditional intentionalists can explain these cases away, but they offer us few positive resources to explain what people are up to in these cases, or why using language would be a good way to do it.

Some of these uses of language seem to pose threats to the basic assumptions of intentionalism—threats that the above responses don't seem to address. The idea that we use language to clarify our thoughts seems to entail that the content of one's utterance is sometimes more articulate than the intention one has in expressing it. But how could this be compatible with the claim that what one says is fully determined by what one intends in saying it? And we seem to be put into a vicious circle by the claim that we sometimes think in natural language together with the intentionalist claim that the meanings of natural-language expressions can be explained in terms of the contents of our thoughts.

Loar articulates a related worry:

> The strong thesis is then open to the reasonable objection that, intuitively, natural language meaning could be constituted independently of the use of language in communication. There are such phenomena as working out ideas on a word processor, thinking out loud in sentences, engaging in inner speech: can we not conceive of settings in which they stand on their own, independently of communication? And, more basically, there is the possibility that we normally think, at least in part, in a natural language, that our beliefs and intentions depend on having internalized some natural language, perhaps even in a way that is not typically phenomenologically available. I doubt that it can be argued persuasively on philosophical grounds that this makes no sense. It does not seem to be an obvious conceptual truth that such private meaningful uses of language would presuppose, even indirectly, communicative intentions or linguistic manifestations thereof. The strong Gricean thesis is not something I am inclined to defend.
>
> (Loar (2001); reprinted in (2017, 124–125))

This is not an objection to any particular Gricean explication. Rather, it is an objection to the whole intentionalist premise that the concepts of speaker meaning—and so, communicative intentions—will play an essential role in explaining semantic notions. The intentionalist's concepts are tailor-made to explain communicative uses of language. Loar raises the possibility that communication is just one use of language among many, and so does not deserve a privileged position in an explanation of how language works. In particular, since all of the uses of language that Loar mentions seemingly depend on the semantic properties of words and sentences, Loar's line of thought raises serious doubts for the idea that the semantic facts can ultimately be reduced to facts about the use of language to communicate, to the exclusion of facts about other uses of language.[23] This is one consideration that led Loar to abandon the version of intentionalism that he had previously defended and to fall back a weaker thesis that, he thought, "is perhaps not terribly exciting" (Loar 2017, 131).

These are serious objections, but I think that the methodological reorientation I have been urging puts us in a position to answer them.

Suppose we approach the problem with an eye toward the mechanisms underlying our linguistic capacities. Confronted with a non-communicative use of language, we must ask several questions. First, what is the point of using language in this way? What are we doing, and why? Second, how do we do it? In particular, what are the psychological mechanisms whose activities and interactions allow us to use language in this way? Thirdly, does our answer to the second question undermine the aims and claims of intentionalism? In particular, does it show that there are mechanisms underlying language use other than those that the intentionalist must posit to explain communicative language use? It is a problem for intentionalism if we can't explain how humans perform a certain linguistic activity in terms of the same mechanisms that intentionalists posit to explain linguistic communication. Otherwise, it's hard to see what this objection really amounts to.

## 9. Some Non-Communicative Uses of Language: A Sketch of an Intentionalist Account

Suppose that the picture of linguistic communication that I sketched in §§4–5 is correct. To communicate is to get an addressee to recognize one's intention to produce an effect in them. When we communicate linguistically, we make use of an informationally isolated language system to encode and decode evidence of our communicative intentions. When someone speaks, their language system takes input from their planning system and encodes a partial and defeasible representation of the mental state they intend to produce, then passes this representation along to a motor system, which turns it into an utterance. When someone perceives a linguistic utterance, their language system decodes from it a semantic representation, which they treat as a partial and defeasible piece of evidence about what kind of effect was intended by the utterance.

This makes it sound as though the language system is a special-purpose device for communicating with others. But note some things that I have *not* claimed: (i) that the only thing for which we use the language system is interpersonal communication; (ii) that the biological function of the language system is communication with others; or (iii) that the language system evolved for communication with others. Although I find the last two of these claims to be plausible, I don't want to commit myself to them here. I see no good reason to accept (i) and some good reasons to reject it. What I need, then, is an account of how a system that plays the communicative role that I have posited it to play can also play various other roles as well. There is nothing mysterious about this: a mechanism can do more than one thing. I normally use my oven to cook food, but I could also turn it on in order to warm up my kitchen. My infant daughter likes to use wooden spoons and measuring cups as bath toys. Similarly, I propose that the language mechanism, as I have already described it, can be used for purposes other than communication.

First, consider what goes into practicing a speech. In this case, my planning system sends the same kind of utterance plan to my language system that it would send if I were actually giving a speech, but it does this as a way of implementing a different kind of plan. When I am actually giving a speech, the utterance plan that my planning system sends to my language system is a subplan of a communicative intention. This utterance plan is the result of means-end reasoning about how to get my point across to my actual addressee (or group of addressees). When rehearsing a speech, I formulate an utterance plan as a subplan of a different kind of intention—an intention to pretend that I am giving a speech to a certain kind of audience. In this case, the representation of the audience that my planning system sends to my language system is a representation of a hypothetical audience that I've imagined up. It is probably a relatively indefinite representation, but this will also be the case when I give a speech to a roomful of people I don't know.

By sending practice speech through my language system in this way, it may be that I can prime my articulatory mechanisms for a smoother and more skillful delivery later on. I can also listen to my own speech, feeding the outputs of my language system back in as inputs. This may allow me to notice problems that were not apparent at the planning stage, and so adjust my utterance plan to be a better means to the communicative ends that I anticipate having later.

Feeding the outputs of my language system back in as inputs probably also has other uses. I write things down and then read them later as a way of storing information outside my head. In the much shorter term, I may remember a phone number long enough to get out a pen and a piece of paper by repeating it out loud to myself over and over. By feeding information back and forth through my language system in this way, I can use it as a form of short-term memory.

Suppose that we sometimes engage in a version of this activity that doesn't involve actually producing an utterance. When I speak, my language system creates a representation of the phonological properties of an utterance, which is then turned into instructions for my motor systems. Sometimes this last step gets suppressed, and the phonological representation is instead fed back into the language system as an input. This process would amount to a kind of inner speech used for short-term memory.

In fact, there is a large body of evidence that an inner-speech mechanism of this kind plays a role in short-term memory. This mechanism, which is sometimes called the "phonological loop" or "articulatory loop", was posited by Baddeley and Hitch (1974) as one component in their influential model of working memory.[24] According to this model, the phonological loop consists of a memory store and a mechanism for either vocal or subvocal rehearsal. The memory store fades quickly but can be refreshed by means of rehearsal. There is substantial evidence that subvocal rehearsal is performed by at least some of the same mechanisms that we use to produce utterances. Speaking out loud, even in a way that would not tax the memory store (such as repeating a single syllable), substantially interferes with verbal working-memory performance, for example (Murray 1968). There is also substantial evidence that the storage and rehearsal mechanisms deal, at least in part, in phonological representations rather than purely semantic representations.[25] Phonologically similar strings of letters, numbers, or words are more difficult to store in verbal working memory than phonologically dissimilar strings, for example—an interference effect that is usually explained by assuming that representations in verbal working memory are stored in a phonological format, at least in part (Conrad and Hull 1964; A. D. Baddeley 1966b, 1966a).

This line of thought suggests an explanation of how the language system, conceived as a modular input-output system along the lines I have defended, could serve a variety of non-communicative functions related to pretense, verbal practice, inner speech, and memory. Such an account requires only a couple of speculative hypotheses beyond what I have already defended. First, the utterance plans that the planning system sends as inputs to the language system are sometimes subplans of genuine communicative intentions, but are sometimes subplans of other kinds of intentions, such as the intention to pretend to communicate or the intention to hold something in memory for a short time. Second, inner speech depends on a capacity to intercept the outputs of the language system and feed them back in as inputs before they are turned into motor instructions, resulting in a use of language that Baddeley (2007) calls "subvocal-rehearsal". These hypotheses aren't obvious or uncontroversial, but they are plausible, and they dovetail with a venerable tradition of research on the role of linguistic processing in working memory.

What I have said so far does not on its own account for the puzzling ways in which we are able to clarify our thoughts by speaking out loud or writing things down. Why should sending my thoughts out through the language system and back in again be a way of making them clearer?

Here is a way of answering this question that requires only one further speculative hypothesis. Suppose that the instructions sent by planning systems to language systems are sometimes imprecise—the product of thoughts that are, in some sense, unclear. In particular, utterance plans of this kind aren't precise enough to fully determine what kind of utterance to produce. But suppose that the language system is adept at taking imprecise instructions of this kind and making more or less arbitrary choices about how to turn them into an utterance. It has to pick *some* words and arrange them into *some* syntactic structure, after all, and so it chooses options that are within the range of what is specified, without crashing when the utterance plan it has been given does not narrow the options all the way down.

If we grant this hypothesis, then we have the makings of an explanation of how linguistic rehearsal—subvocal, vocal, orthographic, or otherwise—could be a process by which we make our thoughts more precise. Suppose I have an unclear intentional state, $\sigma$. I form an intention to clarify $\sigma$ through speech, and this intention serves as a premise in means-end reasoning to an utterance plan of the kind that might otherwise be a subplan of a communicative intention to produce $\sigma$ in someone else. Because $\sigma$ is unclear, this utterance plan underspecifies the utterance to be produced, and so my language system must make some arbitrary choices in designing an output. This output then becomes an input, which my language system turns into a semantic representation—a partial specification of the kind of effect that someone would intend by using the words that my language system chose. In some cases, the result of this process will be a representation of a more precise mental state than I set out to clarify in the first place. And in *some* cases, I might even prefer this clearer mental state to the one with which I began and decide to adopt it as $\sigma$' s replacement. If iterated, this procedure could serve as a selection process by which we hone our thoughts over time.

This is just a sketch of the sort of process by which humans could use a modular language system to clarify their thoughts. This sketch also makes sense of at least one way in which humans could be said to think in language, either inwardly or outwardly. It is a process by which we may sometimes transition from one thought to another, sometimes improved thought. In some cases, the causal pathway of this process is wholly contained within our heads. In others, it follows a trajectory out through articulatory mechanisms and back in through sensory mechanisms. We can say these things without positing a language system that is any more flexible or elaborate than what I have posited to explain linguistic communication. We need only say that we sometimes take advantage of this system's processing capacities for purposes other than communication, and that we do so by sending it the usual sorts of instructions—albeit sometimes less-than-fully-clear ones—but for non-communicative reasons.

Of course, the story I have just told *is* speculative. In particular, a good deal more needs to be said about what it is for one thought to be clearer than another. Although having an unclear thought and clarifying it is something that most of us would say that we regularly do—I am doing it right now!—it is an under-theorized idea.

Still, my aim in sketching this hypothesis has not been to defend it in any detail. I have presented it as an example of how the mechanistic reorientation that I proposed in §3 and implemented in §§4–5 can yield new explanatory resources that give us fresh ways of thinking about old problems. The hypothesis I have offered is promising and deserves to be fleshed out and empirically investigated. It suggests a way of making progress on an issue that has dogged the intentionalist program for over half a century. I, for one, will be pursuing it in future work.

## 10. Conclusions

I have argued that intentionalism should be pursued as a project in mechanistic explanation rather than as a project in explication. Thus conceived, the research program belongs to interdisciplinary cognitive science rather than to philosophical analysis. Its principal aim is to discern the contours of the cognitive architecture underlying our capacity to communicate, rather than to formulate necessary-and-sufficient conditions for statements about actual and possible communicators.

This methodological reorientation has several advantages. It allows us to turn away from the fruitless pursuit of conceptual analyses and from a quest for necessary-and-sufficient conditions that has led to ever greater abstraction at the expense of explanatory ambition. It puts the intentionalist program in contact with theoretical resources from linguistics, the philosophy of action, and cognitive science that allow us to formulate empirical claims that can be tested and iterated. And it dissolves some objections that have perennially dogged intentionalism, such as the problem of non-communicative language use. Instead of clashing intuitions or a downward spiral of counterexamples, we are left with a scientific research program.

As I suggested in §3, I think that this reorientation has been underway among some intentionalists since the 1980s. At the same time, it remains common to encounter new proposed explications of speaker meaning and new intuitive counterexamples to these proposals. I hope that by explicitly describing and defending my proposed methodological reorientation, I can help us to move toward the future of the intentionalist research program while learning from its past.

## Acknowledgements

I am grateful to Eric Mandelbaum, Gary Ostertag, and Elmar Unnsteinsson for comments on an earlier draft.

## Notes

1. In particular, see (Loar 1972, 1976, 1981, 2001) and (Schiffer 1972, 1981, 1982, 1993, 2003, 2006).
2. See, especially, (Grice 1957, 1969; Strawson 1964; Schiffer 1972; Neale 1992; Davis 1992, 2003; Sperber and Wilson 2015; Bach and Harnish 1979).
3. Both this point and the snark accompanying it are unoriginal; for more of both, see Fodor (1981, 1998, chs.3–4). The ur-source of skepticism about analysis is Quine (1951).
4. (Sperber and Wilson 1995, 2002; Carston 2002; Wilson and Sperber 2012; Csibra 2010; Keysar 2007).
5. (Clark 1996; Clark and Marshall 1981; Clark and Carlson 1982; Clark and Schaefer 1987; Brennan and Hanna 2009).
6. (Csibra 2010; Hacquard and Lidz 2018; Bloom 2000; Tomasello 2003).
7. (Scott-Phillips 2014; Tomasello 2008; Sperber 2000; Moore 2015).

8. See, e.g. (Machamer, Darden, and Craver 2000; Godfrey-Smith 2008; Bechtel 2008; Bechtel and Abrahamsen 2005; Bechtel and Richardson 1993).
9. E.g. (Bechtel 2008; Godfrey-Smith 2008; Piccinini and Craver 2011). There are, of course, many more-or-less methodologically self-conscious precursors to this approach to cognitive science, and that is part of the new mechanists' point.
10. I use "plan" and "intention" more or less interchangably, but I take "plan" to have the connotation of complexity. As Bratman puts it, "intentions are, so to speak, the building blocks of . . . plans, and plans are intentions writ large" (1987, 8).
11. See, e.g., (Scott-Phillips 2014; Tomasello 2008). For criticisms of these views, see (Chomsky 1976; Bar-On 2013; Hauser, Chomsky, and Fitch 2002).
12. See, e.g., (Bloom 2000; Hacquard and Lidz 2018; Tomasello 2003).
13. I consider the issue in (slightly) more detail in (Harris 2017).
14. For more detailed versions of these arguments and what I take to be their consequences, see (Harris n.d., 2017).
15. (Perner 1991; Wellman 1990; Gopnik and Meltzoff 1997).
16. (Leslie 1987, 1994; Leslie, German, and Polizzi 2005; Scholl and Leslie 1999, 2001; Fodor 1992; Carey 2009; Baron-Cohen, Leslie, and Frith 1985; Baron Cohen 1997; Frith and Frith 1999; Carruthers 2006).
17. E.g. (Carruthers 2004, 2006).
18. (Heal 1986; Gordon 1986, 2009; Goldman 1995, 2006).
19. See also Loar (1972, 1976, 1981, 2001) and Schiffer (1972, 1982, 1993).
20. I confess that I did the same in my dissertation (Harris 2014, chs.4–5).
21. Some influential versions of this objection include those by Chomsky (1976, 55–77) and Carruthers (1996, ch.3). The objection is also one that tends to come up a lot outside print.
22. The human tendency to anthropomorphize inanimate objects is an active topic of psychological research. We tend to anthropomorphize objects when they violate our expectations, including when they malfunction (Epley, Waytz, and Cacioppo 2007). Mandelbaum and Ripley (2012, 364) argue, for example, that we are much more likely to anthropomorphize a car if it doesn't work well. It is a relatively straightforward prediction of intentionalism that phenomena that cause us to anthropomorphize a non-agent will also make us more likely to direct utterances to it.
23. See also Chomsky (1976, 55ff.).
24. For a recent overview of this model of working memory and the evidence that supports it, see (Baddeley 2007).
25. Following Baddeley (2007, 8), my use of "phonological" is not meant to invoke any particular theoretical claims, including those of mainstream phonology. Rather, it is meant to capture the idea that phonological representations include information relevant to articulation in a verbal medium. Others sometimes use the term "phonetic", "acoustic", or "articulatory" instead.

## References

Bach, Kent, and Robert M. Harnish. 1979. *Linguistic Communication and Speech Acts*. Cambridge, MA: MIT Press.

Baddeley, Alan. 2007. *Working Memory, Thought, and Action*. Oxford, UK: Oxford University Press.

Baddeley, Alan D. 1966a. "Short-Term Memory for Word Sequences as a Function of Acoustic, Semantic and Formal Similarity." *Quarterly Journal of Experimental Psychology* 18: 362–365.

———. 1966b. "The Influence of Acoustic and Semantic Similarity on Long-Term Memory for Word Sequences." *Quarterly Journal of Experimental Psychology* 18: 302–309.

Baddeley, Alan D., and Graham Hitch. 1974. "Working Memory." *Psychology of Learning and Motivation* 8: 47–89.

Bar-On, Dorit. 2013. "Origins of Meaning: Must We 'Go Gricean'?" *Mind and Language* 28(3): 342–375.

Baron Cohen, Simon. 1997. *Mindblindness: An Essay on Autism and Theory of Mind*. Cambridge, MA: MIT Press.

Baron-Cohen, Simon, Alan M. Leslie, and Uta Frith. 1985. "Does the Autistic Child Have a 'Theory of Mind'?" *Cognition* 21: 37–46.

Bechtel, William. 2008. *Mental Mechanisms*. New York; London: Routledge.

Bechtel, William, and Adele Abrahamsen. 2005. "Explanation: A Mechanist Alternative." *Studies in History and Philosophy of Biological and Biomedical Sciences* 36: 421–441.

Bechtel, William, and Robert C. Richardson. 1993. *Discovering Complexity: Decomposition and Localization as Strategies in Scientific Research*. Princeton, NJ: Princeton University Press.

Bloom, Paul. 2000. *How Children Learn the Meanings of Words*. Cambridge, MA: MIT Press.

Bratman, Michael. 1987. *Intention, Plans, and Practical Reason*. Cambridge, MA: Harvard University Press.

Brennan, Susan E., and Joy E. Hanna. 2009. "Partner-Specific Adaptation in Dialog." *Topics in Cognitive Science* 1: 274–291.

Carey, Susan. 2009. *The Origin of Concepts*. Oxford: Oxford University Press.

Carruthers, Peter. 1996. *Language, Thought, and Consciousness: An Essay in Philosophical Psychology*. Cambridge, UK: Cambridge University Press.

———. 2004. "Practical Reasoning in a Modular Mind." *Mind & Language* 19(3): 259–278.

———. 2006. *The Architecture of Mind: Massive Modularity and the Flexibility of Thought*. Oxford: Oxford University Press.

Carston, Robyn. 2002. *Thoughts and Utterances: The Pragmatics of Explicit Communication*. Oxford: Blackwell.

Chomsky, Noam. 1976. *Reflections on Language*. Middlesex: Temple Smith.

Clark, Herbert H. 1996. *Using Language*. Cambridge, UK: Cambridge University Press.

Clark, Herbert H., and Thomas B. Carlson. 1982. "Hearers and Speech Acts." *Language* 58(2): 332–373.

Clark, Herbert H., and Catherine R. Marshall. 1981. "Definite Reference and Mutual Knowledge." In *Elements of Discourse Understanding*, edited by A. K. Joshi, B. L. Webber, and I. A. Sag, 10–63. Cambridge, UK: Cambridge University Press.

Clark, Herbert H., and Edward F. Schaefer. 1987. "Concealing One's Meaning from Overhearers." *Journal of Memory and Language* 26: 209–225.

Conrad, R., and A. J. Hull. 1964. "Information, Acoustic Confusion and Memory Span." *British Journal of Psychology* 55: 429–432.

Csibra, Gergely. 2010. "Recognizing Communicative Intentions in Infancy." *Mind and Language* 25(2): 141–168.

Davis, Wayne. 1992. "Speaker Meaning." *Linguistics and Philosophy* 15(3): 223–253.

———. 2003. *Meaning, Expression, and Thought*. Cambridge: Cambridge University Press.

Epley, Nicholas, Adam Waytz, and John T. Cacioppo. 2007. "On Seeing Human: A Three-Factor Theory of Anthropomorphism." *Psychological Review* 114(4): 864–886.

Fodor, Jerry A. 1981. "The Present Status of the Innateness Controversy." In *RePresentations: Philosophical Essays on the Foundations of Cognitive Science*, 257–316. Sussex: Harvester.

———. 1983. *The Modularity of Mind*. Cambridge, MA: MIT Press.

———. 1992. "A Theory of the Child's Theory of Mind." *Cognition* 44: 283–296.

———. 1998. *Concepts: Where Cognitive Science Went Wrong*. Oxford: Oxford University Press.

Frith, Chris D., and Uta Frith. 1999. "Interacting Minds: A Biological Basis." *Science* 286: 1692–1695.

Godfrey-Smith, Peter. 2008. "Reduction in Real Life." In *Being Reduced: New Essays on Reduction, Explanation, and Causation*, edited by Jakob Hohwy and Jesper Kallestrup, 52–74. Oxford: Oxford University Press.

Goldman, Alvin. 1995. "In Defense of the Simulation Theory." In *Folk Psychology*, 191–206. Oxford, UK: Blackwell.

———. 2006. *Simulating Minds*. Oxford, UK: Oxford University Press.

Gopnik, Alison, and Andrew Meltzoff. 1997. *Words, Thoughts, and Theories*. Cambridge, MA: MIT Press.

Gordon, Robert M. 1986. "Folk Psychology as Simulation." *Mind & Language* 1: 158–171.

———. 2009. "Folk Psychology as Mental Simulation." In *Stanford Encyclopedia of Philosophy (Fall 2009 Edition)*, edited by Edward N. Zalta.

Grice, H. P. 1957. "Meaning." *The Philosophical Review* 66(3): 377–388.

———. 1968. "Utterer's Meaning, Sentence-Meaning, and Word-Meaning." *Foundations of Language* 4(3): 225–242.

———. 1969. "Utterer's Meaning and Intention." *The Philosophical Review* 78(2): 147–177.

Hacquard, Valentine, and Jeffrey Lidz. 2018. "Children's Attitude Problems: Bootstrapping Verb Meaning from Syntax and Pragmatics." *Mind & Language* online first: 1–24.

Harris, Daniel W. 2014. *Speech Act Theoretic Semantics*. PhD Dissertation, City University of New York Graduate Center.

———. 2017. "Speaker Reference and Cognitive Architecture." *Croatian Journal of Philosophy* 17(3): 319–349.

———. forthcoming. "Semantics Without Semantic Content." *Mind & Language*.

Hauser, Marc D., Noam Chomsky, and W. Tecumseh Fitch. 2002. "The Faculty of Language: What Is It, Who Has It, and How Did It Evolve?" *Science* 298: 1569–1579.

Heal, Jane. 1986. "Replication and Functionalism." In *Language, Mind, and Logic*, edited by Jeremy Butterfield, 135–150. Cambridge, UK: Cambridge University Press.

Keysar, Boaz. 2007. "Communication and Miscommunication: The Role of Egocentric Processes." *Intercultural Pragmatics* 4(1): 71–84.

Leslie, Alan M. 1987. "Pretense and Representation: The Origins of 'Theory of Mind'." *Psychological Review* 94: 412–426.

———. 1994. "ToMM, to by and Agency: Core Architecture and Domain Specificity." In *Mapping the Mind*, edited by L. Hirschfeld and S. Gelman, 119–148. Cambridge: Cambridge University Press.

Leslie, Alan M., Tim P. German, and Pamela Polizzi. 2005. "Belief-Desire Reasoning as a Process of Selection." *Cognitive Psychology* 50(1): 45–85.

Lewis, David K. 1969. *Convention: A Philosophical Study*. Cambridge, MA: Harvard University Press.

———. 1975. "Languages and Language." *Minnesota Studies in the Philosophy of Science* 7: 3–35.

Loar, Brian. 1972. *Sentence Meaning*. PhD Thesis, Oxford.

———. 1976. "Two Theories of Meaning." In *Truth and Meaning: Essays in Semantics*, edited by Gareth Evans and John McDowell, 138–161. Oxford, UK: Oxford University Press.

———. 1981. *Mind and Meaning*. Cambridge, UK: Cambridge University Press.

———. 2001. "The Supervenience of Social Meaning on Speaker's Meaning." In *Paul Grice's Heritage*, edited by Giovanna Cosenza. Turnhout, Belgium: Brepols.

———. 2017. *Consciousness and Meaning: Selected Essays*. Oxford, UK: Oxford University Press.

Machamer, Peter, Lindley Darden, and Carl F. Craver. 2000. "Thinking about Mechanisms." *Philosophy of Science* 67(1): 1–25.

Mandelbaum, Eric, and David Ripley. 2012. "Explaining the Abstract/Concrete Paradoxes in Moral Psychology: The Nbar Hypothesis." *Review of Philosophy and Psychology* 3(3): 351–368.

Moore, Richard. 2015. "Meaning and Ostension in Great Ape Gestural Communication." *Animal Cognition* 19(1): 223–231.

Murray, D. J. 1968. "Articulation and Acoustic Confusability in Short-Term Memory." *Journal of Experimental Psychology* 78: 679–684.

Nagel, Ernest. 1961. *The Structure of Science: Problems in the Logic of Scientific Explanation*. New York, Chicago, San Francisco, Atlanta: Harcourt, Brace & World, Inc.

Neale, Stephen. 1992. "Paul Grice and the Philosophy of Language." *Linguistics and Philosophy* 15: 509–559.

Perner, Josef. 1991. *Understanding the Representational Mind*. Cambridge, MA: MIT Press.

Piccinini, Gualtiero, and Carl Craver. 2011. "Integrating Psychology and Neuroscience: Functional Analyses as Mechanism Sketches." *Synthese* 183(3): 283–311.

Quine, W. V. O. 1951. "Two Dogmas of Empiricism." *The Philosophical Review* 60(1): 20–43.

Rowe, Andrea D., Peter R. Bullock, Charles E. Polkey, and Robin G. Morris. 2001. "'Theory of Mind' Impairments and Their Relationship to Executive Functioning Following Frontal Lobe Excisions." *Brain* 124: 600–616.

Schiffer, Stephen. 1972. *Meaning*. Oxford: Oxford University Press.

———. 1981. "Indexicals and the Theory of Reference." *Synthese* 49(1): 43–100.

———. 1982. "Intention-Based Semantics." *Notre Dame Journal of Formal Logic* 23(2): 119–156.

———. 1993. "Actual-Language Relations." *Philosophical Perspectives* 7: 231–258.

———. 2003. *The Things We Mean*. Oxford: Oxford University Press.

———. 2006. "Two Perspectives on Knowledge of Language." *Philosophical Perspectives* 16: 275–287.
Scholl, Brian J., and Alan M. Leslie. 1999. "Modularity, Development, and 'Theory of Mind'." *Mind & Language* 14: 131–153.
———. 2001. "Minds, Modules, and Meta-Analysis." *Child Development* 72(3): 696–701.
Scott-Phillips, Thom. 2014. *Speaking Our Minds: Why Human Communication Is Different, and How Language Evolved to Make It Special.* Basingstoke: Palgrave Macmillan.
Sperber, Dan. 2000. "Metarepresentations in an Evolutionary Perspective." In *Metarepresentations: A Multidisciplinary Perspective*, edited by Dan Sperber, 117–137. Oxford: Oxford University Press.
Sperber, Dan, and Deirdre Wilson. 1995. *Relevance: Communication and Cognition.* 2nd ed. Oxford: Blackwell.
———. 2002. "Pragmatics, Modularity, and Mindreading." *Mind and Language* 17: 3–23.
———. 2015. "Beyond Speaker Meaning." *Croatian Journal of Philosophy* 15(44): 117–150.
Strawson, P. F. 1964. "Intention and Convention in Speech Acts." *The Philosophical Review* 73(4): 439–460.
Tomasello, Michael. 2003. *Constructing a Language.* Cambridge, MA: Harvard University Press.
———. 2008. *Origins of Human Communication.* Cambridge, MA: MIT Press.
Wellman, Henry M. 1990. *The Child's Theory of Mind.* Cambridge, MA: MIT Press.
Wilson, Deirdre, and Dan Sperber. 1988. "Mood and the Analysis of Non-Declarative Sentences." In *Human Agency: Language, Duty, and Value*, edited by Jonathan Dancy, J. M. E. Moravcsik, and C. C. W. Taylor, 210–229. Stanford, CA: Stanford University Press.
———. 2012. *Meaning and Relevance.* Cambridge: Cambridge University Press.

# 2 Loar, Donnellan, and Frege on Descriptions

*John Perry*

## 1. Introduction

In this essay I discuss the theory of reference Brian Loar explains and defends in his 1976 essay, "The Semantics of Singular Terms". Loar defends what he calls a "Fregean view" of reference against two of the early classics of what I will call "referentialism", Saul Kripke's "Naming and Necessity"(1980) and Keith Donnellan's "Reference and Definite Descriptions"(1966). I was fascinated Loar's defense of a Fregean theory when it appeared, and have taken this occasion to return to thinking about his essay. I focus on Loar, Donnellan and Frege, and pretty much ignore later work: Loar's, my own, and that of many other people.

According to Loar, on the Fregean view "the function of a singular term is to introduce an *individual concept* into what is meant or expressed on its particular uses." The referentialist attack rests on cases involving proper names and definite descriptions used "referentially", in which it seems no individual concept is part of what is meant or expressed.

I will focus on definite descriptions. I first remind the reader of Donellan's distinction, explain what Loar says about it, with most of which I agree. Then I express one rather important reservation. I then look at Frege's theory of descriptions. I argue that we can find, in Frege's views, the basis of a variant theory that is an improvement on the one Frege himself provides. We have to combine views Frege held at different times into a single framework. This variant accommodates Loar's insights and Donnellan's distinction.

## 2. Donnellan's Distinction

Donnellan explains his distinction between referential and attributive uses of descriptions with this example. Someone comes across the body of Smith, whom everyone liked, brutally murdered. Without having any idea who did the foul deed she exclaims "The murderer of Smith is insane. That's an *attributive use* of "The murderer of Smith". What is meant basically accords with Russell's analysis: there is a unique person who murdered Smith, and that person is insane.

Now it's later. Jones has been charged with the murder; the evidence is overwhelming. In the courtroom, Jones behaves very oddly. An observer of the trial says, "The murderer of Smith murderer is insane", intending to refer to Jones, to say what they could have said with "Jones is insane". In this case, ". . . the description is simply a means of identifying the person we want to talk about". The description is not essential to saying what we want to say, as it is in the attributive case. In fact, according to Donnellan, we could use "Smith's murderer is insane" to say that Jones is insane, even if Jones were not, in fact the murderer. In that case,

> Jones might . . . accuse us of saying false things about him in calling him insane, and it would be no defense . . . that our description, "the murderer of Smith" failed to fit him.
>
> (Donnellan, 1966, p. 286)

In the original article, Donnellan says that he is not sure whether the distinction is semantic or pragmatic. In his reply to Kripke's (1977) analysis of the distinction, he comes down on the semantic side (Donnellan, 1978).

On a natural semantic interpretation, the two uses involve the expression of different propositions. As Loar says, on this view,

> It is held that to specify the semantical content—the possible worlds truth conditions—of a referential utterance one must specify the referent itself, and that no corresponding individual concept is essential thereto. Hence the semantical content of a referential utterance of "*t* is *G*" is, in an abstract way, identified with the ordered pair <G,x>, where *G* is the predicated property and *x* is the referent to *t*. But on other uses of singular terms—the ones, roughly, which Donnellan calls *attributive*—no particular is essential to content, for one means that the *F*, whatever it may be, is *G*. In assessing the possible world truth conditions of attributive uses, unlike referential uses, no individual of this world is carried through other world.
>
> (355–56)

That is, in terms becoming current when Loar wrote, "The murderer of Smith is insane" expresses a *singular proposition* with Jones is a constituent when used referentially, but a *general* proposition involving only properties when used attributively. Loar call this the "radical two-use theory".

## 3. Loar's Analysis

Loar recognizes Donnellan's distinction, but rejects the radical two-use theory. He argues that referential uses do not actually provide examples of the use of singular terms where no individual concept is involved in what is meant, and so do not provide a counterexample to Loar's Fregean theory of reference. His criticisms of the radical two-use theory occur in section II of the paper; he gives his positive account in sections IV–VI.

Loar sees the paradigm examples of referential and attributive uses of the sort Donnellan provides as extremes in a range of cases arranged along two dimensions. The first dimension is *identifying* versus *generalizing*. It is a matter of degree. The second is *intrinsic* versus *extrinsic*.

Consider the attributive use of "the murderer of Smith is insane". This is a generalizing use. The "referential qualifier", the concept or property of murdering, plays a role in the attribution of insanity. The brutal murder provides evidence for the insanity of whoever did it. But used referentially in the courtroom the attribution of insanity is based on Jones behavior there, not on the fact that he is a murderer. The referential qualifier serves to identify the person that the speaker is talking about, but it doesn't play a role in the attribution of insanity. If Jones had been on trial for drunk driving, a violation many more or less sane people commit, the speaker would still have drawn the conclusion that he was insane on the basis of his behavior in the courtroom.

Suppose we alter the referential case a bit. The speaker doesn't think that the courtroom behavior by itself is overwhelming evidence for insanity. But when he adds to it the fact that Jones is a brutal murderer, he is sure that Jones must be insane. This, as I understand it, would be an intermediate case on the first dimension; to a certain degree the referential qualifier is identifying, and to a certain degree it is explanatory.

In the attributive case, the referential qualifier is *intrinsic* to what the speaker means. If there is no murder—Smith died from injuries sustained in a gory fall into a vat of chili say—then what the speaker meant is not true. On Russell's theory of descriptions, it is false. In Donnellan's referential example, the referential qualifier is *extrinsic*. What the speaker meant to say might be true, even if it wasn't a murder, or even if Jones were innocent. This is shown by the fact that the speaker could supply a clarification of what meant to say, perhaps, "What I meant was the defendant is insane". Further suppose that the speaker had wrongly taken Jones to be the defendant, when he was actually the defendant's erratically behaving lawyer. He can further clarify: What I meant was that *that man*, the fellow over there in a three-piece suit is insane".

Loar's response to the threat to his theory of reference is to argue that even in paradigm cases of a referential uses "the *so-and-so* is *G*" where the *being so-and-so* is neither generalizing nor intrinsic, there will be . . .

> some description "the *H*" such that the speaker could have expressed what he had meant by saying "the *H* is *G*". "The truth of this

> counterfactual would indicate a certain feature of the speaker's original communicative intentions; what he had essentially meant was that the *H*—whatever it is—is *G*. This is the core of the thesis that it is the conventional function of singular terms to introduce individual concepts into what is meant.
>
> (360)

## 4. A Reservation

Loar's distinctions are insightful; they provide tools that help us describe and understand attributive and referential uses, and those in between. Loar's treatment would be completely persuasive, if one shared the view of semantics in terms of which he offers his theory of reference. But the view doesn't seem plausible to me. He says:

> What is it to give a semantical theory for a language? If we were systematically to pair the sentences of a language with the types of communicative intentions with which they are conventionally correlated, that would include the essentials. We would in effect have recursively defined a function from the sentences of a language to certain entities which, in their way, encapsulate the constraints on what communicative intentions a conventional speaker might have in uttering each sentence. These entities might appropriately be counted as the meanings for the sentence-types to which they are assigned by that function—that is, by that language.
>
> (353)

It seems that on Loar's view the rules of natural language are conventions that link sentences to states of intending to convey propositions; these states are the focus of semantics. What I mean is what I intend to convey to my listeners. Reference has its natural home in this body of conventions.

This is in the spirit of Grice's (1957) application of his concept of *non-natural meaning* to the meanings of expressions in language:

> "x meansNN(timeless) that so-and-so" might as a first shot be equated with some statement or disjunction of statements about what "people" (vague) intend (with qualifications about "recognition") to effect by x.
>
> (385)

But the issue with which Donnellan is concerned seems to be not what is meant but what is said. On the two-use interpretation, it would seem that the claim is that different things are said in referential and attribute uses.

What is said in the first case is captured by a singular proposition, in the second by a general proposition.

By what a person means, Loar does not mean what a person intends to *say*.

> Moreover, the notion of what is said should be regarded as a derivative concept of semantical theory. It is to be explicated partially in terms of the concept of what a sentence means, which is a function of conventional regularities which correlate sentential features with aspects of those communicative intentions which are constitutive of what speakers mean. Consequently it is not to be employed in giving the basic semantics of singular term.
>
> (369)

I think this has things backwards. The conventions of language determine truth conditions or other appropriate satisfaction conditions for sentences of the language. These properties, truth conditions established by convention, make the language useful for satisfying various intentions of speakers.

Consider baseball. The conventions in the *Rulebook of Baseball* connect various events on the field with things like scoring runs, making outs, winning, and losing. They don't mention intentions of the players, managers, or spectators. But the whole game, including the rules, evolved so that people could enjoy themselves and exercise their skills by playing, coaching, and managing, and survived for that reason, and it continues to thrive because it turned out people enjoyed watching it, so much they are willing to pay to do so. We cannot understand the institution baseball without putting it in this larger context. But the connection between why players are playing it and why people are watching them shouldn't be made at the level of the rules of baseball.

Somewhat similarly, I think the conventions of language assign references to expressions and truth conditions and other success conditions to types of utterances, based on the sentences uttered and the expressions they contain. This makes the institution of language useful for a variety of purposes, including the ones Grice and Loar emphasize, basically getting people to believe and desire various things, and do various things in virtue of those beliefs and desires.

What one means, Loar's sense, is what one intends to convey. Often, one intends to convey that so and so *by* saying that so and so. The two attitudes are causally connected, but there is a logical independence. On my view, then, reference, in the way the term is used in the philosophy of language, is more or less the contribution that individual expressions make to the truth conditions of the utterances that contain them. This in no way denies that the whole point of the exercise is to have a way of meaning things.

On this conception of semantics, the clarifications available to those who use descriptions referentially, on which Loar bases his defense of his Fregean theory in the face of referential uses, don't seem directly relevant. The fact that one did not *mean* something does not show that one did not *say* it. One might have said it quite unintentionally. The speaker considered above might well have said, "I *said* that the murder of Smith was insane. But that's not what I *meant*". The question is not whether we can avoid singular propositions in understanding what was meant, but whether we can avoid them in explaining what was said.

Consider an example of Kaplan's, (1978) slightly altered. A lecturer thinks he is pointing at a painting of Carnap on the wall behind him, and says, "The picture at which I am pointing is of the greatest philosopher of the twentieth century". But pranksters have replaced the painting of Carnap with a one of Spiro Agnew. We might agree that the speaker, apprised of the prank, is correct when he says that he *meant* that the painting that *used* to be on the wall behind him was of the greatest philosophers of the twentieth century. But this would not commit us to say that the speaker *said* the painting that used to be on the wall behind him was of the greatest philosopher of the twentieth century, or that he *didn't say* that the picture he was pointing at as he spoke was of the greatest philosopher. He didn't say what he meant.

And consider a version of one of Donnellan's examples, "the man with a martini". In this version, the speaker knows that Muggs, someone he recognizes across the room, is wanted on the phone. Muggs is not drinking a martini, but a gimlet garnished with an olive rather than a slice of lime, so it looks like a martini. The speaker is not in a position to leave his position and fetch Muggs. He says to a friend, who is in a position to fetch Muggs, but doesn't know who he is, "The man with a martini is wanted on the phone". It seems that the speaker has conveyed something true, which he intended to convey, by saying something false. When he learns the drink is a gimlet, the speaker can clarify what he meant. He meant that the person drinking something that looks like a martini is wanted on the phone. But it doesn't seem he can claim that he didn't *say* something that implied that someone in the room was drinking a martini. Suppose the host, who has a religious opposition to martinis, overhead him and berated the bartender for serving one. Then it seems that the speaker said something false, which got the bartender in trouble. As in the Kaplan-Carnap case, the fact that drinking a martini was not intrinsic to what the speaker *meant to convey* does not seem to get him off the hook for *saying* something false, if it turns out to be important. (There is a forensic aspect in our concept of saying that is relevant here, discussed in Korta & Perry, 2011).

However, I think we can separate Loar's theory of reference and his insights about the attributive-referential distinction from his conception of semantics. Looking at Frege's theory of descriptions will be helpful in this endeavor.

## 5. Frege's Theory of Descriptions

Considerable attention has focused on whether Frege held something like Russell's view, that proper names were disguised or hidden descriptions. The evidence is in the essays Frege wrote in the early 1890s, introducing his theory of sense and reference. In the only examples in which he provides for senses of proper names, he uses definite descriptions to identify those senses. But, even confining ourselves to those essays, I don't think we should draw the conclusion that Frege thought that names were hidden descriptions.

Frege's view was more likely the opposite, that definite descriptions are proxies for names. This is suggested by a passage in "Function and Concept":

> [Consider] the expression
> "the capital of the German Empire".
> This obviously *takes the place of a proper name*, and stands for [*bedeutet*] an object.
>
> (1952b, 31ff, italics added)

Frege calls definite descriptions "proper names", and provides basically the same semantics for both ordinary proper names and definite descriptions. I'll use "Name", with a capital, for Frege's category, and use "name" the way the rest of us use the term.

In "On Sense and Reference", (1952a) Frege explains only the sense and reference of Names and sentences. He leaves the treatment of concept-words (predicates) to other essays written about the same time. This chart summarizes what he tells us; what the reader naturally assumes about concept-words is in italics:

| Expression | Names (Ordinary names and descriptions) | *Concept-words (predicates)* | Sentence |
|---|---|---|---|
| Sense | Sense of Name | *Sense of Predicate* | Sense of the sentence (Thought) |
| Reference | Object or objects | *Property or relation* | Truth-Value |

(In "Function and Concept" (1952b) Frege gives a more complicated account of concept-words. Intentionally individuated properties and relations are only found at the level of sense. The references of predicates have to be extensionally individuated, at least for the purposes of logic. He emphasizes the importance of what he calls "extensions", which he had decided had to play a large role in his logicist project. His extensions are not what we now call extensions, but an instance of "courses of values". For my purposes in this essay we can set these issues aside.)

An ordinary name has a sense associated by the conventions and other practices of the users of the language of which it is a part; in what Frege calls "perfect" languages in "On Sense and Reference", those suitable for serious science, all users will associate the same sense with a name. For imperfect languages, variations in the senses associated can be "tolerated". (58n) Definite descriptions have senses that are determined by the senses of their parts. In both cases, these senses are, or at least determine, what Loar calls *individual concepts*, that is, properties that pick out the referent.

The chart provides a sort of commutative diagram, two combinations of functions that give the same result. If we start at the top of second and third columns and go down and then across, we go from a pair of senses to a pair of references and from a pair of references to a truth-value (given facts about the world). If instead we go across and then down, the pair of senses gives us a Thought, which then gives us a truth-value (given facts about the world). By either route, we end up in the lower right cell, with the same truth-value.

The sense of a Name then has two important functions. As indicated by the second column, the sense of a Name determines the reference of the Name, the first function. As indicated by the top row, the sense of the name makes a contribution to determining the Thought expressed by the sentence, the second function. This latter contribution is *not* the object referred to. Thoughts do not contain objects; they are complexes of properties and relations. A sentence can express a Thought, even if the Name in it has no reference. The Thought expressed by "The murder of Smith is insane", as far as things are explained in "On Sense and Reference", is essentially the proposition that one and only person murdered Smith, and that person has the property determined by the sense of "is insane".

The theory is elegant. But I think Frege was on the verge of a more elegant theory, which he did not adopt.

## 6. The Variant

A central notion of Frege's theory in his 1879 *Begriffsschrift*, is that of a *circumstance* (*Ümstande*). A circumstance consists of an object having a property (or objects standing in a relation). Circumstances are very much like singular propositions. Some circumstances are facts; some are not. It seems that what belongs in the lower right corner of the chart is not the truth-value, but the circumstance provided by route 2. If that circumstance is a fact, that fact will be an *instantiation* of the Thought provided by route 1. Then the chart would look like this:

*Variation on Frege's Theory*

| Expression | Names (Ordinary names and descriptions) | *Concept-words (predicates)* | *Sentences* |
|---|---|---|---|
| Sense | Sense of Name | *Sense of Predicate* | *Thought* |
| Reference | Object | *Property or relation* | Circumstance |

If the circumstance is a fact, the sentence is true; otherwise it is false.

The cells in the chart tell us what the sentence and the expressions in it provide. The right column gives us two consistent truth conditions for a sentence. The second cell gives us the Thought expressed by the sentence. It is a complex condition on reality, in terms of properties that must be instantiated and co-instantiated. If reality meets the condition, the sentence is true. The third cell gives us a circumstance. If it is a fact, the sentence is true. The conditions are consistent. The senses that determine the constituents of the circumstance are themselves components of the Thought, so if the circumstance is a fact, the Thought will be instantiated and vice-versa. The object referred to will meet the condition required of it, and reality will meet the condition required of it.

## 7. Back to Loar

With a bit of deviation from Loar's picture of semantics, our variation justifies much of his theory, and allows the acceptance of singular propositions in the form of circumstances without giving up the spirit of Frege. We retain his idea that that we utter sentences, paradigmatically, to get others to believe things. We *mean* things, in his sense. But we accept what I said earlier, that the conventions of language give us truth conditions for sentences. They connect indirectly with our meanings. Uttering a sentence is a way of getting others to believe that the truth conditions of the sentence are met.

On the variation, there is a choice of truth conditions. In modern terminology, we can intend our hearer to believe the general proposition in row two or the singular proposition in row three. The routes to either choice of truth conditions go through individual concepts.

In the former case, the general proposition and the referential qualifier are *intrinsic* to what we mean in Loar's sense. If it is false, then not only have we said something false, but what we meant to convey is false. Clarification won't help.

In the latter case, we mean to convey a singular proposition. The referential qualifier is not intrinsic to our meaning, but serves to identify the constituent of the singular proposition. A different referential qualifier that yields the same referent might work as well to convey our meaning, or better.

Now consider the martini case. We have to allow that when the speaker says, "The man with a martini is wanted on the phone", he says something false. Nevertheless, he succeeds in getting his hearer to believe what he wanted to. The referential qualifier was not intrinsic to his meaning. But he succeeded in his main goal; the hearer believed the singular proposition in a way that allowed him to act the way the speaker meant him to.

In the case where the speaker and the hearer both believe the gimlet is a martini, we can say the speaker succeeded in conveying what he meant to convey, just not according to plan. But perhaps the speaker realized it was a gimlet, but assumed the hearer would take it to be a martini, and he didn't want to take time to explain things. Then he succeeded in conveying what he meant, according to plan, but the plan wasn't paradigmatic. Such cases are not rare.

In this case, did the speaker *say* of the man with a gimlet that he was wanted on the phone? It seems to me he did not. He meant to convey, of that man, that he was wanted on the phone, and in this he succeeded. But Loar is right in stressing the importance of meaning in understanding the distinction. In the straightforward case, where the referential qualifier is not intrinsic, but does in fact describe the individual in question, semantics does fine. The speaker means to get the hearer to believe a singular proposition by uttering a sentence which has that proposition as its referential truth conditions. In the one-off cases, we have to take a wider view that takes into account that saying is of value because it provides a way to successfully mean things. I think Loar's picture of meaning allows us to do this, without accepting his account of the conventions of language.

Loar's view is that the referential/attributive distinction allows a range of intermediate cases. The view I am suggesting can agree. The identifying/generalizing distinction is a matter of degree. Consider the example of the person in the courtroom, who wouldn't have thought that Jones was insane simply because he committed the murder, or simply because he was behaving erratically, but given both bits of evidence, was confident that he was.

It is important, in thinking about such cases, to avoid thinking that *saying* is a relation between a speaker at a time and a proposition. Saying is an activity that involves producing a sentence that has truth conditions. Propositions, singular or general, are abstract objects for classifying those truth conditions. I now assert: "The last president was a real gentleman". Given that I was using English, and the meanings of the words in English, my utterance is true if and only if the person who was the previous president, relative to when I spoke, was a real gentleman. If we add to what is given that Obama was the previous president, then my utterance is true if and only if Obama was a real gentleman. These are different truth conditions, logically independent. But they are perfectly consistent, and imply one another, given the additional premise that Obama was the last president. Both propositions are perfectly correct ways of encoding the truth conditions of my utterance, and having them available is useful when we consider the different things I meant to convey. Was I making the point that being president doesn't require not being a real gentleman? Or just saying something about Obama.

If we think that saying is a relation to propositions, rather than merely being an activity that can be usefully classified by propositions, we will think that our courtroom observer must have said *either* the general or the singular proposition. But no such choice is forced on us.

Suppose I climb a tree to pick an orange. What was I doing? Climbing a tree, or picking an orange? Both. Perhaps I am climbing the tree *in order to* pick an orange. Perhaps I was climbing a tree mainly to convince my wife that I was not so decrepit as she thought, and picking an orange was an excuse. Perhaps both reasons were involved. We can classify actions with propositions: he climbed the tree in order to bring it about *that he possessed an orange*. Or, *he picked an orange to convince his wife he could still climb a tree*. Often, all we need to understand about an action for the purposes at hand can be captured by a single proposition which encodes the success conditions of the main intention. Even so, that is only part of what is going on. My action can have a lot of intended results that can be used to describe it for various purposes. One proposition won't always do the trick of describing an action.

This carries over the action of saying something. Often one proposition will do the job. But just as often, it really won't. In such cases, we need to bring in the larger picture Loar put before in order to us to understand what is going on. The speaker means to convey that Jones is a murderer. He also means to suggest that part of his reason for so thinking is that he committed a murder. But he doesn't mean to suggest that his assertion is completely based on the evidence of the murder. He said that Jones was insane *by* saying that the murderer of Smith was insane. He *meant* to convey both. The referential qualifier is generalizing, to a certain extent, and identifying to a certain extent.

If we abandon the picture of saying as a relation to a proposition in favor of the classificatory picture, it is natural to appeal to the wider setting of an utterance, what the speaker *means*, in cases in which there doesn't seem to be a single thing that was *said*. In many cases, both the general and the referential truth conditions will be useful in diagnosing what the speaker meant to do.

## 8. Back to Frege

Loar says that his account is Fregean. Is he right? The accepted story is that Frege gave us an account of *indirect* reference, while the insights of philosophers like Kaplan, Kripke, and many others show that we should see reference as *direct*. Loar argues in effect that we need to separate the core insight of Frege's theory from the particular examples Frege gives, and when we do so we can accept many of the insights of the "direct referentialists". For example:

> There has been a tendency to interpret description theories of names as claiming that, insofar as N names x, there is some one individual concept which is meant on all uses of N to refer to x. My thesis is far less dramatic: on each of N's uses in referring to x some individual concept or other which is satisfied by x is intrinsic to what is thereby meant.
>
> (371)

Frege only requires that the same sense be attached to all its uses for speakers of a *perfect* language, of the sort his *Begriffsschrift* is intended to be, one suitable for use in serious sciences (1952b, 58n). He recognizes that this requirement does not hold for *imperfect* languages, a category which includes all natural languages. He doesn't say much about imperfect languages, admittedly, but a theory of imperfect languages can be Fregean, without incorporating this requirement.

Loar also emphasizes that the individual concepts involved in reference may be implicit (362). Again, this is probably not something Frege would have wanted in perfect languages. But Loar's theory is Fregean in requiring individual concepts for reference, even if they are of a sort Frege didn't think much about and wouldn't countenance in a perfect language.

I think Frege's essential insight was that to get at the cognitive significance of an utterance of a sentence, circumstances or singular propositions won't do the job. By "cognitive significance" I mean what a semantically competent speaker must believe, or more generally have a positive attitude towards, to sincerely utter the sentence, and what a credulous hearer will come to have a positive doxastic attitude towards.

This insight, and Frege's abandonment of circumstances, had to do with Frege's problems with identity in the *Begriffsschrift*.[1] It seems that "Hesperus = Phosphorus" and "Phosphorus = Phosphorus" stand for the same circumstance, consisting of Venus and the relation of identity. But they do not have the same cognitive significance; someone could believe the second but not the first. They do not have the same inferential properties. Given the premise that Hesperus is moonless, the first implies that Phosphorus is moonless, but the second does not. But if they stand for the same circumstance, then on the *Begriffsschrift* account they have the same *conceptual content*.

But on the *Begriffsschrift* account, if they have the same conceptual content, they should also have the same cognitive significance and inferential power. Frege's solution, in §8 of the *Begriffsschrift*, is to abandon "=" in favor of "≡". "Hesperus ≡ Phosphorus" means that the names "Hesperus" and "Phosphorus" co-refer. So it does not refer to the same circumstance as "Phosphorus ≡ Phosphorus". Frege retires "='; it does not appear after §8.

After finishing the *Begriffsschrift*, Frege became aware that the solution doesn't work. (1952b, 29). The problem isn't with the identity sign, which is re-instated in his works. "Hesperus is moonless" and "Phosphorus is moonless" also refer to the same circumstance.[2] Frege realized that circumstances simply don't get at the cognitive significance of sentences. I think Frege was quite right about this, and the same goes for singular propositions. I address the apparent conflict between this point of agreement and my enthusiasm for circumstances in a bit.

So, by the 1890s, Frege thought that reference was *indirect*, mediated by senses. The Name is *associated* with a sense, a condition, and the referent *meets* that condition. I agree with Loar that this is the essence of Frege's insight, and it is *not* refuted simply by showing that Frege's own suggestions for the senses of names aren't very plausible.

So-called theories of direct reference are not direct in any sense that conflicts with Frege's insight. Suppose I refer myself by using "I". On Kaplan's theory, what happens involves a *character*, the meaning of "I". The character plus the context determines a property, *being the speaker in the context* (of the utterance), that an object must have to be the referent. Reference is mediated by this property, and so not direct in a way that conflicts with Frege's insight. By "direct" Kaplan means that the referent is *directly* imported into the proposition expressed, a singular proposition. This conflicts with Frege's overall theory, which no longer recognizes anything like singular propositions, but not with his insight.

Consider the characters in Frege's famous footnote, (1952a, fn 6) speakers of an imperfect language who, he says, associate different senses with the name "Aristotle". Call them Fred and Ethel. Fred believes firmly that Aristotle was the student of Plato and the teacher of Alexander. Ethel isn't so sure about that, but he believes firmly that Aristotle was the famous philosopher born in Stagira. Frege suggests that, in their imperfect language, these beliefs provide the senses.

Some version of the modern causal-historical-informational theories put forward by Geach (1969), Kripke (1980), Donnellan (1972, 1974), Evans (1973) and others is surely more plausible. Here is a simple version. A use of a name N will occur as a part of a causal-historical network of references, each utterance in the network intended to co-refer with some earlier ones. The network will begin with a dubbing of some object with the name; that object is the referent of nodes along the network. Aristotle's parents called him "Aristotle". So, Plato called him "Aristotle", philosophers and commentators and historians and philosophy teachers called him "Aristotle", and, finally, Fred and Ethel called him "Aristotle". There is nothing very direct about this phenomenon, stretching, as it does in the case of "Aristotle", over centuries. Fred and Ethel haven't read Geach, Donnellan, Kripke, or Evans, but they are *attuned* to the way names work. They know the difference between using the name to co-refer with the uses of "Aristotle" in a biography of Jackie Kennedy, and using it to co-refer, say, with its uses in Will Durant's *The Story of Philosophy* (1926), where Fred and Ethel and I all learned it, as it happens. The theory vindicates Frege's insight.

Why did Frege not adopt the variant I suggested? Alternatively, if I agree with Frege that circumstances don't capture cognitive significance, why do I insist on them? The answer is that I think that circumstances, although they don't capture cognitive significance, have another useful classificatory use. They get at what I will call *informational content*. This is what "Hesperus is moonless", "Phosphorus is moonless" and "Venus is moonless" have in common. In communicative situations we often want to share information without much caring about possible differences in cognitive significance. We play what I call "information games." Someone at some time picks up information about an object; he passes the information along to someone else, who uses it at some later time. Sameness of cognitive significance or Thought isn't required for this to work, only a much weaker condition, the realization that different conditions pick out the same object. All sorts human abilities, practices, and institutions are devoted to assuring this condition. I order an Irish Whiskey at the bar and see the bartender pour some in a glass. A bit later, he brings a glass full of some kind of whiskey to my table. Good bartending practice makes me confident it is the same glass, with the same fine whiskey I saw poured into it. Here I play both roles in the information game.

Indeed, Frege's remarks on "imperfect languages", suggest the need for circumstances. Given Frege's analysis, that Fred and Ethel associate different senses with "Aristotle", what makes things tolerable? Not simply that they both use "Aristotle"; Ethel might be referring to Onassis's paternal grandfather, also named "Aristotle" (or so I will pretend). Not that they both refer to Aristotle; this might be an accident. Something in their situation guarantees sameness of circumstance, in a way that it makes sense for them to be confident that they are referring to the same person, in spite of the difference in associated senses, and that's why it's tolerable.

So, we need circumstances and singular propositions in semantics for the same reason we need general ones. In both cases, abstract objects help us keep track of important kinds of equivalence between sentences that play an important role in our use of language. Fred's teacher told the class that the author of *Tom Sawyer* was once a riverboat pilot. But he misses the question, "True or false: the author of *Huckleberry Finn* was a once riverboat pilot" on the exam. He complains to Mary, a more competent student, "She didn't tell us that!" She responds, "Yes she did". Fred is right; the cognitive significance of the question isn't the same as the cognitive significance of what she said in class. General propositions can get at the difference. But Mary is right too. The information she asked for in the exam was *just* what she provided in class. The circumstance that Mark Twain was once a riverboat pilot gets at this equivalence. The teacher relied on the practice of students reading their assignments. But Fred opted out of that particular practice.

Frege gives an argument in "On Sense and Reference" to justify his choice of truth-values as the referents of sentences. It is basically that we are interested whether Names have a referent only when we are interested in truth. When the Name lacks a referent, it will lack a truth-value. This isn't a very convincing argument. The argument doesn't favor truth-values over circumstances. If a Name lacks a referent, there won't be a circumstance to be or not be a fact. But Frege does not even consider circumstances as candidates for the referents of sentences. It's almost as if by the 1890s he wanted to forget that he ever thought about them.

## Conclusion

Loar's essay contains much that seems well ahead of its time. In particular, separating Frege's insight about cognitive significance and individual concepts from the particular examples Frege provides was an insight that has remained largely unappreciated. His framework of intrinsic and extrinsic, general and identifying sheds a great deal of light on examples of referential and attributive uses of descriptions. What he says about names is similarly insightful, although I haven't the time and space to explore it. While I don't like his treatment of the conventions of language, the concept of what one means, and the possibility of clarifying what one means when referential qualifiers are used extrinsically is very illuminating. I wish I had studied his essay more when it first appeared.

I'll end by observing that the approach to descriptions Kepa Korta and I recommend in *Critical Pragmatics* (2011) is not the variation on Frege that I suggested. Unlike Frege, we do not classify definite descriptions with names, but rather with indefinite descriptions. We emphasize utterances, and we rely on the reflexive-referential theory David Israel and I developed years ago which I explained in *Reference and Reflexivity* (2012) and called "critical referentialism". But, given those differences, there are important similarities, and I think Loar's insights could be appreciated on our theory.

## Notes

1. See de Ponte, Korta & Perry (forthcoming).
2. Frege's example is "The morning star has a shorter period of revolution than the earth and "The evening star has a shorter period of revolution than the earth".

## References

de Ponte, M., Korta, K., & Perry, J. (forthcoming) "Four Puzzling Paragraphs."

Donnellan, K. (1966). "Reference and Definite Descriptions." *Philosophical Review*, pp. 281–304.

Donnellan, K. (1972). "Proper Names and Identifying Descriptions." In Davidson, D. & Harman G. (eds.). *Semantics of Natural Language*. Dordrecht: D. Reidel, pp. 356–379.

Donnellan, K. (1974). "Speaking of Nothing." *Philosophical Review*, No. 1, pp. 3–31.

Donnellan, K. (1978). "Speaker Reference, Descriptions, and Anaphora." In Cole, P. (ed.). *Syntax and Semantics 9: Pragmatics*. New York: Academic Press, pp. 47–68.

Durant, W. (1926). *The Story of Philosophy*. New York: Simon and Schuster.

Evans, G. (1973). "The Causal Theory of Names." *Aristotelian Society Supplementary*, Vol. 7, pp. 187–208.

Frege, G. (1879). *Begriffsschrift, eine der arithmetischen nachgebildete Formelsprache des reinen Denkens*. Halle: Nebert.
Frege, G. (1891). *Funktion und Begriff*. Jena: Hermann Pohle.
Frege, G. (1892). Über Sinn und Bedeutung. *Zeitschrift für Philosophische Kritik*, No. 100, pp. 25–30.
Frege, G. (1952). *Translations From the Philosophical Writings of Gottlob Frege*. Edited and translated by Geach, P. & Black, M. Oxford: Basil Blackwell, 1952.
Frege, G. (1952a). "On Sense and Reference." Translation of Frege (1892) in Frege, 1952, pp. 56–78.
Frege, G. (1952b). "Function and Concept." Translation of Frege (1891) in Frege, 1952, pp. 21–41.
Geach, P.T. (1969). "The Perils of Pauline." *The Review of Metaphysics*, Vol. 23, No. 2, pp. 287–300.
Grice, H.P. (1957). "Meaning." *Philosophical Review*, pp. 377–388.
Kaplan, D. (1978). "Dthat." In Cole, P. (ed.). *Syntax and Semantics*, vol. 9. New York: Academic Press.
Korta, K., & Perry, J. (2011). *Critical Pragmatics*. Cambridge: Cambridge University Press.
Kripke, S. (1977). "Speaker's Reference and Semantic Reference." *Midwest Studies in Philosophy*, Vol. 2, pp. 255–276.
Kripke, S. (1980). *Naming and Necessity*. Cambridge, MA: Harvard University Press. Revised transcript of lectures given at Princeton University in 1970.
Loar, Brian. (1976). "The Semantics of Singular Terms." *Philosophical Studies*, Vol. 30, No. 6, pp. 353–377.
Perry, J. (2012). *Reference and Reflexivity*, 2nd edition. Stanford: CSLI Publications.
Russell, B. (1905). "On Denoting." *Mind*, New Series, 14, Vol. 56, pp. 479–493.

# 3 Modes of Presentation in Attitude Reports

*François Recanati*

## 1

In "Quantifiers and Propositional Attitudes" (1956), Quine emphasizes the importance of a distinction between two types of attitude reports: *de re* and *de dicto*, or, as Quine himself puts it, "relational" and "notional". The distinction is based upon a more fundamental distinction at the level of the attitudes themselves.

Some attitudes are relational: they involve a relation between the attitude holder and some other individual. For example, the attitude holder may believe, of his friend John, that he is always late. This is a (triadic) relation between the attitude holder, his friend John, and what the former believes of the latter (viz., that he is always late). It is natural to report that sort of belief (belief in the relational sense, as Quine puts it) by using the "believes of" locution, as I have just done. Other attitudes are not relational in that sense: they do not involve a relation between the attitude holder and some other individual, but only (as far as relations go) a relation between the attitude holder and the propositional content of the attitude. For example, the attitude holder may believe that there are spies. This is a (dyadic) relation between the attitude holder and the proposition that there are spies.

The belief that there are spies is the belief that the property of being a spy is instantiated—the belief that someone or other is a spy. But if I say, "John believes that someone is a spy", that is ambiguous. That can be read either as saying that, according to John, there are spies (non-relational reading: John believes that the concept of spy is instantiated), or as saying that there is someone in particular *of whom* John believes that he is a spy (relational reading). Quine traces the ambiguity to the belief predicate, which can be dyadic or triadic. On the relational reading of "John believes that someone is a spy", "believes" is triadic, and the second argument position (the person of whom John believes that he is a spy) is existentially quantified:

$$\exists x\ B^3\ (\text{John}, x, z \textit{ is a spy})$$

On the non-relational reading the belief is about no one in particular: it is a (dyadic) relation between John and a general proposition, to the effect that someone is a spy.

$B^2$ (John, $\exists x$ *x is a spy*)

The same sort of ambiguity arises if, instead of a quantifier such as "someone", we use an indefinite description. Thus "John wants to marry a woman richer than himself" can be understood in two ways. Understood one way the utterance entails that there is a particular woman richer than himself whom John wants to marry. Understood the other way it does not: John's desire involves the *notion* of a woman richer than himself, but no particular woman corresponding to that notion. As Quine points out, the two readings are formally distinguished in some languages. Thus, in French (as in other Romance languages—Quine's own example is in Spanish)[1] there are two ways of saying that John wants to marry a woman richer than himself, only one of which entails that *there is* a woman richer than himself whom John wants to marry (relational reading):

*Relational:*

Jean veut épouser une femme qui *est* plus riche que lui [indicative]

*Notional:*

Jean veut épouser une femme qui *soit* plus riche que lui [subjunctive]

According to Quine, that sort of ambiguity also arises when we use a singular term, e.g. a name or a definite description, in the content clause of an attitude report. Thus, a belief report such as "John believes that the shortest spy is a spy" can be understood in two ways:

*Relational reading*

$B^3$ (John, the shortest spy, *z is a spy*)

*Notional reading*

$B^2$ (John, *the shortest spy is a spy*)

On the first reading the sentence can be paraphrased as "John believes of the shortest spy that he is a spy"; this is not so on the second reading, where the description "the shortest spy" contributes a notion (the concept of shortest spy) to the content of the ascribed belief. Relationally understood, the "statement affirms a relation between [two] persons, and the persons remain so related independently of the names applied to them" (1961: 142); so substitution of any other designation for the same person cannot affect truth-value. Indeed, on the relational reading of "John believes that the shortest spy is a spy", where it means that John believes of the person who is in fact the shortest spy that he is a spy, if the shortest spy happens to be Jane's second son it can be inferred that John believes of Jane's second son that he is a spy. But if what John believes is the general proposition that (whoever is) the shortest spy is a spy, substitution does not preserve truth-value. Likewise, existential generalization is possible on the relational reading: if John believes of the shortest spy (a.k.a. Jane's second son) that he is a spy, then there is someone whom he believes to be a spy. This is not the case on the notional reading: John may believe that whoever is the shortest spy is a spy without believing of anyone in particular that he is a spy.

Quine applies the distinction to belief reports featuring a proper name, such as "Tom believes that Cicero denounced Catiline". That sentence too may be understood in two ways, he says: either transparently as saying of Cicero that Tom believes he denounced Catiline (relational reading), or opaquely as saying that Tom holds true the sentence "Cicero denounced Catiline".

*Relational reading*

$B^3$ (Tom, Cicero, *z denounced Catiline*)

*Notional reading*

$B^2$ (Tom, *Cicero denounced Catiline*)

Again, substitution of identicals and existential generalization are only possible on the relational reading. That is the criterion Quine offers for telling apart the two readings of attitude reports.

Interesting though it is, Quine's distinction between relational and notional attitude reports suffers from a significant difficulty: a difficulty which Brian Loar detected in his first published paper, "Reference and Propositional Attitudes" (1972). Quine, it seems, has conflated two different distinctions, which are both legitimate but should be kept apart (Recanati 2000a). One is the distinction between those attitudes which target particular individuals (e.g. John's desire to marry a particular woman richer than himself) and those which don't; and the other is the distinction between transparent and opaque attitude reports. The problem for Quine is that singular attitudes targeting particular individuals can themselves be reported "opaquely" as well as "transparently". If one assumes, as many people do, that to hold an attitude targeting a particular individual (as opposed to an attitude with general content) is to stand in a certain relation to that individual, then Quine's conflation of relationality and transparency becomes unacceptable; for it entails that whenever an attitude report is opaque, the attitude it reports must belong to the non-relational variety.[2]

## 2

Let us reconsider the distinction between the two types of attitude: those which involve a relation between the attitude holder and some particular object which the attitude is about, and those which do not involve such a relation. The former are sometimes called "*de re* attitudes". The distinction is well illustrated by Quine's contrast between wanting a particular sloop and wanting mere "relief from slooplessness". The content of the desire is *singular* in one case (involving a particular sloop) and *general* in the other (wanting a sloop, but not anyone in particular). Likewise, some beliefs are purely general, others are singular and involve particular objects. As an example of a general belief, we have the belief that there are spies, or the belief that all swans are black. As Frege put it, those beliefs are about concepts, if they are about anything at all: the first is the belief that the concept "spy" is satisfied by at least one object; the second is the belief that whatever satisfies the concept "swan" satisfies the concept "black". But the belief that Quine was a student of Carnap is a belief about two *individuals*: Quine and Carnap. Because the belief is irreducibly singular and concerns particular individuals, rather than whoever satisfies such and such conditions, having the belief involves being suitably related to the particular individuals in question; and ascribing the belief involves affirming a relation between the believer and these individuals.

The idea that singular belief (belief about particular objects) is fundamentally relational has loomed large in anti-descriptivist theories of reference. Bach, for example, argues as follows:

> If *all* your thoughts about things could only be descriptive, your total conception of the world would be merely qualitative. You would never be related in thought to anything in particular. Thinking of something would never be a case of having it "in mind", as we say colloquially, or as some philosophers have said, of being "*en rapport*", in "cognitive contact", or "epistemically intimate" with it. But picturesque phrases aside, just what is this special relation? Whatever it is, it is different from that involved in thinking of something under a description. If we can even speak of a relation in the latter case, it is surely not a real (or natural) relation. Since the object of a descriptive thought is determined SATISFACTIONALLY, the fact that the thought is of that object does not require any connection between thought and object. However, the object of a *de re* thought is determined RELATIONALLY. For something to be the object of a *de re* thought, it must stand in a certain kind of relation to that very thought.
>
> (Bach 1987: 12)

On this view, singular attitudes (*de re* thoughts, in Bach's terminology) have the singular content they have in virtue of the attitude holder's standing in certain relations to the particular object or objects that feature in the content of the attitude. If the attitude holder was not suitably related to the objects in question, the thought would be purely qualitative and would not target any particular individual. Singular attitudes therefore are necessarily relational attitudes: whoever believes that Quine was a student of Carnap believes *of* Quine and Carnap that the former was a student of the latter. The relevant relations (between the attitude holder and the particular objects involved in the content of singular attitudes) descend from more basic, informational relations such as the relations of perceiving, of remembering or of hearing about. All these relations are genuine relations. If John perceives, remembers, or hears about the table, there is something which he sees, remembers, or hears about. Singular belief is based on, or grounded in, the basic informational relations from which it inherits its relational character. To have a thought about a particular object, one must be "en rapport with" the thing through perception, memory or communication. (Pure thinking does not suffice. Thus, inferring that there is a shortest spy does not put one in a position to entertain a singular belief about the shortest spy, in the relevant sense.)

By and large, Brian Loar accepted the distinction,[3] even though, in his paper "The Semantics of Singular Terms" (1976), he expressed dissatisfaction with the "radical two-use theory" which I have just expounded and which Bach's quotation illustrates. Loar's dissatisfaction sprang from two sorts of consideration. First, he held that even in the relational (*de re*) case, the attitude holder is thinking of the referent through some "individual concept" or mode of presentation; and he took individual concepts to be generally expressible by means of definite descriptions. Second, he thought there was a continuum of cases rather than a sharp division between the two classes.[4] These reservations led Loar to reformulate the distinction as a distinction between two types of individual concepts, those that are and those that are not "identifying", where identifyingness is a graded property. Be that as it may, how exactly we cash out the distinction between the two types of attitude is not what matters for our present purposes. What matters is the relation between that distinction and *another* distinction, between transparent and opaque attitude ascriptions.

Quine more or less conflated the two distinctions: he held that "notional" attitude reports are opaque, and permit neither substitution of identicals *salva veritate* nor existential generalization, while "relational" attitude reports are transparent and allow for both. Thus, as we have seen, "John believes, of the shortest spy, that he is a spy" entails that John believes, of Jane's second son, that he is a spy (assuming the shortest spy = Jane's second son), and also entails that there is someone of whom John believes that he is a spy. "The shortest spy" occurs extensionally in such a statement, whose logical form is

$B^3$ (John, the shortest spy, *z is a spy*)

In contrast, "the shortest spy" occurs nonextensionally in "John believes that the shortest spy is a spy" when this is understood notionally as ascribing to John a thought involving the *concept* of shortest spy. That is why Quine equated the two distinctions, and used nonextensionality as a criterion for non-relationality. But that was a mistake, Loar pointed out. Some relational belief reports are transparent, but not all are.

Loar gives the following example of a belief report that is both relational and opaque:

(1) Michael believes that that masked man is a diplomat.

Suppose the speaker utters (1) while pointing to a certain man (say, Brown) at a costume ball. The speaker thereby refers to Brown, and says of him that Michael believes him to be a diplomat. This looks like a relational belief report. Still, the report may well be opaque. It may be that Michael talked to the masked man during the ball, and inferred from his conversation with him that the man in question (whom he did not recognize as Brown) is a diplomat, even though Michael would strongly deny that Brown (whom he knows to be a dentist) is a diplomat. In this situation, the report in (1) is both relational and opaque. It is relational because Michael is said to believe of a certain man, singled out by a pointing gesture, that he is a diplomat; but it is opaque because, even though that masked man = Brown, substitution of "Brown" for "that masked man" turns (1), which is true, into (2), which is false in that situation:

(2) Michael believes that Brown is a diplomat.

To be sure, (2) is true in that situation if it is understood "transparently", that is, as merely saying that Michael believes of Brown (thought of in some way or other) that he is a diplomat. But (2) is false on the opaque reading, while (1) is true on the opaque reading. The point is precisely that (1) can be construed as opaque, and resisting substitution, while still being a relational belief report ascribing to Michael a belief about a particular individual (thought of in a particular way).

Because substitutivity fails, Quine would say that a belief report such as (1) is non-relational; for if it affirmed a relation between Michael and the masked man, that relation could be affirmed using any another designation for the latter, e.g. the name "Brown". But Loar rebuts that argument. Substitution may be blocked, he says, because the singular term "that masked man" plays a *dual role*; it both refers to the person the belief is about (the masked man, a.k.a. Brown) while mirroring the way Michael thinks of him when he thinks he is a diplomat. Such a dual role, he argues, is similar to the dual role of the name "Giorgione" in Quine's own example

Giorgione was so-called because of his size.

Even though "Giorgione" refers to Giorgione in that statement, it cannot be replaced by another name for Giorgione, say "Barbarelli", *salva veritate*. That is because the name "Giorgione" does double duty in the sentence: it refers to Giorgione (something which "Barbarelli" can also do) but at the same time it is the referent of the demonstrative adverb "so" in "so-called". Substitution (of "Barbarelli" for "Giorgione") changes the interpretation of the adverb and thus affects truth-value:

> Barbarelli was so-called because of his size.

Substitution holds, however, if we *fix* the interpretation of "so-called" so as to make it context-independent. From

> Giorgione was *called "Giorgione"* because of his size

it does follow that

> Barbarelli was called "Giorgione" because of his size.

Likewise for (1): substitutivity is restored if we *fix* the aspect of its interpretation which is context-sensitive and depends on the choice of the referring expression. From

> Michael believes that that masked man, *thought of as that masked man*, is a diplomat

it does follow that

> Michael believes that Brown, thought of as that masked man, is a diplomat.

Accordingly, Loar suggests the following logical form for a report such as (1) which is both relational and opaque:

> $B^3$ (Michael, that masked man, *z is that masked man and z is a diplomat*)

This displays the dual role played by the singular term "that masked man": it refers to the individual Michael is belief-related to, *and* specifies how Michael thinks of that individual when he holds the reported belief.[5]

To be sure, Quine would insist that such a belief report is not *purely* relational; the role of the singular term, "that masked man", is not purely to specify the individual that Michael's belief is about—it has an additional role and contributes the *notion* of masked man to the content of the reported belief. What Quine means by "relational" is, indeed, *purely relational*. Purely relational belief reports are subject to the principle of substitutivity, in contrast to those belief reports that are not purely relational. Verbal matters aside, however, the intuitive distinction between relational and non-relational attitudes which Quine himself appeals to when he gives his initial examples (wanting a particular sloop vs wanting relief from slooplessness, etc.) has to be recognized as distinct from the theoretical distinction that is of interest to him, that between the attitude reports that are transparent and license free substitution of identicals and those that are not. An adequate and comprehensive theory should combine the two distinctions, instead of conflating them.

## 3

In Loar's framework, a belief report such as "John believes that his successor is a linguist" has (at least) three different readings, not two (Loar 1972, 2017: 23, fn. 6).[6] First, it has a transparent reading, paraphrasable as

(i) John believes of the person who is in fact his successor that she is a linguist.

Thus understood the statement does not entail that John realizes that the person he takes to be a linguist is his successor. In that interpretation, the description "his successor" occurs extensionally and supports both substitution and existential generalization. It is *the speaker* who chooses the description "his successor" to refer to the person whom John believes to be a linguist. In other words, the description does not occur in the content of the belief that is ascribed to John. This reading is purely relational, and its logical form is

$B^3$ (John, his successor, *z is a linguist*)

The statement also has a purely notional, attributive reading, where the belief ascribed to John is a general belief about whoever is his successor, rather than a singular belief about a particular person:

(ii) John believes that whoever is/will be his successor is a linguist.

In this case, the description does occur in the content of the belief that is ascribed to John. Neither substitution nor existential generalization are possible. The logical form of the statement on that interpretation is

$B^2$ (John, *his successor is a linguist*)

But there is also a third, intermediate reading, which may be the most natural for that sort of statement. On that reading, as on the first reading, John's belief is about a particular person (so existential generalization is possible): John believes of that particular person, say Mary, that she is a linguist. Yet, in contrast to the first reading, "his successor" does not occur extensionally. As on the second reading, the description does feature in the content of the belief that is ascribed to John:

(iii) John believes of his successor (Mary), *thought of as his successor*, that she is a linguist.

Assuming Mary is Peter's lover, we cannot infer from "John believes that his successor is a linguist", thus understood, that John believes that Peter's lover is a linguist (unless we understand this last report transparently). For John may not know that Mary is Peter's lover, and he may have positive reasons to deny that Peter's lover is a linguist. The third reading corresponds to the following logical form:

$B^3$ (John, his successor, *z is his successor and z is a linguist*)

As we have seen (§1), Quine applies the relational/notional distinction indifferently to belief reports involving definite descriptions, such as "John believes that his successor is a linguist", and to belief reports involving proper names, such as "Tom believes that Cicero denounced Catiline" or "John believes that Mary is a linguist". But definite descriptions, although they can be used referentially, can also be used attributively; and when they are they do not refer to any particular object, in the strong, relational sense of "refer". So, there is a sharp contrast to be drawn between a relational reading of "John believes that his successor is a linguist", such as the transparent reading (i), and a non-relational reading, such as the attributive reading (ii). Proper names, however, differ from definite descriptions in being intrinsically referential (i.e. marked as such).[7] So "John believes that Mary is a linguist" only possesses *relational* readings: the logical form is triadic in all cases and the report states a relation between John, Mary, and what John believes about her. True, the report has two readings, depending on whether it is understood as transparent or opaque, but this is not a contrast between a relational and a non-relational reading (as the contrast between (i) and (ii) is), but a contrast between two relational readings, representable as

$B^3$ (John, Mary, *z is a linguist*)

and

$B^3$ (John, Mary, *z is Mary [or: z is called "Mary"] and z is a linguist*)

Note that the same contrast exists between the two relational readings of "John believes that his successor is a linguist", namely (i) and (iii).

Following Loar, I conclude that we need a more complex picture than Quine's. We need both the distinction between relational and non-relational attitude reports (based upon the distinction between singular or referential attitudes, on the one hand, and general or non-referential attitudes, on the other) and the distinction, within the class of relational attitude reports, between those that are opaque and those that are transparent. Relational attitude reports do, and non-relational attitude reports do not, support existential quantification; but among relational attitude reports, only those that are transparent support substitution of identicals (Figure 3.1).

## 4

In relational belief reports, the speaker refers to the believer (say, Tom) as well as to another individual (say, Cicero), and ascribes to the former a belief about the latter—say the belief that he denounced Catiline. Now, all reference is under a "mode of presentation". For example, Cicero can be referred to as "Cicero", as "Tully", or as the author of *De Senectute.* This applies not only to speech (talking about Cicero) but also to thought (thinking about Cicero). So, when a thought about Cicero is ascribed to Tom, there is a *double* reference to Cicero: the ascribed belief is about Cicero, and that means that the believer is taken to refer to Cicero in thought and to predicate of him the property of having denounced Catliline; but the speaker who ascribes the belief herself refers to Cicero as the person the belief is about. Correspondingly, two modes of presentation are involved: the speaker presents Cicero in a certain way when she ascribes to Tom a belief about him; and the believer, Tom, thinks of Cicero in a certain way when he judges that he denounced Catiline.[8]

In transparent belief reports, the way the believer thinks of the individual that her belief is about is not specified: the report ascribes a belief concerning that individual, without specifying *how* the believer thinks of the individual in question. To be sure, the individual in question is presented in a certain way in the report—as Cicero, as Tully, or as the author

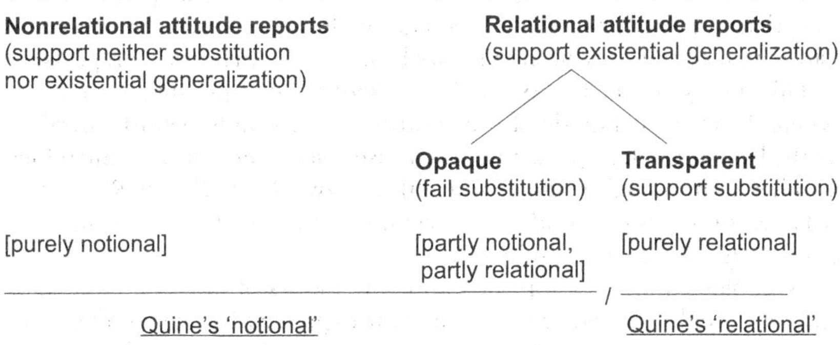


*Figure 3.1* Quine's Picture Amended

of *De Senectute*. But this is irrelevant to the ascribed belief: the speaker chooses a particular way of referring to the individual that the belief is about, but the mode of presentation thus selected is not ascribed to the believer. That is why substitution is possible: since the mode of presentation through which the speaker refers to the individual that the belief is about is not ascribed to the believer, changing the mode of presentation does not affect the belief that is ascribed, hence the truth conditions of the report. In contrast, opaque belief reports are such that the speaker's way of referring to the individual the belief is about is supposed to mirror the ascribee's own way of thinking of that individual. Opaquely understood, therefore, "Tom believes that Tully denounced Catiline" is incorrect if Tom himself does not think of Cicero as "Tully" when he predicates of him the property of having denounced Catiline.

Let me now introduce a bit of terminology. In *Direct Reference* (1993) I distinguished between the *exercised* mode of presentation and the *ascribed* mode of presentation. The ascribed mode of presentation is (unsurprisingly) the mode of presentation which is ascribed to the believer in opaque attitude ascriptions. The exercised mode of presentation is the mode of presentation through which the speaker refers to whatever she is referring to, e.g. the individual the ascribed belief is about. In terms of that distinction we can rephrase Loar's theory as follows. In opaque singular ascriptions, the same mode of presentation is *both* exercised by the speaker in referring to the individual the belief is about *and* ascribed to the believer as part of the content of her belief. That is why, on the opaque reading of "John believes that the F is G" we find *two* occurrences of the description "the F" in the corresponding logical form:

$B^3$ (John, the F, *z is the F and z is G*)

The individual concept "the F" serves both as the exercised mode of presentation and as the ascribed mode of presentation, in opaque belief reports. In transparent belief reports, the mode of presentation only plays the first role: that of exercised mode of presentation. It does not play the other role (since no mode of presentation is ascribed, in transparent belief reports).

This theory is a little too simple, as there are opaque singular reports where the exercised mode of presentation is *not* simultaneously ascribed to the believer. Before presenting such cases, however, I need to introduce another terminological distinction (also drawn from *Direct Reference*) between two types of mode of presentation: that between linguistic and psychological modes of presentation.

Psychological modes of presentation are modes of presentation occurring in thought—whether in the thought expressed by the speaker (and grasped by the understanding hearer), or in the thought ascribed to the believer. Both exercised and ascribed modes of presentation count as psychological modes of presentation. In contrast, the linguistic mode of presentation is the minimal mode of presentation of the referent conventionally encoded by referring expressions. This corresponds to what Loar calls the "referential qualifier" (Loar 1976, 2017: 49). Thus, a description "the F" encodes the property of being F; a pronoun such as "she" encodes the property of being a female individual; a name NN encodes the property of being called NN.

The linguistic mode of presentation is typically poorer and more schematic than the exercised mode of presentation, which fleshes it out. Thus consider the following well-known example from Brian Loar's paper on singular terms:

> Suppose that Smith and Jones are unaware that the man being interviewed on television is someone they see on the train every morning and about whom, in that latter role, they have just been talking. Smith says "He is a stockbroker", intending to refer to the man on television; Jones takes Smith to be referring to the man on the train. Now Jones, as it happens, has correctly identified Smith's referent, since the man on television is the man on the train; but he has failed to understand Smith's utterance. It would seem that, as Frege held, some "manner of presentation" of the referent is, even on referential uses, essential to what is being communicated.
>
> (Loar 1976, 2017: 51)

Here the linguistic mode of presentation is the property of the referent which the pronoun "he" encodes: the property of being a male individual, or possibly a *salient* male individual. But the psychological mode of presentation exercised by the speaker (and the comprehending hearer) is something much more specific like "the man on television". Grasping the exercised mode of presentation, on the basis of the linguistic mode of presentation and the context, is essential for understanding, Loar says.

It is tempting to construe the exercised mode of presentation as a "specifization" or "logical restriction" of the linguistic mode of presentation, as the idea of "fleshing out" suggests. Loar resisted that move, however, and I believe he was right. I follow him in holding that the linguistic mode of presentation *constrains* the exercised mode of presentation, without necessarily being like a skeleton which the exercised mode of presentation fleshes out. In my own story, the exercised mode of presentation is a *mental file* deployed in thinking about the referent, and what the referring expression encodes corresponds to a piece of information in the file. The speaker's file and the hearer's file are coordinated, inter alia, via the constraint that they both have to contain the piece of information encoded by the singular term (e.g. that the referent is called "Cicero").[9]

## 5

What has been said thus far suggests the following picture:

**Loar's Picture**

> In opaque belief ascriptions the mode of presentation exercised by the speaker in referring to the individual the ascribed belief is about does double duty: it is not only exercised by the speaker (and whoever properly understands the utterance) but also ascribed to the believer. So whichever relation the linguistic mode of presentation bears to the exercised mode of presentation (which it constrains), it also bears to the ascribed mode of presentation when the report is understood opaquely.

That picture is not general enough, however. Some opaque belief reports involve a single mode of presentation playing a double role, as in Loar's analysis, but others don't. Accordingly, we need to distinguish between several notions, or types, of opacity.

The notion of opacity we have been operating with so far is the following:

**Opacity in the Narrow Sense**

> In opaque belief ascriptions, the exercised mode of presentation, which the linguistic mode of presentation constrains, is simultaneously ascribed to the believer.

But opacity, in that sense, is not the opposite of the notion of "transparency" which we characterized in section 4:

**Transparency**

> In transparent belief ascriptions, no mode of presentation is ascribed to the believer—only the referent (the object the belief is about) is specified.

The opposite of transparency, thus characterized, would correspond to a broader notion of opacity:

**Opacity in the Broad Sense**

> In opaque belief ascriptions, some way of thinking of the referent is ascribed to the believer.

The difference between opacity in the narrow sense and opacity in the broad sense is this: there is opacity in the broad sense provided that some mode of presentation is ascribed to the believer, *even if that mode of presentation is distinct from the exercised mode of presentation*. There is opacity in the narrow sense only if the ascribed mode of presentation *is* the exercised mode of presentation.

Of course, the difference I have just mentioned will only materialize if there are attitude ascriptions such that (i) some mode of presentation is ascribed to the believer, while (ii) the mode of presentation exercised by the speaker is not ascribed to the believer. Are there such reports? I think there are (and they are far from uncommon).[10]

Think of the following story. King Peter wants to know what his subjects sincerely think of him. So he disguises himself as a beggar and goes to the market place, only accompanied by one guard (also disguised). He mixes with the crowd and engages conversation whenever he can. At some point, he notices a woman who keeps looking at him suspiciously. As the woman turns away to talk to an acquaintance, the King whispers to the guard:

(3) She knows I am the King. We should leave.

Let's suppose the woman's name is "Berta". The propositional attitude which King Peter ascribes to Berta is singular: it's about King Peter himself. He says that she knows that *he* is the King. Is the ascription transparent? Is Berta said to know, of King Peter, that he is the King? Clearly not. Every subject in the Kingdom knows that King Peter is the King, and it follows that they all know of King Peter that he is the King. It is not that trivial bit of knowledge which (3) ascribes to Berta. What (3) ascribes to Berta is a quite specific bit of knowledge: that (e.g.) *the short person looking like a beggar and located at such and such a place* is the King. In other words, Peter takes Berta to have seen through his disguise. The true belief he ascribes to her is opaque in the broad sense: it is a belief about Peter that involves a particular way of thinking of Peter. That way of thinking of Peter is ascribed to Berta. It is the "ascribed mode of presentation".

What about the exercised mode of presentation? In ascribing to Berta a belief about himself, Peter refers to himself. How—under which mode of presentation—does he refer to himself? He uses the first person: "She knows that *I* am the King". So he presents himself (the person Berta's belief is about) as the person making this utterance. This mode of presentation is the linguistic mode of presentation (Loar's referential qualifier): "I" encodes the property of being the speaker. That linguistic mode of presentation constrains the exercised mode of presentation, in the sense that whichever mental files the speaker (King Peter himself) and his hearer (the guard) deploy in thinking about the referent must contain the piece of information that the referent is currently making this utterance. That is, indeed, something of which both King Peter and the guard are aware: they both know that Peter is saying "She knows that I am the King" to the guard. So the exercised mode of presentation is a way of thinking of Peter that somehow involves the awareness that Peter is making this utterance; but Berta is unaware that Peter is making this utterance—she is looking away as Peter whispers aside to the guard. It follows that, in this example, the exercised mode of presentation and the ascribed mode of presentation come apart. The ascription is opaque in the broad sense (it is not transparent—a particular mode of presentation is ascribed to the believer) but it is not opaque in the narrow sense (the exercised mode of presentation is not ascribed to the believer).

I conclude that there are more cases of "relational opacity" than those Loar can analyze by means of his "intermediate" logical form for utterances of the type "*a* believes that the F is G":

$B_3$ (*a*, the F, *z is the F and z is G*)

The case in which there is coincidence between the mode of presentation exercised by the speaker in referring to what the belief is about and the mode of presentation ascribed to the believer as part of the content of belief is only a special case (opacity in the narrow sense). Another type of relational opacity involves two distinct modes of presentation, as per the following logical form:

$B_3$ (*a*, the F, *z is the H and z is G*)

Here the ascribed mode of presentation ("the H") and the exercised mode of presentation ("the F") come apart. That is what we found with example (3), which can be analyzed roughly as

$K_3$ (Berta, the speaker, *z is that person looking like a beggar and z is the King*)

## 6

In the "King" example, the linguistic mode of presentation constrains the way the speaker and his addressee think of the referent, but it does not constrain the mode of presentation ascribed to the believer (Berta does not think of the referent as being the speaker). This suggests that, perhaps, the ascribed mode of presentation is constrained by the linguistic mode of presentation only when it is identical to the exercised mode of presentation, which is so constrained.

But is that true? Or could there be cases in which the ascribed mode of presentation is constrained by the linguistic mode of presentation, even though the ascribed mode of presentation is not identical to the exercised mode of presentation? To answer that question, we need to look at the notion of exercised mode of presentation more closely in order to clarify it.

There are two things we know about the exercised mode of presentation. First the exercised mode of presentation is the way the speaker and/or the understanding hearer think(s) of the referent. The speaker and the hearer need not think of the referent in the same way—obviously, the speaker who says "I" does not think of himself in the same way as the addressee thinks of the speaker—but at least their ways of thinking of the referent are coordinated. The coordination is secured, inter alia, via the linguistic mode of presentation, which constrains both the speaker's way of thinking of the referent and the hearer's. That is the second thing we know about the exercised mode of presentation: it is constrained by the linguistic mode of presentation.

These two things may seem to come apart in a class of cases with the following characteristics. The speaker and the hearer think of the referent in a certain way, while ascribing to the believer a different way of thinking of the referent. Thus far, this is like the example discussed in the previous section. But here comes the difference: in the relevant class of cases, the linguistic mode of presentation constrains the believer's way of thinking of the referent, but not the speaker's or the hearer's. That is the opposite of the situation described in the last section.

Consider the following example. The speaker and the hearer know that Mary is not John's future bride; but John thinks she is. In that situation, the speaker can ascribe to John a singular belief about Mary, thought of as his future bride:

(4) John believes that his future bride is coming tonight.

This is not to be understood as an attributive, purely notional ascription ("John believes that whoever will be his bride is coming tonight"), but as a *de re* ascription: John believes of Mary, thought of as his future bride, that she is coming tonight. This is another instance of opaque-relational report, but it cannot be ascribed the same logical form as Loar's example (1) ("John believes that that masked man is a diplomat") because the description "his future bride" is not exercised by the speaker in referring to Mary (or so it seems). *The speaker does not think of Mary as John's future bride.* We can even imagine that he has compelling reasons to believe that John will actually marry Sofia, so for him the description "John's future bride" refers to Sofia. (Let us additionally suppose that he is right and that John's future bride *is* Sofia.) Still, in uttering (4), he says that John believes of Mary, thought of as his future bride, that she is coming tonight. This cannot be rendered as

$B_3$ (John, his future bride, *z is his future bride and z is coming tonight*)

for the first occurrence of "his future bride" would refer to Sofia! What we need, rather, is something like

> $B_3$ (John, Mary, *z is his future bride and z is coming tonight*)

Here, as in the "King" example, the exercised mode of presentation and the ascribed mode of presentation come apart (or so it seems). But, in contrast to the "King" example, it is the ascribed mode of presentation which the linguistic mode of presentation constrains. Here the property of the referent which is encoded by the singular term is the property of being John's future bride; and it is John himself, not the speaker (nor the hearer), who thinks of Mary as his future bride. So it seems that we have found a class of cases in which the linguistic mode of presentation constrains the ascribed mode of presentation rather than the exercised mode of presentation.[11]

But that may not be the right description of the case. It all depends on what we mean by "exercised mode of presentation" (hence the need for clarification which I mentioned above). In standard cases the exercised mode of presentation is the way the speaker/hearer think of the referent, *and* it is constrained by the linguistic mode of presentation (which helps coordinate the speaker's and hearer's respective ways of thinking). In the situation I have described, however, the two things come apart: the linguistic mode of presentation encodes the property of being John's future bride but the speaker and the hearer do *not* think of the referent as being John's future bride. If we decide that the exercised mode of presentation is the way the speaker and the hearer actually think of the referent, we have to conclude, as I have tentatively done, that sometimes the exercised mode of presentation is not constrained by the linguistic mode of presentation, while the ascribed mode of presentation is. But this conclusion is not forced upon us. We can also *stipulate* that the exercised mode of presentation has got to be constrained by the linguistic mode of presentation. After all, the exercised mode of presentation in a belief report is the mode of presentation one exercises in referring to the individual that the belief is about, and one refers to the individual in question by using an expression which encodes certain of its alleged properties. On this view, nothing is the exercised mode of presentation unless it is constrained by the linguistic mode of presentation—there is a constitutive link between the two notions. It follows that, even though the speaker and the hearer do not *think* of Mary as John's future bride in the situation we have described, still in that context they do refer to Mary *as* John's future bride. The mode of presentation they exercise in referring to Mary is not the way *they* think of Mary, but the way that *John* thinks of Mary. In other words: the mode of presentation through which they refer to Mary is a *vicarious mode of presentation*, in such cases. They refer to Mary from John's perspective, by putting themselves into John's shoes.

Pursuing this line of argument will make it possible to maintain that the ascribed mode of presentation is constrained by the linguistic mode of presentation only when it is identical to the exercised mode of presentation (which is always so constrained).

## 7

In several writings over the past 40 years I mentioned the important phenomenon of *oblique reference*. There is oblique reference to some individual $x$ when the mode of presentation through which the speaker refers to $x$ is not the way the speaker herself thinks of $x$ but the way some other person thinks of $x$. In such cases, to understand the utterance you need to understand that the speaker is, as it were, *echoing* some other person and referring to $x$ as that other person would.[12] That the referring expression is used echoically can be indicated by putting it within quotation marks, as in the following examples:

(5) Hey, "your sister" is coming over!
(6) "Quine" has still not finished his paper.

In example (5), from Recanati 1987a, the speaker refers to Ann, who is not the addressee's sister (and who both the speaker and his addressee know not to be the addressee's sister), but who is believed to be the addressee's sister by a third party, James. The speaker is ironically mocking James by referring to Ann as the addressee's sister, thus echoing James' mistake. That is possible because James' mistake is common knowledge between the speaker and his addressee. In that situation, the speaker says of Ann, vicariously thought of as the addressee's sister, that she is coming over. The hearer can respond, "No, she is not—she has stopped and is retracing her steps", and himself refer to Ann by means of the pronoun "she", which anaphorically picks up its reference from the echoic description. Similarly, in (6), from Recanati (2000b, 2001), the speaker ironically uses the name "Quine" (in quotes) to refer to a philosopher, McPherson, whom a third party has misidentified as Quine a few days ago. In that context (6) says that McPherson has still not finished his paper. The speaker can respond, "He has—he told me over lunch that he's just finished" and himself refer to McPherson by means of the pronoun "he", which anaphorically picks up its reference from the echoic name.

There are at least two (compatible) ways to look at the phenomenon. From a strictly semantic point of view, we can account for the shift of reference of the description "your sister" (which does not refer to the addressee's sister, as it should, but to the person whom James takes to be the addressee's sister) or of the name "Quine" (which does not refer to Quine, as it should, but to the philosopher who was misidentified as Quine by the person the speaker is ironically mocking) by means of a *context-shifting operator* contributed by the (implicit or explicit) quotation marks around the expression. Thanks to the operator, the expression refers to what it would refer to in the shifted context (Recanati 1997, 2000b, 2008, 2010). Or, in more cognitive terms, we can say that the linguistic mode of presentation constrains the exercised mode of presentation, as usual, and therefore imposes that the mental file deployed in thinking about the referent contain the piece of information encoded by the expression (that the referent is Quine—or is named "Quine"—or that the referent is the addressee's sister), but that, in this particular case, the mental file deployed in thinking about the referent is not the speaker's (or hearer's) "regular file" about it but an "indexed file", that is, a vicarious file indexed to some other person (and containing the mistaken piece of information).[13]

Oblique reference is particularly useful when one is describing a person's intentional states or actions: it is natural to take that person's perspective (to put oneself in their shoes) in specifying the object the state or action is directed toward. Thus, consider the following passage from Ruth Millikan's *Varieties of Meaning*:

> When a kitten sees itself in the mirror, it tries to approach the other kitten, to smell it and touch it. Failing in this, it then tries to look behind the mirror.
>
> (Millikan 2004: 123)

What the kitten sees in the mirror is what it tries (but fails) to approach, to smell and to touch. In referring to it, however, the speaker (Millikan) adopts two different perspectives: first, from her own, external perspective on the scene, she describes what the kitten sees as "itself"; then, in trying to make sense of the kitten's actions, she adopts the kitten's own perspective in describing what it is trying to approach, smell, and touch: "the other kitten". Of course there is no other kitten. Still, we don't have to treat the description "the other kitten" which Millikan uses as referentially vacuous. We can maintain that the description refers to what the kitten sees, namely itself, but through a vicarious mode of presentation corresponding to the kitten's own perspective: when it looks at itself in the mirror, the kitten mistakes itself for another kitten. This perspective shift could be made explicit by putting the description within quotation marks:

> When a kitten sees itself in the mirror, it tries to approach "the other kitten," to smell it and touch it.

Or consider the following example, from Pinillos (2011), on which I commented several times:

> We were debating whether to investigate both Hesperus and Phosphorus; but when we got evidence of their true identity, we immediately sent probes there.

In the first clause, the speaker espouses the point of view of the unenlightened (herself and her peers before they came to realize that Hesperus is Phosphorus), and she refers to Venus twice, via two distinct mental files (respectively associated with the names "Hesperus" and "Phosphorus") rather than via a single inclusive Venus-file corresponding to her current point of view. The inclusive Venus-file is associated with the demonstrative adverb "there" at the end of the second clause. That second clause expresses the subject's current point of view while the first clause is phrased from the point of view of the speaker and her peers before they learnt the identity (when they thought there were two distinct stars). The exercised modes of presentation associated respectively with each of the two singular terms "Hesperus" and "Phosphorus" in the first clause are mental files indexed to the speaker and her peers at the time of the deliberation which is reported (before they merged the two files into a single, inclusive file). In contrast, when she refers to Venus for the third time at the end of the second clause, the speaker deploys her regular, inclusive Venus-file. Again, we could make the perspective shift explicit by enclosing "Hesperus" and "Phosphorus" within quotation marks.

When a singular belief report is opaque in the broad sense, that is, when a particular mode of presentation of the individual the belief is about is ascribed to the believer, it is always possible to refer obliquely to that individual by vicariously deploying the very mode of presentation which is ascribed to the believer. Thus, instead of "She knows that I am the King", King Peter could have said: "She knows that *that funny beggar talking to you* is the King". That possibility is exploited in the Pinillos example, and it is the key to understanding example (4), to which I finally return:

(4) John believes that his future bride is coming tonight.

The description "his future bride" can be construed as echoic, and thus as referring not to John's future bride (Sofia) but, obliquely, to *the person whom John takes to be* his future bride (Mary). On that interpretation, the mode of presentation which the speaker (and his understanding hearer) exercise in thinking about Mary is not their "regular file" about Mary, but a vicarious file indexed to John, and containing the mistaken piece of information that she is his future bride. The logical form of (4), thus understood, is

> $B^3$ (John, "his future bride", *z is his future bride and z is coming tonight*)

where the quotation marks around the description filling the second argument slot of the triadic belief relation indicate that the description should be evaluated not with respect to the actual world but with respect to what John takes to the actual world (oblique reference). Since, in all the worlds compatible with John's beliefs, his future bride is Mary, the echoic description "his future bride" refers to Mary, and the report ascribes to John a singular belief about her.

In this type of case, the mode of presentation one exercises in referring obliquely to the object the belief is about is the mode of presentation we simultaneously ascribe to the believer. So, as in Loar's example ("that masked man"), the ascribed mode of presentation and the exercised mode of presentation are identical; but in contrast to Loar's example, it is the exercised mode of presentation which is parasitic on the ascribed mode of presentation (via the mechanism of indexed files and oblique reference). The difference can be presented as follows:

- In the "masked man" type of case the mode of presentation exercised by the speaker in referring to the individual the ascribed belief is about does double duty: it is not only exercised by the speaker (and whoever properly understands the utterance) but also ascribed to the believer.
- In the "future bride" type of case the mode of presentation ascribed to the believer does double duty: it is not only ascribed to the believer but also (vicariously) exercised by the speaker in obliquely referring to what the belief is about.

In both types of case, the ascribed mode of presentation and the exercised mode of presentation are identical. This is in contrast to the "King" type of case, where the mode of presentation ascribed to the believer is distinct from the mode of presentation exercised by the speaker (and by whoever properly understands the utterance).

## 8

In the first half of this chapter I presented Loar's criticism of Quine's distinction between notional and relational attitude reports. I defended the claim that, whenever the content clause of an attitude report contains a genuine singular term referring to some individual that the attitude is about, the report has to be construed as "relational", even if it is opaque and fails substitutivity (Figure 3.1). I fully agree with Loar's views on this matter, and have adopted his more comprehensive picture, based upon "a seemingly acceptable kind of statement of which Quine's analysis fails to make sense, but which our expanded version accommodates without difficulty" (Loar 1972, 2017: 22). In the second half of the chapter, I argued that Loar's alternative picture is still not comprehensive enough, as there are more cases of relational opacity than it can accommodate. I therefore attempted to make the picture more complex. The following chart recapitulates some of the distinctions I have made, and the main examples I have used (Figure 3.2).

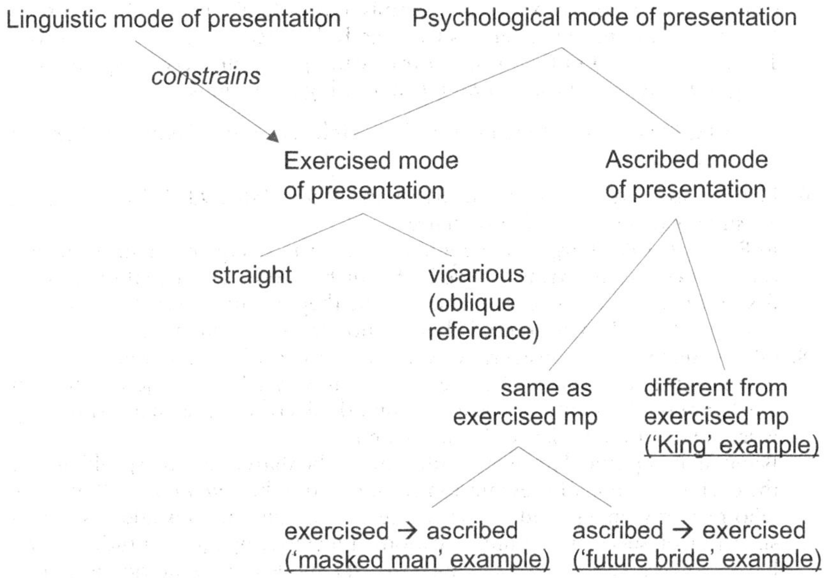


*Figure 3.2* Varieties of Mode of Presentation

## Notes

1. Quine's example is "Procuro un perro que habla" vs "Procuro un perro que hable" (Quine 1956: 177).
2. Thus Quine: "If belief is taken transparently, then 'Tom believes that Cicero denounced Catiline' expresses an outright relation between the men Tom and Cicero . . . .; if belief is taken opaquely, then [that statement] expressly relates Tom to no man" (Quine 1960: 145).
3. "Some belief reports do imply that the believer stands in certain relations to particular items, and these relations are probably at least partially causal relations. Other belief reports do not have such import, but seem to assert something of a rather more general nature about the believer, as well as about his beliefs". (Loar 1972, 2017: 25).
4. "Consider this range of cases. Case (1): we see a large empty shoe; *S* says about its owner, whoever that may be, 'He's rather big'. (. . .) Case (2): we see large footprints on the beach; same utterance. Case (3): we see a mound of sand, which we assume covers a man; same utterance. Case (4): like the last case, except that a leg is protruding. Case (5): we see the man directly; *S* says, pointing, 'He's rather big'". (Loar 1976, 2017: 51–52).
5. Another interesting example Loar gives involves the specific indefinite "a certain":

   Ralph believes that a certain cabinet member is a spy

   This does not mean that Ralph has a general belief to the effect that some cabinet member or other is a spy. As the phrase "a certain" is meant to indicate, there is a particular cabinet member Ralph's belief is about. The belief report, therefore, is relational. However, Loar points out that that statement "will often be taken to imply more than" the purely relational "there is a cabinet member x such that Ralph believes x is a spy" (Loar 1972, 2017: 22). On the most natural reading, Ralph ascribes spyhood to the guy *thought as a cabinet member.* The logical form is:

($\exists x$) ($x$ is a cabinet member & $B^3$ (Ralph, $x$, *z is a cabinet member and z is a spy*))

6. Loar himself says "at least". In Recanati (1993: 386–393) I distinguish six possible readings for such a sentence.
7. In Recanati 1993 I argue that genuine singular terms (proper names, indexicals etc.) convey a lexical feature REF which encodes referentiality. Definite descriptions can be used referentially but they are not lexically referential (they can be "token-referential" but are not "type-referential").
8. Of course, the same considerations which apply to Cicero also apply to Catiline: the speaker presents Catiline in a certain way when she ascribes to Tom a belief about him; and the believer, Tom, thinks of Catiline in a certain way when he judges that Cicero denounced him.
9. Being mental particulars, mental files cannot be shared, strictly speaking. But the exercised mode of presentation is supposed to be *common* to all of those who properly understand the utterance (the speaker and his addressee, in a situation of successful communication). Likewise, opaque attitude reports have just been characterized as such that the mode of presentation exercised by the hearer is ascribed to the attitude holder: that means that the mode of presentation in question is shared by the speaker (and the understanding hearer) *and* the attitude holder. To make sense of these claims, "sharing" has to be understood loosely. On that understanding, a mode of presentation is shared between individuals just in case the mental files they deploy have enough in common, i.e. just in case they all satisfy the constraint set up by the linguistic mode of presentation plus whatever constraints derive from the speaker's communicative intention (in Loar's example: the intention to speak of the man on television). The claim that, in opaque attitude reports (or some of them at least), the exercised mode of presentation and the ascribed mode of presentation are "identical" will have to be understood in the same manner, i.e. as not requiring actual identity but only sufficient similarity.
10. See Morgan (2011: 177) for a detailed example.
11. Another example in the same category is mentioned by Jennifer Hornsby (who, like Loar, argues for the existence of reports that are both relational and opaque): "Bill thinks that the bank manager was rude, but it actually was a clerk about whom Bill reached that conclusion" (Hornsby 1977: 34).
12. The label "echoic" comes from Sperber and Wilson (1981, 1986). Other labels are used for what is essentially the same phenomenon: "polyphony" (Ducrot 1980a, 1980b, 1984, Recanati 1987b), "staging" (Clark 1996: chapter 12) and "protagonist projection" (Holton 1997; Stokke 2013). Davies (1981: 178–179) speaks of "non-literal anaphoric uses".
13. On indexed files see Recanati (2012, 2016).

## References

Bach, K. (1987) *Thought and Reference.* Oxford: Clarendon Press.

Clark, H. (1996) *Using Language.* Cambridge: Cambridge University Press.

Davies, M. (1981) *Meaning, Quantification, Necessity.* London: Routledge and Kegan Paul.

Ducrot, O. (1980a) Analyses Pragmatiques. *Communications* 32: 11–60.

Ducrot, O. (1980b) Analyse de texte et linguistique de l'énonciation. In O. Ducrot *et al.* (eds.) *Les Mots du discours*, 7–56. Paris: Editions de Minuit.

Ducrot, O. (1984) Esquisse d'une théorie polyphonique de l'énonciation. In O. Ducrot (ed.) *Le Dire et le Dit*, 171–233. Paris: Editions de Minuit.

Holton, R. (1997) Some Telling Examples: A Reply to Tsohatzidis. *Journal of Pragmatics* 28: 625–628.

Hornsby, J. (1977) Singular Terms in Contexts of Propositional Attitude. *Mind* 86: 31–48.

Loar, B. (1972) Reference and Propositional Attitudes. *Philosophical Review* 81: 43–62. Reprinted in Loar 2017, 14–28.

Loar, B. (1976) The Semantics of Singular Terms. *Philosophical Studies* 30: 353–377. Reprinted in Loar 2017, 48–68.

Loar, B. (2017) *Consciousness and Meaning: Selected Essays*. Oxford: Oxford University Press.

Millikan, R. (2004) *Varieties of Meaning*. Cambridge, MA: MIT Press.

Morgan, D. (2011) *First Person Thinking*. PhD dissertation, University of Oxford.

Pinillos, A. (2011) Coreference and Meaning. *Philosophical Studies* 154: 301–324.

Quine, W.V.O. (1956) Quantifiers and Propositional Attitudes. *Journal of Philosophy* 53: 177–187.

Quine, W.V.O. (1960) *Word and Object*. Cambridge, MA: MIT Press.

Quine, W.V.O. (1961) *From a Logical Point of View*, 2nd ed. Cambridge, MA: Harvard University Press.

Recanati, F. (1987a) Contextual Dependence and Definite Descriptions. *Proceedings of the Aristotelian Society* 87: 57–73.

Recanati, F. (1987b) *Meaning and Force*. Cambridge: Cambridge University Press.

Recanati, F. (1993) *Direct Reference: From Language to Thought*. Oxford: Blackwell.

Recanati, F. (1997) Can We Believe What We Do Not Understand? *Mind and Language* 12: 84–100.

Recanati, F. (2000a) Opacity and the Attitudes. In Orenstein, A. and Kotatko, P. (eds.) *Knowledge, Language and Logic: Questions for Quine*, 367–406. Dordrecht: Kluwer.

Recanati, F. (2000b) *Oratio Obliqua, Oratio Recta*. Cambridge, MA: MIT Press/Bradford Books.

Recanati, F. (2001) Open Quotation. *Mind* 110: 637–687. Revised version in Recanati 2010, chapter 7.

Recanati, F. (2008) Open Quotation Revisited. *Philosophical Perspectives* 22: 443–471. Revised version in Recanati 2010, chapter 8.

Recanati, F. (2010) *Truth-Conditional Pragmatics*. Oxford: Oxford University Press.

Recanati, F. (2012) *Mental Files*. Oxford: Oxford University Press.

Recanati, F. (2016) *Mental Files in Flux*. Oxford: Oxford University Press.

Sperber, D. and Wilson, D. (1981) Irony and the Use/Mention Distinction. In P. Cole (ed.) *Radical Pragmatics*, 295–318. London: Academic Press.

Sperber, D. and Wilson, D. (1986) *Relevance*. Oxford: Blackwell.

Stokke, A. (2013) Protagonist Projection. *Mind and Language* 28: 204–232.

# 4 Expression-Meaning and Vagueness

*Stephen Schiffer*

In "Two Theories of Meaning," the most important of his papers in the philosophy of language, Brian Loar asked:

> What facts about a sentence constitute its meaning—that is, its meaning in abstraction from any particular utterance, and in so far as it belongs to the language of a particular population?

The answer he proceeded to give was a theory of expression-meaning in support of the Gricean program of intention-based semantics (IBS). IBS is a two-stage program for reducing all questions about the intentionality of speech acts and linguistic expressions to questions about the intentionality of thought: in the first stage a certain notion of *speaker-meaning* is to be taken as foundational in the theory of meaning and defined, without recourse to any public-language semantic notions, in terms of acting with certain audience-directed intentions, and in the second stage the semantic features of linguistic expressions are to be defined in terms of the now defined notion of speaker-meaning, together with certain ancillary notions, such as that of *convention*, also to be defined in terms of nonsemantic propositional attitudes. A widely-held view about the relation between language and thought is that it is only our intentional mental states—believing, intending, and the like—that have *original* intentionality, intentionality that doesn't have its source in something else's intentionality; the intentionality of speech acts and words is *derived* intentionality, intentionality inherited from that of associated mental states. But that derivation story is plausible only if there is a plausible explanation of *how* speech acts and words inherit their intentionality from the propositional attitudes implicated in linguistic behavior. IBS aims to provide that plausible explanation.[1] In the late 60s, when Brian began writing his D. Phil. thesis on *Sentence Meaning*, detailed revisions by Grice (1969) and myself (1972) of Grice's 1957 account of speaker-meaning were available to explain how propositional speech acts inherit their intentionality from the propositional attitudes in terms of which they, the speech acts, were defined, but there was nothing close to a comparably detailed account to show how expression-meaning was definable in terms of a Gricean account of speaker-meaning. The account of expression-meaning Brian advanced in his dissertation was intended to fill that gap, and that is the account a revised version of which finally appeared in print in "Two Theories of Meaning." That account, in my estimation, is probably as good an account of expression-meaning as IBS can hope to achieve. But it shares a certain feature with every other IBS theory, and, as we'll see, that feature proves to be the banana peel under every IBS theorist's heel. The feature to which I allude is that every theory constructed under the IBS banner ignores vagueness, as though it simply didn't exist, and thus makes no attempt to accommodate the vagueness of vague expressions or vague acts of speaker-meaning, notwithstanding that virtually every sentence we utter and virtually every act of speaker-meaning is vague.

Of course, proponents of IBS knew what they were doing. Part of the reason they ignored vagueness was that not to ignore it would require them to have a theory of vagueness, which they didn't have, and couldn't have had, since no IBS theorist had ever worked on vagueness. Yet that doesn't explain why IBS theorists developed their semantic theories under the pretense that there were no vague expressions or vague speech acts, for they might have concluded that, since virtually every expression and speech act was vague, it would be reckless to devise theories of meaning, reference, and speech acts when one had no idea how the vagueness of an expression affected its semantics or how the vagueness of an act of speaker-meaning affected what was meant in its performance. Evidently, however, Grice, Brian, and I must have believed that our ignoring vagueness was nothing worse than a useful idealization, akin, perhaps, to Galileo's ignoring friction in his theories of bodies in motion. *Is* that what we thought? Actually, I'm not sure any of us ever considered the question; at least I can't *recall* a single time in the countless conversations I had about IBS issues with Grice and Brian in the 20 years between 1965 and 1985 that the question even came up. At the same time, I suspect that if the question had been put to us we would have come up with some version of the harmless-idealization line. If that is right, then we were wrong: vagueness, as I will here try to show, defeats the program of intention-based semantics. Brian's account of expression-meaning makes it possible to sketch the architecture of a theory that realizes the IBS program, and once we have that we'll be positioned to see why vagueness defeats IBS. Now, in idealizing vagueness out of their theories IBS theorists were in good company, for virtually every presentation of a foundational semantic or metasemantic theory ignores vagueness, and in seeing why vagueness defeats IBS we'll also see why it defeats nearly every other extant theory of meaning.

## 1. The Architecture of IBS

That architecture has the following parts.

a. The most foundational IBS notion is that of *speaker-meaning*; this is where the semantic makes its first contact with the psychological. Speaker-meaning is the most general kind of illocutionary act, the genus of which all other kinds of illocutionary acts are species (see Schiffer 1972, Ch. IV). There are interrogative and imperatival acts of speaker-meaning, but present purposes will be adequately served if we identify speaker-meaning with *assertoric* speaker-meaning (henceforth simply speaker-meaning), i.e. meaning that such-and-such is the case, as when in uttering 'J'ai faim' Odile meant that she was hungry. IBS takes speaker-meaning to be a relation, *S meant p*, between a person *S* and a proposition *p* that she meant, where a proposition is any abstract entity that has truth conditions, has those truth conditions necessarily, and is mind- and language-independent in that it belongs to no language and wasn't created by what anyone said or thought.[2] That relation, as already noted, is then defined wholly in terms of acting with certain audience-directed intentions. There is no official IBS definition of speaker-meaning, and IBS theorists may disagree among themselves about how exactly the details of that definition should go, but the following toy conditions will highlight the features of an IBS account of speaker-meaning most relevant to this essay:

> For any person *S*, proposition *p*, and utterance *x*,[3] *S* meant *p* in uttering *x* iff for some person *A* and feature *φ*, *S* intended it to be mutual (or common) knowledge between *A* and *S* that *x* has *φ* and, on the basis primarily of that, mutual knowledge that *S* uttered *x* intending her utterance of *x* to result in *A*'s actively believing *p*.

Let's call the value of '*φ*' in an act of speaker-meaning its *inference-base feature* (its *IB-feature*, for short). Acts of speaker-meaning are typically performed by uttering sentences of a language common to the speaker and her audience, and, according to IBS, the IB-features of those sentences are their meanings. If you utter "It's snowing" to communicate that it's snowing, the IB-feature of the sentence "It's snowing" on which you rely is the meaning of that sentence in English. The reason IB-features are typically meaning properties is that meaning properties are *optimal* IB-features: if you want to tell your child that it's snowing, you would do much better to utter "It's snowing" than to attempt to communicate that it's snowing by impersonating a snowflake. At the same time, a *sine qua non* of the IBS account of speaker-meaning is that the only intentional notions mentioned on its right-hand side are ordinary propositional-attitude notions, and, consequently, for a person to mean a proposition, it's not a necessary condition that what she utters has any sort of semantic property as its IB-feature. For example, during a lecture one might communicate to one's friend that one is bored by closing one's eyes and pretending to snore. The fact that the IB-feature needn't be a semantic feature is (supposed to be) what makes it in principle possible to define expression-meaning in terms of speaker-meaning. The IBS strategy for defining expression-meaning is to define it in terms of certain conventional regularities in communicative behavior that *explain* why a sentence's having the meaning it has in a certain population of speakers makes uttering that sentence an optimal way for a member of the population to communicate to another of its members a proposition that conforms to that meaning.

b. Having defined speaker-meaning, the next thing on the IBS agenda is defining all other agent-semantic notions in terms of the now defined notion of speaker-meaning. Here the most important notions are *illocutionary act* and *speaker-reference*. IBS dispatches illocutionary acts simply by identifying each kind of illocutionary act with a particular kind of act of speaker-meaning (see Schiffer 1972, Ch. IV). As for speaker-reference, there are a few interrelated notions of speaker-reference, but the two most important for present purposes are notions of what I will call *primary* (or first-order) speaker-reference (Schiffer 1981b; see also Neale 2016; Schiffer 2016). I'll call the first of these notions *referring-**in*** (*referring*$_i$) and define it thus:

> *S referred*$_i$ to *o* in (the course of) uttering $x$ iff, for some *o*-dependent proposition $p_o$, *S meant* $p_o$ in uttering $x$.[4]

For example,

> In nodding her head in response to the question "Is Henry coming to the party?", Jane meant the Henry-dependent proposition *that Henry was coming to the party*, and thus referred$_i$ to Henry in nodding her head.
>
> In uttering 'He's coming to the party' in response to the question "Is Henry coming to the party?", Jane meant the Henry-dependent proposition *that Henry was coming to the party*, and thus referred$_i$ to Henry in uttering that sentence.

Although in both examples Jane referred to Henry, there is an important difference between them: in the first example, there was no part of Jane's "utterance" (in this case, her nodding) *with which* she referred to him, but in the second example there was; there she referred to him *with* the demonstrative pronoun 'he'. *Referring-**with*** (*referring*$_w$) is the second of the two notions of primary reference to which I alluded, and it may be defined (at least to a first approximation) thus:

> In uttering $x$, *S* referred$_w$ to *o* with the *i*th occurrence of *e* in $x$, $e_{ix}$, iff for some property $\varphi$ and audience *A*, *S* uttered $x$ intending it to

be mutual knowledge between $S$ and $A$ that $e_{ix}$ has $\varphi$ and, on the basis primarily of that, mutual knowledge that $S$ referred$_i$ to $o$ in uttering $x$.[5]

*Primary* speaker-reference, then, is *de re* speaker-meaning. To refer to a thing $o$ in an act of primary speaker-reference is to mean some proposition *about* $o$. In ($n > 1$)th order speaker reference the speaker refers to a thing not in order to mean something about it, but in order to refer to a thing to which she is making an ($n$—1)th order reference. For example, in uttering

That boy next to Mary is noisy

the speaker is making a primary reference to *that boy next to Mary* and a secondary reference to *Mary*; and in

That boy next to that man talking to Mary is noisy

the speaker is making a primary reference to *that boy next to that man talking to Mary*, a secondary reference to *that man talking to Mary*, and a tertiary reference to *Mary*. And so on.[6]

c. Having defined speaker-meaning and all other agent-semantic notions in terms of nonsemantic propositional attitudes, the one remaining thing on the IBS agenda is to define expression-meaning in terms of the already constructed IBS definitions. The strategy for doing this that best suited IBS, and the one Brian adopted, was inspired by David Lewis (1969). That strategy has two parts. In the first part, a language is taken to be a certain kind of abstract object that may or may not be used by anyone—namely, a finitely specifiable function from infinitely many finite strings of sounds (marks, gestures, neural states, whatever) to things of the kind meanings must be. Now, a language may be used in more than one way. Of special importance to an understanding of IBS is that a language may be used in one, or both, of the following two ways. First, it may be used by a population as its *public language*, the language members of the population use to communicate with one another. Second, if, as many suppose, we think—i.e. process information—in a neural system of mental representation, one's "brain's language of synaptic interconnections and neural spikes" (Lewis 1983, p. 346), then a language may be used by a person as her *language of thought*. So an expression $\varepsilon$ can't simply mean $\mu$ for $x$; $\varepsilon$ can only mean $\mu$ for $x$ by meaning $\mu$ in a language $x$ uses as a public language or in a language $x$ uses as a language of thought (or in a language $x$ uses in some other way). Since use as a public language and use as a language of thought are the only two uses that need for present purposes to come into play, it will be convenient to stipulate that:

> $\varepsilon$ means$_P$ $\mu$ for $x$ iff for some language $L$ and population $Q$, (i) $L(\varepsilon) = \mu$, (ii) $L$ is the (or a) public language of $Q$, and (iii) $x$ is a member of $Q$.
>
> $\varepsilon$ means$_T$ $\mu$ for $x$ iff for some language $L$, (i) $L(\varepsilon) = \mu$ and (ii) $L$ is $x$'s language of thought.

Let's say that the *public-language relation* is that relation that must obtain between a language $L$ and a population $Q$ in order for $L$ to be the public language of $Q$, and let's say that the *language-of-thought relation* is that relation that must obtain between a language $L$ and a person $x$ in order for $L$ to be $x$'s language of thought. Then we see that to define expression-meaning$_P$ is just to define the public-language relation, and that to define expression-meaning$_T$ is just to define the language-of-thought relation. The expression-meaning that IBS aims to define in terms of the propositional attitudes that define speaker-meaning is expression-meaning$_P$. So the second part of the Lewis-inspired IBS strategy is to define the public-language relation, and for the IBS theorist this will require defining that relation in terms of the way members of $P$ use $L$ to perform acts of speaker-meaning.

d. An IBS account of expression-meaning$_P$ requires more than defining expression-meaning$_P$ in terms of the propositional attitudes that define speaker-meaning. This is because IBS aims not merely to *define* linguistic intentionality in terms of mental intentionality; it aims to *reduce* linguistic intentionality to mental intentionality. This reductionist aspiration can be achieved only if expression-meaning$_T$ can be explicated without any appeal to the notion of expression-meaning$_P$; that is to say, only if the language-of-thought relation can be defined in terms of notions whose explications require no recourse to the public-language relation. This may be explained in the following way. IBS theorists have no trouble accepting the hypothesis that we think in a language of thought, provided it entails some refinement of the idea that:

> Necessarily, for any proposition $p$ and person $x$, $x$ believes $p$ just in case a sentence which means$_T$ $p$ for $x$ is tokened in $x$'s belief box.[7]

And when a proposition $p$'s being the content of a belief is defined in terms of a mentalese sentence's meaning$_T$, then the most major commitment of IBS may be put by saying that mentalese sentences are "the basic objects of interpretation; their content confers content upon thoughts; and thoughts transmit their content to outer speech" (McGinn 1982, p. 70). So IBS not only needs an account of the public-language relation, it also needs at least to show that a certain kind of account of the language-of-thought relation is possible. But while IBS took itself to have a strategy for defining the public-language relation, its having a strategy for defining the language-of-thought relation was left for a future occasion.

Let's return to the Lewis-inspired IBS strategy for explaining expression-meaning$_P$. The first part of that strategy required defining a language as a finitely specifiable function from finite sequences of sound, marks, whatever, onto things that might be their public-language meanings. In order to implement this part of his strategy, the IBS theorist must first do two things. So far I've characterized IBS as holding that speaker-meaning is a relation between speakers and propositions of some stripe or other. The first thing the IBS theorist must do is settle on the stripe of the propositions we mean; this is essential in order to know what word meanings should be taken to be. IBS theorists may disagree among themselves as to the nature of the propositions that comprise the range of the speaker-meaning relation, but for convenience of exposition I will initially suppose them to be Russellian, structured entities made up of the objects and properties that our speech acts are about. I don't really think they can be Russellian propositions, for I don't think that what a speaker would mean in uttering "J. K. Rowling is the author of the Harry Potter novels" is the same as what he would mean in uttering "Robert Galbraith is the author of the Harry Potter novels", but once I reach the conclusions I need to reach relative to the Russellian assumption, it will be easy to show (in §IV) that those conclusions would also have been reached relative to any other assumption about the nature of the propositions we mean. The second thing the IBS theorist must do is say what expression-meanings must be relative to the assumption that the things we mean are Russellian propositions. Now IBS takes sentences to be devices for performing acts of speaker-meaning, and it takes their meanings to provide bases from which hearers may infer what speakers mean in producing unembedded utterances of those sentences. If declarative sentences were context *in*sensitive, the IBS theorist could take their meanings to be the propositions that, all else being equal, speakers would mean in producing unembedded utterances of them, and it would take the meanings of words and other subsentential expressions to be the objects and properties that compose those propositions. But since hardly any of the sentences we utter are context insensitive, IBS will want to take expression-meanings to be things that *constrain* what speakers can mean in uttering those sentences. This may be spelled out in the following way.

Like virtually every other philosopher who has written about context-sensitive expressions, the IBS theorist recognizes two kinds of meanings, which I'll call *meanings* and *contents*. Meanings are properties of expression-types, contents of expression-tokens (≈ utterances of expressions[8]). The meaning of an expression-type $\varepsilon$ determines, for any $x$ and any token $\varepsilon_\tau$ of $\varepsilon$, what is required for $x$ to be the content of $\varepsilon_\tau$. Contents of declarative sentence tokens are (we're supposing) Russellian propositions, and if a proposition is the content of an unembedded token of a declarative sentence, then that proposition is what the speaker *said* in producing the token, if she said anything in producing it. The content of every expression token is its contribution to the content of the unembedded sentence token in which it occurs (an unembedded sentence token counts as occurring in itself). The meaning of a context-*in*sensitive expression will assign the same content to every token of the expression which has a content, whereas the meaning of a context-sensitive expression will permit different tokens of the expression to have different contents. I'll call this way of understanding meanings and contents the *meaning/content model* (the M/C model, for short).

Given the M/C model it's useful to represent the meaning of an expression as a function from its tokens to their contents; to define such a function is to specify, for any possible content $c$ and expression $\varepsilon$, the conditions that must be satisfied in order for $c$ to be the content of a token of $\varepsilon$.[9] So conceptualized, the meaning of a context-insensitive expression will be a constant function that maps every token of the expression onto the same content, and the meaning of a context-sensitive expression will be a nonconstant function whose values may differ from one token of the expression to the next. Since IBS takes a language to be a *finitely specifiable* function that maps its expressions onto their meanings, it is committed to taking the meaning of a complex expression to be a syntax-determined function of the meanings of its constituent words (or other morphemes); consequently, the only meanings that must be specified in defining a language are those given in the base-clauses for the language's morphemes. Specifying the meaning of a context-insensitive word merely requires saying what unique content each of its tokens must have. For example, the theorist might say that the meaning of "Saul Kripke" is that function $f$ such that, for any token $\tau$ of "Saul Kripke", $f(\tau)$ = Saul Kripke. As for context-sensitive words it will prove useful to see specifications of the functions that are their meanings as completions of the schema

For any token $\varepsilon_\tau$ of $\varepsilon$ and any x, $f(\varepsilon_\tau) = x$ iff

(1) [*eligibility* condition] . . .;
(2) [*selection* condition] . . .,

where the eligibility condition for an expression specifies the condition that something must satisfy in order for it to be eligible to be the content of a token of the expression, and the selection condition selects which of the things eligible to be the content is the content. For example, one might specify the meaning of the demonstrative 'she' thus:

$x$ is the content of a token $\tau$ of "she" iff

(1) [eligibility condition] $x$ is female;
(2) [selection condition] $x$ is uniquely such that the speaker who produced $\tau$ referred to $x$ with $\tau$.

The schema admits the possibility of two kinds of limiting cases. At one limit, the eligibility condition is such that only one thing can satisfy it, and in this case the eligibility condition also does the work of the selection condition. The meaning of 'I' is like this if the content of a token of "I" is the speaker who produced it. At the other limit, the eligibility condition imposes no restriction on the kind of thing that can be a content, and in this case the selection condition also does the work of the eligibility condition. Perhaps no word is at this limit, although "it", when used as a demonstrative pronoun, would be if all it takes for a thing to be the content of a token of "it" is that the speaker referred to it with the token.[10]

Having defined a language as a finitely specifiable mapping of sounds onto meanings, the IBS theorist sets out to complete his account of expression-meaning by defining the public-language relation, the relation that must obtain between a population *P* and a language *L* in order for *L* to be a public language of *P*. There were known to be problems that arose in attempting to define the public-language relation, perhaps the biggest being what David Lewis (1975) dubbed the *meaning-without-use problem*, and they were the problems that Brian sought to solve in "Two Theories of Meaning." Now, in order for a definition of the public-language relation to provide an *IBS* account of expression-meaning its defining conditions must involve no ineliminable semantic notions, but only those propositional-attitude notions that, according to IBS, define speaker-meaning and convention, and elsewhere (2017) I have argued that that requirement can't be met, and that therefore there can be no correct IBS account of expression-meaning. Be that as it may, however, I will now present a new argument to show why no IBS account of expression-meaning can be correct. This argument will have relevance well beyond IBS, however; for, if it's sound, it will show that no account of expression-meaning that presupposes the M/C model can be correct, and a corollary of this will be that natural languages don't have the kind of compositional semantics that nearly every philosopher of language and semanticist supposes they must have.

## 2. Penumbral Shift and Context Sensitivity

How might the M/C model accommodate vague terms when it's not ignoring their vagueness? Many vague expressions are obviously context sensitive, whether or not their vagueness is taken into account, and they therefore can be accommodated in the model only if it can assign them meanings that are specifiable by instances of the schema:

For any token $\varepsilon_\tau$ of $\varepsilon$ and any x, $f(\varepsilon_\tau) = x$ iff

(1) [eligibility condition] . . .;
(2) [selection condition)] . . . .

Such terms include, for example, "here", "fast", "tall", and "intelligent". But other vague expressions will be treated by the model as context insensitive when their vagueness is ignored. Such terms include "boy", "bachelor", "bald man", "neurotic", "logician", "athlete", and "triangular". For example, when its vagueness is being ignored (and the things we mean are taken to be Russellian propositions), the IBS theorist would say that the meaning of "boy" is a constant function that maps every token of the word onto the property of being a boy. Let's call such terms *predicates**. What can the model say about predicates* when it's *not* ignoring their vagueness? Let's start by noticing that every predicate* has a feature, consequent on its being vague, such that, owing to its having that feature, the predicate* can be accommodated in the M/C model only if it can be assigned a context-sensitive meaning, i.e. a meaning that is specifiable as an instance of the just displayed schema. I call this feature *penumbral shift*, and it may be explained in the following way.

The notion of penumbral shift is defined in terms of the notion of a *penumbral profile*. Every token of every predicate* has a penumbral profile, where two predicate* tokens have the same penumbral profile just in case if either applies to a thing, then so does the other; if either is such that it's indeterminate whether it applies to a thing, then so is the other; if either is such that it's indeterminate whether it's indeterminate whether it applies to a thing, then so is the other; and so on.[11] We may think of a predicate* token's penumbral profile as determining the token's *penumbra*, where a vague predicate* token's penumbra is the range of things to which the token's application is anything other than unqualifiedly correct or unqualifiedly incorrect. Thus, a vague predicate* token's penumbra includes the token's borderline cases, borderline cases of its borderline cases, borderline cases of its borderline cases of its borderline cases, and so on.[12] *Penumbral shift* is then the fact that the penumbral profiles, and thus the penumbras, of a predicate*'s tokens may shift somewhat from one token to the next; that is to say, two tokens of a predicate* may have somewhat different penumbral profiles, and thus two different penumbras. The "somewhat" qualification is important. Typically, there will be numerous things of which every token of a predicate* must be true, and even more things of which every token of it must be false. For example, if Clyde is a man whose scalp is as hairless as a billiard ball and on whose scalp no hair can grow, then every token of "bald man" must be true of Clyde, and if Clyde is blessed with a head of hair like the one Tom Cruise appears to have, then every token of "bald man" must be false of him. At the same time, penumbral shift makes it possible for there to be three simultaneous tokens of any predicate*, one of which is true of the thing to which it's applied, another of which is false of the thing to which it's applied, and still another of which is such that it's indeterminate whether it's true of the thing to which it's applied. Here are three examples:

- At a party, George is asked whether Henrietta came to the party with anyone, and he replies "She came with some bald guy". That utterance would most likely be accepted in the context in which it occurred as true, even if it transpires that the man in question shaves his scalp but wouldn't be said to be bald if he let his hair grow out. In another conversation, however, in which the discussion is about hereditary baldness, someone might correct a remark about the same man by saying "No; he's not bald; he just shaves his scalp", and that utterance, in that context, would very likely count as true. In still another context the question is raised whether a man who shaved his scalp would be bald if no one would take him to be bald if he stopped shaving his scalp and let his hair grow out, and in that context, it might be true to say "That's undetermined by the use of 'bald' in everyday speech; such a man would be neither determinately bald nor determinately not bald".

- In a community in which people typically marry before the age of 20, an utterance of "He's a bachelor" may count as true when said of an unmarried 18-year-old male, whereas in a conversation among New Yorkers, where for both men and women the average age for a first marriage is between 30 and 35, an utterance of "He's a bachelor" would most likely not count as determinately true when said of an unmarried 18-year-old male, and may even count as false.
- An utterance of 'Mary is getting married to a boy from Boston' would count as false if the male whom she is about to marry is 52 years old, but is apt not to count as false if he is 27 years old. At the same time, if every one of the seven male professors in one's department is over 40 except Henry, who is 27, an utterance of "Six men and one boy are professors in my department" would count as a misuse of "boy".

Let's take "boy" as our exemplar of a predicate* and ask how a theorist might attempt to accommodate it in the M/C model when its vagueness is taken into account.

We may start by asking what the IBS theorist might say about the content of the token of "boy" uttered by Jack in the following example.

> Jack and Jill are on a first date, and at the moment are telling one another about their respective families. Jack has just told Jill that he has a sister who has a 7-year-old child named 'Morgan", and then, realizing that "Morgan" is a unisex name, adds "Morgan is a boy".

IBS holds that the things we mean, and thus the contents of declarative sentence tokens, are propositions, and we are provisionally assuming that IBS takes those propositions to be Russellian propositions. If an IBS theorist were ignoring vagueness, she would say that what Jack meant in uttering "Morgan is a boy", and the content of the token of that sentence he uttered, is the singular proposition <Morgan, the property of being a boy>;[13] for if the theorist is ignoring vagueness, then she would say that "boy" is context insensitive, and that its meaning is that function $f$ such that for any token $\tau$ of "boy" and any $x$, $f(\tau) = x$ iff $x =$ the property of being a boy, and that therefore the content of the token of "boy" Jack uttered is the same as every other token of "boy", viz. the property of being a boy. But now we are supposing the theorist not to be ignoring vagueness, and "boy" is vague. It's vague because even if the token of "Morgan is a boy" that Jack uttered is determinately true or determinately false, it might have been neither: Morgan might have been a borderline case of a thing to which "boy" applies, either because Morgan is a borderline case of a male, or of a human being, or because he's of an age such that it's indeterminate whether "boy", as uttered by Jack, applies to a human male of that age. So what can the theorist say about the content of the token of 'boy' Jack uttered? All that we can say at this point is that its content can't be the property of being a boy, and this because there can be no such property as *the* property of being a boy. For if there were such a property, then it would have to be the content of every token of "boy", and penumbral shift secures that no property has to be the content of every token of the word. Because of penumbral shift, the M/C model must treat "boy" as a context-sensitive term; that is to say, if the model is to account for the word's meaning in a way that takes account of its vagueness, then it can do so only by finding a true completion of the schema:

> For any token $\tau$ of "boy" and any property $\varphi$, $f(\tau) = \varphi$ iff
>
> (1) [eligibility condition] . . .;
> (2) [selection condition] . . . .

What options does the M/C model have for achieving such a completion? In order to answer this, we would first have to know what options are available to the model for saying what the contents of tokens of "boy" are, given the provisional assumption that the contents of declarative sentence tokens are Russellian propositions. We can make this question more tractable by returning to the example of Jack's utterance of "Morgan is a boy" (above p . . .) and asking what the M/C model can say about the content of the token of "boy" Jack uttered. However, since properties, like propositions, are mind- and language-independent entities, the M/C theorist can't say what the content of a token of 'boy' might be without first taking a stand on the issue of ontic vagueness, or vagueness in the world, at least as regards properties.

## 3. Ontic Vagueness and the Meaning of "Boy"

The issue of ontic vagueness is a contest between a view we might call *no-vagueness-in-the-world* and one we might call *vagueness-in-the-world*. What exactly is at issue in this contest doesn't escape vagueness, but I think the following gloss should be good enough for present purposes.

No-vagueness-in-the-world holds that vagueness is exclusively a feature of language and thought and that, therefore, nothing outside of language and thought can be vague in its own right, independently of the vagueness of language and thought, while vagueness-in-the-world holds that vagueness isn't exclusively a feature of language and thought and that, therefore, properties or things outside of language and thought may be vague in their own right. I'll say that things that aren't vague in their own right are *metaphysically precise*, and that things that are vague in their own right are *metaphysically vague*. A Russellian proposition is metaphysically precise just in case each of its constituent properties or objects is metaphysically precise, and metaphysically vague just in case one or more of its constituent properties or objects is metaphysically vague. Since our concern now is to characterize the kind of property that might function as the content of the token of "boy" Jack uttered when he uttered "Marlon is a boy", we need only to engage the issue of ontic vagueness as regards properties. So, what would it be for a property to be metaphysically precise or vague? What, to begin, would it be for a property to be metaphysically vague? Some philosophers doubt whether we can make coherent sense of vagueness-in-the-world, but in order to give the views against which I'll be arguing the best run for their money, I will assume that vagueness-in-the-world is a view to be reckoned with. Consequently, when I ask what it would be for a property to be metaphysically vague, I'm really asking what is the best answer to that question that a proponent of vagueness-in-the-world might give. How would such a theorist say what a metaphysically-vague property is?

One thing the theorist will want to say is that $\varphi$ is a metaphysically-vague property *only if* it's possible for there to be a metaphysically-precise object *o* such that it's metaphysically indeterminate whether *o* has $\varphi$, where that means that there is no fact of the matter as to whether *o* has $\varphi$.[14] But the theorist won't be able to say that $\varphi$ is metaphysically vague *if o* is metaphysically precise and it's metaphysically indeterminate whether *o* has $\varphi$. This is because no-*vagueness*-in-the-world doesn't entail no-*indeterminacy*-in-the-world and we can't rule out that there might be a precise object *x* and a precise property $\varphi$ such that, while *x* can't be a borderline instance of $\varphi$, it's nevertheless metaphysically indeterminate whether *x* has $\varphi$—for example, it may be metaphysically indeterminate that a given alpha particle will decay within a certain period, where that metaphysical indeterminacy can't be explained by attributing vagueness to any object or property. What must a vague property be like so that its being metaphysically indeterminate whether a thing has that property can be explained in terms of the property's vagueness? In explaining penumbral shift in §II, I said that every token of a predicate* has (what I called) a *penumbral profile* which determines the token's *penumbra*, which is to say, the range of things to which the token's application is anything other than unqualifiedly correct or unqualifiedly incorrect. I believe that what the proponent of metaphysically-vague properties needs to say is that a vague property is a property that has a penumbral profile which determines a penumbra for the property, where that is the range of things to which the property's application is anything other than unqualifiedly correct or unqualifiedly incorrect. If $\varphi$ is a metaphysically-vague property of a kind that enters into normal discourse, then we should expect there to be numerous things to which $\varphi$ unqualifiedly applies, and even more things to which $\varphi$ unqualifiedly doesn't apply. But *the property of being a thing to which $\varphi$ unqualifiedly applies/doesn't apply must* evidently also be vague. This means that not only can there be no precise cutoff as regards the things which have $\varphi$, there can also be no precise cutoff as regards the things such that it's metaphysically determinate that they have $\varphi$. A metaphysically-vague property will not have a precise condition of application at any order of vagueness. By contrast, a metaphysically-precise property will have an absolute, unconditionally precise condition of application, even if it's possible for there to be things for which it's metaphysically indeterminate whether they satisfy that condition. Now, there are reasons to question whether the foregoing characterization of metaphysically-vague properties is coherent, but my concern hasn't been to show that there are, or even that it's metaphysically possible for there to be, metaphysically-vague properties; my concern has been merely to say what I think the proponent of vagueness-in-the-world needs to say about what it is for a property to be metaphysically vague.

In any case, we are now positioned to say that if the vagueness of "boy" can be accommodated in the M/C model relative to the assumption that Russellian propositions are the contents of declarative sentence tokens, then the following options (in which $\beta$ is the token of "boy" Jack uttered and we're back to a pretheoretic use of 'determinate' and its cognates) are the ones worth taking seriously:

(A) Some metaphysically-precise property is the content of $\beta$.
(B) No metaphysically-precise property is such that it's determinately the content of $\beta$, but myriad metaphysically-precise properties are each such that it's indeterminate whether it's the content of $\beta$.
(C) Some metaphysically-vague property is the content of $\beta$.
(D) No metaphysically-vague property is such that it's determinately the content of $\beta$, but myriad metaphysically-vague properties are each such that it's indeterminate whether it's the content of $\beta$.

Although (A)-(D) are the only answers we need to consider, logical space contains infinitely more possible answers. In fact, for every answer *X* contained in logical space, logical space also contains the answer that it's indeterminate whether X, so that, for example, in addition to (A), logical space also contains the answers:

(A2) It's indeterminate whether (A).
(A3) It's indeterminate whether (A2).
(A4) It's indeterminate whether (A3)
⋮

But once our critical examination of (A)-(D) is concluded it will be clear why we have no need to consider permutations of them induced by higher-order vagueness.[15]

Now that we know the options available to the M/C model as regards the content of the token of 'boy' Jack uttered, we can discuss, relative to each of those options, the prospect of achieving a correct completion of the schema:

> For any token $\tau$ of 'boy' and any property $\varphi$, $f(\tau) = \varphi$ iff
>
> (1) [eligibility condition] . . .;
> (2) [selection condition] . . . .

**Re (A)** [Some metaphysically-precise property is the content of $\beta$ (the token of "boy" Jack uttered)]. The token of "Morgan is a boy" Jack uttered is vague. It's vague because even if it's determinately true or determinately false, it might have been neither; it might have been borderline true/false. The vagueness of the sentence token is entailed by the vagueness of $\beta$, the token of "boy" contained in it, and, let's suppose, that is the only source of the sentence's vagueness. Given that and the assumption that Russellian propositions are the contents of declarative sentence tokens, the content of the sentence token Jack uttered is the metaphysically-precise proposition <Morgan, $\varphi$>, if (A) is correct and $\varphi$ is the metaphysically-precise property that is the content of $\beta$. But how can the token of "Morgan is a boy" be vague if its content is a metaphysically-precise proposition? That is possible if, and, I should think, only if, the epistemic theory of vagueness is correct. For that theory holds that a borderline sentence is true or else false, and we cannot know which. The fact that (A) presupposes the epistemic theory is already enough to make (A) problematic (see e.g. Schiffer 2003, pp. 183–184), but we can put that polemical remark aside, because, as we're about to see, we can show that (A) is false without having independently to show that the epistemic theory is false.

Penumbral shift entails that there is no such property as *the* property of being a boy. If there were such a property, it would be the content of every token of "boy", and that is precisely what penumbral shift precludes. Given penumbral shift, if (A) is true, then different tokens of "boy" may have different metaphysically-precise properties as their contents. In fact, the content of a particular token of "boy" would have to be one of uncountably many metaphysically-precise properties that are equally eligible to be the content of a token of "boy". Let's ignore the fact that "male" and "human being" are vague and pretend that they express metaphysically-precise properties. Let's also pretend that for each person there is a precise instant of time at which he or she came into existence. Then a good candidate for being the content of $\beta$ if (A) is correct would be, say, *the property of being a male human being whose age in seconds* ≤ *531,066,240*. But if that is a good candidate, then so is *the property of being a male human being whose age in seconds* ≤ *531,066,240.1*, *the property of being a male human being whose age in seconds* ≤ *531,066,240.01*, *the property of being a male human being whose age in seconds* ≤ *531,066,240.001*, *the property of being a male human being whose age in seconds* ≤ *531,066,239*, *the property of being a male human being whose age in seconds* ≤ *531,066,239.05733*, *the property of being a male human being whose age in seconds* ≤ *536,000,674*, *the property of being a male human being whose age in seconds* ≤ *527,000,674.7009*, . . . —well, you get the point. Let's suppose (for *reductio*) that (A) is true and that among the uncountably many equally good candidates for being the content of $\beta$ the one that happens to be its content is *the property of being a male human being whose age in seconds* ≤ *530,802,239.057*. Call this property $\varphi^*$. It can't be a brute inexplicable fact that $\varphi^*$ is $\beta$'s content; there must be some feature that $\varphi^*$ alone among the countlessly many equally good candidates has which makes *it* the content of $\beta$. What might that feature be? It can't be that Jack *intended* to express $\varphi^*$ with $\beta$.[16] It can't be any *causal relation* that relates $\beta$ to $\varphi^*$ but to no other equally good candidate. And it's preposterous to suppose it's somehow miraculously determined by the use of "boy" among speakers of English. I submit that there is *nothing* that could make one alone of these countlessly many candidate properties the content of $\beta$, and that, therefore, (A) is false.

There is another, independent, reason why no metaphysically-precise property can be the content of $\beta$. If (A) were true, then, owing to penumbral shift, the meaning of "boy" would have to be a function that was specifiable as an instance of the schema:

> For any token $\tau$ of "boy" and any metaphysically-precise property $\varphi$, $f(\tau) = \varphi$ iff
>
> (1) [eligibility condition] . . .;
> (2) [selection condition] . . . .,

The considerations rehearsed in the preceding paragraph show that there can be no correct selection condition. But we can also see that there can be no correct eligibility condition. For let's continue to pretend that "male" and "human being" express metaphysically-precise properties and that for each person there is a precise instant of time at which he or she came into existence. Then in order for there to be a correct eligibility condition for "boy" there would have to be real numbers $j$, $k$ such that (a) $j$ is the largest number such that, necessarily, *every* token of "boy" is determinately true of every human male whose age in seconds $\leq j$ and (b) $k$ is the smallest number such that, necessarily, *every* token of "boy" is determinately false of every human male whose age in seconds $\geq k$. If there were such numbers, then we could specify the eligibility condition by saying that:

> For any token $\tau$ of "boy" and any metaphysically-precise property $\varphi$, $f(\tau) = \varphi$ *only if*, for some real number $j' \geq j, < k$, a male human being has $\varphi$ iff his age in seconds $\leq j'$.

But there being such a $j'$ is precluded by the fact that there can be no determinate cutoffs at any order of vagueness: owing to high-order vagueness, there can be no greatest lower bound or least upper bound to determine the metaphysically-precise properties that are eligible to be the content of a token of "boy".

(Some theorists, however, are evidently committed to rejecting the argument just concluded. The dominant model in formal semantics takes a compositional semantics for a language $L$ to be a compositional type-driven functional-application possible-worlds truth-theoretic semantics for $L$ constructed in terms of the formal semanticist's proprietary language of the typed lambda calculus. This semantic model, like every other foundational semantic model, has been developed as an idealized model that prescinds from the vagueness of vague expressions, but some formal semanticists have attempted to show how at least certain kinds of vague expressions may be accommodated in a compositional semantics of the kind just mentioned. The most prominent such attempt is the semantics for vague gradable adjectives Christopher Kennedy (2007) offers. On that semantics, the meaning of "tall" involves a contextually-determined measure function which determines a scale of measurement for height and a precise degree of height on that scale so that an utterance of "John is tall" in context $c$ is true if John's height surpasses the degree-of-height threshold determined by c, false otherwise. Since for Kennedy an utterance of "John is tall" is either true or false, it's impossible for anyone to know the precise contextually-determined threshold John's height must surpass in order for the utterance to be true. So, as Kennedy recognizes, his account of vague gradable adjectives is an epistemic theory according to which, even though the context in which "John is tall" is uttered determines a measure function which in turn determines a precise threshold that John's height must surpass in order for the sentence to be true relative to that context, it's impossible for anyone to know what that function or threshold is (for if one could know what the function was one could in principle know the threshold it determined, and if one could know that, then one could in principle determine whether the token of "tall" produced in an utterance of "John is tall" was true of any given individual, in which case nothing could be a borderline case of a thing of which the token was true, whereas the epistemicist, to account for what makes a predicate vague, must say that every utterance of a vague predicate admits the possibility of borderline cases). Even though it's impossible to know the measure function a context of utterance determines, we should still expect to be told *something* about how a context determines such a function. Yet all Kennedy tells us—by way of telling us how his theory provides a "contextualist" solution to the sorites paradox generated by a vague gradable adjective—is that if an utterance of "tall" is being applied to a pair of individuals whose heights are very similar, then the context can't determine a measure function that determines a degree of height that only one of the pair of individuals meets or exceeds. In another much-cited article, Chris Barker (2002) suggests that a dynamic component be added to the semantics of vague gradable adjectives, but his account, like Kennedy's, requires a contextually-determined precise threshold, and, like Kennedy's again, it offers no account of how that threshold is determined.[17])

**Re (B)** [No metaphysically-precise property is such that it's determinately the content of $\beta$, but myriad metaphysically-precise properties are each such that it's indeterminate whether it's the content of $\beta$.] Let $D$ be the determinately operator, so that $DP$ means that *it's determinately the case that P*. As already remarked (see n. 11), we don't want $P$ to entail $DP$ because we don't want $\neg DP$ to entail $\neg P$. Nevertheless, one can't be *warranted* in *asserting* $P$ unless one would be equally warranted in asserting that it was determinately the case that $P$—whence the infelicity of "Morgan is a boy but it's indeterminate whether or not he's a boy". Similarly, if one has the concept of a proposition's being determinately true and one knows that one knows that $p$ is true, then one knows that $p$ is determinately true, and if one is justified in believing that one is justified in believing that $p$ is true, then one is justified in believing that $p$ is determinately true. In the just concluded discussion of (A) I offered two arguments to show that every metaphysically-precise property is such that it couldn't be the content of $\beta$. I could not coherently have reached that conclusion and then added "But while the foregoing argument shows that every metaphysically-precise property is such that it couldn't be the content of $\beta$, it's still an open question whether or not there is a metaphysically-precise property such that it's indeterminate whether it's the content of $\beta$". This is because to whatever extent those arguments justify me in concluding that no metaphysically-precise property is the content of $\beta$, to that same extent they justify me in concluding that it's determinately the case that no metaphysically-precise property is the content of $\beta$: Now, if it's determinately the case that no metaphysically-precise property is the content of $\beta$, then every metaphysically-precise property is such that it's determinately not the content of $\beta$; and if that is so, then no precise property is such that it's indeterminate whether it's the content of $\beta$. In short, the considerations that show (A) to be false also show (B) to be false.

It's also important to notice that the very same eligibility-condition problem that arises for (A) also arises for (B). This is because in order for a property to be such that it's indeterminate whether it's the content of a token of $\beta$, "boy" must have a meaning that determines what must be the case in order for a property to be the content of a token of "boy", and such a meaning, as we've seen, requires a correct eligibility condition for "boy". So the impossibility of such a condition falsifies (B) as well as (A).

Re (C) [Some metaphysically-vague property is the content of $\beta$]. If there are metaphysically-vague properties they are every bit as finely individuated as metaphysically-precise properties. So if a metaphysically-vague property $\varphi$ is a good candidate for being the content of $\beta$, then so are countlessly many metaphysically-vague properties that are virtually indistinguishable from $\varphi$. For example, suppose that metaphysically-vague properties $\varphi$ and $\psi$ are identical except that, whereas it is indeterminate whether $\varphi$ applies to a human male whose age in seconds is 522,000,000, it is merely indeterminate whether it is indeterminate whether $\psi$ applies to him. Then we should expect that if either property is a good candidate for being the content of $\beta$, then so is the other. (A) was shown to be false by the fact that there was nothing to explain what would make any precise property such that it alone among the uncountably many equally eligible precise properties was the content of $\beta$. In the same way, (C) is shown to be false by the fact that there is nothing to explain what would make any metaphysically-vague property such that it alone among the uncountably many equally eligible metaphysically-vague properties was the content of $\beta$.

Also like the falsity of (A), the falsity of (C) is overdetermined. If (C) were correct, there would be a correct completion of the M/C schema

> For any token $\tau$ of "boy" and any metaphysically-vague property $\varphi$, $f(\tau) = \varphi$ iff
>
> (1) [eligibility condition] . . .;
> (2) [selection condition] . . .,

but the argument of the preceding paragraph shows that there is no correct selection condition for this schema, just as the corresponding argument for metaphysically-precise properties showed that there could be no correct selection conditions for those properties. The discussion of (A) also contained an argument to show that there could be no correct eligibility condition for metaphysically-precise properties, and the same argument is available, *mutatis mutandis*, to show that there also can't be a correct eligibility condition for metaphysically-vague properties. If a metaphysically-vague property is the content of $\beta$ and Morgan has that property, then Jack's utterance of "Morgan is a boy" is true, and if Morgan doesn't have that property, then the utterance is false, and if Morgan is a borderline instance of the property, then it's indeterminate whether the utterance is true. What matters as regards an eligibility condition are the conditions a property imposes on its determinate application. So, if we continue to pretend that "male" and "human being" express metaphysically-precise properties and that for each person there is a precise instant of time at which he or she came into existence, then, as before, in order for there to be a correct eligibility condition for the just-displayed schema there would have to be real numbers $j$, $k$ such that (a) $j$ is the largest number such that, necessarily, every token of "boy" is determinately true of every human male whose age in seconds $\leq j$ and (b) $k$ is the smallest number such that, necessarily, every token of "boy" is determinately false of every human male whose age in seconds $\geq k$. And if there were such numbers, then we could specify the eligibility condition by saying that:

> For any token $\tau$ of 'boy' and any metaphysically-vague property $\varphi$, $f(\tau) = \varphi$ *only if*, for some real number $j' \geq j, < k$, a human male has $\varphi$ iff his age in seconds $\leq j'$.

But there being such a $j'$ is precluded by the fact that there can be no determinate cutoffs at any order of vagueness: owing to high-order vagueness there can be no greatest lower bound or least upper bound to determine even the metaphysically-vague properties that are eligible to be the content of a token of "boy". Therefore, every metaphysically-vague property, like every metaphysically-precise property, is such that it's not the content of $\beta$.

**Re (D)** [No metaphysically-vague property is such that it's determinately the content of $\beta$, but myriad metaphysically-vague properties are each such that it's indeterminate whether it's the content of $\beta$]. (D) stands to (C) as (B) stands to (A). I claim that the discussion of (C) warrants concluding that (C) is false, and to whatever extent it warrants holding that no metaphysically-vague property is the content of $\beta$, to that same extent it warrants holding that it's determinately the case that no metaphysically-vague property is the content of $\beta$, and that therefore each metaphysically-vague property is such that it's determinately not the content of $\beta$, and therefore no metaphysically-vague property is such that it's indeterminate whether it's the content of $\beta$. Just as the case against (A) is simultaneously a case against (B), so the case against (C) is simultaneously a case against (D).

## 4. The Argument Extended

The options (A)-(D) don't presuppose IBS. They are, I submit, the options available to *any* theorist who thinks the M/C model can accommodate vagueness and who takes Russellian propositions to be the contents of tokens of vague sentences (or to sentences relative to "contexts of utterance"). Would (A)-(D) fair better on another conception of propositions? When I provisionally supposed we were addressing a view on which the contents of sentence tokens were taken to be Russellian propositions I said that that was merely an expository convenience, since the arguments to be deployed to show that Russellian propositions couldn't be the contents of tokens of vague sentences could be redeployed to show that no propositions of any other kind could be their contents either. The idea is this: The arguments against (A)-(D) are effectually arguments against any theory that takes contents of tokens of vague predicates like 'boy' to be metaphysically-precise or metaphysically-vague properties. A theorist who takes the contents of sentence tokens to be propositions construed as functions from possible worlds to truth-values will construe properties as functions from possible worlds to sets of things in those worlds (e.g. she would represent the property of being a tiger as the smallest function that maps every possible world onto the set of things in that world that are tigers). It's not clear to me how the possible-worlds theorist might represent the notion of a metaphysically-vague property, but if we continue to pretend that "male" and "human being" express metaphysically-precise properties and that for each person there was a precise instant of time at which he or she came into existence, then the theorist would say that an example of a function eligible to be the content of $\beta$ (the token of "boy" Jack uttered) might be, say, that function that maps each possible world onto the set of human males in that world whose age in seconds $\leq$ 530,156,794. But if such a function is eligible to be the content of $\beta$, then so is the function that maps each possible world onto the set of human males in that world whose age in seconds $\leq$ 530,156,795, the function that maps each possible world onto the set of human males in that world whose age in seconds $\leq$ 530,156,794.0057, and so on for countlessly many other functions that differ only in some irrelevant way from them. But then the sort of considerations which show that there is nothing that could make one alone of the countlessly many equally eligible properties the content of $\beta$ would also show that there was nothing that could make one alone of the countlessly many equally eligible functions the content of $\beta$, and it should be obvious that the considerations pertaining to higher-order vagueness that make it impossible for there to be a correct eligibility condition for properties would make it equally impossible for there to be one for the functions that are the possible-world theorist's surrogates for properties. If anything is the content of $\beta$—or if anything is such that it's indeterminate (or indeterminate whether it's indeterminate, or . . .) whether it's the content of $\beta$—and it's not a property or property-surrogate, then it would have to be something that *determines* a property in the way that a Fregean "mode of presentation"/"way of thinking" of a property is supposed to do. But then there would be countlessly many equally eligible such things, and it should by now be obvious that they, too, would fail for the same sort of reasons that the other candidate contents fail.

From this I conclude that, if there are such *things* as the contents of tokens of vague sentences, then they aren't propositions of any kind. At the same time, it would surely have been correct to report that, in uttering "Morgan is a boy", Jack told Jill, and thus meant, that his sister's child Morgan was a boy, and from this we may further conclude that speaker-meaning isn't a relation, *S meant p*, between a speaker *S* and a proposition *p* that she meant;[18] for if it were, then propositions *would* be the contents of sentence tokens. And, I should think, we may also conclude that there are no such *things* as the contents of vague sentence tokens or the things we mean; for if there were such things they would evidently have to be language- and mind-independent things that have truth conditions, and that just is the generic sense of "proposition" (see above p. 80).

Davidsonians, however, claim that semantics has no need for such *things* as "contents", and that the only semantics a public language needs is an extensional compositional truth theory, where, roughly speaking, an extensional compositional truth theory for a language *L* is a finitely statable theory of *L* that generates for each truth-evaluable sentence of *L* a theorem of the form "An utterance of $\sigma$ is true iff . . . ", where 'iff' is the material biconditional. Could such a semantics accommodate the vagueness of "boy"? Some theorists would say the answer is yes, and they would support that answer in the following way:

> The words "snow" and "white" are vague, and therefore so is the sentence "Snow is white". Yet that doesn't affect the truth of the "T-sentence"
>
> (T) "Snow is white" is true iff snow is white,
>
> and this because the vagueness of (T)'s right-hand side cancels out the vagueness of its left-hand side, in that each side matches the other "umbra for umbra and penumbra for penumbra".
>
> (Quine 1960, p. 37; quoted in Lepore and Ludwig 2005, p. 139)

But this is wrong; it's falsified by the context sensitivity induced by penumbral shift. Not only is (T) not true, it's also the case that every assertive utterance of it is false. For suppose the displayed token of (T) was assertively uttered. The left-hand side of that token ascribes truth to the sentence *type* "snow is white". If a sentence type is true, then every assertively uttered token of it is true, and whatever is required for the truth of the sentence type is also required for the truth of every assertively uttered token of it. In this way, we could have more precisely expressed what is supposed to be expressed by (T) by:

> (T′) For every (assertively uttered) token $\tau$ of "snow is white", $\tau$ is true iff snow is white.

The problem with (T′) is that *every* assertive utterance of *it*—i.e. of (T′) itself—is *false*. For suppose the displayed token of (T′) was assertively uttered. Let's call that token '$(T')_\tau$'. Then every assertively uttered token of "snow is white" would have exactly the same truth and falsity conditions as the token of "snow is white" on the right-hand side of $(T')_\tau$. But since "snow is white" is vague, it's subject to penumbral shift, and a consequence of that is that there may be assertively uttered tokens of "snow is white" with different truth-values, in which case the penumbral profile of the token of "snow is white" on the right-hand side of $(T')_\tau$ wouldn't determine the truth conditions of every assertively uttered token of "snow is white", and from that it follows that $(T')_\tau$ is false, and the same goes for every assertively uttered token of (T′). In effect, an assertive utterance of (T′) would be in the same sort of pickle as an assertive utterance of

> For every (assertively uttered) token $\tau$ of "she is French", $\tau$ is true iff she is French

in which the token of "she" on the right-hand side referred to a particular female named Sabine. Just as what would be needed to accommodate "she" in a compositional truth theory would be a finitely statable meaning for "she" that specified what must be the case in order for a token of 'she' to refer to a particular thing, so what would be needed to accommodate the vague sentence "snow is white" in a compositional truth theory would be a finitely statable meaning for the sentence that specified what must be the case in order for any token of "snow is white" to be true; but if we could achieve such a specification, then we could show how the M/C model is able to accommodate vague terms like "snow", "white", and "boy". As regards "boy", for example, what kind of base axiom should we expect a compositional truth-theoretic semantics to have for the word in order for it to capture the word's penumbral-shift-induced context sensitivity? Well, let's continue to pretend that "male" and "human being" have precise extensions and that for each person there was a precise instant of time at which he or she came into existence. And let's also pretend that there are real numbers $j$, $k$ such that $j$ is the largest number such that every token of "boy" is determinately true of a male human being whose age in seconds $\leq j$ and $k$ is the smallest number such that every token of "boy" is determinately false of every male human being whose age in seconds $\geq k$. *Then* we could devise a base axiom for "boy" in a compositional truth theory *provided* we could find a condition $C$ such that:

> For any $x$, token $\tau$ of "boy", and time $t$, $\tau$ is true of $x$ at $t$ iff at $t$ $x$ is a male human being whose age in seconds = some real number $n$ such that:
>
> (1) (eligibility condition) $j \geq n < k$;
> (2) (selection condition) $n$ alone of the countlessly many eligible numbers—i.e. the uncountably many between $j$ and $k$—satisfies condition $C$.

But, of course, we already know that no such base axiom is to be found, for there can be no upper or lower bounds to serve as witnesses for "$j$" and "$k$" in the displayed conditions, and even if there were there would be no condition to do the job required for there to be a correct selection condition.

## 5. What Now?

A *compositional meaning theory for a language L* would be a finitely statable theory of $L$ that generates for each expression $\varepsilon$ of $L$ a theorem that assigns to $\varepsilon$ its meaning in $L$, where, for any possible content $c$ and any token $\varepsilon_\tau$ of $\varepsilon$, that meaning determines what must be the case for $c$ to be the content of $\varepsilon_\tau$. A *compositional truth theory for a language L* would be a finitely statable theory of $L$ that generates for each truth-evaluable sentence of $L$ a theorem that species what must be the case for a token of that sentence to be true. If everything I've so far said in this paper is correct (a big if, to be sure), then neither kind of compositional semantics can accommodate the vagueness of vague expressions, and since virtually every sentence of every natural language is vague, this means that no natural language can have either kind of semantics. Might natural languages have some other kind of semantics? In order to address this question, we should have on board two further, but so far unmentioned, features of vagueness—namely, what I will call *penumbral ignorance* and *penumbral indifference*.

*Penumbral ignorance* is the fact that speakers tend to have very little, if any, awareness of the penumbral profiles of the vague expression tokens that they utter. Many adults are probably unaware that most of the words they use are vague (in the sense that they admit of possible borderline cases), and it's *possible* for someone to count as a competent speaker of a language even if he doesn't even have the concept of a vague expression. My guess is that the concept of a borderline case isn't one a child acquires until fairly late in her linguistic development, well after she is regarded as a competent speaker.[19] That is the most extreme form of penumbral ignorance. But fully competent speakers of a language also manifest penumbral ignorance. One typical manifestation is illustrated in the following example. Jane, an intelligent native speaker of English, is asked if she has any children, and she replies, "Yes. I have a 7-year-old boy". Although different tokens of "boy" may have different penumbral profiles, Jane's child is such that every token of "boy" must be true of him. Now suppose that, after explaining to her what the question means, we ask Jane, "What must be true of an individual in order for it to be a borderline case of a thing to which 'boy', as you just now used it, applies?" That is not a question Jane considered in making her utterance, nor did she have any reason to consider it: she knew that what she said was most definitely true, so she had no reason to wonder what sort of state of affairs would have made her utterance merely borderline true. What Jane *ought* to say in response to the question is that, never having considered what would count as a borderline boy, she is in no position to answer it. If Jane did venture an answer, it would have no special authority, either about the truth of her answer or about what she would say in relevant counterfactual circumstances.[20] I hazard, first, that most utterances of vague sentences are like Jane's in that, all else being equal, when a rational speaker applies a vague predicate to a thing, she is confident that the predicate is definitely true of the thing, and, second, that if in such cases the hearer doesn't believe what the speaker said, it won't be because the predicate she uttered is vague. These speakers have no reason to consider what something would have to be like in order for it to be a borderline case of a thing to which the token of the predicate she uttered applies. Penumbral ignorance is a consequence of this. But even when a speaker applies a vague predicate to a thing and her interlocutors deem that application to be merely borderline correct, they won't have considered what something would have to be like in order for it to be a borderline case of a borderline case of a thing to which the predicate, as uttered by the speaker, applies. Penumbral ignorance is a consequence of this too.

*Penumbral indifference* is the fact that we don't regard it as a barrier to knowing what someone said in uttering a vague sentence that we know very little about the utterance's penumbral profile and that, consequently, typically when a person $x$ says something using a vague expression $\varepsilon$ and another person $y$ uses $\varepsilon$ in reporting what $x$ said, $y$ pays no attention to whether the penumbral profile of her utterance of $\varepsilon$ matches that of $x$'s utterance of $\varepsilon$. For example, if $A$ assertively utters "Jane's child is precocious" and $B$, reporting on the speech act $A$ thereby performed, utters "$A$ told me that Jane's child is precocious", $B$'s utterance may count as true even though the penumbral profile of her utterance of "precocious" is different from that of $A$'s. Related to this is the fact that when, as we would say, we "believe what so-and-so said", it's unlikely that the belief we acquire will have exactly the same penumbral profile as the one to which the speaker gave voice in her utterance.[21] Penumbral indifference has limits, of course. For example, if I know that Leona believes that "home" can't be true of apartments, but only of houses, then I would be very reluctant to report her utterance of "Morris is homeless" by uttering "Leona said that Morris was homeless". If there was any information that I thought was transmitted by her utterance it would be information I would express with the sentence "Morris doesn't live in a house". But what are these limits? If a speaker assertively utters a sentence in which a vague predicate $\varphi$ is predicated of a certain thing, when will one find it unproblematic to use $\varphi$ in reporting what she said or the information acquired from her utterance? I think two already noticed facts about our use of vague terms will help to answer that question. The first is that however much the penumbral profiles of two tokens of a vague predicate may differ, there will normally be myriad things to which every token of the predicate must apply and even more things to which no token of it can apply. Let's call things of the first kind the vague predicate's *positive anchors* and things of the second kind its *negative anchors* (penumbral shift occurs in the area between the positive and negative anchors), while recognizing that there can be no determinate set of positive or negative anchors. The second fact about our use of vague terms is that, all else being equal, a rational speaker won't apply a vague predicate to a thing unless she is confident that the predicate is definitely true of the thing and would be recognized as such by others apprised of the facts on which her assertion was grounded, and she expects that if her hearer doesn't accept her assertion, it won't be because of its vagueness. I think this explains why, when a speaker predicates a vague predicate of a thing, we are normally comfortable in using that same predicate to report either what the speaker said or the knowledge we acquired from her utterance.

The point about positive and negative anchors might seem to suggest that, even if vagueness precludes our language from having a correct compositional truth theory that, for *every* truth-evaluable sentence $\sigma$, issues in a theorem of the form.

For any token $\sigma_\tau$ of $\sigma$, $\sigma_\tau$ is true iff . . .,

the fact that most single-word vague predicates have positive and negative anchors would make it possible for our language to enjoy a correct compositional truth theory that, for *most* truth-evaluable sentences $\sigma$ that will ever be uttered, issues in theorems of the forms

For any token $\sigma_\tau$ of $\sigma$, $\sigma_\tau$ is true if . . .
For any token $\sigma_\tau$ of $\sigma$, $\sigma_\tau$ is false if . . .

The possibility of this sort of compositional truth theory is suggested by the following line of reasoning. What stands in the way of the more ambitious compositional semantics is the impossibility of getting correct base axioms for single-word vague predicates. For example, such a base axiom for "boy" would have to be a completion of the form

For any $x$, token $\tau$ of "boy", and time $t$, $\tau$ is true of $x$ at $t$ iff . . .,

and if what I have argued is correct, no such completion is available. At the same time, 'boy' has positive and negative anchors; that is to say, there are numerous individuals—e.g. your 9-year-old son Charlie—of whom every token of "boy" must be unqualifiedly true and numerous individuals—e.g. Ruth Bader Ginsberg—of whom every token of "boy" must be unqualifiedly false. This evidently entails that there are numerous conditions $\Omega$ such that:

(1) For any $x$, token $\tau$ of "boy", and time $t$, $\tau$ is true of $x$ at $t$ *if* $x$ satisfies $\Omega$ at $t$

and numerous conditions $\Omega'$ such that:

(2) For any $x$, token $\tau$ of "boy", and time $t$, $\tau$ is false of $x$ at $t$ *if* $x$ satisfies $\Omega'$ at $t$.

Further, given that there are such conditions, then it's apt to seem that there should be specifications of them, such as, for example:

(3) For any $x$, token $\tau$ of "boy", and time $t$, $\tau$ is true of $x$ at $t$ *if* at $t$ $x$ is a 9-year-old male human being.
(4) For any $x$, token $\tau$ of "boy", and time $t$, $\tau$ is false of $x$ at $t$ *if* at $t$ $x$ is an 86-year-old female human being.

And if there are such specifications of sufficient conditions for the application or non-application of "boy", then there would be analogous sufficient conditions for nearly every other single-word vague predicate, and there would evidently be nothing standing in the way of achieving a limited compositional truth theory of the kind described. The hope would then be that this limited compositional semantics could be put to work to explain some of the things compositional truth-theoretic semantics is thought to be needed to explain.

That line of reasoning, and the hope it aims to sustain, is problematic in at least two ways. One problem is that even if most single-word vague predicates have positive and negative anchors that enabled us to fashion base axioms for those predicates of the kind in question, the limited compositional semantics which that made possible wouldn't go far enough in explaining what makes utterances of vague sentences true; for, as we know from the discussion of penumbral shift, utterances of vague predicates can be true of things, and known to be true of them, even though the things of which they are true are not among the predicate's positive anchors (for example, owing to penumbral shift, there could be two simultaneous predications of "bald" to a certain man, one of which was true of him while the other which was false of him). A second problem is more serious. It may be illustrated in terms of our running example of the vague word "boy". The problem comes to light when we notice that, while it is plausible that there are numerous conditions $\Omega$ such that:

(1) For any $x$, token $\tau$ of "boy", and time $t$, $\tau$ is true of $x$ at $t$ *if* $x$ satisfies $\Omega$ at $t$

the sentence

(3) For any $x$, token $\tau$ of "boy", and time $t$, $\tau$ is true of $x$ at $t$ *if* at $t$ $x$ is a 9-year-old male human being.

is not the true substitution instance of the open sentence (1) that it appears to be, and when we see why this is so we'll see why no sentence would provide a substitution instance. In order for (3) to be a substitution instance of (1) that is true, "is a 9-year-old human male" in (3) must express a condition that satisfies the open sentence (1). But owing to its penumbral-shift-induced context sensitivity, the expression *type* "is a 9-year-old human male" in (3) doesn't express any condition. What about *tokens* of that expression? Although different tokens of it may express somewhat different conditions, won't it nevertheless be the case that every token of "boy" must be true of every token of every individual of whom *any* token of "is a 9-year-old human male" is true? No. There *could* be such predicates; for example, I should think that every token of "boy" must be false of every individual of whom any token of "is an 86-year-old female human being" is true. But it's not the case that every token of "boy" must be true of every individual of whom any token of "is a 9-year-old human male" is true. One reason this is so is that "male" is vague and there may be two tokens of the term one of which is true of a certain individual while the other is false of that individual, and in that case there might easily be a token of "boy" that is false of someone of whom a particular token of "is a 9-year-old human male" is true. What all this suggests is that, while there are indeed numerous conditions $\Omega$ such that, for any person $x$, token $\tau$ of "boy", and time $t$, $\tau$ is true of $x$ at $t$ *if* $x$ satisfies $\Omega$ at $t$, it may not be possible to articulate any of these conditions! One way this could happen would be if no-vagueness-in-the-world were true. For then we should expect there to be metaphysically-precise properties whose possession by a person was sufficient for every literal utterance of "boy" to be true of him. Then, even though we couldn't know what any such metaphysically-precise property was, we might still be able to know when someone had such a property. After all, you already know that every literally uttered token of "boy" is true of your 9-year-old son Charlie, even though you might not be able to specify any property of Charlie that makes that the case. In any event, if sufficient conditions for the application of a vague predicate token are inarticulable, then it won't be possible for anyone to *articulate* even a limited compositional theory with a base axiom for "boy" that stated a sufficient condition for any token of "boy" being true of every individual who satisfied that condition. This is an important point because many theorists hold that if a compositional theory is to explain language understanding, then a representation of it must be implicated in the information processing language understanding requires; but it won't be possible for there to be a *representation* of such a theory if the conditions the theory needs to assign to vague predicates in the theory's base axioms are inarticulable.

Where does all this leave us? From my vantage point, the next question to ask is: If what I have said in this paper is correct, what facts about a language that seemed to implicate the need for the language to have a compositional semantics remain to be explained, and what kind of theories are needed to explain them? This is not an easy question to answer. For example, one thing that remains to be explained is the fact that we are able to understand indefinitely many sentences of our language upon encountering them for the first time. What must be true of the sentences and of us for this to be so? What makes this a difficult question to answer is that in order to make progress on it we first need to know in what "understanding" a sentence consists. When vagueness is being ignored a ready answer is that to understand a sentence is to know the kind of speech act that would be performed in a literal and unembedded utterance of the sentence, and the kind of content that speech act must have. That may seem to be a reasonable thing to say, at least as a starting point, even when vagueness isn't being ignored; only now we have to tackle the question of what talk of the content of an utterance can come to when there are no such *things* as "contents" (speaker-meaning can no longer be thought of a relation between a speaker and a proposition she means), especially given penumbral ignorance and indifference.

In any case, the question of understanding novel sentences may not be the most pressing question to be tackled. Suppose we think—i.e. process information—in a language-like neural system of mental representation, Mentalese. Then our spoken language will have a compositional semantics if Mentalese does, but we won't need a compositional semantics to explain our "understanding" of Mentalese because we don't need to know anything about the "brain's language of synaptic interconnections and neural spikes" (Lewis 1983, p. 346) in order to think in it. So why might one think there is something about our thinking in Mentalese whose explanation requires it to have a compositional semantics? If there is nothing about Mentalese whose explanation requires the neural language to have a compositional semantics, then we won't need a compositional semantics for our spoken language to explain our ability to understand its sentences, since sentence understanding may be understood as a wholly nonsemantic process whereby spoken sentences are mapped onto their Mentalese correlates.[22] If Mentalese needs a compositional semantics, it will be to explain how our beliefs are realized by tokenings of Mentalese sentences. Fodor argues that Mentalese will need a compositional semantics precisely to explain that. But the way he formulates the argument suffers from his ignoring vagueness:

> Mentalese must . . . be productive. The reasoning is . . . familiar: On the one hand, propositional attitudes derive their semantical properties (their 'intentional contents') from the semantics of the Mentalese expressions. . . . And, on the other hand, there are infinitely many psychologically possible propositional attitudes. . . . What needs to be explained is that (synonymy aside) each of the infinitely many syntactically distinct expressions of [Mentalese] has its distinctive truth conditions.
>
> (1990a, p. 421)

In other words, if Harold has a belief that is true iff snow is white, then that is because a Mentalese sentence that is true iff snow is white is tokened in his belief box. Since there are infinitely beliefs Harold might have, each with its distinctive truth condition, there must also be infinitely many Mentalese sentences, each with its distinctive truth condition. So let's suppose Harold thinks in English. Then his Mentalese will need a compositional semantics that generates for the Mentalese sentence "Snow is white" the T-sentence

> "Snow is white" is true iff snow is white,

and similarly for each of the infinitely many other sentences of his Mentalese. But, if what I argued in §IV is correct, not only is that T-sentence not true, every token of it is false.

Notwithstanding that, something still remains to be explained, and the challenge for me is to show how to explain it in a way that is consistent with the arguments that I've given. If we continue with the Mentalese story, the fact standing in need of explanation may be put like this:

> Suppose Harold believes that Jane's car is white. Suppose, too, that that belief is realized by the Mentalese sentence "Jane's car is white" being tokened in Harold's belief box. Then the fact that the sentence's tokening results in his having that belief must be explained at least partly in terms of properties of the syntax and words that compose the sentence. What remains to be explained is what those properties are and how it is that, owing at least in part to them, the sentence's tokening in Harold's belief box realizes his believing that Jane's car is white.

So far, so good; but, you'll recall, the challenge at this point is to assume that what I have argued in this paper is correct and then to determine (i) what remains to be explained given that assumption and (ii) whether what remains to be explained can be explained in a way that is compatible with the assumption. One can't begin to speculate about how the tokening in Harold's belief box of "Jane's car is white" realizes his belief that Jane's car is white before one has some hypothesis about how to understand the claim that *Harold believes that Jane's car is white*. This is no easy task on the assumption that what I have argued is correct, for, on that assumption, we can't understand Harold's believing *that Jane's car is white* as his standing in the belief relation to the proposition that Jane's car is white nor, indeed, to anything else, and we must recognize that the penumbral profile of one's uttered token of "Jane's car is white" in one's uttered token of "Harold believes that Jane's car is white" is very unlikely to be the same as the penumbral profile of the token of "Jane's car is white" tokened in Harold's belief box. The starting point in these investigations, I believe, should be with the conceptual roles of Mentalese expressions and syntactic structures, where these are nonsemantic properties that determine the conceptual roles of the sentences that those words and structures compose, where the conceptual role of a Mentalese sentence details how that sentence is counterfactually related to sensory stimulations, to other Mentalese sentences, and to bodily movements. One feature of these conceptual roles may be that whenever a sentence $\sigma$ is tokened in one's belief box, so too is the sentence ⌜I believe that $\sigma$⌝. How one goes on from there is, alas, an open question.[23]

## Notes

1. Much of the appeal of IBS for Brian lay in what he saw as its place in reducing *all* intentional notions to nonintentional notions. Once IBS succeeded in reducing semantic intentionality to mental intentionality, the task, as Brian conceived it, was then to reduce mental intentionality, and thereby all intentionality, to functional notions that enjoy wholly physical realizations. The aim of his book *Mind and Meaning* (1981) was to fulfill that physicalistic ambition.
2. As we will later see (in §IV), for present purposes it doesn't matter to which kind of proposition—Fregean, Russellian, functions from possible worlds into truth-values, whatever—the propositions we mean are taken to belong, provided they can be assigned in a compositional truth-theoretic semantics, but for simplicity of exposition I will often write as though they are taken to be Russellian propositions, i.e. structured entities whose basic components are the objects and properties our speech acts are about.
3. Here, following Grice (1957), I use 'utterance' and its cognates as a technical term that applies both to linguistic and to non-linguistic items and behavior.
4. An *o*-dependent proposition is one that is individuated partly in terms of *o* and wouldn't exist if *o* didn't exist.
5. This borrows from Stephen Neale's improvement of a definition I gave in (1981b) (see Neale (2016), p. 281).

6. Schiffer (1981b) contains a recursive definition of speaker-reference devised by Brian and myself which accommodates speaker-reference at any order.
7. Talk of a Mentalese sentence's being tokened in one's belief box is a metaphor for one's standing in that functional relation to the sentence that is constitutive of the sentence's being tokened as a belief (see my (1981a).
8. Sometimes, for stylistic reasons, I'll speak of the content of an utterance of an expression, rather than of a token of the expression.
9. On David Kaplan's (1989a, 1989b) version of the M/C model, meaning is called *character*, and is represented as a function from "contexts of utterance" to Russellian contents, where a "context of utterance" is a sequence of exactly the things needed to determine the content of *any* context-sensitive expression relative to such a "context." But (i) the representation of an expression's meaning as a mapping of the expression's tokens onto their contents is merely a notational variant of Kaplan's characters *if* there really are sequences of things capable of determining the contents of context-sensitive expressions, since in that case any function from tokens to contents would have to be defined in terms of the way Kaplan's sequences determine the contents expressions have relative to them; (ii) it can't be assumed that there are Kaplanian sequences to determine the content of any context-sensitive expression, so Kaplan's representation of expression meanings begs questions that aren't begged by the IBS construal of how the meaning/content model should represent meanings; and (iii) it's arguable that for all but a few indexical expressions—e.g. 'I' and 'yesterday' (but *not* 'here' and 'now')—most of the work in determining the reference of a speaker's utterance of a demonstrative or indexical is done by the speaker's referential intentions (e.g. it's *very* arguable that in a speaker's utterance of 'He doesn't love her', the referent of 'he' is the male to whom the speaker referred with 'he' and the referent of 'her' is the female to whom the speaker referred with 'her'), and this, in fact, is the view Kaplan came to accept in (1989b); but then there is no need for a technical conception of "contexts of utterance" as Kaplanian sequences if the references of context-sensitive terms are determined by speakers' referential intentions (see Schiffer 2003, §3.7). Kaplan does offer an argument (1989a, §XIII) to show that we won't be able to have a logic capable of accounting for the validity of arguments formulated with sentences containing demonstratives or indexicals if we represent those arguments as containing *utterances/tokens* of those expressions, but the soundness of Kaplan's argument is discussable. It's also worth remarking that the practice among formal semanticists of representing referential pronouns and demonstratives as free variables and then giving the truth conditions for the sentences containing them relative to "contextually-determined assignment functions" isn't incompatible with taking the meaning of an expression to be a function from its tokens to their contents.
10. I realize that my gloss of the labels *eligibility condition* and *selection condition* isn't exactly precise, but I don't think it needs to be more precise to be useful in the informal intuitive way I intend the labels to be useful.
11. My use of 'vague', 'determinate', 'indeterminate', and 'borderline' throughout this essay is pretheoretic in that nothing I say will rely on any particular philosophical theory of vagueness or indeterminacy but will instead remain neutral on that score. So, for example, as far as this essay is concerned it's not assumed that 'It's indeterminate whether Harold is bald' entails 'It's neither true nor false that Harold is bald'. I will, however, assume that: (i) '*x* is borderline *F*' entails 'It's indeterminate whether *x* is *F*'. (ii) 'It's indeterminate whether *x* is *F*' doesn't entail '*x* is borderline *F*'. For example, if, as many suppose, it's indeterminate whether the continuum hypothesis is true, that

wouldn't entail that it was borderline true or even vague. (iii) If it's indeterminate whether *x* is *F*, then it's impossible for anyone to know whether *x* is *F*. If, for example, it's indeterminate whether Harold is bald, then nothing can count as one's discovering that Harold is in fact bald or that he is in fact not bald. If one did come to know that Harold was bald, then one would thereby come to know that it wasn't indeterminate whether Harold was bald. (iv) One might wonder what the difference is supposed to be between *x*'s being *F* and *x*'s being determinately *F*. What, for example, is the difference between its being true that it's raining and its being determinately true that it's raining? If they are two distinct facts, in what can the difference between them consist? Are we to imagine that it's raining harder if we suppose that it's determinately true, as opposed to being merely true, that it's raining? Of course not. It's not that one might know that Sadie is lethargic and then wonder whether she's also determinately lethargic. To understand my vagueness-related use of the jargon expressions 'determinate' and 'indeterminate' it's enough to know that, while I assume that '*x* is determinately *F*' entails '*x* is *F*', I don't assume that '*x* is *F*' entails '*x* is determinately *F*'. For '*x* is not determinately *F*' must be consistent with 'It's indeterminate whether *x* is *F*', and we don't want to assume that that entails '*x* is not *F*'. So we can't deny that it's indeterminate whether *x* is *F* by claiming that *x* is *F* or that *x* isn't *F*, but we can deny it by claiming that *x* is determinately *F* or that *x* is determinately not *F*. The usefulness of '*x* is determinately *F*/not *F*' resides in its incompatibility with 'It's indeterminate whether *x* is *F*'.

12. *Every* token of a vague predicate has a penumbral profile and penumbra, and is also subject to a version of what I'm about to call *penumbral shift*. My focus on predicates* is for expository economy.
13. For convenience of exposition I will ignore syntax-determined temporal reference when nothing turns on it.
14. We need the qualification about a metaphysically-precise *object* because if an object is metaphysically vague (whatever that might mean) it may be that it's entirely owing to its vagueness that it's a borderline case of a thing that instantiates a certain property.
15. Another option in logical space not worth taking seriously is that 'boy' has a constant meaning that changes from moment to moment.
16. For Jack to have such an intention he would have to have some way of thinking of the property under which he had that intention, but he clearly has no such way of thinking of it. See the discussion of *de re* intentions in Schiffer (2019).
17. Una Stojnić and Matthew Stone (manuscript) claim to offer an account of how the Kennedy-required precise cutoffs are determined. They propose that the work, or the better part of it, can be done by mechanisms of discourse coherence, but while they might show how discourse-coherence considerations affect the determination of thresholds, I don't see that they even attempt to show how Kennedy-required precise thresholds are determined.
18. There is a freestanding argument for this conclusion in Schiffer (2019).
19. Susan Carey (p.c.) believes that no one has studied this question.
20. 'Midtown' is the name of a vaguely defined area of Manhattan: if you're in Times Square, you're definitely in Midtown and if from there you move in a straight line far enough in any direction you will eventually definitely not be in Midtown, but at no point will you have crossed an invisible line on one side of which you're definitely in Midtown and on the other side of which you're definitely not in Midtown. Nevertheless, I've found that when I ask savvy Manhattanites what the boundaries of Manhattan are, they don't hesitate to tell me—although no two of them tell me the same thing. A lawyer

once told me the southern boundary was 34th St., but I got her to retract her statement when I asked, "You mean Madison Square Garden isn't in Midtown?"

21. If we think in a *lingua mentis*, the penumbral profile of a belief is the penumbral profile of the mentalese sentence whose tokening in one's belief box realizes the belief.
22. For the full story on this, see my (1987, Ch. 7, "Compositional Semantics and Language Understanding) and Jerry Fodor's defense of my argument in his (1990a).
23. I'm grateful to Crispin Wright for helpful discussions on the topics of this paper. Some of this material was presented in the NYU Mind and Language Seminar that Cian Dorr and Jim Pryor gave in spring 2018. I benefited from their comments and from the comments made by Chris Barker and others during the general discussion.

## Works Cited

Almog, J., Perry, J., and Wettstein, H. (eds.). (1989). *Themes from Kaplan* (Oxford University Press).

Barker, C. (2002). "The Dynamics of Vagueness," *Linguistics and Philosophy*, 25 (1): 1–36.

Capone, A. (ed.). (2019). *Further Advances in Pragmatics and Philosophy, Part II* (Springer).

Davidson, D. (2001). "Theories of Meaning and Learnable Languages," in *Inquiries into Truth and Interpretation* (Oxford University Press): 3–15.

Evans, G. and McDowell, J. (eds.). (1976). *Truth and Meaning: Essays in Semantics* (Oxford University Press).

Fodor, J. A. (1990a). "Stephen Schiffer's Dark Night of the Soul: A Review of *Remnants of Meaning*," in Fodor (1990b): 177–193.

———. (1990b). *A Theory of Content and Other Essays* (MIT Press).

Grice, H. P. (1957). "Meaning," *Philosophical Review*, 66: 377–388.

———. (1969). "Utterer's Meaning and Intentions," *Philosophical Review*, 78: 147–177.

Gunderson, K. (ed.). (1975). *Minnesota Studies in the Philosophy of Science* (University of Minnesota Press).

Hale, R., Wright, C., and Miller, A. (eds.). (2017). *Blackwell Companion to the Philosophy of Language*, Volume 1, Second Edition (Wiley-Blackwell).

Kaplan, D. (1989a). "Demonstratives: An Essay on the Semantics, Logic, Metaphysics, and Epistemology of Demonstratives and Other Indexicals," in Almog et al. (1989).

———. (1989b). "Afterthoughts," in Almog et al. (1989).

Kennedy, C. (2007). "Vagueness and Grammar: The Semantics of Relative and Absolute Gradable Adjectives," *Linguistics and Philosophy*, 30: 1–45.

Lepore, E. and Ludwig, K. (2005). *Donald Davidson: Meaning, Truth, Language, and Reality* (Oxford University Press).

Lewis, D. (1969). *Convention: A Philosophical Study* (Harvard University Press).

———. (1975). "Languages and Language," in Gunderson (1975): 3–35.

———. (1983). "New Work for a Theory of Universals," *Australasian Journal of Philosophy*, 61: 343–377.

Loar, B. (1975). "Two Theories of Meaning," in Evans and McDowell (1975).

———. (1981). *Mind and Meaning* (Cambridge University Press).
McGinn, C. (1982). *The Character of Mind* (Oxford University Press).
Neale, S. (2016). "Silent Reference," in Ostertag (2016): 229–342.
Ostertag, G. (ed.). (2016). *Meanings and Other Things: Themes from the Work of Stephen Schiffer* (Oxford University Press).
Quine, W. V. O. (1960). *Word and Object* (MIT Press).
Parret, H. and Bouveresse, J. (eds.) (1981). *Meaning and Understanding* (de Gruyter).
Schiffer, S. (1972). *Meaning* (Oxford University Press).
———. (1981a). "Truth and the Theory of Content," in Parret and Boveresse (1981).
———. (1981b). "Indexicals and the Theory of Reference," *Synthese*, 49: 43–100.
———. (1987). *Remnants of Meaning* (MIT Press).
———. (2003). *The Things We Mean* (Oxford University Press).
———. (2016). "Reply to Neale," in Ostertag (2016): 495–501.
———. (2017). "Intention and Convention in the Theory of Meaning," in Hale et al. (2017): 49–72.
———. (2019). "Vague Speaker-Meaning," in Capone (2019).
Stojnić, U. and Stone, M. (manuscript). "Vague Utterances in Context."

# 5 Limning the External Dimensions of Meaning[1]

*Arthur Sullivan*

Early on in the fervent, epochal debates prompted by the externalist arguments of Kripke (1972), Putnam (1975), and Burge (1979) (among others), Brian Loar (1976, 1981, 1982) draws some characteristic distinctions, upon which he continues to build throughout his career. Namely, (in broad strokes) Loar distinguishes between certain externalist theses about reference and truth conditions on the one hand, and on the other hand certain internalist theses about meaning and content. These distinctions were apt to seem idiosyncratic and obstinate, back when the loudest voices in the field were engaged in binary debate between monolithic versions of causal-externalism and descriptivist-internalism. However, to Loar's credit, they now seem fairly unassailable, and are linked to real significant progress in our understanding of reference, meaning, and surrounding issues.

In §1, I will discuss some motivations for externalism about reference, and consider the range of cases to which these motivations aptly apply. §2 is dedicated to exploring certain internalist theses about meaning. In §3, I turn to Loar's distinctions between "socially deferential" concepts and various others which lack that feature (such as "recognitional concepts" (1990, 1991), "subjective concepts" (1994, 1995), or "narrow concepts" (Loar 2003)). Finally, in §4 I summarize how these distinctions afford an insightful synthesis of the considerations raised in §§1–2.

## 1. Externalism About Reference

To be an externalist, in one pertinent sense of the term, is to reject a supervenience thesis. Internalists about some property $\Phi$ hold that intrinsic duplicates are equivalent with respect to $\Phi$, while externalists about $\Phi$ hold that intrinsic duplicates might still differ in relevant respects. So, for example, Lewis (1983, p. 197) cites "shape" and "charge" as examples of properties about which internalism is uncontentious, and "being a sibling" and "being in debt" as examples of properties about which only externalism is viable.

Narrowing our focus to the case of semantic properties, the general idea motivating semantic externalism is that traditional approaches to language tended to mistakenly assume that all semantic properties are intrinsic properties, whereas it has become evident that at least some of them are to some extent relational. So far, that sentiment leaves open a wide variety of possible externalist theses.[2] One could be an externalist about reference, but not meaning, about truth conditions but not about all aspects of content. (Both "reference" and "meaning" are variously used. I will say more to sharpen my usage of both terms shortly.) Or, along a different dimension: one could be an externalist only about the semantic properties of socially deferential terms (such as "aluminum", "arthritis"), but not about all terms.[3]

For another dimension along which varieties of semantic externalism could be plotted, note that no one is a complete, unqualified externalist (i.e., nobody holds that semantic properties are entirely constituted by external factors). For example, Davidson (1968, p. 136) discusses a sequence of sounds which would express distinct meanings in different languages. Surely such cases could be multiplied indefinitely, and could be instanced alike in writing (e.g., the word-form "formidable" corresponds to quite distinct words in French vs. English). This suggests that semantic properties are not purely constituted by material events or properties external to the agent.[4] Or, again: "incomplete mastery" cases are an important part of the case for externalism (i.e., agents of whom there is considerable reason to count as competent with a term, but who nonetheless do not possess the criteria for its correct application—such as Putnam (1975) on "beech"/"elm"), but presumably all agree that someone who thinks that ketchup is a kind of marsupial should not be counted as competent with the term.[5] If so, then all agree that there are internal aspects required for successful participation in the semantic enterprise, that semantic properties are not purely externally constituted. Refined externalists roll up their sleeves and work toward distinguishing the aspects and dimensions which supervene on the agent from those which do not.

Let us take "reference-externalism" to be the thesis that reference does not supervene on intrinsic properties of the agent.[6] That is, reference-externalists hold that two different agents, or the same agent in different contexts, could—while tokening the same (non-indexical) term, and while being intrinsic duplicates—nonetheless refer to different things. (We set aside indexicality on the presumption that it is a distinctive, circumscribed sub-case wherein sameness of term is obviously compatible with a difference in reference.) The thesis is aptly called "externalism" because the upshot is that reference irreducibly depends on extrinsic factors. Prevalent candidates for external factors which play roles in the determination of reference include: (i) the causal-historical chain of transmission of the term tokened, (ii) facts about the actual nature of the ambient environment which may be inaccessible to ordinary speakers (e.g., gold vs. iron pyrites, $H_2O$ vs. XYZ), and (iii) the states and doings of certain specific sub-sets of the linguistic community in which the speaker is immersed (such as Putnam's (1975) "experts", or Evans' (1982) "producers").

The case for reference-externalism is especially strong when it comes to uses of proper names with whose referent the agent is unfamiliar (Donnellan 1970; Kripke 1972). Exactly who or what a name (as tokened in context) refers to need not, it seems, supervene on anything intrinsic to the agent. The general recognition of this externalist foothold comes in the wake of a battery of familiar lines of argument for distinguishing the semantic relation between a proper name and its referent from that between a compositionally structured noun phrase (including especially a definite description) and whatever might happen to satisfy it (Kripke 1972; Kaplan 1977).[7] There are fairly strong grounds for holding that intrinsic duplicates, who happen to be in distinct possible worlds in respects which are not at all salient to them, might refer to different individuals with otherwise-as-similar-as-possible uses of "Homer", "Jonah", "Columbus", "Einstein", etc.

Attempts to extend reference-externalism to other elements of the category of singular terms raise other complications, and so are generally considered to be not as strong as the case for proper names (cf., e.g., Perry (2009), Bach (2012)). Natural kind terms, however, are very much amenable to this line of reference-externalist argument (Kripke 1972; Putnam 1975), as are certain other sorts of general terms (Putnam 1975; Burge 1979). Exactly to what a use in context of "beech", "arthritis", etc. refers need not, it seems, supervene on anything intrinsic to the speaker, and so intrinsic duplicates might be referring to different kinds. Given the actual availability of indiscernible (to non-experts) though semantically distinct "gold" vs. "iron pyrites" contexts, or "arthritis" vs. "tharthritis" contexts (Loar 1988, p. 100), the point can be made without even the cost of a trip to twin earth.

A crucial pillar of reference-externalism is an account of how reference is determined which does not rely on resources intrinsic to the agent. Thus consider Kaplan (1989, pp. 602–603):

> [O]ne of the most important contributions of contemporary theory of reference . . . [is] the historical chain picture of the reference of names. . . . The notion of a historical chain . . . offer[s] an alternative explanation of how a name in local use can be connected with a remote referent, an explanation that does not require that the mechanism of reference is already in the head of the local user.

This helps to explain why incomplete mastery does not need to pose a debilitating barrier to successful reference by name. So, why would certain general terms be relevantly similar? Well, notwithstanding many significant differences between them,[8] more or less everything said above about the external "mechanisms of reference" for proper names can also be applied to the case of certain general terms. The explanation for the failure of the reference-internalist supervenience thesis is standardly taken to be very much parallel across the two cases. (There is some discussion of *Which general terms?* and *Why, exactly?* below in §3.)

Even given a persistent and unremitting commitment to a core strand of Fregeanism (more on which below in §2), and the increasing focus on certain first-person, subjective aspects of content in his later work (cf. §3), Loar is in this sense a reference-externalist. Explicit commitments to reference-externalism can be found throughout his corpus—e.g., (1981, p. 229, 1982, p. 274, 1987, p. 115, 1991, p. 222, 1994, p. 53, 2003, p. 229). Even further, reference-externalism is a *sine qua non* for some of Loar's most famous contributions, such as the distinction between social and psychological content (1988), which itself paves the way for the phenomenological concept strategy for understanding the explanatory gap (1990, 1999). Endorsements along the following lines are ubiquitous throughout Loar's works:

> "the reference of our words is in part a social fact" (1981, p. 229); "reference derives . . . from the language I speak, from the social-semantic relations I draw on" (1991, p. 221); "reference is externally determined and not descriptively or satisfactionally determined" (1994, p. 57); "there are good reasons to count reference as constituted by externally determined relations" (1995, p. 62); "reference . . . [is] constituted by relations that, at least in part, are externally determined, whether socially or not" (2003, p. 235).

Loar (1995, p. 54) also holds that "socially deferential names (Julius Caesar, Richard Wagner)" and "socially deferential kind terms (aluminum, arthritis)" instance more or less the same "external reference relation". Clearly, throughout his diverse career, Loar holds that counterexamples to the reference-internalists' supervenience thesis abound.

Note, by way of segue, that there are at least two different things to which reference-externalism is opposed—there is internalism about reference (i.e., reference is determined by the intrinsic states and properties of language-users) and there is individualism about reference (i.e., the isolated individual agent is the autonomous determinant of reference). The two are commonly lumped together, for many traditional approaches to language contain elements of both internalism and individualism,[9] and lots of contemporary theorists are indiscriminate in their rejection of both of them. However, they are not equivalent in general, or in Loar's work in particular (cf., e.g., 1987, note 5). So, for example, an internalist could be an anti-individualist by accommodating reference-borrowing (e.g., Strawson 1959, p. 182)). Kripke (1986) does a masterful job of exposing the instability of this kind of anti-individualist internalism,[10] but still the two things are distinct. Going forward, it will be crucial to distinguish considerations which weigh against individualism (i.e., semantically relevant communal factors which are external to the agent's head) from considerations which weigh against internalism (i.e., semantically relevant environmental factors which are external to everybody's heads).

## 2. Internalism About Meaning

Even more than the case of "reference" (cf. note 6), technical usage of "meaning" varies considerably. Meanings are notoriously difficult to talk about in a non-contentious, non-tendentious way. There are influential skeptics about meaning (e.g., Quine 1960), (Chomsky 1993)), and there are lots of non-trivial differences between the non-skeptics, as to how the notion should be understood. For example, an illustrative but not exhaustive list of fundamental bases for meaning, according to distinct theoretical orientations, might include: ideas, sense, reference, truth conditions, use, intentions, causation, and teleology.

At the broadest limit, as it were, the meaning of an expression might be taken to include any and all of its semantically relevant properties (where of course "semantically relevant" is, as of yet, vague and diversely understood). So, for example, Frege's (1892, p. 60) "three levels of difference" between terms—i.e., idea/ sense/ reference—might be seen as three dimensions of meaning (perhaps even among some others). At the opposite, narrowest limit, there is the referentialist approach to meaning which just simply identifies the meaning with the reference. Problems for referentialism are familiar and easily multiplied—for example, in the form of cases wherein sameness of reference does not seem to suffice for synonymy ("renate"/"cordate", "Hesperus"/"Phosphorus"), or cases wherein lack of reference does not seem to entail lack of meaning ("phlogiston", "Vulcan"). The challenge for a discriminating notion of meaning is where to draw the line—i.e., Exactly which properties should be taken to constitute meaning? Differing conceptions of meaning correspond to differing conceptions of the scope of semantic theory itself—i.e., there are certain questions (some of which will come up below) which a broad conception of meaning would account for semantically, but which would not be counted as semantically relevant on a narrow conception of meaning (and so perhaps farmed out to syntax, pragmatics, or psychology for explanation).

A canonical Frege/Russell contrast is pertinent here. A Russellian approach to meaning is referentialist, individuating meaning as coarsely as truth conditions—"Mont Blanc itself is a component part of what is actually asserted in the proposition, Mont Blanc is more than 4000 meters high" (letter to Frege 12/12/1904); and so " . . . if one thing has two names, you make exactly the same assertion whichever of the two names you use . . ." (Russell 1918, p. 245). For Frege, in contrast, there is more to meaning than reference or truth conditions, and so interchanging co-referential parts can change the meaning. (Given that truth conditions are compositionally determined by the reference of the parts, the relation between reference and truth conditions parallels the relation between atomic terms and molecular sentences.)

The term "mode of presentation" is used to designate the dimension along which co-referential terms might differ in meaning. Accordingly, "*Hesperus is far from Missouri*" is arguably not synonymous with "*Phosphorus is far from Missouri*", even though all corresponding parts are co-referential, because of the difference in mode of presentation. And I will call the doctrine that modes of presentation are semantically relevant "Frege's constraint". While all would agree that the belief that *Hesperus is larger than Phosphorus* involves a less serious error than the more drastically confused belief that *Hesperus is larger than Hesperus*, only proponents of Frege's constraint distinguish between the operative meanings. There are lots of other (pre-, post-, or otherwise extra-semantic) attempts to account for this difference, which do not involve distinctions of meaning (cf. note 11).

As is well known, Russell's position on Frege's constraint is actually rather convoluted—for one thing, the above-cited (1918, p. 245) quote which transgresses it is explicitly limited to Russell's infamous notion of a "logically proper name". Relatedly, Russell often seems to completely agree with Frege's criterion for the individuation of meanings, but to accommodate it with a heavy-handed approach to telling people what they really mean (i.e., some/ most/ all things that agents mistakenly take to be names, in their own thought and talk, are actually "disguised" or "truncated" descriptions). Another thing which is also clear from the historical record, and pertinent to present purposes, is that reference-externalism is often taken to fit with or suggest a narrow, Russellian conception of meaning (Kaplan 1977, 1989).[11] For if modes of presentation do not determine reference, then why keep them on the semantic payroll?

In work which spans decades, from at least (1976) to (2003), Loar swims against that tide. Not only is reference-externalism compatible with respecting Frege's constraint, but further, a satisfactory notion of meaning must accord with Frege's constraint[12]—otherwise it cannot respect, let alone illuminate, evident constitutive connections between linguistic meaning and the agent's intentions and attitudes. This is a requirement in order to capture the causal-explanatory links between meaning and intentional action. A theory that identifies meanings which have different constitutive links to intentional action, or distinguishes meanings which have the same links to intentional action—for the case of a rational, non-culpable, though finite and fallible, agent—is thereby problematic.

Recent iterations of these debates over Frege's constraint may strike observers as litany, with opposing factions insisting on opposing tenets regarding synonymy and substitutivity, correlative to their contrastive stances on the semantic relevance of modes of presentation (cf., e.g., Schiffer [1987, 2006, 2016] vs. Salmon [1989, 2006, 2016]). However, Loar famously goes a distinctive step beyond that, introducing a case in which understanding the utterance requires recognition of the operative mode of presentation:

> Suppose that Smith and Jones are unaware that the man being interviewed on television is someone they see on the train every morning and about whom, in that latter role, they have just been talking. Smith says "He is a stockbroker", intending to refer to the man on television; Jones takes Smith to be referring to the man on the train. Now Jones, as it happens, has correctly identified Smith's referent, since the man on television is the man on the train; but he has failed to understand Smith's utterance. It would seem that, as Frege held, some 'manner of presentation' of the referent is, even on referential uses, essential to what is being communicated.
>
> (1976, p. 357)

Surely every case is potentially a "stockbroker" case—though Loar is ingenious in his isolation of variables, all the required ingredients are mundanely available. This suggests that, contra the referentialist—and independently of tendentious claims about synonymy or substitutivity—to characterize the truth conditions does not suffice to limn the meaning.

If we define "meaning-externalism" as the view that meaning supervenes on factors extrinsic to the agent, then above I have claimed that no one is a (complete, unqualified) meaning-externalist (i.e., recall the points above about "formidable", "Madagascar", and "ketchup").[13] That does, though, allow for a sharp contrast with a bold Lockean meaning-internalism, which holds that meaning supervenes on intrinsic factors. We could then plot a continuum of views between these poles, on which the referentialist is decidedly more externalist than those who endorse Frege's constraint (at least on the standard assumption that modes of presentation supervene intrinsically, which is explicitly endorsed by Loar (1976, 1987, 1991, 2003, etc.)). One is a meaning-internalist, in this sense, to the extent that one countenances factors which are (i) instrinsic to the agent and (ii) semantically relevant.

Some respects have already emerged in which Loar's meaning-internalism, too, like his reference-externalism, play a major role in some of his distinctive philosophical contributions. Both are essential ingredients of the (1988) distinction between social and psychological content, for example, and Loar's (1987, 1990, 1991, 1994, 1995, 2003) attendant explorations of certain first-person, subjective aspects of content are a center-piece of recent meaning-internalist theorizing. ("Our primitive notion of aboutness is subjective, and this is the foundation of the semantic" (1987, p. 116).) Marked internalist dimensions stretch back through Loar's (1982) functionalist intentional realism—e.g., the express aim of countering the "enthusiasm for reference over meaning" (pp. 3–5), within a physicalist approach.

Next, we will dive into some of the nuances of Loar's meaning-internalism—involving as it does fine distinctions between different kinds of concepts, contexts, and intentions, as well as attendant refinements when it comes to differences between anti-individualist and anti-internalist considerations.

## 3. Loar on Kinds of Terms

As understood here, reference-externalism and meaning-internalism are surely consistent. Absolutely and unequivocally, one could hold that what a token of "Wagner", "water", or "arthritis" refers to, in context, does not supervene on factors intrinsic to the agent, and yet there are aspects of their meaning which do so supervene. After all, to reason from "X is irrelevant to reference" to "X is irrelevant to meaning" is to expressly presuppose meaning-referentialism, and so would be a *non sequiteur* on any broader conception of meaning. (That would be to capitulate to the "enthusiasm for reference over meaning" (1982, p. 3).) To the contrary, Loar's considered aim is to "introduce a social element into determining reference and fixing belief contents, without implying that all meaning and content are socially constituted" (2006, p. 88).

Toward that end, let us next consider distinctions which Loar draws between different kinds of terms, along some relevant dimensions. (This parallels remarks from Kripke and Putnam mentioned in note 3; though Loar mines this vein more deeply.) There is a category of terms which Loar calls "socially deferential", including some proper names[14] and general terms. (For the latter case, Loar (2003, §3) gives a familiar representative list: "water", "tiger", "arthritis".) This category is distinguished in a preliminary way by Loar (1988, p. 107) as the sort of case in which "conceptual roles are distinct from truth conditions", and it plays a key role throughout Loar's later works. Loar (2003, §14) says that socially deferential terms "involve conceptions of other speakers and of the shared language", and (1988, p. 109) that their "fundamental usefulness" consists in the way in which they allow us "to impose a grid of socially regularized information on the vagaries of individual psychology"—i.e., to "describe people as conveyors of more or less determinate information, which remains constant even as the contents of their states vary".

Socially deferential terms are of course (and not accidentally) the very cases for which the reference-externalist arguments are the strongest. While the semantic significance of deference is anticipated by, say,

Kripke's (1972, p. 94) stressing the importance of the agent's "connection with other speakers in the community", or by Putnam's (1975, p. 231) "division of linguistic labour"—or, less proximately, by the marked anti-individualist strands in Wittgenstein (1953)—Burge (1979) is often credited with articulating the general importance of semantic deference, and exploring its externalist consequences. As Burge (1979) stresses, a key indicator for the presence of deference is openness to correction: to the extent to which agents are open to changing their linguistic habits if they came to see themselves as deviating from the norm, social deference is at work. For example, alluding back to note 14, it would not take much to convince Loar that he had been mistaken about exactly to whom "Boltzman" or "Bukharin" refer, but it would be much harder to convince him that he was mistaken about the reference of what he had always taken to be the name for his brother, or for the street on which he grew up.

Regarding the scope or range of social deference in everyday language use, Burge's view is that the notion:

> has extremely wide application . . . [beyond the signature case of] "arthritis". . . . We could have used an artifact term, an ordinary natural kind word, a color adjective, a social role term, a term for a historical style, an abstract noun, an action verb, a physical movement verb, or any of various other sorts of words. . . . The [externalist] argument can get under way in any case where it is intuitively possible to attribute a mental state or event whose content involves a notion that the subject incompletely understands. . . . [Incomplete mastery] is the key. . . . The phenomenon is rampant in our pluralistic age.
>
> (1979, p. 80)

I am not so sure about "rampant", for its negative connotations. ("Rampant", related to "rampage", ≈ flourishing + lamentably so. For an opposite sentiment cf. Kaplan (1989, pp. 603–604) on "vocabulary power as epistemological enhancement".) Surely, social deference is ubiquitous and prevalent. No doubt, there are interesting stories to be told about why it might be more prevalent at some times and places than others, and the prevalence of social deference may be completely incompatible with some versions of internalism and/or individualism. However, I see no evident reason to lament the phenomenon *per se*. (How else am I supposed to ask questions about platypuses, neutrinos, or the House of Hapsburg?[15])

Natural kind terms, in their standard usage by non-experts, are a paradigm case to illustrate the (non-contingent) overlap of reference-externalism and social deference (as are uses of proper names with whose referent the agent is unfamiliar). That is, on such uses, terms like "tiger" or "water" are used to refer to a mind- and language-independent kind of thing or stuff, the precise criteria of identity for which is typically unknown to speakers who may nonetheless count as competent with the term. Typically, and tellingly, such non-expert speakers are relatively open to correction by experts, when it comes to the exact criteria for the term's correct application. Where there is social deference, there is purchase for the division of linguistic labour to kick in—for the external mechanisms of reference determination to play their role in affording determinate content to the thoughts and utterances of incompletely-mastering agents.

There are of course lots of non-typical uses of these terms, as of any others. (As Loar 1991, p. 120) observes: "Social meanings do not deprive me of autonomy when I insist on it.") For one thing, there are water-experts, who know more about water than most anyone else (and know that they do so); they would likely react non-deferentially to the discovery that they deviate from any statistical norms of "water"-usage. For another, ordinary non-experts also exhibit myriad non-natural kind uses of natural kind terms—i.e., many uses of "water" are not deferential and essence-targeting, but rather relatively crude practical kind terms uses (i.e., water ≈ whatever it is that flows out of this tap, or whatever I can use to do the laundry, or etc.) On a deferential, natural kind use of "tiger", only the (normal) offspring of tigers could (clearly) count; on a looser usage, toys, statues, etc. can also perfectly well count as tigers.[16]

So, strictly speaking, there is no such thing as a socially deferential term, but rather "socially deferential" applies to usage, or tokens of terms. It is intentions in context, openness to correction, that matters. (This is perhaps clearest in the case of proper names—there is no such thing as a socially deferential proper name, but there are socially deferential uses of names. After all, whoever Bukharin was, if it weren't for "Bukharin"-producers, there would be no "Bukharin"-consumers (in something like Evans' (1982) sense of those terms).). "Socially deferential term" is then short-hand for: "a term which is typically or commonly used in a socially deferential way", and "socially deferential proper name" is a short-hand way to designate terms which are almost entirely used in socially deferential ways, within a specific community.

Consider next now how social deference, on the one hand, relates to anti-individualism vs. anti-internalism, on the other. I take it that semantic deference is immediately and unequivocally anti-individualist. To the extent that anti-individualist internalism is a coherent option, then deference is not necessarily anti-internalist; however, if it is not (cf. note 10), then deference also turns out to have anti-internalist entailments. Kripke (1972), Putnam (1975), and Burge (1979) are all thoroughly anti-individualist (in keeping with the prevailing tides within post-Wittgensteinian philosophy of language), but only explicitly anti-internalist about certain sorts of usage, or specific sorts of term. (Remember note 3, and the pro-internalist remarks about "foolish", "doctor", "chair", etc.) Clearly though, the two core semantic externalist cases of uses of proper names with whose referent the agent is unfamiliar and deferential essence-targeting uses of natural kind terms by non-experts are both anti-individualist (involving deference to communal factors) and anti-internalist (involving deference to environmental factors).

We turn now to the sorts of usage of sorts of terms which, according to Loar, should not be thought of as "socially deferential". To begin, consider Loar (2003, §3) on "narrow concepts":

> for which reference is context-independent, that is, independent of contexts that transcend "internal conceptual role" and the like. Paradigms are the logical connectives. If a connective has the conceptual role of "and" or "all" it eo ipso expresses conjunction or the universal quantifier. There are no twin-Earth reference-shifts for logical connectives. Presumably mathematical and modal concepts belong here as well. (It will be convenient, if somewhat inelegant, to include in this group indexicals that pick out internal states: "this sensation", "this thought"; for their referring arguably does not consist in externally determined relations.)

Narrow concepts are meaning-internalist in our ongoing operative sense—there is no deference-induced gap between their conceptual role (for the agent) and what determines their reference (in the community). This is why they are twin-earth-proof—i.e., counterfactual variance of factors in the ambient environment which are inaccessible to ordinary speakers will not alter their reference. As Loar (1994, p. 73) says of such cases: "semantical-intentional fact and appearance are identical". Narrow concepts are not as obviously or strongly individualistic—a child or a foreigner learning English could surely exhibit incomplete mastery of "and". But still the relation between conceptual role and reference-determination is quite different from, say, a standard case of non-expert usage of a natural kind term, or an Intro to Classics student wondering who Homer was. Incomplete mastery of "and"—akin to "yellow", "chair", etc., and as distinct from "elm"—is tantamount to incompetence.[17]

So, these non-socially-deferential terms are internalist, in that their conceptual role does not diverge from what determines their reference. This renders them impervious to twin-earth shift. However, the relations between absence of deference and individualism are more complex. In socially deferential cases, incomplete mastery is compatible with competence; in non-socially-deferential cases this is less obviously so. These are of course shades of grey, not binary categories, and so for example perhaps Putnam's (1962, 1975) "pencil" or Salmon's (1989) "ketchup" illustrate the terrain near the middle of the range—i.e., they are considerably distant both from "and" on the one hand and from "aluminum" on the other, when it comes to relations between conceptual role and truth conditions. (Here compare (Loar 1987, p. 111) on anti-individualism, competence, and "roast chicken".)

Next up: Are there sub-varieties of non-socially-deferential usage or terms that ought to be distinguished? If so, along which dimensions? I will take as **NSD(i) logical terms** (e.g., "and", "all"), described by Loar (above) as a paradigm case of narrow concepts. (Here, again, semantic-intentional appearance = semantic-intentional fact. If it licenses the characteristic inferences, then QED, it is "and".) Loar (2003, §3) alludes to similarities exhibited by "mathematical and modal concepts", but I will not work to define precise boundaries here (in some measure, because of skepticism as to whether "precise boundaries" would get much purchase in this terrain). Instead I will briefly describe a few other sub-varieties, to illustrate some other members of the non-socially-deferential species.

**NSD(ii) recognitional terms:**Loar (1988, p. 107) follows up an above-cited remark about certain (deferential) cases in which conceptual roles can be distinct from truth conditions by specifying as a sort of case in which that possibility does not seem to arise "certain demonstrative judgements involving perceptual discriminative concepts". A little bit later, he (1990, §2) goes much deeper into:

> a wide class of concepts that I will call recognitional concepts. They have the form "x is one of that kind"; they are type-demonstratives. These type-demonstratives are grounded in dispositions to classify, by way of perceptual discriminations, certain objects, events, situations. Suppose you go into the California desert and spot a succulent never seen before. You become adept at recognizing instances, and gain a recognitional command of their kind, without a name for it; you are disposed to identify positive and negative instances and thereby pick out a kind. These dispositions are typically linked with capacities to form images, whose conceptual role seems to be to focus thoughts about an identifiable kind in the absence of currently perceived instances. An image is presumably "of" a given kind by virtue of both past recognitions and current dispositions.
>
> Recognitional concepts are generally formed against a further conceptual background. In identifying a thing as of a recognized kind, we almost always presuppose a more general type to which the kind belongs—four-legged animal, plant, physical thing, perceptible event. A recognitional concept will then have the form "physical thing of that (perceived) kind" or "internal state of that kind" etc.

Recognitional terms play some key roles in Loar's later research projects. Rather than trace that trajectory, though—or delving into the nearby vein that demonstrative reference is "the fundamental case of reference" (Loar 1995, p. 55)—the present job is to explain why recognitional terms are illustrative of the non-deferential variety.

Well, first, no social or otherwise external relations need be relied on here, to secure a link between term and referent. No deference is appropriate, when one tokens a thought along the lines of "I think that is another instance of *that* kind"—where "*that* kind" is employed as a recognitional term. (Compare note 14 about what distinguishes the socially-deferential proper names from their complement.) The conceptual role determines the truth conditions, rendering recognitional terms also twin-earth proof (i.e., counterfactual variance of factors in the ambient environment which are inaccessible to ordinary speakers will not alter their reference). So, if "water" is used as a recognitional term and not as an essence-targeting natural kind term, then the content of "I think *that water* is Φ" is indifferent to whether the stuff is in fact $H_2O$ or XYZ.[18]

As for some differentia within the non-socially-deferential genus: Recognitional terms are not only internalist but also relatively individualist, for who is in a position to correct me about "*that* kind", on this sort of recognitional usage? (Of course, such questions as whether my term "*that* kind" corresponds to a category countenanced by experts, and if so which expert category, are very different things, and much more straightforwardly linked to social deference.) As Loar (1990, §2) recognizes, this aspect gives rise to familiar worries within the philosophy of language (". . . a red flag for many who are aware of the vexing . . . problems about referential scrutability, rule-following, naturalizing intentionality . . ."). However, while there is a relative sort of individualism here, it falls far short of any troubling kind of infallibility—surely, I could be just plain wrong to think that a new candidate instance should be counted as an instance of *that* kind, even despite a lack of social deference. (See Loar (1991, §VI, "False Ascriptions of Recognitional Concepts") for detailed discussion.)

**NSD(iii) subjective terms:** Attendant upon the distinction between social and psychological content (1988) and the subsequent exploration of phenomenal concepts (1990), one of Loar's (1994, 1995) next moves is to delve more deeply into the subjective, first-person perspective. Consider for example the following opening preamble:

> In the first person, it is not easy to regard scepticism about reference seriously. Seeing a tree one thinks "that is an oak"; and it makes little apparent sense to wonder whether the trunk or the bark are equally as good candidates as the tree itself for being what one's thought is about. There is a modem tradition of discounting the first-person perspective, and of counting it essential to a proper understanding of semantic properties and relations that they be seen from the third person, as objective. But the seeming security of the first-person perspective ought to raise the question whether it might not be the right perspective from which to think about semantic properties and relations . . . . [R]eference, while externally determined, is also in a deep sense constituted from the first person perspective.
>
> (1994, p. 51)

One element at play here is a wrestling match with the waning influence of behaviorism within the philosophy of language. A part of Loar's point here is that Quine's (1960) "gavagai" worries get no traction whatsoever from the subjective point of view. This suggests that perhaps the entire "inscrutability" problematic depends on the presumption that the third-person or objective point of view is semantically authoritative. Behaviorists had some manner of justification for that presumption, but since the days are long gone when that was the received paradigm in the philosophy of psychology, it is not clear what credentials remain for that purported justification.

The above excerpt also contains a characteristic Loarian distinction between "determining" and "constituting" reference. So, for example, the antics of botanical experts can play a role in *determining* the reference of a token of "oak", but they need not thereby play the same kind of role in *constituting* an instance of reference. Reference is constituted from the first person, subjective perspective (1994, p. 51, 1995, pp. 71–72); objective indeterminacy is compatible with subjective determinacy, and does nothing to undermine the constitution of reference (1995, p. 73). Again, though—rather than delving further into such historical veins or refined distinctions—the present order of business is: do subjective terms provide an example of the non-socially-deferential species?

Well, again, for a case like "that is an oak" (as described above), one may or may not be deferential about "oak" (cf. note 16), but not so for "that". There is no social deference to "that" experts, no gap between conceptual role and truth conditions, nothing much that could constitute incomplete mastery of "that". There are of course significant debates about what determines the referent of a token of "that" (see, e.g., Perry [2009] and Bach [2012]), but they are very different from the complications involved in determining the reference of "water", "tiger", "arthritis", or, in general, any term which targets and categorizes mind- and language-independent phenomena. It is hard to even begin to imagine how to convince someone that they were wrong about which object, among the available candidates, they intended to designate by "that"—that is up to the agent, and is not under the influence of other elements of their community.

Hence, as in the case of logical and recognitional terms, there are subjective usages (and sorts of terms which are particularly amenable to such) which do not exhibit social deference. There is no openness to correction, no incomplete mastery, no role to be played by external social relations in affording determinate content. Hence, such cases differ markedly from the semantic externalist paradigms (of uses of proper names with whose referent the agent is unfamiliar and essence-targeting uses of natural kind terms by non-experts) when it comes to questions about externalism and anti-individualism.

**NSD(iv) common, non-technical terms**: Loar's latest research did not delve much further into questions about externalism, reference, and meaning *per se*, but rather moved on into some powerful and penetrating work on the metaphysics of mind (cf. Schiffer (2017)). I know of no other place (in addition to some already mentioned excerpts stretching from 1987, p. 111, to 1995, p. 73) where Loar explicitly addresses how these above considerations apply to ordinary non-technical terms—i.e., How do the externalist arguments apply, if at all, to "chair", "yellow", "happy", "widow", etc.? So the following is just brief speculation (though not without warrant) about Loar's views on the on the kinds of question first broached in note 3. Within the ongoing general project of "introduc[ing] a social element into determining reference and fixing belief contents, without implying that all meaning and content are socially constituted" (2006, p. 88), which sorts of usage or terms are going to line up as more like the name of a recently met neighbor than like "Boltzman" or "Bukharin" (from note 14)?

Well, as for "all" or "and", it would take some audacity to try to twin-earth up a reference shift for "chair", "happy", "grandmother", "widow", etc.—i.e., for a vast range of the common terms employed in everyday thought and talk.[19] What makes them twin-earth-proof is the absence of deference. A non-deferential internalism about meaning (though not, thereby, individualism) seems rather plausible for such ubiquitous, mundane terms. (After all, in your house as in mine, there are a lot more chairs than tigers.) Incomplete mastery is compatible with competence only to the extent that the speaker is deferential; this will differ significantly (in degree) for distinct types of term, as well as for distinct types of usage for any given term. Incomplete mastery can still amount to semantic incompetence, in lots of mundane cases, wherein deference is absent, and the semantical-intentional appearances limn the semantical-intentional facts.

## 4. Conclusion

To sum up this study of Loar, externalism, and meaning:

First, many fine distinctions are drawn between meaning, reference, individualism, and internalism, in these urbane times, and on this front, we owe much to Loar's careful digging and sorting. Second, reference externalism is compatible with meaning internalism; and once we distinguish between socially deferential terms and terms, usage, and contexts which lack that feature, then it becomes clear that the balance between these externalist/internalist factors can play out differentially, in different contexts, and across different sub-categories of the lexicon. Third, social deference opens the gap between conceptual role and truth conditions; where deference is absent, externalist arguments don't get much traction. Incomplete mastery is compatible with semantic competence only where there is this deference-induced gap.

In general, social deference directly and immediately entails anti-individualism; the link to anti-internalism is more complex and mediate.

Deference only implies anti-internalism in specifically targeted respects or contexts (for the sorts of usage about which facts about the actual nature of the ambient environment, which may be inaccessible to ordinary speakers, are semantically relevant). The absence of deference entails internalism. Given all that, in non-deferential terrain, a significant degree of meaning-internalism is natural and fairly unassailable.

## Notes

1. I had the enormous good fortune of studying with Brian Loar at Rutgers in the Fall terms of 1996 and 1997, as a visiting PhD student under his supervision. This was an amazing opportunity, and Brian remains to me a role model for mentorship in philosophy. He was unfailingly kind, generous, exacting, and demanding. I cherish memories of being struck as if by lightning, on the way home at the end of the day, with waves of recognition of the significance of what Brian had been saying to me earlier. (It was too much to digest, all at once.) This paper runs along the lines of our frequent discussions in those days—which continued, on an off, whenever the opportunity arose.
2. For general discussion of the many questions and issues which tend to be tangled up in the debates over semantic externalism, cf. Sawyer (2011) and Gertler (2012). Some paradigm cases of traditional semantic internalism include Plato (1928, pp. 324A–343A), Locke (1690, Bk III), Frege (1892), and Russell (1918).
3. For example, Kripke (1972, pp. 127–128) cites "foolish", "fat", and "yellow" as examples of terms to which the ongoing externalist considerations (specifically pertaining to natural kind terms) may not apply. Relatedly, Kripke (1979, p. 256) holds that there are kinds of terms which could not give rise to the puzzle about belief:

   > Not that the puzzle extends to all translations from English to French. [. . . It] seems to me that Pierre, if he learns French and English separately, without learning any translation manual between them, *must* conclude, if he reflects enough, that "doctor" and "medecin", and "heureux" and "happy" are synonymous, or at any rate, coextensive; and potential paradox of the present kind for these word pairs is blocked.

   So, Kripke might be an externalist about proper names and natural kind terms, but not about terms like "doctor", "foolish", "fat", "happy", or "yellow". Similarly, Putnam (1975, p. 233) says that "some words do not exhibit any division of linguistic labour: 'chair', for example". Further, he also concedes that the externalist case ". . . has more plausibility . . ." with respect to "cat" than to "pencil" (1975, p. 248). Finally, Burge (2007, pp. 160–161) also qualifies his commitment to externalism in a significant way.
4. Evans' (1973) "Madagascar" example is a classic case which also suggests this conclusion. Cf. Loar (1987, p. 120): "the world contains no relations that are semantic just by virtue of their objective roles".
5. Cf. Salmon's (1989) attempt to run a Fregean "Hesperus"/"Phosphorus" case on "catsup"/"ketchup". Salmon's externalist claim is that one could be competent with both terms while believing that they differ in reference.
6. There are many significant dimensions along which technical usage of "reference" differs. For [1], some use it strictly to apply to the relation between singular terms and designata, while others use it more broadly, such that any independently meaningful expression *eo ipso* refers to a semantic value (and

so predicates refer to properties, logical connectives refer to truth-functions, etc.). For another, [2] some use "reference" exclusively to designate language-world relations, whereas others also apply it to intentional mental phenomena (e.g., concepts). Or again, [3] some treat reference as a two-place relation between a term and a referent, whereas others hold that it is a pernicious oversimplification to presume that referring is something that terms do—rather, reference is something that an agent in a context uses a term to do.

For present purposes, I will be quick with [1] and [3]—I'll use "reference" broadly, such that reference applies to any independently meaningful term, and I will take it to be a four-place relation involving a term, an agent, a context, and a referent. [2] is harder, both in general due to the complexity of the impending questions about relations between language and thought, and in the particular case of Loar scholarship, since over the course of decades of work his focus and orientation evolved (cf. Schiffer (2017)). Herein, I will assume that terms involved in the reference relation can be either linguistic expressions or mental concepts. So, it is well-formed to ask what the reference is for tokens of the expressions "and", "arthritis", or "Arthur"; and it is well-formed to ask what the reference is for an agent's "and", "arthritis", or "Arthur" concepts. I will not get into questions about relations between the two.

7. Dissenters exist (e.g., Hawthorne & Manley 2012) but I believe their arguments can and should be countered (cf. Sullivan 2013)). In Kaplan's (1989, pp. 571–573) terms, the paradigm of the variable replaced the paradigm of the description in the theory of reference; in Bach's (1987, Chpt 1) terms, there are significant differences between relational vs. satisfactional intentional connections. According to Loar (2006, p. 79): "Russell's distinction between reference and denotation is well-motivated; reference is a semantic primitive while denotation is not".
8. For example, proper names refer to discrete particulars while the referents of kind terms are taken to be either repeatable (and hence abstract entities) or else discontinuous, scattered, inconstant aggregations. Relatedly, there are significant metasemantic differences between baptizing a child (I dub thee "Norbert") and introducing a term for a kind (let's use the term "tiger"/"gold" to designate the kind of thing of which this is an instance). For that matter, there are also serious differences between different sub-types of natural kind terms—for instance, biological species are distinct from chemical kinds in being subject to evolution over time. ("Was there a first tiger?" is a relevantly weirder question than "Was there a first hydrogen atom?") And so on.
9. For example, the following passage from Locke (1690, Bk III, 2, ii) clearly endorses both internalism and individualism: "A man cannot make his words the signs either of qualities in things, or of conceptions in the mind of another, whereof he has none of his own. Til he has some ideas of his own, he cannot . . . use any signs for them: for thus they would be signs of he knows not what, which is in truth to be signs of nothing".
10. Kripke's (1986) case goes something like this: Suppose that, of the set of people who use the name "Peano", almost all just (mistakenly) think of him as the founder of the Peano axioms. A small sub-set of experts know that Dedekind founded the Peano axioms, and have other means of singling out Peano. Now suppose all those experts are together at a conference, and the venue gets bombed, and they all perish. Anti-individualist internalism about reference has the unpalatable consequence that, at this moment of tragedy, "Peano" changes from a name of Peano to a name of Dedekind. Only on reference-externalism can the name still refer to Peano after the tragedy.

11. Here Kaplan (1978, p. 296) articulates the guiding idea, musing that perhaps modes of presentation "should not be considered part of the content of what is said, but should rather be thought of as contextual factors which help us interpret the actual physical utterance as having a certain content." Approaches which reject or qualify Frege's constraint include Salmon (1989), Millikan (1994), Devitt (1996), Soames (2002), and Williamson (2007). (Cf. note 13.)
12. For a typical flat-footed, unapologetic motivation of Frege's constraint, see Loar (1987, p. 105). Others with whom Loar is in agreement here include Evans (1973, 1982), Schiffer (1987, 2006), Perry (1988, 2009), Recanati (1993, 2010). Note that Kripke, for one, is emphatically agnostic on Frege's constraint—"no firm doctrine regarding the point should be read into my words" (Kripke 1980, pp. 20–21).
13. Examples in which extreme meaning-extermalism is approached are provided by Soames (2002, pp. 70–71, 2011, pp. 92–93), Williamson (2007, pp. 66–67, 128–129), in which general unqualified claims about semantic competence are motivated only with quick remarks about how one could be competent with, say, "furze" and "gorse" without knowing that they are co-extensive. (Note that "furze" and "gorse" are externalist-friendly natural kind terms—much more on the relevance of this point in §3.) Soames (2011, p. 97) also discusses, as further motivation, Salmon's (1989) aforementioned "ketchup"/"catsup" case, claiming that the agent in question "understands both words" even while thinking that they designate distinct condiments. Even if we were to grant that, surely we would need more than "furze" and "ketchup" to extend the scope of these externalist conclusions to "meaning" in general. It is a long way from this small hand-picked selection of cases to "and", "all", "yellow", "happy", "chair", "grandmother", etc.
14. Namely, those which are "reflexively constrained by a distinctive relation, a socially mediated relation between a token-use (by me) of a name *N* and an object *O*" (Loar 1994, p. 66). Illustrative examples given are "Boltzman", "Sarah Bernhardt" and "Bukharin". Loar's example given of a non-socially deferential name is "the name of a recently met neighbor" which would involve "a complex memory demonstrative, along with some descriptive elements". In the latter sort of case the link between *N* and *O* need not rely on social deference.
15. As Burge (1979, note 1) himself insists, "employ[ing] before mastery" is a crucial part of the "process of mastery". Cf. Burge (1986) for more exploration into relations between competence, understanding, and openness to correction; and cf., e.g., Wikforss (2004), Sawyer (2011) for extended critical discussion.
16. To delve further into this issue, consider Putnam's (1962) thought experiment which concerns the surprising discovery that cats are actually Martian robots. Putnam (1962, p. 661) points out that intuitions may be divided between two different reactions to this surprising discovery:

    i. Wow! It's turned out that cats are not animals after all!
    ii. Wow! It's turned out that there aren't and never were any cats!

    One fundamental difference between [i] and [ii] concerns exactly how the term 'cat' is used. [i] involves a deferential, essence-targeting use of the term; whereas [ii] involves a more autonomous, my-meaning-determines-my-extension, use of the term.

    We need not even go to such far-fetched thought experiments to illustrate this point. For example, reactions [i] and [ii] might surely have applied to the scientific recognition that whales are mammals and not fish, or, more recently, to the de-classification of Pluto as a planet in 2006. (This is a nice recent illustrative example: media reports I encountered about the decision to de-classify Pluto from the ranks of the planets tended to include a stubborn person-on-the-street insisting "As far as I am concerned, Pluto will always be a planet!" This is an autonomous, non-deferential response.)

17. One of the critical factors at play here is that, at least in many cases, what these narrow concepts (as opposed to, say, natural kind terms) target, and intend to sort, is not purely mind- and language-independent; hence there is no determinate objective reference for the sense to fail to fit. They are constituent elements of a conceptual scheme, not targets to be sorted by a conceptual scheme. Cf. Sullivan (2018, Ch. 6) for further exploration of this point.
18. Here compare Loar (1988, p. 105) on the indifference of the content of "No swimming today; the water is too rough" to whether it occurs in a $H_2O$ or XYZ context. "It is not that we switch rapidly back and forth between two explanations . . .".
19. Williamson (2007, pp. 95–96) tries to come up with something akin to a twin-earth reference shift for the case of "and"; I discuss his attempt in Sullivan (2018, §6.2).

## References


Bach, K. (1987). *Thought and Reference*. Clarendon Press.

Bach, K. (2012). Context Dependence. In M. García-Carpintero & M. Kölbel (Eds.), *The Continuum Companion to the Philosophy of Language*. Continuum.

Burge, T. (1979). Individualism and the Mental. *Midwest Studies in Philosophy*, *4*, 73–121.

Burge, T. (1986). Intellectual Norms and Foundations of Mind. *Journal of Philosophy*, *83*, 697–720.

Burge, T. (2007). "Postscript" to (1979). In *Philosophical Essays*, Volume 2. Oxford University Press.

Chomsky, N. (1993). *Language and Thought*. Moyer Bell.

Davidson, D. (1968). On Saying That. *Synthese*, *19*, 130–146.

Devitt, M. (1996). *Coming to Our Senses*. Cambridge University Press.

Donnellan, K. S. (1970). Proper Names and Identifying Descriptions. *Synthese*, *21*, 335–358.

Evans, G. (1973). The Causal Theory of Names. *Aristotelian Society Supplementary*, *47*, 187–208.

Evans, G. (1982). *The Varieties of Reference*. Clarendon.

Frege, G. (1892). Sense and Reference. In P. Geach & M. Black (Eds.), *Translations from the Philosophical Writings*. Blackwell.

Frege, G. (1980). *Philosophical and Mathematical Correspondence*. Blackwell.

Gertler, B. (2012). Understanding the Internalism-Externalism Debate. *Philosophical Perspectives*, *26*, 51–75.

Hawthorne, J., & Manley, D. (2012). *The Reference Book*. Oxford University Press.

Kaplan, D. (1977). Demonstratives. In J. Almog, J. Perry, & H. Wettstein (Eds.), *Themes From Kaplan*. Oxford University Press, 1989.

Kaplan, D. (1978). Dthat. In P. Cole (Ed.), *Syntax and Semantics*. Academic Press.

Kaplan, D. (1989). Afterthoughts. In J. Almog, J. Perry, & H. Wettstein (Eds.), *Themes From Kaplan*. Oxford University Press.

Kripke, S. (1972). *Naming and Necessity*. Cambridge University Press.
Kripke, S. (1979). A Puzzle About Belief. In A. Margalit (Ed.), *Meaning and Use*. Reidel.
Kripke, S. (1980). *"Preface" to the 2nd Edition of (1972)*. Cambridge University Press.
Kripke, S. (1986). A Problem in the Theory of Reference. In *Proceedings of the XVIIth World Congress of Philosophy*. Editions Montmorency.
Lewis, D. (1983). Extrinsic Properties. *Philosophical Studies*, *44*, 197–200.
Loar, B. (1976). The Semantics of Singular Terms. *Philosophical Studies*, *30*, 353–377.
Loar, B. (1981). Conceptual Role and Truth Conditions. *Notre Dame Journal of Formal Logic*, *23*, 272–283.
Loar, B. (1982). *Mind and Meaning*. Cambridge University Press.
Loar, B. (1987). Subjective Intentionality. *Philosophical Topics*, *15*, 89–124.
Loar, B. (1988). Social Content and Psychological Content. In R. H. Grimm & D. D. Merrill (Eds.), *Contents of Thought*. University of Arizona Press.
Loar, B. (1990). Phenomenal States. *Philosophical Perspectives*, *4*, 81–108.
Loar, B. (1991). Can We Explain Intentionality? In B. M. Loewer & G. Rey (Eds.), *Meaning in Mind: Fodor and His Critics*. Blackwell.
Loar, B. (1994). Self-Interpretation and the Constitution of Reference. *Philosophical Perspectives*, *8*, 51–74.
Loar, B. (1995). Reference from the First Person Perspective. *Philosophical Issues*, *6*, 53–72.
Loar, B. (1999). Should the Explanatory Gap Perplex Us? In *The Proceedings of the Twentieth World Congress of Philosophy*. Philosophy Documentation Center.
Loar, B. (2003). Phenomenal Intentionality as the Basis of Mental Content. In M. Hahn & B. Ramberg (Eds.), *Essays on the Philosophy of Tyler Burge*. MIT Press.
Loar, B. (2006). Language, Thought, and Meaning. In M. Devitt & R. Hanley (Eds.), *The Blackwell Guide to the Philosophy of Language*. Blackwell.
Loar, B. (2017). *Consciousness and Meaning: Selected Essays*. (K. Balog & S. Beardman, Eds.). Oxford University Press.
Locke, J. (1690). *An Essay Concerning Human Understanding*. Routledge, 1995.
Millikan, R. G. (1994). *White Queen Psychology*. MIT Press.
Perry, J. (1988). Cognitive Significance and New Theories of Reference. *Noûs*, *22*, 1–18.
Perry, J. (2009). Directing Intentions. In J. Almog & P. Leonardi (Eds.), *The Philosophy of David Kaplan*. Oxford University Press.
Plato. (1928). Seventh Letter (trnsl. Harward). *Classical Quarterly*, 143–154.
Putnam, H. (1962). It Ain't Necessarily So. *Journal of Philosophy*, *59*, 658–671.
Putnam, H. (1975). The Meaning of 'Meaning'. In K. Gunderson (Ed.), *Language, Mind, and Knowledge*. University of Minnesota Press.
Quine, W. V. (1960). *Word and Object*. MIT Press.
Recanati, F. (1993). *Direct Reference: From Language to Thought*. Blackwell.
Recanati, F. (2010). In Defense of Acquaintance. In R. Jeshion (Ed.), *New Essays on Singular Thought*. Oxford University Press.
Russell, B. (1918). The Philosophy of Logical Atomism. In R. C. Marsh (Ed.), *Logic and Knowledge*. Allen & Unwin, 1950.

Salmon, N. (1989). Illogical Belief. *Philosophical Perspectives*, *3*, 243–285.
Salmon, N. (2006). The Resilience of Illogical Belief. *Noûs*, *40*, 369–375.
Salmon, N. (2016). Constraint with Restraint. In Ostertag (Ed.), *Meanings and Other Things*. Oxford University Press.
Sawyer, S. (2011). Internalism and Externalism in Mind. In J. Garvey (Ed.), *The Continuum Companion to Philosophy of Mind*. Continuum.
Schiffer, S. (1987). The 'Fido'-Fido Theory of Belief. *Philosophical Perspectives*, *1*, 455–480.
Schiffer, S. (2006). A Problem for a Direct-Reference Theory of Belief Reports. *Noûs*, *40*, 361–368.
Schiffer, S. (2016). De Re Subtleties. In Ostertag (Ed.), *Meanings and Other Things*. Oxford University Press.
Schiffer, S. (2017). *Introduction to Part 1 of Loar (2017)*. Oxford University Press.
Soames, S. (2002). *Beyond Rigidity*. Oxford University Press.
Soames, S. (2011). Kripke on Epistemic and Metaphysical Possibility. In A. Berger (Ed.), *Saul Kripke*. Cambridge University Press.
Strawson, P. (1959). *Individuals*. Methuen.
Sullivan, A. (2013). *Reference and Structure*. Routledge.
Sullivan, A. (2018). *The Constitutive a Priori*. Rowman & Littlefield.
Wikforss, Å. M. (2004). Externalism and Incomplete Understanding. *The Philosophical Quarterly*, *54*, 287–294.
Williamson, T. (2007). *The Philosophy of Philosophy*. Blackwell.
Wittgenstein, L. (1953). *Philosophical Investigations*. Blackwell.

# Part II

# On Content in the Philosophy of Mind

# 6 Relational vs Adverbial Conceptions of Phenomenal Intentionality

*David Bourget*

Much theorizing on intentionality has proceeded on the assumption that intentionality can be fully explained in terms of functional role and causal/informational/correlation-type relations, i.e. that it can be "naturalized". This assumption remains widespread, but it has come under increased scrutiny over the past couple of decades. Brian Loar (1995) was among the most influential critics of the naturalization project, arguing that intentionality cannot be fully understood without the first-person perspective. He also articulated a picture of the mind on which all intentionality either is or originates from *phenomenal intentionality,* a kind of intentionality that arises from consciousness alone (2002, 2003). Since Loar's papers on this topic began circulating in the 90s, many philosophers have joined the phenomenal intentionality camp.[1] His rich and inspiring work has been highly influential, helping to usher into the mainstream what is increasingly being perceived as a main contender for a theory of intentionality.

So far, proponents of phenomenal intentionality have been more concerned with defending their common view than adjudicating their differences. I think it is time to look more closely at internal disagreements within the phenomenal intentionality camp. One such disagreement runs particularly deep: according to *relationalists*, phenomenal intentionality is a kind of relation to mind-independent entities (for example, propositions); according to *adverbialists* (or, as I prefer to call them, *aspect theorists*), it is purely non-relational. The choice between these two fundamentally different conceptions of phenomenal intentionality is a crucial but largely overlooked one for the phenomenal intentionality research program. This paper aims to shed some light on this choice.

Loar advocated for a non-relational conception of phenomenal intentionality. I happen to favor a relational view, but I recognize that this view faces many challenges. To echo Loar's words, "my homage to [Loar] will be expressed by my being driven to extremes" in defending a relational view of phenomenal intentionality in the face of his and others' objections to such views.[2] I will start by laying out the issue I want to talk about more precisely.

## 1. The Relation and Aspect Views

*Phenomenal states* are mental properties that there is something it is like to instantiate and that are individuated by what it is like to instantiate them (their *phenomenology*). *An experience* is an event consisting in the instantiation of a phenomenal state by an individual at a time (or over a period of time). Correspondingly, *to experience* is to instantiate a phenomenal state at a time.

Proponents of *phenomenal intentionality* (PI) take at least some phenomenal states to give rise to intentionality in that they ground or otherwise necessitate some "aboutness" or "directedness". I will refer to phenomenal states that give rise to intentionality as *phenomenal intentional states*, or *PI states*. The *content* of a PI state is what the directedness it gives rise to is directed towards. The claim that there are PI states is neutral on whether intentionality is explanatorily or metaphysically prior to consciousness (or vice versa).[3]

A wide range of phenomenal states plausibly give rise to intentionality. For example, the phenomenal state instantiated in a visual experience of a red ball seems to in some way be about a red ball or about there being a red ball. It is "directed" at a red ball, red-ball-ness, or there being a red ball. This seems to be an essential feature of this state that cannot be separated from its phenomenology: change the phenomenology to that of a blue square experience, and the red-ball content is gone; change the target of the directedness to something having to do with blue squares, and the red-ball phenomenology is gone. It is not just visual experiences in normal conditions that are instances of PI states. Plausibly, all perceptual experiences are, and so are episodes of imagery and conscious thoughts.

The *relation view* takes PI states to be states that consist in standing in a relation to their contents, which are distinctly existing entities. For example, one might say that the PI state of experiencing a red ball consists in standing in a relation to the property of being a red ball, whose existence is not tied to that of the experience. The relevant relation might be the same across all PI states, or there could be several relations (for example, one per sensory modality). For present purposes, I am going to assume that there is only one relation (if any) that satisfies the relation view, and I am going to call it *phenomenal representation*.[4] Nothing here turns on the uniqueness assumption except ease of exposition.

It is non-trivial to explain what it means to say that a state consists in standing in a relation to something as opposed to instantiating a monadic property. One point that is often made is that relations differ from monadic properties in requiring the existence of two or more entities (objects or other kinds of relata), but this isn't quite right since some binary relations are not irreflexive. However, if A's being F implies the existence of a thing B distinct from A, and A existing itself does not have this implication, this is at least an indicator that F is a relational property involving B. We can also take it as partly definitional of relations that if A and B stand in a relation, then A and B exist. In my opinion, the key tenet of the relation view (the part of the view that its proponents care the most about) is the claim that phenomenal states have non-mental entities as essential constituents. Whatever a relation is, this is the main point that the relationalist aims to convey in describing experience as "relational".

We can read Russell (1912) as proposing a relation view in terms of "acquaintance", though this is no doubt a debatable exegetical claim. More recent and explicit proponents include Chalmers (2006), Pautz (2007, 2009b, 2009a, 2010, 2013), Speaks (2015), Woodling (2016), and me (2010b, 2017a, 2018, 2019). Tracking representationalism (Dretske 1995; Tye 1995; Lycan 1996, 2001) may also be counted as a kind of relation view, but my focus here will be on non-reductive relation views.[5]

It is crucial not to conflate the relation view of phenomenal intentionality with naïve realism, the view that experiences occurring as part of veridical perceptual episodes are relationships to external objects or facts involving external objects. Both views ascribe an aboutness-underpinning relational structure to at least some phenomenal states: PI states in the case of the relation view, states instantiated in veridical experiences in the case of naïve realism. However, PI states and the states instantiated in veridical experiences need not (and almost certainly don't) coincide, so naïve realism and the relation view don't necessarily ascribe a relational structure to the same mental states. For this reason, neither view entails the other. In addition, naïve realism takes the relata of relational experiences to be ordinary objects like chairs and tables or facts involving such objects, whereas the relation view carries no such commitments. The relation view is consistent with *abstractivism,* the view that PI states are relationships to abstracta such as properties or general propositions. In my opinion and that of many proponents of the relation view, abstractivism is the most plausible form of the relation view, and that is precisely because naïve realism's commitment to experiences of ordinary objects is not very plausible (see Bourget 2019).

We must also distinguish the relation view from externalism about PI states or consciousness. The claim that PI states have a relational structure is at least prima facie conceptually independent from the claim that they are wide (not supervenient on a subject's internal state). This is easiest to see if we assume an abstractivist view of the contents of PI states: there seems to be no inconsistency in the idea that facts about one's brain determine that one stands in the phenomenal representation relation to an abstract entity outside of space and time. Phenomenal representation is in this respect like some non-mental relations to abstract objects. For example, something can stand in the relation *X is the mass of Y in kg* to the number 2 simply in virtue of its intrinsic properties.

The main alternative to the relation view that I will be concerned with is the *aspect view*. According to this view, the contents of PI states are aspects of these states rather than relata. An aspect of a mental state might be the mental state itself, a monadic property of the state, a monadic property of a monadic property of the state, or some other monadic property that is intuitively an aspect of the state. Kriegel (2007, 2008, 2011a), Pitt (2009), Mendelovici (2018, ch. 9), and Banick (forthcoming) endorse variants on the aspect view. Crane (2013) defends a non-relational view of "objects of thought", which is related in many ways to the aspect view of phenomenal intentionality, assuming certain relationships between thought and phenomenal intentionality. For present purposes, I will focus primarily on Mendelovici and Kriegel's views, which are the most developed competitors to the relation view of phenomenal intentionality with respect to the issues discussed here.

Let us now consider the evidence for and against the relation and aspect views. I will consider what seem to me to be the weightiest evidence on each side, starting with evidence favoring the relation view.

## 2. For the Relation View

### 2.1. *The Argument From Introspection*

#### *2.1.1 The Argument*

When I introspect, I typically find that I am undergoing various experiences. For example, I might find myself in a state that I want to describe as an experience *of a red ball*. I could use other words that have the same meaning as "a red ball" (e.g. "une balle rouge"), but there is no substitute for words meaning *a red ball* to report what I find introspectively.

Whatever it is that I denote with the phrase "a red ball" when I report on my experience, it is neither my mental state itself nor any intrinsic, non-relational aspect of my mental state. My words "red" and "ball" pick out properties of sorts that we expect external objects to have, not mental properties or features.[6,7] Moreover, these words do not seem to describe a contingent relational feature of my experience. For example, I am not saying that I am having an experience of a type sometimes caused by a red ball. When I say that I am experiencing a red ball, I am giving a non-contingent description of the phenomenal nature of my experience.

How can I give a non-contingent description of the phenomenal nature of my experience using terms such as "red" and "ball", which refer to non-mental properties? I can think of only two possible explanations (and they are closely related). First, it could be that my experience is constituted at least in part by entities to which the terms "red" and "ball" refer (let us assume that these are the properties of being red and being a ball, respectively). Second, it could be that my experience has as a constituent something that has the properties to which these terms refer, that is, an actual red ball. Of course, both possibilities might obtain together. So, my experience is at least partly constituted by an actual red ball or red-ball-y properties or both. From there, it is a short step to the conclusion that my experience consists in a relationship to these entities (or to one or more entities that have these entities as constituents), since it is hard to see how else my experience could be partly constituted by these entities. More specifically, it seems that these entities, or one or more entities they at least partly constitute, constitute the content of my experience, which is a relatum of the phenomenal state that my experience instantiates. Since these entities are plausibly mind-independent (and so exist distinctly from my experience), this establishes the relation view with respect to my experience of a red ball. Parallel observations apply to all or at least many PI states, which strongly supports the relation view.[8]

### 2.1.2. *An Objection*

One reply to this argument goes something like this:

> What introspection seems to reveal is an actual red ball (say, red ball B1) or that *some* red ball is a constituent of your experience. But we know that the same experience could have occurred in the absence of a red ball. So, introspection is known to be wrong. Why should we take its claims regarding the nature of intentionality seriously?[9]

This objection makes two main claims. First, it claims that the apparent revelations of introspection regarding red ball experiences go too far: they imply that a red ball is a constituent of one's experience when this is not the case. In other words, introspection seems to endorse naïve realism, but naïve realism is false. Second, since introspection is wrong in this respect, we should dismiss what it says about such experiences entirely.

I disagree with both of these claims. Regarding the first claim (that introspection endorses naïve realism and naïve realism is false), note first that the fact that what introspection "says" is correctly reported by my saying that *I am experiencing a red ball* (RED_BALL) does not show that introspection is committed to a red ball being a constituent of my experience. There are three possible construals of RED_BALL and its relation to what introspection says. On the *singular reading*, this report is elliptical: what introspection says is that I am experiencing red ball B1 (say). This interpretation takes introspection's claim to be best rendered as *Experiencing* (*I*, *o*) in predicate logic, where "o" is a name for a specific red ball. The other two possible construals of what introspection says take RED_BALL to be a literal statement of it. These interpretations are generated by two different understandings of the quantification apparently introduced by the quantified noun phrase "a red ball" in

RED_BALL. On the *de re* understanding, "a red ball" is used as in "I am kicking a red ball": $\exists x(RedBall(x) \wedge Experiencing(I, x))$ This reading and the singular reading entail that a red ball is a constituent of my experience if introspection is right. However, RED_BALL can also be given a *de dicto* reading similar to the salient interpretation of "I ordered a red ball". In this case, there need not be a red ball for the sentence to be true. Montague's (1974) treatment of such constructions tells us that this is because (on the dicto reading) "a red ball" refers to a generalized quantifier (a property of properties) rather than being a use of such a quantifier. Without putting too much weight on this particular semantic view, "a red ball" seems to denote some abstract entity on the de dicto reading of RED_BALL (a generalized quantifier or some other abstract entity). The overall logical form of the de dicto reading is *Experiencing (I, ARedBall)*, where "ARedBall" names some abstract entity (not a red ball).

Arguably, the de dicto reading of RED_BALL is the one that correctly captures what introspection tells me. There are at least three good arguments for this claim:

First, I do not detect any inconsistency between what introspection tells me and the hypothesis that there is no red ball. Pace some naïve realists, it seems clear that I can identify my relevant state of awareness and coherently think *this could be just like it is in the absence of a red ball.*

Second, there is no introspective evidence that perceptual experiences of red balls make us aware of the features of red balls that individuate them. Since there are no haecceities, experiencing red ball B1 as opposed to a qualitatively identical ball B2 would presumably require experiencing the essence of B1—likely a complex property having to do with the constitution, space-time trajectory, and/or origin of B1. The essence of B1 is the only difference between B1 and B2, so there is no sense in which one can experience B1 as opposed to B2 without experiencing this essence; if one didn't experience the essence of B1, we should say that what one is experiencing is something common to B1 and B2 (e.g. the property of being a red ball), not B1. However, we don't find any introspective evidence pertaining to such properties in introspection. When we reflect on what it would take to experience a specific red ball, it becomes clear that we don't have introspective evidence that we do this (notwithstanding the fact that we easily lapse into describing experiences as if we did, a practice that is facilitated by the grammar of perceptual experiences; see (Bourget 2019)).

Third, the de re and singular readings do not even capture the phenomenology. If I say *there is a red ball, and I am experiencing it,* or *I am experiencing red ball B1* (making explicit the de re and singular readings, respectively), I am not saying *how* I am experiencing the ball. For example, these statements are consistent with my experiencing the red ball as blue or square.[10] The de re and singular readings of RED_BALL at once say too much (that there is a red ball) and too little (nothing on phenomenology) to capture what I might find introspectively. These observations are discussed in more detail in (Bourget 2017a, 2019).

For all of the above reasons, the correct reading of RED_BALL (understood as a phenomenological description directly supported by introspection) is the de dicto reading. This reading is not falsified by the fact that my experience could have occurred in the absence of a red ball, which undercuts the objection at hand.

Even if introspection did claim that a red ball is a constituent of my experience, I don't think we should take this to discredit it to the point that we cannot get supporting evidence for the relation view from it. On my objector's interpretation of what introspection says, we can break up introspection's claim into two parts: my experience is constituted by a certain "foreign object" distinct from my mental states, and that "foreign object" is a red ball. Even if introspection is wrong about the second claim, it might be right about the first. It could be that my experience is a relationship to some property involving red-ball-ness, and I somehow get confused and take it to be about an actual red ball.

## 2.2. *The Argument From Language*

### 2.2.1. *The Argument*

Another argument for the relation view is that the language we use to describe experiences encodes a relational structure. There are many reasons for thinking that RED_BALL, on the intended (de dicto) reading, has a relational logical form, binding together a polyadic property with two (or more) entities. Since I have developed parallel reasons for ascribing a relational structure to other de dicto perceptual ascriptions in detail in (Bourget 2017a, 2019), I will go over this quickly.

First, notice that RED_BALL supports existential generalization with respect to "a red ball" even on the de dicto reading. From RED_BALL, it follows that there is something I experience. Even when I am hallucinating a red ball, it is correct to say that I am experiencing *something*. What does not follow is that I am experiencing an actual red ball, i.e. that there is a red ball such that I am experiencing it. But that is just to say that the intended reading of RED_BALL is not de re. Even on the de dicto reading, there is still something I am experiencing, but not an actual red ball. One hypothesis suggested by Montague's treatment of these constructions is that I am experiencing the following generalized quantifier: the property of being a property had by a red ball.

Relatedly, RED_BALL licenses inferences that would not be valid were it not relational. For example, suppose I know that, due to some apparatus connecting our brains, you experience *everything* that I experience. It seems to follow from this claim and RED_BALL that you experience a red ball. I can see that this follows even if I don't know what a red ball is. This suggests that this follows in virtue of the very logical form of the claims in question. This explanation requires that we take "a red ball" to fill an argument place in RED_BALL.

Consider also that some overtly relational statements seem to be made true by de dicto "experiencing" ascriptions. For example, take *COLOR*, the claim that I am experiencing *something* involving a color. COLOR seems to be made true by the fact expressed by RED_BALL. If so, it seems that COLOR and RED_BALL must involve the same use of "experiencing", referring to the same property (whether a monadic or polyadic one). But "experiencing" clearly refers to a relation in COLOR, so it must refer to a relation in RED_BALL as well.[11]

Granted that RED_BALL has a relational logical form along the lines of *Experiencing(I, ARedBall)*, how does this show that experiences have a relational structure? There is a logical gap between linguistic expressions having a relational form and the mental states they ascribe having a relational form.

There is more than one way to bridge the gap. The way that I favor first points out that the logical form of RED_BALL is plausibly the logical structure of the proposition it expresses. This seems quite plausible assuming a structured view of propositions. Next, we observe that the form of the proposition expressed is also the form of the fact that putatively makes RED_BALL true. This is prima facie plausible, and this falls out of a natural understanding of facts as true propositions: if facts are simply true propositions, then the proposition expressed by RED_BALL just *is* the fact that makes it true, and the structure of the proposition is the structure of the fact. Since the direct object of RED_BALL refers to a property or similar mind-independent entity, this establishes the relation view with respect to the ascribed phenomenal state. We can repeat the argument with multiple ascriptions to convince ourselves that the relation view holds generally.

Another way of bridging the logical gap is inductive. The above arguments show that "to experience" is not merely apparently transitive but also genuinely transitive, contributing a relational form like other transitive verbs. All other verbs that contribute a relational form express relational facts, so it is reasonable to take the relational form of expressions such as RED_BALL to indicate that they ascribe relational properties.

### 2.2.2. Objections

One might object that the argument from language adds nothing to the argument from introspection. The argument from language is based on how we describe experiences, whereas the argument from introspection is based on how they strike us introspectively. Since the manner in which we describe experiences is likely directly guided by how they strike us, one might say that I am double counting the evidence: all that I have offered evidence for is that experience strikes us as relational in introspection.

I don't think this is quite right. Introspection is subject to various influences, including in particular the influence of theory. It seems probable that theorists are prone to introspectively see different things depending on their theories. In contrast, language might be based in some way on introspection, but it encodes how experiences have reliably struck countless users of the language before any theorizing about the question under discussion took place.[12] In this way, the structure of language offers objective evidence regarding how experience appears to us naively and collectively, which one might argue is more valuable and weighty than specific introspective observations made by us today, now that we have adopted views on the question at hand.

While I discuss the language of experiential ascriptions as part of the argument from introspection, the key point there was that we used terms for worldly properties (e.g. "ball") when describing these experiences. The analysis of logical form that enters into the argument from language offers additional evidence beyond this point.

Another objection is that the relational analysis of experiential ascriptions given above is not clearly correct because such ascriptions can also be glossed using monadic language, as suggested by adverbialists in response to similar arguments. For example, one might say that "I experienced a red ball" should be glossed as "I experienced-red-ball-y".

This reply misses the point of the argument. The mere possibility of paraphrasing perceptual or experiential ascriptions without using monadic expressions would not show that such ascriptions are not correctly glossed using explicitly relational terms (it is trivial to produce such paraphrases[13]). What one needs to show is that the explicitly relational glosses of perceptual and experiential ascriptions given above (and in Bourget 2019) are *incorrect,* not just *non-mandatory.* Showing this would require taking on the arguments given above that purport to show that at least one correct gloss of the logical form of the relevant expressions is relational. Suppose one were to offer strong evidence that "John eats" is correctly glossed as *Eats(John)* in predicate logic (for example, one might point out that the inference from "John eats" to "Someone eats" seems valid). A paraphrase reply to the argument from language would be like dimissing such evidence on the grounds that "John eats" can be glossed as "P" in propositional logic.[14]

Mendelovici (2018, pp. 268–269) suggests that the argument from language offered in (Bourget 2019), which is similar to the present argument, is susceptible to a debunking reply. The reply casts doubt on the significance of the relational form of experiential ascriptions on the grounds that we would describe mental states using relational language whether or not the relation view was true. According to Mendelovici, we would employ relational language to describe our mental states even if the aspect view were true because this would allow us to economize on words and concepts by reusing words and concepts that purportedly pick out external things.

I don't think it is very plausible that we would speak (and think) relationally even if the aspect view were true. One reason is that it is unclear how we could speak relationally *and* succeed in picking out mental aspects. If the aspect view is true, every phenomenal state is a purely monadic property of subjects. No phenomenal state is partly constituted by a red ball, the external property of being red, or the external property of being a ball. It is unclear how we might succeed in talking about such monadic states using grammatically and logically relational statements such as RED_BALL, in which "red" and "ball" purport to refer to the properties of being red and being a ball. Recall that "red" and "ball" do not merely provide a contingent description of the mental state in question. If "red" and "ball" refer to properties that are not merely contingently related to the mental state picked out, their referents have to be essential constituents of the mental state picked out, but this is inconsistent with the aspect view unless they refer to mental features, not external properties. It seems clear that "red" and "ball" refer to external properties—if those terms don't aim at external properties, we are unable to refer to *any* external properties. So, the only way that RED_BALL could avoid ascribing a relational state is by "red" and "ball" failing to refer, but this would clearly lead to a failure to ascribe a mental state, not an ascription of an aspectual state. It is at best unclear how relational expressions whose constituents purport to refer to mind-independent properties could be used to refer to mental aspects.

Another problem with the debunking reply is that it is unclear that it would be possible to speak relationally at all on the aspect view (let alone refer to monadic states *by* speaking relationally). On this view, we don't have the kind of awareness of the world that we naively think we have: we are not in contact with external properties like being red or being a ball, much less external objects. As we will see in the next section, it is unclear how experiences could have truth conditions or refer to (or even purport to refer to) external entities on this view. But Mendelovici's debunking argument rests on the premise that we start by referring to (or purporting to refer to) external properties, then we form thoughts about our experiences by reusing conceptual resources geared toward thinking about a mind-independent reality. This is why we are supposed to find it economical to describe phenomenal states using relational constructions. Insofar as the aspect view makes it unclear how we can think and talk about a mind-independent reality in the first place, it undermines the main premise of the debunking argument.

### *2.3. Accounting for Truth-Aptness*

PI states seem intrinsically, essentially capable of being true or false, or accurate or inaccurate. (For ease of exposition, I will talk about "truth conditions" and "truth-aptness", but this is intended to cover accuracy conditions and satisfaction conditions as well.[15] The important point is that there are worldly conditions that experiences are by nature suited to "aim at".[16]) Assuming that PI states are essentially truth-apt, we might ask whether the relation view or the aspect view best accounts for this feature. In this section, I suggest that the relation view offers the most plausible explanation.

#### *2.3.1. The Relational Account*

One relational account of truth-aptness claims that experiences are relationships to propositions, where propositions just *are* truth conditions in the form either of sets of possible worlds or intensions (functions from possible worlds to truth values). On this view, it seems trivial to explain how experiences can be true or false. For example, if we take propositions to be sets of possible worlds, we can say that an experience is true when the actual world is a member of the proposition to which it relates the subject.

However, this view is phenomenologically implausible: experiences don't introspectively seem like relationships to sets of possible worlds or intensions; introspection does not reveal sets of possible worlds or functions from possible worlds (Kriegel 2007). Moreover, this view seems ontologically problematic because experiences being relationships to sets of possible worlds or intensions ties the existence of experiences to the existence of merely possible worlds.[17]

These concerns could be avoided by taking sets of possible worlds and intensions to *model* mental contents or propositions instead of *constituting* mental states. But if sets of possible worlds and intensions merely model the truth conditions of experiences, they cannot explain these conditions in the way described above: we need a substantive explanation of how experiences acquire the modeled truth conditions.

An alternative to sets of possible worlds and intensions is to take the contents of PI states to be *possible states of affairs* (PSOAs), which are logical combinations of universals and (optionally) particulars.[18] This view is much more phenomenologically plausible than the preceding views. At least, it relates us to entities that we might reasonably be thought to encounter introspectively, such as the property of being red and the property of being a ball. I will come back to the PSOA view's phenomenological plausibility in §3.3.4.

The PSOA view naturally goes with the following account of truth conditions: an experience that relates one to PSOA X is true just in case

X is a fact (or *obtains*). This simple *identity theory of truth* assumes that PSOAs and facts are the same kind of thing.[19]

Mendelovici (2018, §9.3.4) anticipates this account and rejects it on the grounds that obtaining and non-obtaining states of affairs are fundamentally different: the obtaining ones are concrete states of the world, whereas the non-obtaining ones are mere abstract objects (at best).

I disagree that obtaining and non-obtaining states of affairs are fundamentally different. Obtaining is an accidental feature of facts. When X is a fact, it is that very combination of objects and properties, whose nature allows that it not be a fact, that is a fact, not some other state of affairs.[20] Otherwise, every PSOA that does not obtain would necessarily not obtain, but everyone should agree that it is contingent that it is not a fact that zebras eat aluminum. *So long as* we admit possible states of affairs in our ontology, we have to agree that some that don't obtain *could* have obtained, so it cannot be part of their nature to be non-obtaining, and the difference between obtaining and non-obtaining states of affairs has to be an accidental feature.

In any case, we can allow that PSOAs are a different kind of thing than facts. This requires us to specify the obtaining property as a kind of correspondence, which we can do. For example, the PSOA <there is a red ball bouncing> consists in the properties *being red*, *being a ball,* and *bouncing* bound together by the existential quantifier. For it to obtain is for there to be something that instantiates these three properties. It is easy to provide a recursive definition of the obtaining property along these disquotational lines for all PSOAs that we might reasonably be thought to experience. On this approach, instantiation is the bridge between abstract objects and concrete reality.

### 2.3.2. *The Aspectual Account*

Let us now turn to the aspect theorist's account of truth conditions. If experiences are not relationships to PSOAs, universals, or anything of the sort, they are not composed of properties or other non-mental items that occur in the external world. This makes it hard to see how we can account for the truth conditions of experiences.

Mendelovici (2018, Ms) offers an aspect-theoretic account of the truth conditions and reference conditions of PI states (I will continue to focus on truth conditions, but everything I say below extends almost unchanged to her account of reference conditions). Her proposal hinges on a distinction between the superficial character and the deep nature of mental states. The *deep nature* of a mental state is what it "really is", *au fond*. For example, on some views it is part of the deep nature of mental states that they "carry information" about things in the environment. In contrast, "[t]he *superficial character* of an intentional state or content is the set of superficial features that characterize it as the intentional state or content that it is"

(Mendelovici 2018, p. 25; original emphasis). It is critical that superficial characters are properties of contents or mental states. Mendelovici also stresses that superficial characters are properties of contents and mental states of sorts that we have an introspective, pre-theoretic grip on.

Mendelovici offers a *matching theory* of the truth conditions of contents: a content C is true just in case there is an item (presumably a fact) distinct from C that instantiates C's superficial character. Superficial characters, being properties, can be shared between two or more things, including potentially between mental states and external, non-mental items. This account is offered as part of a broader internal theory of truth, according to which it is in some sense up to us to decide what are the truth conditions of our mental states or contents. Mendelovici takes the matching theory to be what most of us have decided to adopt as our criterion of truth, but the internal theory allows variations.

One consideration in favor of the matching theory (noted by Mendelovici) is that it seems to be in line with how we naively think of truth: we naively think of truth as the world being *like* what we think, where this "like" seems to be the "like" of similarity. The relevant similarity does not seem to be similarity with respect to deep nature (the world need not be mental in order for a mental state to be true!) but rather similarity with respect to superficial character.

The matching theory faces at least two significant challenges. One challenge is that contents can be shared between mental states; as a result, Mendelovici's theory seems to predict that two experiences with the same content make each other true (because they match each other) even if their shared content intuitively has nothing to do with mental states. It is tempting to try to avoid this problem by requiring that the matching item be something non-mental, but this would have the unwelcome consequence that mental states representing mental states could never be true. It seems that we need a conditional criterion that goes something like this: if C is about a mental state, then C's truth requires a (distinct) matching mental state or fact; otherwise, C's truth requires a matching non-mental fact (Mendelovici anticipates that this may be required; see appendix H in her 2018). A worry with this proposal is that it does not accommodate mixed contents such as <an experience caused a movement>. Adding a third condition for such mixed contents along the lines of the above conditions would not work because we need to guarantee that the mental and non-mental parts are made true by mental and non-mental aspects of reality, respectively. Another worry with the conditional criterion is that it seems viciously circular, since being *about* a mental state seems to be a matter of *referring* or at least *purporting to refer* to a mental state. We are here considering only the case of truth conditions, but Mendelovici must and does offer a parallel criterion for reference (a mental state refers to what matches its superficial character), and that criterion for reference also has the problem of being satisfied by mental items when it should not. This criterion of reference cannot without circularity be improved by saying that all and only mental states that refer or purport to refer to mental items must match mental items. To make the conditional criterion viable, it seems that Mendelovici must specify an understanding of "being about a mental state" that differs from its natural reading in terms of reference. It is not clear how this might be done.

A second, more basic challenge for the matching theory is that we don't seem to have the intellectual resources to apply it to even a single case. On Mendelovici's view, when you have an experience there is an intrinsic aspect of your experience that is its content. Contents are "[t]hings of the same kind as what we are tempted to describe as what our mental states are 'directed at' or what they 'say' when we introspect on paradigm cases of intentionality" (Mendelovici 2018, glossary). Your experience is true if the superficial character of its content is matched by a relevant item. The difficulty here is that locutions such as "what my mental state is directed at" or "what my mental state says" are relational through and through, and their relata introspectively seem to be non-mental things such as PSOAs or facts (to naïve realists). So, it seems that their superficial characters should be PSOAs. *If* this were the case, it would be easy to see how the superficial characters of contents match worldly facts, for reasons adduced above. But Mendelovici denies that the superficial characters of contents are PSOAs or facts. On her view, this understanding of the superficial characters of contents as worldly or abstract entities must be cast aside. Here the best I can do is to focus on the content of my mental state as it strikes me (a PSOA that I have in consciousness) and imagine that its nature as a PSOA is illusory: in fact, it is an aspect of my mental state. When I do this, I need to think of certain features of my content as illusory while preserving others. The problem is that *everything* about the PSOA that I seem to have in consciousness is non-mental. I don't know what the result of imagining that *this* is an aspect of my mental state should be. This is a little bit like trying to imagine that winter tires are a kind of beverage—what sort of beverage is this? Should I imagine a dark beverage? Why should I suppose that basically everything about my idea of winter tire beverages is mistaken except the color? I can conceive in the abstract that the superficial characters of my contents are features of my mental states that are shared with external items, but I cannot verify this in any particular case because I don't know how to imagine my contents as mental aspects.[21]

## 3. For the Aspect View

I now turn to considerations that seem to support the aspect view.

### *3.1. Arguments From Externalism and Physicalism*

Loar (2002, §5) considers and rejects a view on which certain phenomenal states are relationships to property complexes, a variation on the

PSOA view. Such phenomenal states, Loar seems to hold, would refer to properties in virtue of being relationships to entities that have these properties as constituents. I will call this kind of reference *constitutive reference*. Loar suggests that thought experiments such as the brain in a vat (BIV) and the inverted spectrum show that phenomenal states cannot constitutively refer to properties in this way. According to him, a BIV's mental states cannot refer to properties such as being red or being a ball because reference is determined by external relations. Since a BIV can share phenomenal states with a normally embedded individual, it follows that phenomenal states are not relationships to properties such as being red or being a ball.

From the point of view of the phenomenal intentionality theory, the weakest premise of this argument seems to be the assumption that all reference depends on external relations. It is hard to see how the traditional arguments for externalism extend to the kind of constitutive reference in question.

A related argument takes it starting point from physicalism: i) physicalism is true; ii) if physicalism and the relation view are true, consciousness can only be explained in terms of informational-causal relations; iii) consciousness cannot be explained in terms of informational-causal relations (because it is narrow); therefore, the relation view is false.[22]

The overall problem with this argument is that there is a tension between physicalism and endorsing (ii) or (iii). It seems to be widely accepted that defending physicalism against conceivability arguments requires endorsing the phenomenal concept strategy advocated by Loar (1990, 1997), which centrally involves denying that we have a sufficient grip on the nature of consciousness through our introspectively-grounded phenomenal concepts to be able to assess its relationships to physical facts a priori. Accordingly, a physicalist should not put much weight on thought experiments purporting to show that consciousness is narrow, which undermines much of the motivation for (iii). One should also not be confident that one is able to imagine how consciousness can be explained (against [ii]). For these reasons, the argument is dialectically ineffective.

### 3.2. *Problems for Aristotelian Abstractivism*

For reasons briefly discussed in §2.1, it is not very plausible that PI states have particulars as constituents of their contents. This means that we are left with an abstractivist view, on which the contents of PI states are properties, property complexes, general PSOAs composed of properties and quantifiers (which can themselves be seen as properties), or other sorts of abstract objects that don't involve concrete particulars. The rest of this paper focuses on objections to abstractivism. I will focus more specifically on the combination of abstractivism and the PSOA view, i.e. the view that PI states relate us to PSOAs composed of properties and quantifiers only.

A key choice point for the abstractivist (especially the proponent of the PSOA view) is what general outlook on the metaphysics of properties to adopt. There are two main views of properties: the Aristotelian view and the Platonic view. The Aristotelian view takes properties to exist solely in their instances. This makes the existence of properties dependent on the existence of instances. In contrast, the Platonic view takes properties to exist independently of their instances. The choice between the Aristotelian and Platonic conceptions of properties seems to pose a dilemma for the abstractivist, as each kind of abstractivism faces objections. The rest of this section discusses the problems that Aristotelian abstractivism faces; the following section discusses the Platonic alternative.

### *3.2.1. Inventory Problems*

One problem with Aristotelian abstractivism is briefly touched upon by Loar (2002, 2003). Any experience, it seems, is of a phenomenal type that can occur quite independently of the presence of matching objects. In the extreme case, a BIV that spontaneously appeared in an empty universe could have experiences of the same phenomenal type as ours. This seems to show that the properties that one is related to in experience, if any, are "abstract objects that are unanchored in real resemblance" (2002, §8), that is, not Aristotelian. As noted in the preceding section, proponents of the phenomenal concept strategy (including most physicalists) should reject the BIV intuitions that this argument rests on, but this is an argument that we need to contend with if we do not endorse this strategy.

Mendelovici (2018) offers a different but related argument against the Aristotelian relation view. She points out that some properties that are good candidates for being the contents of experiences are not good candidates for being Aristotelian. She refers to this as *the inventory problem*. Take the red ball example again. On the face of it, the content of this experience involves a certain color-like property, red*. Red* seems to be a warm, vivid quality that can spread homogeneously over surfaces.[23] Plausibly, the only instantiated properties that have to do with colors (or colors*) are broadly electromagnetic properties, whether monadic or relational, for example, the property of reflecting electromagnetic radiation of about 650 nm (EM650). The problem is that EM650 and all other physical properties of this sort are prima facie distinct from red*. On the face of it, no actually instantiated property (or related fact) matches the phenomenology of experiences of red.[24]

This argument, too, is one that a phenomenal concept strategist would probably reject. In fact, one of the most plausible developments of the phenomenal concept strategy, due to Tye (1999), argues that phenomenal concepts get their special character from our concepts of presented qualities. If one takes this view, one should reject appeals to intuitions of non-identity between red* and EM650.[25] However, a relationalist who does not have in her arsenal this general protection against a priori arguments seems forced to endorse Platonic abstractivism.[26]

### 3.2.2. Ontological Objections

Aristotelian abstractivism might seem to require a dubious ontology: even if Aristotelian properties are not ontologically questionable, one might think that false PSOAs or propositions constituted of such properties are questionable, and it seems that relationalism requires that such entities be the contents of inaccurate experiences. Accounting for experiences of impossible scenes seems to be especially problematic, since we don't want to accept that all impossible states of affairs exist (Kriegel 2011a).

I can think of two promising responses to this objection that are consistent with Aristotelianism about properties. First, there is Russell's (1912) response. Russell was moved by this concern, and this led him to deny the existence of mind-independent propositions. He suggested that what seem like states of acquaintance with propositions are actually complex mental acts relating us to more than one universal at a time.[27]

There is a natural way of developing this view in more detail. The PSOAs or propositions that we experience are arguably limited to certain types. For example, there do not seem to be any experiences of disjunctive contents (e.g. <something is red or green>), negated contents (e.g., <something is not green>), or universal contents (<everything is green>).[28] Suppose for a moment that there are also no experiences of relations: at the most fundamental level of analysis, the contents of experiences boil down to predications of monadic properties. If the contents of experiences really are subject to the preceding limitations, they can be modeled using a simple state space whose dimensions are the experienceable spatial and temporal dimensions and other basic experienceable properties such as colors. A (fully or partially defined) position in this state space represents a simple, point-like experienced object with some basic experienceable properties. Volumes or sets of positions in this space represent complex experienced objects constituted of more basic objects. It could be that what seem like experiential representations of complex PSOAs are in fact sets of unified experiences, each of which is a relationship to a volume in this phenomenal state space. Even if we have to allow that all the positions and volumes within the state space in some sense exist, this seems like an ontologically parsimonious picture.

Of course, it is not clear that the contents of experiences are devoid of relations. It is natural to say that we experience an object moving another and other simple relations of this sort. There are two possible ways to maintain the state space approach in the face of this phenomenological datum. First, it might be possible to analyze such relational experiences as, for example, experiencing one object instantiating the monadic property of being a mover at space-time position L while experiencing (as part of the same unified experience) another object instantiating the monadic property of being moved at a space-time position adjacent to L.[29] Second, it might be that the dimensions of the phenomenal state space can be dynamically enriched to include properties such as *causing effect A*. An account of the origins of the space's dimensions would have to supply this.

This response to the ontological concerns about PSOAs and propositions depends on substantive and debatable claims regarding the nature of the contents of experiences; however, it seems to me that the state-space story is sufficiently plausible on its face that anyone who is moved by parsimony considerations might reasonably consider endorsing the required assumptions about the nature of the contents of experiences in order to achieve parsimony. There might also be other ways of giving an ontologically minimalistic account of all relevant PSOAs that can accommodate a wider variety of PSOAs.

The alternative to Russell's approach is to argue that PSOAs built from a sparse ontology of properties are ontologically acceptable. So long as we start with a relatively sparse ontology of the constituting properties, it might be OK to admit into our ontology all the PSOAs (true or false) constituted by such properties through a finite set of quantifiers and operators. Since quantifiers and operators can be construed as higher-order properties, all that we need to admit in our ontology are set-theoretic constructions out of (existing) properties. Seen in this light, PSOAs have a very thin existence, somewhat like mereological sums of objects.

Even if neither of the two preceding responses can be made to work, we should not put too much weight on the ontological objection. Physicists talk about branching universes and superpositions of concrete states. For all we know, the world really has a kind of modal structure, with mere possibilities somehow interacting with actual, "concrete" states of the world and each other. We should keep an open mind on ontology.

Relatedly, we should bear in mind that considerations of parsimony can only recommend a theory over another when the two theories are at least roughly matched in explanatory power (including the theories' fit with observations and ability to make accurate new predictions). We are far from having a complete relational theory of experience, but our sketch of a theory explains the linguistic and introspective evidence discussed earlier, as well as PI states' truth-aptness. It fits fairly well with all observations so long as we allow false PSOAs to exist. Making a case from parsimony against the relation view requires articulating an alternative theory with comparable explanatory power. So far, the aspect view does not seem to have anywhere near as much explanatory power: it can at best explain away the linguistic and phenomenological evidence using auxiliary hypotheses, and it is not clear that it can explain the truth-aptness of experience.

### *3.3. Problems for Platonic Abstractivism*

In the preceding section, we saw that Aristotelian abstractivism faces objections that can all plausibly be addressed, but only from within a physicalist framework committed to the phenomenal concept strategy (the inventory problems can be avoided only if we can appeal to the phenomenal concept strategy). For theorists who do not endorse the phenomenal concept strategy, Platonic abstractivism is the only option: they are forced to accept that the properties that are constitutive of experienced PSOAs are Platonic objects. This view comes with its own problems.

#### *3.3.1. Additional Ontological Objections*

Traditionally, a central objection to Platonism is that it seems ontologically extravagant. In this vein, Platonic abstractivism seems forced to posit a vast world of causally impotent Platonic entities just to accommodate the apparent relational structure of experience; isn't it more plausible that this apparent relational structure is illusory? This objection from parsimony might seem to have even more bite than that faced by Aristotelian abstractivism with respect to false PSOAs.

The first thing to note in response is that the set of properties that we can in practice experience (colors, shapes, etc.) is quite limited compared to the set of all possible properties. Add the properties that other kinds of actual conscious beings plausibly experience, and we still have only a finite and relatively small sample of possible properties. One might argue that giving a relational explanation of actual experiences requires only these Platonic properties to exist and that there is no major ontological extravagance there.

One might think that Platonic abstractivism cannot make do with a limited set of Platonic properties because it must accommodate all possible experiences, and all (or a lot of) possible properties are possible contents of experiences. I agree that we want a theory such as relationalism to be applicable to merely possible experiences as well as actual experiences, but I disagree that this requires that the contents of possible experiences exist. Take, for example, the (correct) theory that high-fiving is relational. This theory's applicability to merely possible high-fivings doesn't require that every person that one could possibly high-five be actual. Possible applications of a theory merely require possible objects.[30]

Of course, the preceding remarks at best establish that Platonic abstractivism only commits us to a limited set of Platonic properties. Platonic abstractivism might still incur unacceptable ontological commitments when it comes to the representation of full propositions or PSOAs. However, the points made about the ontology of PSOAs and propositions in the context of Aristotelian abstractivism carry over to Platonic abstractivism. It might be possible to analyze PSOAs and propositions away when giving a more fundamental description of experience, and one might reasonably claim that PSOAs and propositions composed of a limited set of properties are parsimonious enough. An additional answer that is available to the Platonist is that PSOAs are simply properties of everything or the world as a whole (Speaks 2015). If Platonic properties of objects are ontologically unproblematic, then so should be properties of the world. As before, we should also bear in mind that ontology is hostage to its applications.

One might object that a handful of Platonic properties is as bad as an infinite number of them. I think this depends on whether there is a plausible explanation for why only some possible Platonic properties exist. The reconstruction of experienced (and possibly Platonic) properties as dimensions in a phenomenal state space suggested above seems to provide a possible justification for a sparse view of Platonic properties. Perhaps other explanations are possible.

Regarding this last issue as well as the overall ontological question, we should bear in mind that our views on these questions might be largely shaped by the limits of human categories and imagination. We don't really know what a Platonic object *is*. We know that they are supposed to constitute the contents of experiences (if Platonic abstractivism is correct), but this leaves their nature largely open. The term "Platonic" evokes imagery of translucent objects floating in a dark space, but clearly that is not what a Platonic object is. When it comes to grasping the nature of Platonic objects, we seem to be stuck between incomplete and misleading ideas. It could be that these objects make sense ontologically, but we have to form a better understanding of them to see this. It seems wise to keep an open mind on Platonic objects until we are confident that we are not merely butting against the limits of human understanding.

### 3.3.2. *Efficacy and Explanation*

One objection to the ontology-minimizing strategy proposed in the preceding section is that this response seems to require some kind of interaction between abstract objects and concrete mental states: how does nature make sure that we only represent those abstract objects that exist? Given that the Platonic properties in question exist outside of space and time, the suggestion that mental states are restricted to representing those that exist seems mysterious.[31]

This objection is a variant on a general objection to Platonic abstractivism to the effect that abstracta cannot play any role in explanations of concreta (whether causal or constitutive explanations). Papineau (2014) writes: "My conscious sensory feelings are concrete, here-and-now, replete with causes and effects. How can their metaphysical nature essentially involve relations to entities that lie outside space and time?"

(p. 7) Kriegel (2007, 2011b) similarly suggests that concreta cannot even be partly explained by abstracta.

Here it is important to bear in mind that the relationalist is only required to adopt a full-blown Platonic view of the contents of experience if she cannot appeal to the phenomenal concept strategy to solve the inventory problems. Since physicalism requires this strategy, it is reasonable to answer the present objection assuming dualism about consciousness.

Within a dualist framework, we might reasonably suppose that there are psychophysical laws governing interactions between experiences and physical states.[32] We should also expect that the laws predict and constrain what can be experienced. Plausibly, if we knew the relevant laws, we would find that there is no residual mystery regarding how nature selects contents that exist. The laws could simply be laid down to match existing Platonic objects, or they could quantify over the domain of existing Platonic objects. There would also be no mystery how states that consist in relationships to abstract objects can be causally efficacious: they would figure in psychophysical laws, which is enough for efficacy. Similarly, abstracta would be part of explanations of concreta in virtue of figuring in psychophysical laws. Of course, we don't currently have plausible psychophysical laws, and the fact that it is very unclear how such laws could be formulated does speak against dualism, but this is not the relationalist's problem. If dualism can't be made to work, she will have to accept physicalism, which is consistent with the relation view and supports Aristotelian abstractivism.

### 3.3.3. *Mystery*

A related objection to Platonic abstractivism is that it seems to posit a mysterious reaching out of the mind towards abstract objects. How exactly can concrete mental states incorporate Platonic objects? This seems wholly mysterious.[33]

The objection is simple, and so is the response: of course it is mysterious! The relation view points out that consciousness has a relational structure, but it is not an explanation of consciousness. It does not purport to close the explanatory gap nor to shed any light on how experiences arise from non-experiential goings-on. Given that it is already maximally mysterious how consciousness arises, it does not seem to be a significant cost if the relation view posits a prima facie mysterious relation that bridges the world of concreta and the world of abstracta.

Without closing the explanatory gap, abstractivism plausibly makes the problem of consciousness just a little more tractable. It allows us to redescribe PI states (which arguably include all phenomenal states) in terms of worldy properties (properties such as colors and shapes). This reveals a built-in connection between phenomenal states and the world of mind-independent objects, which cannot hurt in explaining how consciousness arises from the interactions of mind-independent objects. The relation view also articulates the internal structure of the phenomenal to some extent, which is promising. Presumably, the first step in explaining consciousness will be a suitable articulation of the internal structure of phenomenal states. Without some way of breaking up phenomenal states into simpler components, it is hard to see how they could ever be explained. The relation view is a small but significant step in the right direction.[34]

### 3.3.4. *Phenomenology*

Kriegel (2007) raises a phenomenological objection against (Platonic) abstractivism about conscious thoughts: "phenomenologically, the entities we are aware of when we think of dragons and parrots present themselves to us, from the first-person perspective, as external concreta, not as abstracta or mental concreta". This objection is even more plausible when applied to perceptual experiences as suggested in (Kriegel 2011a).

To a first approximation, concrete objects (concreta) are objects that have (non-trivial) spatial and temporal properties (they are in space and time). Abstracta are things that don't have (non-trivial) spatial and temporal properties. Kriegel claims that the objects of our thoughts (or experiences), such as the dragons that dragon thoughts are about, seem to be concreta. That is to say that when I introspect a thought (or experience) of a dragon, I find myself thinking of it as being about a dragon in space and time.

It is not clear that this claim is in tension with Platonic abstractivism. On the Platonic view, phenomenally representing that there is an F is a matter of standing in a certain phenomenal representation relation to the PSOA <there is an F>. In some cases, F might be a spatiotemporal property such as *being a dragon at position L now*. This makes the representation a representation of a concrete dragon, not an abstract dragon. Since, on the relation view, representing a concrete object is a matter of being related to a spatiotemporal property as opposed to a non-spatiotemporal property, it seems that the theory can accord with the revelations of introspection regarding the concrete nature of represented dragons.

However, there is a further concern that runs deeper than Kriegel's objection (on my interpretation). This is a concern about the abstractness of the contents of experiences (e.g. propositions) rather than the things that are part of the contents of experiences (e.g. dragons). The point of the relation view is to account for the nature and feel of experiences in terms of the relata of a special relation, the phenomenal representation relation. If so, it seems that the nature of what one is related to in the phenomenal representation relation should be reflected in the phenomenal nature of one's experience. Presumably, it is part of the nature of Platonic entities to be abstract, but we do not find any abstractness when we introspect our experiences.

I think one can reasonably deny that we find nothing abstract in introspection. When I introspect my current visual experience, there is a sense in which I am aware of a way the world could be. But I cannot find anything non-repeatable as part of my experience—no trace of a specific time, location, or even a particular object (as Kriegel 2011b, pp. 163 argues). As a result, it doesn't seem implausible to say that what I am aware of are abstract ways the world could be and/or Platonic properties that constitute such PSOAs. Of course, it takes a little reflection to conceptualize what one is aware of in that way (to come to put it in terms of abstractness and so on). But this only goes to show that we don't have a perfect innate reflective grasp of the nature of our own mental states, which is to be expected.

### *3.3.5. Epistemology*

Kriegel (2011a) suggests that Platonic abstractivism (or a more general form of the view targeted at all intentionality) has unacceptable epistemological consequences, whereas adverbialism (his version of the aspect theory) does not. The first claim is justified by pointing out that Platonic abstractivism is inconsistent with a view on which beliefs about particulars can be acquired and (in some sense) justified simply by endorsing perceptual experiences. The reason Platonic abstractivism is supposed to be inconsistent with the endorsement model for perceptual justification is that, on this abstractivist view, experiences have nothing to do with particulars. This seems to require that perceptual beliefs about particulars be justified by some kind of inference. This is reminiscent of naïve realists' claim that singular (and so object-dependent) perceptual contents are necessary to account for demonstrative thought.

I am happy to grant that we do not have singular thoughts about particulars that arise simply by endorsing perceptual experiences. I think it is far from obvious that Russell's view that we know external particulars by description has disastrous epistemological consequences. The part of Kriegel's argument that I take issue with is the claim that adverbialism is better off than abstractivism.

Kriegel correctly notes that adverbialism can preserve an endorsement account of perceptual justification by postulating that perceptual beliefs (not just experiences) are adverbial. This preserves the endorsement model because it is easy to see how beliefs can arise through endorsement of perceptual experiences if they are essentially the same in nature as these experiences. However, this preserves endorsement at the cost of extending the alleged problem to beliefs, which is something that the relationalist can also do. Kriegel suggests that we can restore parity between perceptual beliefs and experiences by supposing that beliefs have the same adverbial (and non-object-involving) nature as perceptual experiences, but a parallel move is also open to the abstractivist, who might say that the contents of perceptual beliefs are abstract like those of perceptual experiences. What the abstractivist can't do is get singular contents out of perceptual experiences, and the adverbialist has the same problem. In fact, the adverbialist has a much larger problem with respect to accounting for the apparent features of the contents of perceptual beliefs: she not only has trouble accounting for singular contents through an endorsement model, she has trouble accounting for the truth conditions of perceptual experiences generally (as we saw above), which makes it hard to see how *any* perceptual beliefs could be justified through endorsement.

There is a large literature surrounding the idea that views along the lines of the abstractivism defended here have disastrous epistemological consequences. Since all of these arguments apply in spades to the aspect view, this is not the place to discuss them.[35]

## 4. Conclusion

This paper explored considerations for and against the relation and aspect views of phenomenal intentionality. On the one hand, the relation view seems to best fit with the phenomenological and linguistic evidence we started with. It also enables a more promising approach to truth conditions. On the other hand, physicalism and externalism might seem to militate against the relation view, and the relationalist is forced to choose between Aristotelian and Platonic abstractivism, each of which faces objections. I have argued that the challenges from externalism and physicalism can be defused, and that relationalists who endorse Loar's celebrated phenomenal concept strategy can successfully defend Aristotelian abstractivism, whereas those who don't (and should therefore endorse dualism) can successfully defend Platonic abstractivism.

## Notes

1. Proponents of this view (or something close to it) include McGinn (1989), Searle (1990, 1992), Siewert (1998), Horgan and Tienson (2002), Kriegel (2003, 2011b), Loar (2002, 2003), Pitt (2004), Horgan et al. (2004), Farkas (2008), Mendola (2008), Mendelovici (2010, 2018), Chalmers (2010), Bourget (2010a, 2017c, 2018), Smithies (2012), Pautz (2013), Speaks (2015), and Montague (2016). For an overview, see (Bourget & Mendelovici 2016) and (Mendelovici & Bourget 2014).
2. Loar uses the quoted passage in (Loar 2003), which was written as an homage to Tyler Burge.
3. For an introduction to phenomenal intentionality and more discussion of the priority question, see (Bourget & Mendelovici 2016).
4. I defend this assumption in (Bourget 2010b, 2017b, 2017d).
5. By "non-reductive" I mean *not committed to reduction.*
6. This echoes Harman's (1990) transparency claims, but only to a limited extent. In particular, I am not claiming that I cannot introspect my experience itself or anything intrinsic about it.

7. One might say that "red" and "ball" have indirect reference like the objects of "that"-clauses on Frege's theory of indirect reference, but a) this would not make a large difference to my argument since abstract objects are not mental aspects, b) Frege's theory of indirect reference has essentially been refuted (Soames 2002), and c) any expression that normally refers to the property of being red or a ball can be substituted salva veritate for "red" or "ball" in "I am experiencing a red ball", which shows that these terms don't have indirect reference in this context.
8. Chalmers (2006) makes a similar argument for (relational) Russellian contents.
9. Something like this objection can be found in (Mendelovici 2018, §9.3.1).
10. One might say that what I find is that there is a red ball and I am experiencing it *as* a red ball. This captures the phenomenology, but this seems revisionist because we do not feel compelled to add the "as" qualification when reporting on our experiences.
11. For more arguments along these lines, see (Bourget 2017b, 2019).
12. I am not sure that the use of the verb "to experience" exhibited above is entirely pre-theoretic. However, it predates theorizing about the structure of consciousness. In any case, the argument can also be made using fully pre-theoretic perceptual language (Bourget 2017b, 2019).
13. Define the *dash-ly* operator as follows: any sentence containing expressions of the form "A—B . . . —Z—ly" (with any number of "—"-separated terms) is true iff the ordinary English sentence obtained by removing all occurrences of "—" and the trailing "—ly" is true. With the help of dash-ly, we can construct arbitrarily complex adverbial expressions that leave nothing out. For example, "I am experiencing—a—red—ball—next—to—a—blue—triangle—ly" is true iff "I am experiencing a red ball next to a blue triangle" is true in ordinary English.
14. Recent discussions of the paraphrase strategy can be found in (Kriegel 2007, 2011b), (Dinges 2015), (Grzankowski 2018), and (Banik forthcoming).
15. Crane (2009) rightly points out that accuracy conditions are quite different from truth conditions. However, I think Crane is wrong in saying that experiences cannot be true. This strains ordinary usage, but we can easily see how the term "true" applies to experiences (see the next footnote).
16. I don't think experiences essentially have a direction of fit. Experiencing is a kind of representation that is, on its own, neither desire-like nor belief-like. For this reason, it can be a little strained to talk about "truth conditions": desire-like or other non-belief-like states are not naturally described as having truth conditions. However, all experiences are such that they can constitute belief-like states. Add the right attitude-conferring ingredient (perhaps functional features) to an experience, and you have a belief-like state. When I talk about experiences having truth conditions, I am thinking of the truth/satisfaction conditions they would have were one to add a belief/desire-like attitude to them.
17. This may not be entirely clear in the case of intensions, but the existence of intensions implies the existence of possible worlds if functions are sets of ordered pairs, which is a common view of functions.
18. I include particulars to remain neutral on certain questions, but I don't think the contents of experiences involve particulars.
19. This account needs to be qualified because not all experiences have PSOAs as contents. Only *basic* experiences have PSOAs as contents, where a basic experience is one that does not consist simply in having one of a set of distinct experiences. In my view, all experiences that we ascribe using locutions of the form "experiencing NP", where NP is a noun phrase, are non-basic.

For example, experiencing a red ball is non-basic. This is because this ascription is silent on what the red ball is doing (bouncing, sitting there, etc.). I don't think it is possible to merely experience a thing doing nothing in particular. So, experiencing a red ball is really a matter of having one of a wide range of distinct experiences: those experiences that involve a red ball doing something. In contrast, experiential ascriptions that have clauses as objects (e.g. "I am experiencing a red ball bouncing") plausibly ascribe basic experiences. See (Bourget 2019) for more discussion.

20. Following Fine (1994), I'm assuming that not all properties that something has necessarily are essential properties it has.
21. For more arguments for the relation view, see Pautz (2007), Speaks (2015, chapters 2–9), Woodward (forthcoming). Another consideration that I find important but had to set aside for space reasons is that the relation view articulates the internal structure of experience in a way that seems helpful for the project of explaining consciousness. I develop this line of argument in my dissertation (Bourget 2010b). It is also briefly discussed in (Bourget & Mendelovici 2014) and (Bourget 2019). Mendelovici (2018) addresses these considerations, and Woodward (ibid.) raises concerns with Mendelovici's discussion of experiential structure, which Mendelovici (forthcoming) addresses.
22. One might be tempted to attribute something like this reasoning to Loar given that he was a staunch physicalist and seemed to endorse the other premises of this argument. However, I am reluctant to attribute the argument to Loar because he does not make this argument explicitly and the argument is flawed for reasons that Loar should have been aware of.
23. I am setting aside the question whether red* is what we normally call "red" in English.
24. See also (Chalmers 2006).
25. The point here is that *if* one is wedded to physicalism and its implications, one should find it easy to resist the inventory problem using the phenomenal concept strategy. I don't actually think it is reasonable to be wedded to physicalism, and I think the mismatch between red* and EM650 is a case that brings this out. This is why in (Mendelovici & Bourget forthcoming) I take the position that this mismatch speaks strongly against tracking theories of intentionality.
26. Kriegel (2011b) raises a version of the inventory problem involving necessarily uninstantiated properties, such as being an Escher triangle. If experiences represent such properties, the relation view seems committed to their existence. But such properties cannot be Aristotelian. As far as I can tell, all necessarily uninstantiated properties apparently represented by experiences are complex properties: they seem to reduce to combinations of simpler properties. For this reason, I think these properties can be dealt with in the same way as PSOAs.
27. The overall strategy is the same as the reductionism advocated by Crane (2013).
28. Famously, we experience absences, but this can be glossed as a certain thing being "missing" instead of "not being here".
29. I have previously argued that we experience relations (2017b), and I have built an argument against intramodal representationalism on this basis. I had not considered the alternative gloss suggested here. I think the ontological concerns under discussion might be sufficient reason to favor this gloss. It might still be possible to run the argument from (2017b) with revisions.
30. One might say that Platonic properties are necessary existents, so the mere possibility that a Platonic property is experienced entails that it exists in the

actual world. I don't think we need to assume that Platonic properties exist necessarily. In any case, this way of being committed to the existence of vast numbers of Platonic properties is independent of the relation view, as an aspect theorist might also have to agree that it is possible that they exist; the question whether necessarily existent Platonic properties are *possible* seems to go beyond the present debate.

31. Angela Mendelovici raised this objection in conversation.
32. Those might be stochastic laws as envisaged in (Bourget forthcoming).
33. Mendelovici (2018, pp. 264–266) makes this argument in an indirect way. She suggests that it is mysterious how content can be "psychologically involved" on the relation view, where one sufficient condition for being psychologically involved is being manifested in phenomenology. This is indirectly a complaint that it is mysterious how content can be manifested in phenomenology on the relation view. This is essentially the problem of consciousness if we take the view that phenomenal intentional states are constituted by their contents.
34. For more on this topic, see (Bourget and Mendelovici 2014) and (Bourget forthcoming) on the mapping problem.
35. Bill Fish (2009) distills such arguments, and I address his and John McDowell's arguments in Bourget (2010b).

## References

Banick, K. (forthcoming). How to be an adverbialist about phenomenal intentionality. *Synthese*:1–26.

Bourget, D. (2010a). Consciousness is underived intentionality. *Noûs*, 44(1):32–58.

Bourget, D. (2010b). *The Representational Theory of Consciousness*. PhD thesis, Australian National University, Canberra, Australia.

Bourget, D. (2017a). Intensional perceptual ascriptions. *Erkenntnis*, 82(3):513–530.

Bourget, D. (2017b). Representationalism and sensory modalities: An argument for intermodal representationalism. *American Philosophical Quarterly*, 54(3):251–268.

Bourget, D. (2017c). The role of consciousness in grasping and understanding. *Philosophy and Phenomenological Research*, 95(2):285–318.

Bourget, D. (2017d). Why are some phenomenal experiences 'vivid' and others 'faint'? Representationalism, imagery, and cognitive phenomenology. *Australasian Journal of Philosophy*, 95(4):673–687.

Bourget, D. (2018). The rational role of experience. *Inquiry: An Interdisciplinary Journal of Philosophy*, 61(5–6):467–493.

Bourget, D. (2019). Implications of intensional perceptual ascriptions for relationalism, disjunctivism, and representationalism about perceptual experience. *Erkenntnis*, 84(2):381–408.

Bourget, D. (forthcoming). Anomalous dualism: A new approach to the mind-body problem. In Seager, W., editor, *The Handbook of Panpsychism*. Abingdon, UK: Routledge.

Bourget, D., and Mendelovici, A. (2014). Tracking representationalism. In Bailey, A., editor, *Philosophy of Mind: The Key Thinkers* (pp. 209–235). London: Continuum.

Bourget, D., and Mendelovici, A. (2016). Phenomenal intentionality. In *The Stanford Encyclopedia of Philosophy*. Stanford: CSLI.

Chalmers, D. J. (2006). Perception and the fall from eden. In Gendler, T. S. and Hawthorne, J., editors, *Perceptual Experience* (pp. 49–125). Oxford: Oxford University Press.

Chalmers, D. J. (2010). *The Character of Consciousness*. New York: Oxford University Press.

Crane, T. (2009). Is perception a propositional attitude? *Philosophical Quarterly*, 59(236):452–469.

Crane, T. (2013). *The Objects of Thought*. Oxford: Oxford University Press.

Dinges, A. (2015). The many-relations problem for adverbialism. *Analysis*, 75(2):231–237.

Dretske, F. (1995). *Naturalizing the Mind*. Cambridge, MA: MIT Press.

Farkas, K. (2008). Phenomenal intentionality without compromise. *The Monist*, 91(2):273–293.

Fine, K. (1994). Essence and modality. *Philosophical Perspectives*, 8:1–16.

Fish, W. (2009). *Perception, Hallucination, and Illusion*. Oxford: Oxford University Press.

Grzankowski, A. (2018). The determinable-determinate relation can't save adverbialism. *Analysis*, 78(1):45–52.

Harman, G. (1990). The intrinsic quality of experience. *Philosophical Perspectives*, 4(n/a):31–52.

Horgan, T., and Tienson, J. (2002). The intentionality of phenomenology and the phenomenology of intentionality. In Chalmers, D. J., editor, *Philosophy of Mind: Classical and Contemporary Readings*, pages 520–533. Oxford, USA: Oxford University Press.

Horgan, T. E., Tienson, J. L., and Graham, G. (2004). Phenomenal intentionality and the brain in a vat. In Schantz, R., editor, *The Externalist Challenge*. Hawthorne: De Gruyter.

Kriegel, U. (2003). Is intentionality dependent upon consciousness? *Philosophical Studies*, 116(3):271–307.

Kriegel, U. (2007). Intentional inexistence and phenomenal intentionality. *Philosophical Perspectives*, 21(1):307–340.

Kriegel, U. (2008). The dispensability of (merely) intentional objects. *Philosophical Studies*, 141(1):79–95.

Kriegel, U. (2011a). The veil of abstracta. *Philosophical Issues*, 21(1):245–267.

Kriegel, U. (2011b). *The Sources of Intentionality*. Oxford, USA: Oxford University Press.

Loar, B. (1990). Phenomenal states. *Philosophical Perspectives*, 4(n/a):81–108.

Loar, B. (1995). Reference from the first person perspective. *Philosophical Issues*, 6:53–72.

Loar, B. (1997). Phenomenal states II. In Block, N., Flanagan, O., and Güzeldere, G., editors, *The Nature of Consciousness: Philosophical Debates*. Cambridge, MA: MIT Press.

Loar, B. (2002). Transparent experience and the availability of qualia. In Smith, Q. and Jokic, A., editors, *Consciousness: New Philosophical Perspectives*. Oxford: Oxford University Press.

Loar, B. (2003). Phenomenal intentionality as the basis of mental content. In Hahn, M. and Ramberg, B., editors, *Reflections and Replies: Essays on the Philosophy of Tyler Burge*, pages 229–258. Cambridge, MA: MIT Press.

Lycan, W. G. (1996). *Consciousness and Experience*. Cambridge, MA: MIT Press.

Lycan, W. G. (2001). The case for phenomenal externalism. *Philosophical Perspectives*, 15(s15):17–35.

McGinn, C. (1989). *Mental Content*. Cambridge: Blackwell.

Mendelovici, A. (2010). *Mental Representation and Closely Conflated Topics*. PhD thesis, Princeton University, Princeton, NJ.

Mendelovici, A. (2018). *The Phenomenal Basis of Intentionality*. New York, USA: Oxford University Press.

Mendelovici, A. (forthcoming). Reply to Woodward's review of the phenomenal basis of intentionality. *Philosophical Psychology*.

Mendelovici, A. (Ms). *Phenomenal Intentionality and an Internal Theory of Truth and Reference*.

Mendelovici, A., and Bourget, D. (2014). Naturalizing intentionality: Tracking versus phenomenal intentionality theories. *Philosophy Compass*, 9(5):325–337.

Mendelovici, A. and Bourget, D. (forthcoming). Consciousness and intentionality. In Kriegel, U., editor, *Oxford Handbook of Philosophy of Consciousness*. New York, USA: Oxford University Press.

Mendola, J. (2008). *Anti-Externalism*. Oxford: Oxford University Press.

Montague, M. (2016). *The Given: Experience and Its Content*. Oxford, UK: Oxford University Press.

Montague, R. (1974). Towards a proper treatment of quantification in english. In Thomason, R. H., editor, *Formal Philosophy*. New Haven, CT: Yale University Press.

Papineau, D. (2014). The presidential address: Sensory experience and representational properties. *Proceedings of the Aristotelian Society*, 114(1pt1):1–33.

Pautz, A. (2007). Intentionalism and perceptual presence. *Philosophical Perspectives*, 21(1):495–541.

Pautz, A. (2009a). A simple view of consciousness. In Koons, R. C. and Bealer, G., editors, *The Waning of Materialism*, pages 25–66. Oxford: Oxford University Press.

Pautz, A. (2009b). What are the contents of experiences? *Philosophical Quarterly*, 59(236):483–507.

Pautz, A. (2010). Why explain visual experience in terms of content? In Nanay, B., editor, *Perceiving the World*, pages 254–309. Oxford: Oxford University Press.

Pautz, A. (2013). Does phenomenology ground mental content? In Kriegel, U., editor, *Phenomenal Intentionality*, pages 194–234. Oxford: Oxford University Press.

Pitt, D. (2004). The phenomenology of cognition, or, what is it like to think that p? *Philosophy and Phenomenological Research*, (1):1–36.

Pitt, D. (2009). Intentional psychologism. *Philosophical Studies*, 146(1):117–138.

Russell, B. (1912). *The Problems of Philosophy*. New York: Barnes & Noble.

Searle, J. R. (1990). Consciousness, explanatory inversion and cognitive science. *Behavioral and Brain Sciences*, 13(1):585–642.

Searle, J. R. (1992). *The Rediscovery of the Mind*. Cambridge, MA: MIT Press.

Siewert, C. (1998). *The Significance of Consciousness*. Princeton, NJ: Princeton University Press.

Smithies, D. (2012). The mental lives of zombies. *Philosophical Perspectives*, 26(1):343–372.

Soames, S. (2002). *Beyond Rigidity: The Unfinished Semantic Agenda of Naming and Necessity*. Oxford: Oxford University Press.

Speaks, J. (2015). *The Phenomenal and the Representational*. Oxford, UK: Oxford University Press.

Tye, M. (1995). *Ten Problems of Consciousness: A Representational Theory of the Phenomenal Mind*. Cambridge, MA: MIT Press.

Tye, M. (1999). Phenomenal consciousness: The explanatory gap as a cognitive illusion. *Mind*, 108(432):705–725.

Woodling, C. (2016). The limits of adverbialism about intentionality. *Inquiry*, 59(5):488–512.

Woodward, P. (forthcoming). Primer, proposal, and paradigm: A review essay of mendelovici's the phenomenal basis of intentionality. *Philosophical Psychology*.

# 7 Phenomenal Intentionality and the Perception/Cognition Divide

*Uriah Kriegel*

## 1. Introduction: Phenomenal Intentionality and Cognitive Phenomenology

There is a line of thought, at one time almost orthodox, that divides the mind-body problem into two parts: the problem of consciousness and the problem of intentionality. The problem of consciousness concerns how to fit into physical reality the phenomenal character of perceptual experiences, bodily sensations, and other paradigmatically phenomenal states. The problem of intentionality concerns how to fit into physical reality the intentional directedness of belief, desire, and other propositional attitudes—paradigmatically intentional states.

Radical versions of this line of thought take phenomenal character and intentional directedness to have non-overlapping extensions: mental states divide into phenomenal and non-intentional states such as feeling ticklish and intentional but non-phenomenal states such as thinking that the weather is nice. This is what Horgan and Tienson (2002) have called "separatism".[1] These specially radical versions go beyond the basic idea I want to focus on here, which may be formulated as follows: phenomenal character and intentional directedness are *ontologically independent features*. (This can be the case even if phenomenality and intentionality are perfectly coextensive.) What this means depends on one's approach to ontological (in)dependence. On a traditional modal approach, it means that for any determinate phenomenal character and intentional content, it is possible for a mental state to exhibit the former without the latter and vice versa. On the newfangled ground-theoretic approach, it means that intentional content is never exhibited by a mental state in virtue of that state's phenomenal character, and vice versa.

The mutual ontological independence of phenomenality and intentionality has recently come under attack from two directions. One view, often referred to as "representationalism" (see Dretske 1995), holds that intentional content grounds phenomenal character; or perhaps more precisely, that there is *a kind* of intentional content such that phenomenal character is grounded in it. Another view, often referred to as the "phenomenal intentionality view" (see Loar 1987 for an early statement of the basic idea and Loar 2003 for the *term* "phenomenal intentionality"), holds that phenomenal character grounds intentional content; or perhaps more cautiously, that there is *a kind* of intentional content such that phenomenal character grounds it. The idea is that purely in virtue of its phenomenal character, and without need of interpretation, a perceptual experience as of a red square to the right and a blue circle to the left, say, has *accuracy conditions*, hence a kind of intentional content (Siewert 1998).

The core difference between representationalism and the phenomenal intentionality view (henceforth, PIV) pertains to the direction of grounding: representationalism holds that phenomenal character is had in virtue of (the right kind of) intentional content, PIV that (the right kind of) intentional content is had in virtue of phenomenal character. There is also a more ancillary difference, which does not quite *fall out* of these views but does seem to be a robust and natural accompaniment. This concerns the question of whether conscious thoughts, judgments, and other propositional attitudes exhibit a kind of sui generis phenomenal character that does not simply derive from the phenomenal character of inner speech, visual imagery, and the like sensory phenomena. At a purely sociological level, it seems that representationalists have not on the whole embraced this idea of a proprietary "cognitive phenomenology", whereas proponents of PIV almost universally have (Strawson 1994, 2011; Siewert 1998, 2011; Horgan and Tienson 2002; Pitt 2004; Bayne and Montague 2011; Chudnoff 2015; Kriegel 2015; Bourget 2017; Montague 2017). It is a fair question why this sociological alignment is so tight, but from a neutral standpoint, the following makes sense: if perceptual states' intentional content is not a primitive feature but is grounded in something, and if cognitive states have a similar kind of intentional content, then we should expect the intentional content of cognitive states to be non-primitive as well, and indeed to be grounded in the same kind of thing that the content of perceptual states is. So, if one holds that the perceptual states' intentional content is grounded in their phenomenal character, one is naturally led to hold that the intentional content of (conscious) cognitive states is grounded in their own phenomenal character.

This combination does produce a special challenge, however: that of accounting for the evident difference between the phenomenal characters of conscious perception and cognition. For someone who holds that perceptual experiences are phenomenal but not intentional and cognitive states are intentional but not phenomenal, there is a simple and clear line of demarcation here. But for someone who holds that both perceptual experiences and conscious thoughts exhibit phenomenal intentionality, something else must be said to account for the manifest difference between the two. Perhaps the answer is that perceptual and cognitive states simply exhibit *different kinds of phenomenal intentionality*. But the question is how to give an informative account of the difference between the phenomenal intentionality characteristic of perceptual experience and the phenomenal intentionality characteristic of conscious thought.

Compare a perceptual experience of a brown dog and a conscious thought about a brown dog. (Note well: by "conscious thought" I mean not a visual image of a brown dog, but a properly intellectual state.) The untutored introspective impression is that there is a clear experiential difference between the two. Moreover, it seems that, at least in normal circumstances, we can easily tell whether our current brown-dog-representing conscious state is a perceptual experience or a thought. The natural explanation is that we do so by picking up on the phenomenal character of our brown-dog-representing conscious state—picking up, that is, on whether it is a perceptual or a cognitive phenomenal character.

At one level, the difference between perceptual and cognitive phenomenology is straightforward. The question is how to capture this difference in a literal and informative manner. We might say, for instance, that in perception objects are *directly* present to us, whereas in thought they are not; or that perception *presents* its objects, whereas thought merely *re*-presents them. Husserl seems to hit the nail on the head when he says that while perceptual experiences present their objects *in the flesh* ("*in persona*", he writes), thoughts do not. But what do such formulations exactly *mean*? Our problem is how to get underneath such suggestive expressions and provide a substantive, informative account of the difference between the phenomenal intentionality of perception and that of thought. Given that the difference between perception and thought is such a bright a line within the field of conscious phenomena, addressing this challenge ought to be one of the central items on the agenda of the phenomenal intentionality research program.

In the 1970s and 80s, many sophisticated accounts of the perception/cognition divide were offered by philosophers and psychologists. But these tended to draw the distinction in terms of subpersonal or architectural features that do not seem phenomenally manifest—whereas what PIV needs is precisely a phenomenally manifest difference between the two. Consider the notion that perceptual processes are "modular" whereas cognitive ones are "central". Fodor (1983) adduced *nine* features distinguishing modular from central states, most prominently domain-specificity, informational encapsulation, and fixed neural implementation. However, Fodor did not *intend* any of these to be in any way associated with phenomenal character, and they certainly do not seem to be. But for the phenomenal intentionality fan who accepts cognitive phenomenology, there should *also* be a purely phenomenal, first-personally appreciable difference between the two. This first-personally appreciable difference could—indeed, probably is—grounded in some difference at the level of subpersonal mechanism; but the question before us concerns the nature of the phenomenal difference thus grounded, not the nature of the underlying mechanistic difference. Thus, our question can be seen as transforming the old problem of drawing the perception/cognition divide from a problem about kinds of subpersonal architecture to a problem about kinds of phenomenal intentionality.

What I will argue is that there is in fact no easy way to do this. I will consider three main types of approach (each branching into a number of subtypes): that the key difference is between perception's low-level contents and thought's high-level contents (§2); that it is the difference between nonconceptual and conceptual content (§3); that it is the difference between an "objectual" and a propositional content (§4). I will conclude that none of these works, and will consider PIV's options for where to go from there (§5).

Before starting, two housekeeping comments. First, I will use the expressions "cognition" and "thought" interchangeably, and have in mind the exercise of the characteristically intellectual capacities involved in conceptual thought, judgment, reflection, and so on. There is a use of the term "cognition" that makes it considerably wider, covering mental imagery, episodic memory, and any other stimulus-independent mental phenomena (see Phillips forthcoming). There is even a use of "cognitive" where it means essentially the same as "mental" (see under: "cognitive science"). I will not be using the term "cognitive" in these more extended senses, because that is not the sense relevant to the phenomenology of thought, judgment, and other cognitive states. Secondly, I will use the locution "thinking about" to cover both thinking-that and thinking-of. The locution "thinking *that*" tends to figure in reports of mental states that take a stand on the truth of that-which-is-thought, such as judgment, belief, and perhaps acceptance. In contrast, the locution "thinking *of*" tends to figure instead in reports of mental states that do not take a stand on the question of truth, such as considering, entertaining, or contemplating something. Since the difference between the two will not matter to us here, I will usually use the locution "thinking about", which seems to me neutral between the two.[2]

## 2. Low-Level vs. High-Level Contents

A straightforward approach to the difference between the phenomenal intentionalities of perception and thought is to claim that perception and thought simply *represent different things*. In particular, it might be suggested, perception represents *low-level properties*, such as color and shape, whereas thought represents *high-level properties*, such as being a Labrador and being illegal.

Setting aside debates over whether perception might represent some high-level properties as well (Siegel 2010), the main problem here is that thought can clearly represent *low-level* properties. You can see red, but you can also *think* about red; you can smell the odor of freshly ground coffee, but you can also think about it. Again, by this I mean not just that you can *imagine* that color and that odor. I mean that you can also form *judgments* about them. Indeed, it is commonly thought that one way we can form judgments or beliefs is simply by endorsing our perceptual experiences. If I seem to see that there is a red triangle in front of me, and take at face value my visual experience—i.e., *endorse* it—I thereby form a judgment that there is a red triangle in front of me. The result is a cognitive state that represents the same low-level properties that the visual experience did.

It is true, of course, that there is still this general difference between thought and perception: thought *can* represent some properties that perception cannot. It is possible to *think* that virtue is its own reward, but impossible to smell or see anything of the sort. However, this does not help us to distinguish a dated token perceptual experience of a red triangle from a dated token thought about a red triangle. It may help us distinguish the *faculties* of perception and thought (if there are such things), or the *natural kinds* Perceptions and Thoughts (ditto). But given an individual perceptual experience of some sensible entity and an individual thought formed by mere endorsement of that perceptual experience, the two will represent the same (low-level) properties.[3]

Might someone insist that, in fact, the redness-related properties represented in perception and in thought are not exactly the same? This is certainly a coherent option. Perhaps the claim could be that perception represents *apparent* redness (understood as a property of external objects—see Shoemaker 1994; Egan 2006), whereas thought represents *real* redness. One problem with this strategy is that we are left with no obvious way to account for the apparent possibility of forming thoughts via endorsement, since the properties represented by color perceptions and color thoughts are systematically different. But more deeply, it is unclear what prevents me from thinking about *whatever* feature I am currently visually aware of—*if only under that description*.

This suggests that the real issue here cannot be *what* property is being represented, but *how* it is represented. Thus, just as one may have two concepts for Venus, a Phosphorescent concept and a Hesperescent concept, one may also have two concepts of red, a perceptual concept and a cognitive concept. It might be suggested, then, that a perceptual experience of a red triangle deploys perceptual concepts of redness and triangularity, while a conscious thought about a red triangle deploys cognitive concepts of redness and triangularity.

Put this way, the account is not particularly illuminating. All it does is pass the buck from the difference between perceptual and cognitive *states* to the difference between perceptual and cognitive *concepts*. This does not quite advance our understanding of the essential difference between the perceptual and the cognitive; it only shifts the locus of the distinction from the realm of states to that of concepts.

The phenomenal intentionalist may, of course, attempt to offer a more informative account of the distinction between perceptual and cognitive concepts. However, it is important to stress that such an account could not appeal to sub-personal or unconscious phenomena that are not manifest in the phenomenology. For what we are trying to account for is the difference between perceptual and cognitive *phenomenology*. Thus, an account in terms of difference between the functional or inferential roles of perceptual and cognitive concepts would be problematic: on the face of it, functional/inferential role is a dispositional property, whereas phenomenal character is occurrent.

Furthermore, *whatever* account of the difference between perceptual and cognitive concepts the phenomenal intentionalist offers, the notion that this is what explains the phenomenal difference between perception and thought has the unfortunate consequence that thoughts can never be formed by endorsement, that is, by taking at face value certain perceptual experiences. Suppose you see a red triangle before you, and then think that there is a red triangle before you. Your perception will have a content C, featuring as constituent the perceptual concept of red, whereas your thought will have a different content C*, featuring as constituent a cognitive concept of red. Thus, the formation of thoughts by simple endorsement of perceptual experiences becomes mysterious.

For all these reasons, it seems unlikely that the phenomenal difference between perception and thought comes down to the difference between representing low-level vs. high-level properties, or to the difference between low-level vs. high-level concepts used to represent properties.

The phenomenal intentionalist might then suggest that the difference between a perceptual way and a cognitive way of representing red goes deeper than the use of different concepts. In fact, she might suggest, the perceptual way represents without the use of concepts at all, whereas the cognitive way is conceptual. Let us consider this approach next.

## 3. Nonconceptual vs. Conceptual Content

The notion that perception has *nonconceptual* content whereas thought has *conceptual* content is widely held among representationalists (Dretske 1995; Tye 1995). There is no reason why PIV cannot avail itself of the same idea. On this view, a perception and a thought may both represent red, but the cognitive representation deploys the concept RED, whereas the perceptual representation does not.

One immediate issue in evaluating this suggestion is the absence of any consensus on what the conceptual/nonconceptual distinction exactly amounts to. The variety of theories in this area is bewildering, but broadly speaking, there are two general ways to construe the conceptual/nonconceptual distinction (Heck 2000). On the *content-based* distinction, a *conceptual* representation of a brown dog has a content of which both the concept BROWN and the concept DOG are constituents; a *nonconceptual* representation of a brown dog has a categorically distinct kind of content, one that does not have concepts for constituents (more on this in §3.2). On the *state-based* distinction, a conceptual representation of a brown dog is a representational state a subject cannot be in unless she possesses the concepts BROWN and DOG; a nonconceptual representation is a representational state the subject can be in even if she does not possess BROWN and DOG.

It is commonly agreed (see Byrne 2005; Speaks 2005; Heck 2007) that in relevant discussions, the state-based distinction has been more central. Accordingly, I start by considering using that distinction to capture the phenomenal difference between perception and thought (§3.1); then I consider using the content-based distinction (§3.2).

### 3.1. *Perception, Cognition, and the State-Based Conception of (Non)Conceptuality*

If we use the state-based distinction, the suggestion becomes effectively this: a perceptual experience of a brown dog is a phenomenal-intentional state we can be in even if we do not possess the concepts BROWN and DOG; an occurrent thought about a brown dog is a phenomenal-intentional state we cannot be in unless we possess BROWN and DOG. Certainly among representationalists this seems to me the most common approach to the difference between conscious perception on the one hand and cognition on the other; this is explicit in Tye's (1995) PANIC theory, and implicit in Dretske's (1981) notion that perception employs an *analog format* whereas thought employs a *digital format*. The idea is that perception presents us what it does in a much finer-grained fashion than thought does, as our capacities for perceptual discrimination typically far outstrip the concepts we possess, so our perceptual awareness can capture details that thought cannot.

This approach seems initially promising, but my view is that its allure is due to purely contingent facts about human perception and thought that shed no light on the deep *natures* of perception and thought. To show this, let me present a two-step problem for the view.

The first step is to note that failure to possess a concept for feature F is not a necessary condition for having a perceptual experience of F. Imagine a creature whose visual field is a perfect square (say, because of the peculiar shape of its visual organs) and who has a visual experience of a pure white Ganzfeld. The only features she is visually experiencing are thus the color white and perhaps the shape square—two features for which most of us, and, let us stipulate, this creature, do possess the concepts. It would be odd to suppose that as soon as this creature acquires the concepts WHITE and SQUARE, she loses the ability to have a visual experience when standing in front of a uniformly white wall.

Indeed, we can also conceive of a supersentient creature who, amazingly, possesses a concept for every shade of red and every polygon up to the megagon (the million-sided polygon). Call this creature Lynceus (after the Greek god of whom he reminds). Lynceus can discriminate $red_{273}$ from $red_{274}$, recognize a sample as $red_{273}$ a year after last seeing it, and draw appropriate inferences about $red_{273}$ objects. Some philosophers hold that such capacities are *constitutive* of possessing the concept $\text{RED}_{273}$, others that they are merely *evidence* of possessing it; I do not take a stand on this here, but I stipulate that Lynceus possesses both the capacities and the concept. Imagine now that Lynceus is presented with a $red_{273}$ chiliagon. It would be perverse to say that Lynceus cannot perceptually experience the $red_{273}$ chiliagon (can only *think* about it) because of his *increased* perceptual acuity and processing power. From this perspective, it seems to be a merely contingent fact about *us* that we fail to possess concepts for some features we can perceive; it is not in the *nature* of perception to outstrip the perceiving subject's conceptual repertoire.

There is an objection to this reasoning, which invites the promised second step. The objection is that the state-based conception of nonconceptuality does not *require* a perceptual experience to outstrip our conceptual repertoire; all it says is that a nonconceptual state is one that the subject *can* be in even if she does not possess the relevant concepts. And although Lynceus possesses the concepts CHILIAGON and $\text{RED}_{273}$, the perceptual state he is in when presented with a $red_{273}$ chiliagon is one he *could* be in even if he *failed* to possess those concepts. That is, although in the world we just envisaged Lynceus possesses both CHILIAGON and $\text{RED}_{273}$, there is another world W where (i) Lynceus does *not* possess the concepts CHILIAGON and $\text{RED}_{273}$, but (ii) Lynceus is in the same mental state.[4]

The second step of the problem starts from granting that there is a world like W. But its existence raises the following question: *What makes it the case* that Lynceus' mental state in W is *the same as* (type-identical to) the state in which he is in the world we originally envisaged (the world where he does possess CHILIAGON and $\text{RED}_{273}$)? In particular, what makes it the case that in both worlds it is a *perceptual* state—as opposed to being a perceptual state in W and a cognitive state in the originally envisaged world? If Lynceus' state is perceptual even in the world in which Lynceus possesses the concepts CHILIAGON and $\text{RED}_{273}$, what makes it the case that it is perceptual? However one answers this question, the answer will effectively preempt nonconceptuality as the criterion for perceptuality. In other words, the assumption that Lynceus can have perceptual experiences of F both in worlds where he possesses the concept of F and in worlds where he does not presupposes that there is some feature, more basic than concept-possession, that accounts for the *perceptuality* of a conscious state.

For example, suppose one said this: the reason Lynceus' state is the same in (type-identical across) both worlds, and therefore is a perceptual state even in the world where Lynceus possesses the concepts CHILIAGON and RED$_{273}$, is that in both worlds it represents low-level properties (colors and shapes). Then one's defense of the conceptual/nonconceptual account of the difference between perception and thought presupposes the low-level/high-level account. The latter is in a sense one's *real* account. Now, the fact that we have already argued against the low-level/high-level account is not what matters to me here. What matters is the fact that the conceptual/nonconceptual account cannot stand on its own, given the possibility of creatures like Lynceus. It must rely on a more fundamental account.[5]

The upshot is that once we admit that a mental representation of F can be perceptual despite the subject possessing the concept of F, there must be some deeper reason for its status as perceptual (as opposed to cognitive) than nonconceptuality understood in the state-based way. The difference between the conceptual and the nonconceptual can no longer be the *ultimate* difference between perception and cognition.

### *3.2. Perception, Cognition, and the Content-Based Conception of (Non)Conceptuality*

The content-based distinction between conceptual and nonconceptual content generates the following view: a conscious thought that the dog is brown has for content a structured proposition whose constituents include the concepts DOG and BROWN; a perceptual experience of the dog being brown has for content a categorically different kind of entity. *What* categorically different entity? Well, there are three importantly different alternatives to a structured proposition whose constituents are concepts: (a) a structured proposition whose constituents are *not* concepts; (b) an *un*structured proposition; (c) an entity other than a proposition. Each may be plugged into a content-based attempt to capture the phenomenal difference between perception and thought in terms of (non)conceptuality.

Option (a) holds that while the conscious thought that the dog is brown has for content the structured proposition whose constituents include DOG and BROWN, the corresponding perceptual experience has for content a similar structure, but featuring as constituents not the concepts DOG and BROWN, but some nonconceptual analogs thereof—perhaps the *nonconceptual modes of presentation* **dog** and **brown**.

An immediate worry here is that it is far from clear what modes of presentation exactly *are*. If they are constituents of proposition-like structures, and if these structures are abstract entities, then presumably they are themselves abstract entities, though not quite the same abstract entities that concepts are. But we really know next to nothing else about the kind of things they are.

More worryingly, from our perspective, the difference between the abstract structures <BROWN + DOG> and <**brown** + **dog**> does not seem to be of the right kind to capture the phenomenal difference between perception and thought.[6] For it is hard to see how the difference between those two structures could deliver the difference between presentation of a brown dog *in the flesh* and presentation of the same dog not in the flesh. What is it about the abstract structure <**brown + dog**> that makes the dog present to us in the flesh? Just invoking that abstract structure and distinguishing it from the conceptual abstract structure <BROWN + DOG> does not get us any closer to answering that question. We can, of course, simply use the expression "nonconceptual mode of presentation" as a *label* for presentation-in-the-flesh. But if this is all we are doing, we are offering nothing that *gets underneath* the observation that perceptual experiences have the kind of content that presents in the flesh while conscious thoughts have the kind of content that does not. We are renaming the explanandum, not explaining it.

Alternative (b) is worse still. The idea here is that when we speak of the proposition <the dog is brown>, there are really two distinct entities we may be referring to: (i) a structured proposition with conceptual constituents and (ii) an unstructured proposition. Perceptual experience of the dog being brown carries (ii), conscious thinking about the dog being brown carries (i). I should stress that nobody in the literature has ever proposed this; I am considering this possibility merely for the sake of exhaustiveness.

The view obviously indulges an extravagant ontology of propositions. We need not endorse a general principle of "explanatory closure of the concrete realm" (Kriegel 2011) to feel uncomfortable about positing all those different denizens of the Platonic heaven *just to account* for the concrete phenomenal difference between seeing a brown dog and thinking about a brown dog. Furthermore, it is hard to see how this view accommodates the idea that we can form a thought simply by endorsing a perceptual experience. The view requires endorsement to be a special procedure that transubstantiates unstructured propositions into structured ones. In addition, the distinction between structured and unstructured propositions seems no more fitted to capture the difference between a phenomenology of presenting-in-the-flesh and a phenomenology of presenting-not-in-the-flesh than the distinction between propositions composed of concepts and propositional structures composed of nonconceptual modes of presentation. These distinctions just do not seem to have the right shape to capture the distinctively in-the-flesh character of perceptual presentation.

To my mind, alternative (c) is the most promising. Here the idea is that while the thought content <the dog is brown> features a constituent structure with concepts as building blocks, perceptual content does not consist in the proposition <the dog is brown> at all, nor any other proposition, conceived of either as unstructured or as structured out of nonconceptual ingredients. Instead it involves a *non-propositional* content.

What exactly is non-propositional content? The natural thought is that perceptual experience has *objectual* content, somewhat as love and fear are often claimed to do (Forbes 2000; Montague 2007). Intuitively, loving one's child is irreducible to loving that *p* for *any p*. And likewise, one might plausibly suspect, seeing a brown dog is irreducible to seeing that *p* for any *p*. Using chevrons to designate contents, whether propositional or not, we might say that while the thought has content of the form <the dog is brown>, the corresponding perceptual experience has content of the irreducibly objectual form <brown dog>. We consider this option next.

## 4. Objectual vs. Propositional Content

In truth, the propositional/objectual distinction can be interpreted either as a distinction concerning *what* is represented or as a distinction concerning *how* what is represented is represented. However, the former leads to an implausible account of the perception/cognition divide. It leads to the notion that while perceptions represent objects, thoughts represent propositions. Now, if the idea is that thoughts represent *Russellian* propositions—essentially, states of affairs—then it is not clear why perception should be incapable of doing the same. Looking at a red rectangle, I see not only the rectangle but also its redness. What I *cannot* see are rather *Fregean* propositions, understood as non-spatial, abstract structured entities inhabiting "the third realm". These are plausibly invisible, and more generally imperceptible. However, Fregean propositions make equally poor candidates for what *thoughts* represents—for *that-which-thoughts-are-about*. When I think that Max is a Labrador, *that which I am thinking about* is the specific dog Max and the kind of dog he is, not some shapeless and colorless counterpart of Max in the "third realm". The point becomes even more salient when we consider other propositional attitudes, such as desire. When you desire that your mother be happy, *what* you desire involves your actual mother; the fate of some corresponding abstractum is none of your concern. This is not to say that Fregean propositions have no role to play in the theory of propositional attitudes, including thoughts. Hesperus/Phosphorus phenomena suggest that they rather do. But the relevant role is *not* that of capturing that-which-is-thought-about.

The other interpretation of the propositional/objectual distinction allows that a perceptual experience and a thought may represent the same state of affairs—say, some rectangle's being red—but represent it *differently*. In particular, the thought involves a *propositionally structured* way of representing that state of affairs, whereby the redness is *predicated of* the rectangle, whereas the perception represents the state of affairs in a pre-predicative way, as an unstructured whole so to speak. We might write: the thought represents the rectangle's being red, whereas the perceptual experience represents the rectangle's-being-red (where the hyphens signal that "red" is a not a syntactic, but only a morphological, part of "rectangle's-being-red").

In this form, this seems to me the most promising of the PIV approaches we have discussed. It is a natural thought that what distinguishes merely sentient creatures from sapient ones is the latter's ability to "put together" ideas (the intellect's "power of synthesis") in the way characteristic of predication. Nonetheless, several considerations should worry us about the view's ultimate plausibility. I will present these as a series of queries to the view's proponent. I do not rule out that a satisfactory answer could be given to all of them, but going through them will bring out the tall order facing the view.

Firstly, is it so obvious that *no* perception has predicative content? Folk psychology certainly makes allowances not only for *objectual* perceptual reports, such as "He sees a brown table", but also *propositional* perceptual reports, such as "She sees *that* the table is brown" ("She hears *that* the mailman has arrived", "She smells *that* the coffee is ready", etc.). The latter ostensibly report predicative states. It might be retorted that the mental states reported in such constructions can be neatly factorized into two components, a purely perceptual one that is pre-predicative and a fully cognitive one that is predicative. But showing that this is so is very hard. The challenge is put very clearly by Søren Klausen:

> Seeing that the rose is red is quite different from simultaneously seeing a red rose and thinking that a rose is red . . . [If perceiving-that] consisted of two distinct intentional states, there could be a genuine question about whether one was in fact thinking of the rose which one also happened to see.
>
> (Klausen 2008: 453)

When you perceive that the table is brown, there seem to be no *possible* daylight between the table you perceive and the table of which brownness is predicated. But such daylight would be possible if the factorizing strategy were correct.

Secondly, there is a converse question, albeit perhaps less pressing: Might there not be objectual cognitive attitudes? Folk psychology does make use of belief-*in* reports, wherein the psychological verb takes an objectual complement (as in "Junior believes in Santa Claus"). Now, the obvious response here is that "belief-in" reports are at bottom just lackadaisical ways of reporting existential beliefs-that: when we say that S believes in ghosts, all we mean is that S believes *that* there are ghosts. Nonetheless, some philosophers have explicitly argued *against* this analysis, claiming that at least *some* belief-in reports resist paraphrase into belief-that reports (Szabó 2003; Textor 2007; as well as Brentano 1874).

Thirdly, is the difference between a structured and an unstructured representation of a state of affairs a *phenomenally manifest* difference? A phenomenal difference is one that we might reasonably expect to be able to pick up on by the use of introspection, at least in favorable circumstances and given the right "phenomenal contrasts". If, using the right phenomenal contrasts and being sufficiently attentive, we could pick up on a subtle but phenomenally real *act of predication* that is built into our thoughts but is absent from our perceptual experiences, that would constitute important evidence for the account under consideration. But to my knowledge, no such evidence has been provided to date.

Fourthly, granting that perceptual phenomenology lacks a predicative dimension present in cognitive phenomenology, could this difference really *exhaust* the difference between the two types of phenomenology? A reason for skepticism is that that would again constitute a merely *negative* characterization of perceptual phenomenology. When a naïve subject "tells" introspectively that she is having a perceptual experience of a brown dog, rather than a thought about a brown dog, she seems to pick up on something positive that is present in her conscious state, not just on some absence.

Finally, and relatedly, is the difference between predicative and pre-predicative content the *right kind* of difference to capture the phenomenal difference between thought and perception? It is unclear why and how the absence of a predicative structuring of one's representation of something would "spark into life" all those colors and sounds, nor why the presence of such predicative structuring make them fade away. It is hard to see the connection between the distinctive in-the-flesh character of perceptual awareness and predication.

## 5. Conclusion: Where Do We Go From Here?

If none of the aforementioned accounts of the phenomenally manifest difference between perception and thought is satisfactory, what are our options?

The most optimistic option is to hope that some other PIV account will be more successful than those we have considered here. Obviously, I have not considered *every* possible PIV account, and one of them might just work. This is of course possible, but would have to be shown.

Another option is to *go primitivist*. The idea is that there is a difference between perceptual phenomenal-intentional content and cognitive phenomenal-intentional content, but there is no way to get underneath that difference. We can use various metaphors, such as "presenting in the flesh", to make the difference vivid, but we cannot hope to offer any substantive account of the difference. Such primitivist moves are of course always available, and sometimes they are *true*; but always they are less theoretically satisfying than substantive accounts.

A more desperate option is to *deny the datum*. This could take the form of either (a) denying that there is a difference between perceptual phenomenology and cognitive phenomenology or (b) denying that there is a proprietary cognitive phenomenology to begin with. That is, even if perceptual experience has phenomenal intentionality, thought does not. Personally, both options strike me as frankly unbelievable, though I am aware that I have provided no argument against them.

A different way forward is to drop the claim that there is a difference between perception and thought at the level of phenomenal-intentional content, but insist that there is still a phenomenal-intentional difference, namely at the level of *attitude* or *mode*. The idea is to posit a cognitive experiential modality alongside the perceptual modalities (or, alternatively, a *plethora* of cognitive modalities, perhaps corresponding to cognitive propositional attitudes that can be conscious—judging that *p*, accepting that *p*, suspecting that *p*, conjecturing that *p*, etc.). Underlying this move is the thought that phenomenal intentionality is really a two-faceted phenomenon, in which content is only one facet and another facet is attitude. On this view, attitudes are just as phenomenally manifest as contents, and a conception of phenomenal intentionality which does not take them into account is perforce incomplete (Horgan and Tienson 2002: 522; Kriegel forthcoming §2). I find this the most natural lesson to draw from this paper's discussion. However, in a companion piece (Kriegel 2019), I argue against a number of attitude-based approaches to the phenomenal difference between perception and thought.

Obviously, there is one last way forward here, which is to give up on the phenomenal intentionality view, on the grounds that it is unable to account for the phenomenally manifest difference between perception and thought. This seems to me an overreaction, however: I would sooner adopt a primitivist account of the difference than claim that phenomenal character does not ground any kind of intentional directedness.[7]

## Notes

1. A particularly radical version, propounded for instance by Rorty (1970), sees "the mental" as a hodgepodge category that forces together all states that happen to exhibit either phenomenality or intentionality, though these have intrinsically little to do with each other.
2. On the one hand, "thinking about" can be used to report a thought of an object, or even a proposition, in a contemplative mode. Thus, when we say, "Jimmy is thinking about the proposition that the weather is nice", we do not mean to imply that Jimmy takes it to be *true* that the weather is nice. On the other hand, we can use the "think about" locution to report a part of a more committal belief-like state. Thus, if Jimmy judges consciously that the weather is nice, we can say—correctly—that Jimmy is thinking about the weather, or even that he is thinking about the weather being nice.
3. It might be suggested that if the possibility of representing (sufficiently) high-level properties is admitted to distinguish the *faculties* of perception and

thought, then we could always propose that perceptual experiences are the products of the perceptual faculty whereas thoughts are the products of the faculty of thought. But the problem is that being-produced-by-faculty-F does not seem like a phenomenal property, the kind of property that could distinguish perceptual from cognitive phenomenology.

4. There is a related but more superficial objection, according to which even if the Lyncean creature *possesses* the concept CHILIAGON, it may not *deploy* that concept when merely perceiving a chiliagon. To this it could be responded that it is quite hard to refrain from applying a fitting concept one possesses and knows to be fitting (try to see your mother's face not *as* your mother's face!), and in any case, we can stipulate that on occasion the creature fails to refrain from automatically applying the concepts. I think the objector will insist here that even if the creature always applies the concept CHILIAGON as soon as she perceives a chiliagon, the two things are logically separate. But what this means, really, is that the creature *could* have had the same perceptual experience without applying or even possessing the relevant concepts. Thus, the objection we are considering in the main text ultimately underlies the objection just raised. If we can respond to the one, we can respond to the other.
5. By the way, the worst answer we could give to the question "What makes it the same mental state, perceptual in both cases, in both worlds?" is "The phenomenology is the same in both worlds, and is rather a perceptual phenomenology". For our hope was to use the conceptual/nonconceptual distinction to *get underneath* the distinction between perceptual and cognitive phenomenology, a gambit that would be frustrated if defending the conceptual/nonconceptual account presupposes a phenomenal difference between perception and cognition.
6. The plus sign is supposed to denote what accounts for the "unity of the proposition"—a potential can of worms that I am setting aside here.
7. This work was supported by the French National Research Agency's grant ANR-17-EURE-0017, as well as by grant 675415 of the European Union's Horizon 2020 Research and Innovation program. For comments on a previous draft, I am grateful to Géraldine Carranante, Ben Phillips, and Enrico Terrone. I have also benefited from presenting the paper at Columbia University, the National University of Singapore, the University of Luxembourg, the University of Milan, and conferences on phenomenal intentionality (Paris, March 2017), perceptual awareness (Paris, July 2017), and perception and observation (Kirchberg, August 2017); I am grateful to the audiences there, in particular Ben Blumson, Davide Bordini, Géraldine Carranante, Marian David, Arnaud Dewalque, Anna Giustina, Gabriel Greenberg, Martin Lin, Tricia Magalotti, Olivier Massin, John Morrison, Takuya Niikawa, Elisa Paganini, Mike Pelczar, Jesse Prinz, Susanna Schellenberg, Enrico Terrone, Alfredo Tomasetta, and Nick Young.

## References

Bayne, T. and Montague, M. (Eds.). (2011). *Cognitive Phenomenology*. Oxford: Oxford University Press.

Bourget, D. (2017). 'The Role of Consciousness in Grasping and Understanding.' *Philosophy and Phenomenological Research*, 95, 285–318.

Brentano, F.C. (1874). *Psychology from Empirical Standpoint*. Edited by O. Kraus. English edition L.L. McAlister. Translated by A.C. Rancurello, D.B. Terrell, and L.L. McAlister. London: Routledge and Kegan Paul, 1973.

Byrne, A. (2005). 'Consciousness and Nonconceptual Content.' *Philosophical Studies*, *113*, 261–274.

Chudnoff, E. (2015). *Cognitive Phenomenology*. London: Routledge.

Dretske, F.I. (1981). *Knowledge and the Flow of Information*. Oxford: Clarendon.

Dretske, F.I. (1995). *Naturalizing the Mind*. Cambridge, MA: MIT Press.

Egan, A. (2006). 'Appearance Properties?' *Noûs*, *40*, 495–521.

Fodor, J.A. (1983). *The Modularity of Mind*. Cambridge, MA: MIT Press.

Forbes, G. (2000). 'Objectual Attitudes.' *Linguistics and Philosophy*, *23*, 141–183.

Heck, R.G. (2000). 'Nonconceptual Content and the Space of Reasons.' *Philosophical Review*, *109*, 483–523.

Heck, R.G. (2007). 'Are There Different Kinds of Content?' In J. Cohen and B. McLaughlin (Eds.), *Contemporary Debates in the Philosophy of Mind*. Oxford: Blackwell.

Horgan, T. and Tienson, J. (2002). 'The Intentionality of Phenomenology and the Phenomenology of Intentionality.' In D.J. Chalmers (Ed.), *Philosophy of Mind*. New York: Oxford University Press.

Klausen, S.H. (2008). 'The Phenomenology of Propositional Attitudes.' *Phenomenology and the Cognitive Sciences*, *7*, 445–462.

Kriegel, U. (2011). 'The Veil of Abstracta.' *Philosophical Issues*, *21*, 245–267.

Kriegel, U. (2015). *The Varieties of Consciousness*. New York: Oxford University Press.

Kriegel, U. (2019). 'The Perception/Cognition Divide: One More Time, with Feeling.' In C. Limbeck-Lilienau and F. Stadler (Eds.), *The Philosophy of Perception and Observation*. Berlin and Boston: De Gruyter.

Kriegel, U. (forthcoming). 'The Three Circles of Consciousness.' In M. Guillot and M. Garcia-Carpintero (Eds.), *The Sense of Mineness*. Oxford: Oxford University Press.

Loar, B. (1987). 'Subjective Intentionality.' *Philosophical Topics*, *15*, 89–124.

Loar, B. (2003). 'Phenomenal Intentionality as the Basis for Mental Content.' In M. Hahn and B. Ramberg (Eds.), *Reflections and Replies: Essays on the Philosophy of Tyler Burge*. Cambridge, MA: MIT Press.

Montague, M. (2007). 'Against Propositionalism.' *Noûs*, *41*, 503–518.

Montague, M. (2017). 'Perception and Cognitive Phenomenology.' *Philosophical Studies*, *174*, 2045–2062.

Phillips, B. (forthcoming). 'The Shifting Border between Perception and Cognition.' *Noûs*.

Pitt, D. (2004). 'The Phenomenology of Cognition: Or What Is It Like to Think That P?' *Philosophy and Phenomenological Research*, *69*, 1–36.

Rorty, R. (1970). 'Incorrigibility as the Mark of the Mental.' *Journal of Philosophy*, *67*, 399–429.

Shoemaker, S. (1994). 'Phenomenal Character.' *Noûs*, *28*, 21–38.

Siegel, S. (2010). *The Content of Visual Experience*. Oxford and New York: Oxford University Press.

Siewert, C. (1998). *The Significance of Consciousness*. Princeton: Princeton University Press.

Siewert, C. (2011). 'Phenomenal Thought.' In Bayne and Montague 2011.

Speaks, J. (2005). 'Is There a Problem about Nonconceptual Content?' *Philosophical Review*, *114*, 359–398.

Strawson, G. (1994). *Mental Reality*. Cambridge, MA: MIT Press.
Strawson, G. (2011). 'Cognitive Phenomenology: Real Life.' In Bayne and Montague 2008.
Szabó, Z.G. (2003). 'Believing in Things.' *Philosophy and Phenomenological Research*, 66, 584–611.
Textor, M. (2007). 'Seeing Something and Believing IN It.' In M.M. McCabe and M. Textor (Eds.), *Perspectives on Perception*. Frankfurt: Ontos.
Tye, M. (1995). *Ten Problems of Consciousness*. Cambridge, MA: MIT Press.

# 8 Cognitive Phenomenology, Sensory Phenomenology, and Rationality[1]

*Michelle Montague*

## 1. Introduction

Almost everyone accepts the following two claims:

(1) Conscious experience essentially involves phenomenology.
(2) Our conscious lives include conscious perception, conscious thought, and conscious emotion.

Taken together, (1) and (2) give rise to a question about the kinds of phenomenology necessary for the occurrence of these different types of conscious states.

Phenomenology can be characterized in a familiar way as the phenomenon of there being "something it is like", experientially, to be in a mental state, something it is like for the creature who is in the mental state.[2] It is a matter of a state's having an experiential, phenomenological character. There is (for example) something it is like to taste Marmite, or feel annoyed, or faintly queasy, or suddenly remember that today is your sister's birthday, or find something funny.

My focus in this paper will be on conscious thought and the phenomenology necessary for it, although it will at certain points be necessary to discuss conscious perception. I am using "conscious thought" widely to include conscious believing, thinking, wondering, entertaining, desiring, etc.[3]

Many have argued that the kind of phenomenology necessary to account for conscious thought is cognitive phenomenology, a *sui generis* non-sensory kind of phenomenology.[4] According to proponents of cognitive phenomenology, there is something it is like to think that London is having the warmest summer on record, or to wonder if a life with only small amounts of pleasure is worth living, something phenomenological that is irreducible to any sensory phenomenology that may be associated with these thoughts.

The existence of cognitive phenomenology calls for an extension in the way analytic philosophers have typically applied the term "phenomenology", because although most accept the existence of sensory phenomenology, many have been skeptical about cognitive phenomenology. I will speak of "phenomenological properties", and in particular of "cognitive-phenomenological properties" and "sensory-phenomenological properties", as characterizing experiential properties of conscious experience.

One source of skepticism about cognitive phenomenology stems from a question about how cognitive-phenomenological properties of thought are modally related to other mental properties of thought. One version of this question runs as follows. Suppose it is agreed, if only for the sake of argument, that sensory-phenomenological properties typically accompany conscious thought. My conscious thought that grass is green may for example be accompanied by an image of "greenish" phenomenology, or by wispy word images. Now we can ask: Can any cognitive-phenomenological property be combined with any sensory-phenomenological property in a given particular conscious thought? For example, can the conscious thought that grass is green with its associated cognitive phenomenology be combined with reddish sensory phenomenology?

Another version of the question is the following. Thoughts possess rational properties, both practical and theoretical. A conscious belief that there is white wine in the fridge combined with a conscious desire for white wine typically leads to going to the fridge for white wine. It's rational to infer the thought that it will rain from the thought that if there are clouds, then it will rain and the thought that there are clouds. Now we can ask: can any cognitive-phenomenological property be combined with any rational-cum-causal/functional property in a given particular conscious thought? For example, can the conscious desire for white wine with its associated cognitive phenomenology systematically lead to beer-seeking behavior or white wine avoidance behavior?

The issue of how these different properties are modally related in thought is crucial for the overall cognitive phenomenology debate, because it concerns the inherent complexity of conscious thought. Any view that asserts the existence of cognitive phenomenology must give a satisfactory account of this complexity.

To address these questions, I will present a series of cases, which I will call "mix and match" cases,[5] that attempt to describe circumstances in which sensory-phenomenological, cognitive-phenomenological, and rational-cum-causal/functional properties are mixed and matched in various ways. Some mix and match cases have been presented as objections to the idea that there is such a thing as cognitive phenomenology. Goff (2018), for example, argues that a state's cognitive-phenomenological properties are only contingently related to its rational properties, and that this leaves the proponent of cognitive phenomenology with the burden of explaining why we obey rational norms. Pautz (2013) argues that those who believe in cognitive phenomenology are committed to accepting combinations of cognitive-phenomenological and sensory-phenomenological properties that are in fact impossible.

I will argue that these mix and match cases pose no difficulty for the proponent of cognitive phenomenology. Doing so involves two tasks. The first includes providing clear definitions of "sensory phenomenology" and "cognitive phenomenology". The second requires explicating how each of the mental properties in question—cognitive-phenomenological, sensory-phenomenological, and rational—are related to the intentional content of conscious thought. Most of the work in answering the mix and match cases relates to the second task. I will argue that whereas the sensory-phenomenological properties of conscious thoughts can float free from their intentional content, both their cognitive-phenomenological and rational properties are essentially connected to their intentional content.[6] I will call this combination of claims the "Content View" (CV for short), since it focuses on how cognitive-phenomenological, sensory-phenomenological, and rational properties relate to the intentional content of thought. Not every proponent of cognitive phenomenology will accept this combination of theses, but the central claim of this paper is that the mix and match cases under consideration are not a problem for CV.

The plan is as follows. §2 demarcates sensory phenomenology from cognitive phenomenology. §3 outlines and motivates a certain view of the relationship between thoughts' cognitive-phenomenological properties and intentional content. §4 lists and clarifies the kinds of properties being tested for modal independence. §5 presents four mix and match cases and argues that they are unproblematic for CV.

## 2. Demarcating Sensory Phenomenology From Cognitive Phenomenology

A failure to clearly demarcate cognitive and sensory phenomenology leads to unnecessary confusion. I will mention two sources of confusion; the first concerns what is sometimes called "high-level" perception and the second concerns imagery.

It is helpful to begin with a list of uncontroversial examples of sensory phenomenology such as there being something it's like to experience red, or hear middle C, or feel soft skin, or taste pineapple, or smell a rose. These examples lead naturally to restricting sensory phenomenology to conscious perceptual representations of what are sometimes called low-level properties, e.g. color properties, sound properties, texture properties, and so on.[7]

Do we have any reason to extend this definition of sensory phenomenology? Siegel (2010) argues that the representation of so-called high-level properties such as natural kind properties in conscious perception should also be considered a matter of sensory phenomenology. I have argued that extending sensory phenomenology in this way leads to confusion.[8]

Briefly put, the argument runs as follows. [1] The representation of high-level properties in conscious perception requires the deployment of concepts in conscious perception. [2] The deployment of concepts in conscious experience, perception or otherwise, necessarily involves cognitive phenomenology.[9] Therefore, [3] The representation of high-level properties in perception necessarily involves cognitive phenomenology. On the present view, representing a blackbird's color in conscious perception need only involve sensory phenomenology, but representing a blackbird *as a blackbird* in a conscious perception essentially involves cognitive phenomenology, whatever other phenomenology it may also involve.

Once the connection between cognitive phenomenology and concept deployment is made clear we can avoid another area of confusion relating to how to characterize imagery, for example, visual and auditory imagery, including "inner speech" imagery. Imagery experiences can be construed as instances of pure sensory phenomenology in the following sense. Inner speech experience, construed in a purely sensory manner, is just experience of particular kinds of sounds with no meaning attached to those sounds. Visual imagery, construed in a purely sensory manner, is just e.g. color and shape phenomenology with no "meaningful object" attribution. People sometimes use the notions of visual imagery and inner speech in a way that treats them as already imbued with concepts and therefore with cognitive phenomenology, without acknowledging this explicitly. On the present terms, if one construes inner speech as already meaningful, and accepts that the phenomenon of its occurrence's being meaningful to the speaker somehow involves the occurrence of some sort of phenomenology, one has already attributed more to inner speech than merely sensory phenomenology. If one takes a visual image of a gas station, for example, to be "presenting" a meaningful object, one has taken or construed that image in a way that essentially involves more than mere sensory phenomenology.

## 3. Cognitive Phenomenology and Intentional Content

It is standard practice to treat beliefs, thoughts, and desires as structured in terms of "intentional attitudes" and "intentional contents". According to the standard approach to thought, it has the structure Rab, where a and b are names for things and R is the name of a relation. There is (i) the thinker, a, (ii) the thing designated by the "that"-clause, b, and (iii) the thinking (etc.) relation R in which a stands to b, which I will call the "intentional attitude". On this view, the thinking (etc.) is a two-place relation between the subject and whatever is designated by the "that"-clause.[10]

Proponents of cognitive phenomenology have argued that there are distinctive cognitive-phenomenological properties associated with different intentional-attitude types, and not only with different intentional contents.[11] In this paper, however, I am concerned only with the relationship between cognitive-phenomenological properties and intentional content.

Once one accepts that cognitive-phenomenological properties are associated with the intentional contents of thought, there is a very difficult question about the nature of this association, and one can hardly make progress on this question without saying something about what intentional content is. I can't hope to give an adequate account of the nature of intentional content here, but providing some clarification on the question of how intentional content gets "fixed" or "determined" will be helpful for discussing the types of objections to cognitive phenomenology with which I am concerned.

To start, we can divide content-determination views into "externalist" and "internalist". Very roughly, externalists about content-determination hold that the intentional content of a mental state directed at the external world is determined wholly by external relations between the subject and the subject's ambient environment.[12] Internalists about content-determination claim that internal (or intrinsic) features of a subject determine the intentional content of the subject's mental states.

Some philosophers think this is an exclusive either-or matter, and that one must be either an all-out internalist or an all-out externalist. But it's perfectly possible—and commonsensical—to hold a hybrid position: to allow that conscious mental states, at least, have both internal and external content. Here, however, I'm going to put hybrid views aside, in order to focus on the role of internalist intentional content in this debate. Accordingly, I will use the phrase "internal intentional content" when discussing CV.

There are many ways to be an internalist about intentional content, but my focus is on a kind of internalist who holds that the intentional content of a conscious state is determined by that state's phenomenological properties. Loar's (2003) seminal paper "Phenomenal Intentionality as the Basis of Mental Content" was a forerunner of such a view. He says (2003: 230):

> Conceptions of mental content in the analytic tradition have tended to be phenomenologically impoverished, largely because of the emphasis on language and reference. And when we turn to the phenomenology, as I will try to show, we do get a grip on internal intentionality.

According to what Loar calls "phenomenal intentionality", internal phenomenological features of certain experiences have intentionality, directedness, or aboutness, that can't be accounted for by appeal to external objects in one's environment.

Loar focused on perceptual experiences, but many philosophers have thought that the central interest of the purported existence of cognitive phenomenology is the possibility of cognitive-phenomenological properties determining intentional-content types quite generally.[13]

I'll call this the "determination thesis". Pautz (2013: 210) summarizes it as follows:

> for at least some cognitive phenomenal properties P, there is a unique content c such that it is metaphysically necessary that, if an individual has P, then he has an occurrent belief (or desire) with content c.

One reason for focusing on the determination thesis is that it provides an internalist view that can seemingly solve certain content-determinacy problems that have vexed wholly externalist approaches to intentionality. The content-determinacy problems for externalist theories are well known, so I won't rehearse them here.[14] Rather, I'll just outline one of the ways in which cognitive phenomenology is supposed to secure determinacy of content.

The general solution starts with the idea that phenomenological features of experience are themselves determinate: when a subject has a phenomenological experience of seeing red or tasting chocolate, for example, there is (necessarily, trivially) a definite way that that phenomenology seems to the subject. The next step is to claim that there is a certain kind of intentionality that is wholly determined by phenomenology alone. The idea here is that given the phenomenology of a visual experience as of a red ball, for example, there is a kind of intentional content that can be "read" off that phenomenology, such that any experience with that exact same phenomenology will have the exact same intentional content. Finally, it is argued that phenomenology is "narrow" or "internal". The general argumentative strategy for this claim is to point out that subjects can possibly share the same phenomenology even if they have radically different, qualitative and quantitative, external environments.

These three steps promise a solution to content-determinacy problems. There is a kind of intentional content that is wholly determined by phenomenology alone. And because phenomenology itself is determinate and internal (narrow), the kind of intentional content it determines is equally determinate and internal (narrow). Note that I haven't explicitly mentioned cognitive phenomenology in summarizing this style of argument. The idea is that similar reasoning will apply to it. Once so applied, we reach the determination thesis.[15]

My aim in this paper is not to assess the prospects for internalist or externalist solutions to content-determinacy problems. Rather, for the reasons sketched above, I will restrict my attention to a view that endorses both cognitive phenomenology and the determination thesis. Endorsing this connection between cognitive phenomenology and intentional content results in a strong version of CV since cognitive-phenomenological properties determine intentional content rather than being only essentially connected to intentional content.

In discussing cognitive phenomenology, it is often useful to talk in term of concepts, so I want to say a word about the relationship between the internal intentional content of thought and concepts. This will help clarify what is at stake in the mix and match cases. I take it that all thought constitutively involves the deployment of concepts, and so accordingly all *conscious* thought constitutively involves the *conscious* deployment of concepts. Clearly there is a very close relationship between the internal intentional content of thought and the deployment of concepts. Concepts—deployments of concepts in thought—constitute the occurrence of the internal intentional contents of thought. It therefore seems plausible to associate cognitive-phenomenological properties and concepts. My conscious thought *that* 2+2=4 and my conscious thought *that the earth revolves around the sun* are constituted by distinct concepts. The deployment of these distinct concepts is associated with distinct cognitive-phenomenological properties, and so in turn these thoughts are associated with different cognitive-phenomenological properties. Once this connection between concepts and cognitive phenomenology is made, we can restate the determination thesis in terms of concepts as follows:

> the instantiation of a particular cognitive-phenomenological property *P* metaphysically necessitates the deployment of a particular concept *C*.

## 4. Features Being Tested for Modal Independence

Since there are a number of features involved in discussing the mix and match cases, it will be helpful to list them before going on.

(i) Cognitive-phenomenological properties: *sui generis* phenomenological properties that are necessary to characterize what it is like to consciously think for example that Kentish Town is a good place to live or that yellow is the color of happiness.
(ii) Sensory-phenomenological properties: the kind of phenomenology associated with the representation of low-level properties, including visual and verbal imagery.

The *sui generis* nature of cognitive-phenomenological properties and sensory-phenomenological properties implies the modal independence of these properties. If certain features are modally independent from one another, then they can be freely combined. For example, consider the following modally independent features of color and shape: {Being red, being purple} and {being square, being round}. Being red can be combined with either being square or being round, and being purple can be combined with being round or being square.

(iii) Internal intentional content: a kind of content that is determined by narrow or intrinsic factors of a subject.

*CV Accepts*

(iv) The determination thesis: "for at least some cognitive phenomenal properties P, there is a unique content c such that it is metaphysically necessary that, if an individual has P, then he has an occurrent belief (or desire) with content c".[16]

We are also concerned with rationality and its governing norms. I can't here give a full explication of rationality, and I'll operate with the standard division into theoretical and practical rationality summarized in (v) and (vi).

(v) Theoretical rationality: inferential links between conscious thoughts and beliefs, including rational (valid) links.
(vi) Practical rationality: links between conscious beliefs/desires and action, including causal/behavioral dispositions.

Two important points about rationality. First, in discussing practical rationality, two kinds of desire must be distinguished. Some desires are related to action and some are not. My desires that it rain or that God exist are not essentially related to action. In contrast, decisions, intentions, volitions are special kinds of desires essentially related to action. As Brentano succinctly put it (1874/1995: 200): "Every volition or striving in the strict sense refers to an action. It is not simply a desire for something to happen but a desire for something to happen as a result of the desire itself". In discussing practical rationality, we are concerned with action-related desires.

Second, rationality raises a key issue about how the notions *internal* and *intrinsic* are typically used in this debate. I'm using internal and intrinsic interchangeably. A standard gloss on the notion of internality is the following: internal features of a subject's overall mental condition are constitutively independent on anything outside of her brain. A related gloss is that internal features of a subject's mental being are those features shared by perfect phenomenal duplicates. (Subject A is a complete phenomenal duplicate of subject B if and only A's total experience is phenomenologically identical to B's.) There is a question about whether inferences, whether they are between mental states, or whether they are part of something that leads to an action, are internal or intrinsic.

In offering the standard externalist view of beliefs and desires, Pautz (2013: 162–163) classifies inferences as non-intrinsic (non-internal) features of subjects:

> The contents of (occurrent and non-occurrent) beliefs and desires are always determined by non-intrinsic factors: factors such as behavioral dispositions, wide relations to the environment, causal or inferential relations among internal states, what sentences one accepts

and their contents as determined by their overall pattern of use in the language, and so on.

I think this passage is in danger of equating intrinsic factors with non-relational factors. A relational property of an entity *can be* an intrinsic feature of that thing in the case in which the relation holds between two internal states of the entity. For our purposes, the obtaining of inferential relations between mental states can be accurately classified as intrinsic features of a subject. For example, my phenomenal duplicate shares all of my inferential relations among her mental states.

In his discussion of physical reality Strawson (2012: 13) provides another clear example of the way in which relational/structural features can be intrinsic:

> We may certainly take it that the purely mathematically describable structure of physical reality is part of its intrinsic nature, so that physics really does describe features of the ultimate intrinsic nature of physical reality, in giving a purely logico-mathematical description of its structure. In giving structural characterizations of reality, physics really has descriptive content: it has . . . structural descriptive content.

## 5. Four Mix and Match Cases

I'll now consider four mix and match cases involving the features listed in (i)-(vi) and argue that none of them pose a threat to CV. The first two cases concern how sensory phenomenology is related to the intentional content of thought, and the second two cases concern how rational properties are related to the intentional content of thought.

### *Case #1*

Consider the possibility of a subject having the conscious thought that 2+2=4 without any accompanying sensory phenomenology. This would be a case of a conscious thought which had cognitive-phenomenological properties in the absence of any sensory-phenomenological properties.

This seems possible to me, but I don't think a proponent of CV should worry too much if it isn't possible. It may not be possible for creatures like us to have thoughts without any accompanying sensory phenomenology given the fact that we're biological creatures with our sensory modalities partly constituting the kinds of biological creatures we are. This fact certainly doesn't entail that there is some kind of strong modal dependence between cognitive-phenomenological and sensory-phenomenological properties.

The important point for CV is that ultimately sensory phenomenology is irrelevant to the metaphysical nature of what constitutes a conscious thought's content. That is, no amount of sensory phenomenology that may somehow be tied up with or integral to the occurrence of a thought or belief can account for that thought or belief's being conscious or being the particular thought or belief that it is. Why not? Because no amount of sensory phenomenology that may be tied up with or seemingly integral to a conscious thought or belief can ever satisfy what I call the "conscious content principle" or CC for short.

> [CC] If an occurrent thought T or belief B is to be a conscious thought or conscious belief, the intentional content of that thought or belief must in some manner be consciously occurrent, it must be consciously entertained.

I take CC to be intuitively obvious. It is very difficult to see what one could mean by conscious thought or conscious belief if the intentional contents of such conscious episodes weren't themselves somehow consciously entertained.

Proposals according to which wholly sensory phenomenology can satisfy CC typically appeal either to inner speech or to a causal relationship between non-conscious intentional content and sensory phenomenology.[17] Here I will only briefly discuss these sensory proposals and why I think they fail.[18]

First, as I understand it, the sensory phenomenology associated with inner speech is a matter of various "internal" sounds, which are themselves intrinsically non-meaningful, just as the words and sentences of any public language are intrinsically non-meaningful. So either a conscious thought consists in some non-conscious content causing the tokening of some inner speech, or inner speech somehow makes the content of the conscious thought conscious. The first option fails to satisfy CC. The second option begs the question, because now we need to hear more about what a content's being conscious consists in.

As for the second proposal, it seems clear that appealing to a (the) causal connection between the intentional content of the thought and the associated sensory phenomenology is just not enough to establish the right type of connection. One possibility is that the intentional content of the thought should simply cause one to have some sensory phenomenology without making the thought conscious at all. Consider the thought that grass is green and the claim that sensory phenomenology somehow makes this thought conscious. The intentional content [green grass] might simply cause a (possibly co-occurring) green patch image or perhaps a thought about green patches rather than the conscious thought that grass is green. Moreover, it is hard to see how the fact that a particular instance of sensory phenomenology is an effect of some cause can make that cause, e.g. some unconsciously tokened intentional content, conscious.

*Case #2*

This case concerns the possibility of mixing and matching cognitive-phenomenological properties and sensory-phenomenological properties. Consider the case Pautz (2013) offers about a thinker called Charlie. In accordance with the determination thesis defined above, suppose that there is a cognitive-phenomenological property P that metaphysically necessitates Charlie consciously believing the content

> *There is a picture on the wall behind me.*

In the actual case, Pautz supposes that the cognitive-phenomenological property P is associated with certain sensory-phenomenological properties:

> for instance, having the sentence "there is a picture on the wall behind me" run through one's interior monologue, and imagining (or being disposed to imagine) a picture on the wall behind one.
>
> (2013: 212)

If P is distinct and modally independent from all sensory-phenomenological properties, according to the modal independence claim, then it is possible that P be associated with a completely different set of sensory-phenomenological properties from those with which it's actually associated. If this is true it should be possible that while Charlie has P, the sentence *"there is a clock on the wall"* runs through his interior monologue, and he is disposed to form a sensory image of a clock on a wall. Pautz claims that such a case is impossible.

As described, the case is ambiguous, but once disambiguated, it is either unproblematically possible or it implicitly assumes the existence of cognitive phenomenology. On the one hand, if we construe sensory phenomenology narrowly in the way I have suggested as involving only shapes, colors, and imagery, including visual and auditory imagery, there seems to be no reason to deny that all the sensory phenomenology that is actually associated with Charlie's belief *that there is a picture hanging on the wall behind him* can be changed without altering Charlie's belief and its associated cognitive phenomenology. There seems to be nothing about changing the phenomenology of mere shapes and colors, or inner speech understood to be meaningless sounds that would conflict with Charlie's belief about a picture being on the wall.

On the other hand, if Charlie's inner speech and visual imagery are partly constituted by concepts, then of course Charlie's cognitive phenomenology will be different given the essential connection between the deployment of concepts and cognitive phenomenology. That is, if Charlie understands the sentence "there is a clock hanging on the wall behind him" as we do, this will implicate the CLOCK concept and the WALL concept and their associated cognitive phenomenology.[19] But this change in cognitive phenomenology poses no problem for CV.

*Case #3*

This case, offered by Goff (2018), concerns a subject called "inverted Ian". Suppose inverted Ian has a desire to have his body damaged. According to the proponent of CV, inverted Ian will have certain cognitive-phenomenological properties that partly constitute this desire. But rather than this desire being linked to being disposed to damage his body and thus leading to bodily damage type behavior, the laws in his world are such that inverted Ian's cognitive-phenomenological properties somehow hook up to Ian's being disposed to avoid bodily damage and thus inverted Ian manifests avoiding bodily damage type behavior. The result is that inverted Ian behaves just like "normal Ian" on earth who has a desire to avoid bodily damage.

Rather than being concerned with the possibility of mixing and matching cognitive-phenomenological properties and sensory-phenomenological properties, this case is concerned with the relationship between cognitive-phenomenological properties and rational cum causal/behavioral dispositions. The idea is that what's rational, given one's desires and beliefs, is that one acts in such a way so as to satisfy those desires (or have dispositions to satisfy those desires). Alternatively, what's irrational given one's desires and beliefs, is to act in such a way that would not satisfy those desires (or have dispositions to satisfy those desires). Accordingly, the Ian in our world ("normal Ian") is rational and inverted Ian is not.

Goff argues that if inverted Ian is possible, then cognitive phenomenology and rational behavior are modally independent. Although normal Ian and inverted Ian can share the exact same cognitive-phenomenological properties because they share the same relevant beliefs and desires, normal Ian is rational when it comes to his seeking or avoiding bodily damage and inverted-Ian is not. Since normal Ian and inverted-Ian share the same cognitive phenomenology, Goff claims proponents of cognitive phenomenology incur an explanatory debt: they must give an account of why we here on earth obey rational norms and inverted Ian does not.

The short response to Goff's example is that I don't think inverted Ian is possible. The content of inverted Ian's desire cannot be separated from causal/dispositional properties in the way the thought experiment requires. The basic idea is that action-related desires have the causal/dispositional properties they have in virtue of the content they have. And according to CV, the internal intentional content of desires is determined by their particular cognitive-phenomenological properties. So, cognitive phenomenological properties and rational properties are essentially linked.

To see why the internal content of desires and beliefs can't be separated from their causal/dispositional properties, it will be helpful to consider briefly the relationship between casual properties, content, and rationality. I can't hope to give a complete analysis of the complexity of this relationship here. Rather, my goal is to outline a plausible picture according to which it is clear why inverted Ian is impossible.

We can begin by asking, what is it for a thing to have a causal power? Roughly, it is what a thing will do given a certain situation. It concerns how a thing will interact with another thing or how distinct parts of the same thing will interact with each other.

Why does a thing interact with other things in the ways that it does? One plausible answer, and the one I favor, is that it is because of what a thing is intrinsically that it interacts with other things in the way that it does. That is, it is because of what a thing is that it has the causal powers it does. It is therefore impossible to separate what a thing is from the causal powers that it has. This is to accept the Shoemaker-Swoyer view according to which, the basic causal features of fundamental physical properties are essential to them,[20] and to reject the Lewisian view according to which the laws of nature can somehow be separated from an entity's intrinsic physical nature, thereby possibly changing its causal powers.[21] The coherency of Goff's thought experiment relies on the Lewisian view.

In our world, part of what beliefs and desires (including their intentional content) do is enter into rational relations, both theoretical and practical. If what a thing does is in virtue of what it is, then part of what content is involves it entering into rational relations. It is therefore impossible to separate content from its rational properties. Can more be said about the connection between content and rationality such that the two cannot be pried apart?

The central idea is that all rationality is grounded in content. We can begin by considering the logical connectives of first-order logic to see the way in which content and rationality are necessarily connected. The content of the logical connectives, what the logical connectives are, grounds or fixes theoretical rationality. It can't be the case that the logical connectives "and", "or", and "if . . . then" and so on remain what they are while systematically giving rise to different valid inferential transitions.

Similarly, the content of beliefs and desires help ground practical rationality. We can see this by considering in more detail what a desire is, and in particular what an action-related desire is.

(1) Every desire essentially involves wanting the world to turn out a certain way.
(2) The way the subject wants the world to be is specified by the content of the desire.
(3) Since we are concerned with practical rationality, we are concerned with desires that are connected to action. So, the kind of desire in

question is not simply that the world turn out a certain way, but for the world to turn out that way as a result of that desire.

(4) The world turning out a certain way as a result of the desire in question just is the desire having dispositions that lead a subject to act in certain ways and the success of those actions.

(5) The disposition to act in certain ways such that the desire is satisfied is partly determined by the content of the desire. That is, which actions are the relevant actions to satisfy the desire is determined by the content of the desire.

(6) So the content of the desire grounds the dispositional/rational properties of the desire.

The basic idea is a desire of the kind that is connected to action couldn't be what it is if the connection between the content of the desire and the relevant actions which would satisfy it were completely severed. In attempting to sever this connection in the way Goff's thought experiment does, the idea that the desire is an action-related desire is completely undermined. One cannot have the idea of the world turning out a certain way as the result of the desire in question if it is impossible for the world to turn out that way as a result of that desire.

To be clear, the picture of desire I'm advocating in no way provides a reduction of internal intentional content to causal/dispositional properties. Indeed, it is the reverse. Cognitive-phenomenological properties determine the desire's internal intentional content, which in turn determines the desire's causal/dispositional properties.

Goff continues to argue that even if one accepts this non-Lewisian view of causal powers, there would still be some explanatory work for the cognitive phenomenology view to do. He says:

> There is a normatively appropriate match between the phenomenally-constituted content of the state (which we apprehend when conceiving of it in terms of what it's like) and the behavioral effects of the state (which we apprehend when conceiving of it qua dispositional state). It is rationally appropriate for a cognitive state with the content of being a desire for burgers to be matched with a dispositional state of seeking out burgers: it is incumbent [on the] cognitive phenomenalist to explain the fact that there is a rationally appropriate match between the two ways of describing the state.
>
> (2018: 111)

I'm not sure I see Goff's worry here. Characterizing the content of a desire for burgers, for example, delivers the causal powers intrinsic to this content; referring to causal properties is part of saying what a desire for burgers is. Maybe the point can be put in the following way. If the categorical nature of beliefs and desires can't be separated from their causal powers, and if causal powers have something to do with rational transitions, there's nothing more to say, and therefore there's nothing more to explain.

It may be true that there seems to be two ways of describing a state, in terms of its phenomenological properties and in terms of its causal/rational properties, but once we see that we cannot adequately describe the causal/rational properties without adverting to the content, and that an adequate description of the content requires cognitive-phenomenological properties, we can see that there is an appropriate match.

In fact, attributing causal powers to an object or a mental state is plausibly just an abstraction from a description of the interaction between two objects or two mental states. That is, there really aren't causal powers *as such*. There are just things, what things intrinsically are, and how they interact given what they are. Saying here is an object, here is what it is intrinsically, and then adding that it has certain causal powers in addition to what it is intrinsically is a mistake. Causal power talk only comes into play when there is a description of two things interacting, but how that interaction occurs is completely down to the intrinsic nature of the object or the objects in question.

### *Case #4*

This final case is offered by Pautz in communication as follows.

> Whenever you hear "That is a vixen", you have the cognitive-phenomenological experience that that is a bachelor. But, because you are totally screwed up, instead of inferring to the cognitive-phenomenological experience that that is a man and the cognitive-phenomenological experience that that is unmarried, you infer to the cognitive-phenomenological experience that that is a fox and the cognitive-phenomenological experience that that is female. And so on and so forth. So you have a deeply secret and super irrational belief that the thing is a bachelor—even though you infer and behave and imagine exactly as if it is a female fox! It's not just secret in the sense of not having the normal outward effects, but also in the sense of not having the normal "inward" effects on other mental states, etc.

Pautz proposes to use case #4 as part of the following argument against cognitive phenomenology. If CV is correct, case #4 is possible. Case #4 is impossible. So CV is incorrect.

This case is complex and involves interactions between many of the features listed in (i)-(vi) above, so it is worth working through the example in stages.

> *Stage One*: Whenever I hear the sentence "That is vixen" I have the cognitive-phenomenological experience that that is a bachelor.

Since I take it that auditory speech sounds and auditory imagery are instances of sensory phenomenology, there is no intrinsic meaning attached to sentences of a public language or to inner speech experience. As a result, there is no problem combining the sound phenomenology associated with saying the English sentence "that is a vixen" with the cognitive-phenomenological experience associated with thinking that *that is a bachelor*.

> *Stage Two*: The cognitive-phenomenological experience of thinking that that is bachelor leads to inferring to the cognitive-phenomenological experiences that that is a female and that that is a fox, rather than leading to inferring to the cognitive-phenomenological experiences that that is a man and that that is a bachelor.
>
> *Stage Three*: I behave and imagine exactly as if the thing I am thinking about is a female fox.

It's not clear from the description of stage two whether the inferences in question are one-off inferences or if they are inferences I consistently make. I'm assuming that they have to be inferences I consistently and persistently make. If they weren't, my purported belief that that is a bachelor would not remain secret for very long. However, given the assumption that the inferences are supposed to be consistent and persistent, I think it would very implausible to credit me with having a thought about a bachelor at all. That is, consistently inferring from bachelor to female foxes is very good evidence that I don't know what a bachelor is and thus do not possess the concept of a bachelor and so cannot be accredited with thoughts about bachelors. So, I agree with Pautz that this case is impossible, but not in a way that threatens CV.

In a certain respect this case is similar to Goff's inverted Ian case. The subject is supposed to have certain cognitive-phenomenological properties that determine the intentional content *that that is a bachelor*, but this content is by hypothesis blocked from entering into any of the rational relations it typically enters into. So like Goff, Pautz is trying to drive a wedge between a thought's content and its rational properties. But as my response to Goff makes clear, this is impossible. A thought's content is necessarily connected to its rational properties. If in Pautz's case it is impossible for the subject to enter into any of the rational relations that are necessarily paired with a particular intentional content, the subject simply cannot be said to have a thought with that content.

In conclusion, mix and match cases illustrate something very important about our conscious thoughts, namely that they are complex phenomena, which typically have a variety of distinct and interacting mental properties. Thus, they are good test cases for views about cognitive phenomenology such as CV, but I have argued that none of the cases considered here pose a problem for it.[22]

## Notes

1. In the summer of 2002, the summer before I started my first job, I attended a six-week NEH summer institute on consciousness and intentionality in Santa Cruz, California. Brian Loar was a member of the faculty. The direction of my research totally changed that summer from a focus on the logic of intentional reports to the nature of the relationship between consciousness and intentionality. Loar's work was an essential force behind that change, and I have been pursuing that work ever since. This paper is a continuation of that work.
2. The term "phenomenology" was originally used to designate a method of theorizing famously employed by e.g. Brentano (1874), Husserl (1900–1901/2001), Sartre (1943/1956), and de Beauvoir (1949) according to which one studies conscious mental phenomena from the "first-person" perspective.
3. For the purposes of this paper, I'm putting aside views that construe beliefs as essentially disposition. See e.g. Crane (2013). Accordingly, I'll use "judgment" and "conscious belief" interchangeably.
4. Characterizing cognitive phenomenology as non-sensory is only a partial characterization, since many have argued there are other *sui generis* kinds of non-sensory phenomenology (see e.g. Strawson 1986; Bayne 2011; Mylopoulos 2015 on agentive phenomenology and see e.g. Montague 2009, 2014, 2016 on evaluative phenomenology).
5. I borrow this label from Goff (2018).
6. In §3 I'll say more about the nature of this essential connection.
7. I'm putting aside non-representational views of sensory phenomenology. Nothing of importance hinges on this exclusion.
8. See Montague (2017).
9. I'll explicate the connection between concept deployment and cognitive phenomenology in §3.
10. Elsewhere I argue that there is no attitude/content distinction as standardly conceived, but I'll put this issue aside.
11. See e.g. Horgan and Tienson (2002).
12. See e.g. Dretske (1981) and Tye (2000).
13. See e.g. Horgan and Tienson (2002) and Pitt (2004).
14. See e.g. Dretske (1981), Kripke (1982), Boghossian (1989), and Fodor (1990).
15. See e.g. Searle (1987) and Horgan and Graham (2012) for this kind of internalist solution to content-determinacy problems. See also Strawson (2008a).
16. Pautz (2013: 210).
17. See e.g. Prinz (2011).
18. See Montague (2016: 197–203) for detailed treatments of the failure of these sensory proposals to satisfy CC.
19. I am using small capitals for concept names.
20. Shoemaker (1980), Swoyer (1982), Martin and Heil (1999), Heil (2003, 2010), Strawson (2008b), and Morch (forthcoming).
21. Lewis (1973).
22. I would like to thank Arthur Sullivan for editing this volume in honor of Brain Loar. For useful feedback and discussion I would like to thank David Bourget, Steven Gubka, Angela Mendolivici, Adam Pautz, David Pitt, Brad Saad, Charles Siewert, Declan Smithies, Bronwyn Stippa, and Galen Strawson.

## References

Bayne, T. (2011). The Sense of Agency. In F. Macpherson (ed.) *The Senses: Classical and Contemporary Philosophical Perspectives*. Oxford: Oxford University Press: 355–374.

Boghossian, P. (1989). The Rule-Following Considerations. *Mind* 98 (392): 507–549.
Brentano, F. (1874/1995). *Psychology from an Empirical Standpoint* (L. McAlister, A. Rancurello, & D. B. Terrel, Trans.). London: Routledge and Kegan Paul.
Crane, T. (2013). Unconscious Belief and Conscious Thought. In U. Kriegel (ed.) *Phenomenal Intentionality: New Essays*. Oxford: Oxford University Press: 156–173.
de Beauvoir, S. (1949/1977). *The Second Sex* (H.M. Parshley, Trans.). London: Vintage.
Dretske, F. (1981). *Knowledge and the Flow of Information*. Cambridge, MA: MIT Press.
Fodor, J. (1990). *The Theory of Content and Other Essays*. Cambridge, MA: MIT Press.
Goff, P. (2018). Conscious Thought and the Cognitive Fine-Tuning Problem. *Philosophical Quarterly*: 98–122.
Heil, J. (2003). *From an Ontological Point of View*. Oxford: Oxford University Press.
Heil, J. (2010). Powerful Qualities. In A. Marmordo (ed.) *The Metaphysics of Powers: Their Grounding and Their Manifestations*. Abingdon, UK: Routledge.
Horgan, T. and Graham, G. (2012). Phenomenal Intentionality and Content Determinacy. In R. Schantz (ed.) *Prospects for Meaning*. Berlin/Boston: De Gruyter: 321–344.
Horgan, T. and Tienson, J. (2002). The Intentionality of Phenomenology and the Phenomenology of Intentionality. In D. Chalmers (ed.) *Philosophy of Mind: Classical and Contemporary Readings*. Oxford: Oxford University Press: 520–533.
Husserl, E. (1900–1901/2001). *Logical Investigations* I and II, translated by J.N. Findlay with revised translations by Dermot Moran. London and New York: Routledge.
Kripke, S. (1982). *Wittgenstein on Rules and Private Language*. Cambridge: Harvard University Press.
Lewis, D. (1973). Causation. *Journal of Philosophy* 70 (17): 556–567.
Loar, B. (2003). Phenomenal Intentionality as the Basis of Mental Content. In M. Hahn and B. Ramberg (eds.) *Reflections and Replies: Essays on the Philosophy of Tyler Burge*. Cambridge, MA: MIT Press: 229–258.
Martin, C.B. and John Heil (1999). The Ontological Turn. *Midwest Studies in Philosophy* 23 (1): 34–60.
Montague, M. (2009). The Logic, Intentionality, and Phenomenology of Emotion. *Philosophical Studies* 145 (2): 171–192.
Montague, M. (2014) Evaluative Phenomenology. In S. Roeser and C. Todd (eds.) *Emotion and Value*. Oxford: Oxford University Press: 32–51.
Montague, M. (2016). *The Given: Experience and Its Content*. Oxford: Oxford University Press.
Montague, M. (2017). Perception and Cognitive Phenomenology. *Philosophical Studies* 174 (8): 2045–2062.
Morch, H. (forthcoming). The Evolutionary Argument for Phenomenal Powers. *Philosophical Perspectives*.
Mylopoulos, M. (2015). Agentive Awareness Is Not Sensory Awareness. *Philosophical Studies* 173 (3): 761–780.
Pautz, A. (2013). Does Phenomenology Ground Mental Content? In U. Kriegel (ed.) *Phenomenal Intentionality: New Essays*. Oxford: Oxford University Press: 194–234.

Pitt, D. (2004). The Phenomenology of Cognition or What It Is Like to Think That P? *Philosophy and Phenomenological Research* 69: 1–36.

Prinz, J. (2011). The Sensory Basis of Cognitive Phenomenology. In T. Bayne and M. Montague (eds.) *Cognitive Phenomenology*. Oxford: Oxford University Press: 174–196.

Sartre, J.-P. (1943/1956). *Being and Nothingness*, translated by H. Barnes. New York: Philosophical Library.

Searle, J. (1987). Indeterminacy, Empiricism, and the First Person. *The Journal of Philosophy* 84: 123–146.

Shoemaker, S. (1980). Causality and Properties. In P. van Inwagen (ed.) *Time and Cause: Essays Presented to Richard Taylor*. Dordrecht: Reidel.

Siegel, S. (2010). *The Contents of Visual Experience*. New York: Oxford University Press.

Strawson, G. (1986). *Freedom and Belief*. Oxford: Oxford University Press.

Strawson, G. (2008a). Real Intentionality 3: Why Intentionality Entails Consciousness'. In his *Real Materialism and Other Essays*. Oxford: Oxford University Press: 281–306.

Strawson, G. (2008b). The Identity of the Categorical and the Dispositional. *Analysis* 68 (4): 271–282.

Strawson, G. (2012). Real naturalism, Romanell Lecture. *Proceedings of the American Philosophical Association* 86: 125–154.

Swoyer, C. (1982). The Nature of Natural Laws. *Australasian Journal of Philosophy* 60 (3): 203–223.

Tye, M. (2000). *Consciousness, Color, and Content*. Cambridge, MA: MIT Press.

# 9 Loar's Compromised Internalism

*David Pitt*

In a series of subtle and penetrating papers spanning four decades, Brian Loar developed a distinctive two-factor theory of mental content.[1] On Brian's account, an individual's conceptual mental states have a kind of content that is determined entirely by factors internal to the individual—a *narrow* ("psychological") content, as well as a kind of content that is determined by (natural and) social factors external to the individual—a *wide* ("social") content. A distinguishing feature of Brian's theory is the foundational role it gives to qualitative experience—*phenomenology*—in the determination of narrow content. His guiding insight was that an adequate theory of mental intentionality (including mental reference) must take into account the individual's *experience* of his or her intentional states, from the *subjective* point of view. This is essential to capturing psychological content, which is constituted by how an individual "conceives the facts, how he conceives the world as being" (Loar 1987, 2017, 165).[2]

Brian was thus a pioneer in the research program in analytic philosophy of mind that has come to be called "Phenomenal Intentionality". Brian (Loar 2003b) was one of the first to use this term. See also Horgan and Tienson 2002). Though a given in the Phenomenological tradition, the idea that conscious qualitative experience has something to do with conceptual representational capacities borders on heretical for most analytic philosophers of mind. If Brian (and the Phenomenologists, Horgan and Tienson, and Searle, among others) are right, the project of *naturalizing* intentionality cannot proceed without naturalizing consciousness and qualitative experience—which is, needless to say, not something that will be accomplished by the middle of next week (if it can be done at all). (Jerry Fodor proclaimed acceptance of an essential link between intentionality and consciousness "intellectual suicide".[3]) Though Brian was no dualist, he saw clearly that the impossibility of giving a naturalistic explanation of consciousness and phenomenology with presently available resources did not justify ignoring it or its foundational role in the determination of intentional content. We should, he thought, "give[] up the idea that naturalism requires that intentionality be explicated in objective and externalist terms" (1991, 236). Such an explanation may arrive at some point in the future; but the theory of content cannot wait for it. The facts about intentionality *as we experience it* are there before us ("there for the noticing" (Loar 2003b, 2017, 293)), to be discounted at one's theoretical peril.

As bold as his insistence on the importance of phenomenology and the subjective point of view was, in the face of mainstream analytic philosophy of mind and its central commitment to naturalizability as a condition of acceptable theorizing, I think Brian did not go far enough. I think he was prevented from following his internalist insights where they inevitably lead by his acceptance of widely-held views on the semantics of singular terms, the sociolinguistic determination of conceptual content, and the scope of phenomenality. I think these views are either not inevitable, not well motivated, or short-sighted, and, in any case, ought to be rejected by anyone who, like Brian, recognizes the central role phenomenology plays in the constitution of intentionality. In accommodating these views, Brian's internalism is compromised.

In this paper, I will focus on the second and third of Brian's compromises, concerning sociolinguistic determination of conceptual content, and the restriction of phenomenality to the familiar sensory kinds. I will argue that the thesis that an individual's concepts have social content in addition to psychological content is not supported by the thought experiments that Brian (like so many others) relies on, in "Social Content and Psychological Content" (1988), that it has unpalatable consequences, and that, in any case, Brian's conclusion about the role of that-clauses in capturing psychological content is too hasty. Then I will argue that the perception-based theory of conceptual content that Brian advocates in his paper "Phenomenal Intentionality as the Basis of Mental Content" (2003b) cannot account for conceptual content, and that an internalist must embrace a broader conception of phenomenology that includes a *sui generis* kind of phenomenology proprietary to conceptual thought.[4]

Though this paper is critical, I want to emphasize how much I admire Brian's work, and how much I have learned from studying it. Brian was a deep and subtle thinker.

## 1. Social Content and Psychological Content

In "Social Content and Psychological Content", Brian argues that the following principle is false:

(A) Sameness of *de dicto* or oblique occurrence of a general term in two belief ascriptions implies, if everything else is the same, sameness of the psychological content of the two beliefs thus ascribed.

(Loar 1988, 2017, 153)

and he concludes from this that there are two different kinds of contents that beliefs have, *social* content, which is determined by the socially determined meanings of the terms in the ascriptions, and *psychological* content, which is determined by the way an individual subjectively conceives things as being (which involves the psychological, including inferential, role the state has for the individual). Psychological content is, according to Brian, entirely subjective (and grounded in phenomenology), and is not determined by sociolinguistic facts external to the thinker. Social content, which is what is captured by that-clauses, on the other hand, is sociolinguistically determined. Though only the former kind of content, which captures how things are from the thinker's point of view, is relevant to psychological explanation, Brian maintains that beliefs (and their constituent concepts) *also* have socially determined contents.

Brian's rejection of (A) is based on cases in which univocal ascriptions fail to capture personal psychological differences. Some of these cases involve translation and proper names, which I would reject for tendentious reasons that I will not defend here. (I do so in *The Quality of Thought*.) So I will focus on the cases involving general terms.

There is an initial question about how (A) is to be interpreted. There is a reading of it on which it means that for an individual to apply the same belief ascription to different individuals is for him to attribute the same belief to them. Use of the same of that-clause implies that the ascriber means to be attributing the same belief. In the ordinary case, this is true—perhaps even trivially so. Without some special reason to the contrary, we assume that the same words mean the same thing when one uses them on different occasions. If I say that two individuals believe that cats are furry, I am ascribing the same belief to them. Brian's intended interpretation, I take it, is, rather, that if two ascriptions using the same that-clause are *true*, it follows that the ascribees believe the same thing. And this is what he claims is not the case. The focus, then, is on the truth of the ascriptions.

Brian is here (and throughout his work on the philosophy of content) relying heavily on the Burgean idea that there are cases in which it is *appropriate* to use an ascription that does not capture subjective content, but in which we should nonetheless take the ascriptions to be *literally true*. He imagines a case in which an individual, Paul, associates two different concepts with the word "cat", wrongly thinking that there are two different kinds of animals that go by the same general name (1988, 2017, 157–158). No one knows this, however; so when Paul says, for example, "I like cats", he is interpreted by his audience as meaning by "cat" what they mean by "cat"—i.e., what "cat" means in the language they speak. And when they attribute this belief to him, on the basis of what he has said, they use the word "cat" as they understand it (with its socially determined meaning).[5] But while the ascription may be appropriately made and true, its that-clause content need not match the particular conception of cats that Paul had in mind when he said that he likes cats. In a case where it does not, Paul's belief has a social content (the content of the that-clause used to report what he believes) and a different psychological content (Paul's personal conception).

I think there are two serious problems for Brian's argument, and, hence, for the two-factor view of intentionality he constructs as a compromise between his internalism and the falsehood of (A). The first is that the Burgean principle it relies on—that ascriptions it is appropriate (intuitively natural) to make are, all things equal, literally true—does not apply in *any* of the cases that are supposed to show that content (for Brian, a *kind* of content) is determined by factors extrinsic to an individual. The second is that in allowing that a psychological state can have two different kinds of content, Brian condones a practice that allows that we may all be massively incoherent, or at least duplicitous, in what we believe—that our beliefs have inconsistent socially and psychologically determined contents. In the next two sections I develop these complaints, beginning with the second.

Before doing that, however, I want briefly to take issue with Brian's claim that that-clauses *cannot* capture subjective psychological content. He maintains that it is "*impossible*" . . . "to explain that-clause ascriptions in internalist terms", (1987, 2017, 178; my emphasis), and that "we lack forms of words conventionally designed for reporting personal conceivings" (*id.* 179).

This seems very implausible. If the contents of attitudes are propositions, and that-clauses express (or denote) propositions, then how could there be *no* that-clause that captures psychological content? How could an individual have a *conception* of things without employing *concepts*? And how could a conception not be constituted by what an individual *thinks*—i.e., which propositions he entertains?

In taking up a first-person perspective on intentionality, I think Brian should have been more careful in distinguishing the various functions propositional attitude ascriptions have, and avoided their role in third-person explanation and prediction of behavior. That-clauses *can* capture subjective intentional content, even if that is not their only, or even primary, function in our ascription of propositional attitudes to each other. The practical purposes typically served by such ascriptions do not require that we specify precisely what someone is thinking. Often enough, information about what an ascribee is referring to, what properties are being attributed to it, and what the ascribee intends to do with it or to it, are sufficient. This is the basic information we need in order to anticipate others' behavior, especially as it might affect ourselves, and to communicate our findings to relevant parties. Details about how an individual is conceiving of objects and properties may not matter if we are just trying to get a bead on what he is likely to do, to what, or to whom. Inexact attributions can count as *true for practical purposes*, even if they are not literally true.

But it does not follow from this that a that-clause *cannot* capture what someone is thinking, the way he is thinking it. For an individual, from the subjective perspective, there is no thinking of a thing and attributing a property to it that does not involve some specific *ways* of thinking of the thing and the property. Unless one supposes that individuals never accurately grasp the socially-determined meanings of terms in the language they speak, and which they use to express their thoughts, then it ought to be possible for a that-clause ascription—especially a *self*-ascription—to express (or denote) the very same proposition that an individual grasps from the subjective point of view. (Indeed, this seems presupposed by the case presented above in which Paul associates two concepts with "cat".) Brian does discuss situations in which our primary concern *is* precisely describing individuals' mental states *as they have them*; but he says that in such cases we *project* from our own case, and what we are projecting cannot be captured by that-clauses. I do not think he has provided sufficient support for this claim.

### 1.1. *Epidemic Duplicity*

Suppose that one of the concepts Paul associates with "cat" is the standard one—say, *feline mammal*—while the other is very idiosyncratic—say, *feline amphibian*. He thinks that some cat-like creatures are in fact cat-mimicking giant salamanders (*Andrias catus*) (he once watched *Planet Earth* while tripping). Though he thinks these are native to East Asia, he suspects that some have been smuggled into the US and sold as pets. In fact, he thinks his neighbor has one. (It spends a lot of time near her bird bath, which Paul finds suspicious.) He knows the difference between mammals and amphibians, and that the classes *Mammalia* and *Amphibia* are, logically, mutually exclusive (nothing can be both a mammal and an amphibian).

One day, Paul's aunt Lydia overhears him muttering "There's that cat again; stalking crickets, no doubt!" and attributes to him the belief that a cat is stalking crickets in the neighbors' yard. If we accept this attribution as literally true (by Lydia's lights), we are committed to Paul's believing that there is a feline mammal in the neighbors' yard. From a subjective perspective, however, what Paul believes is that there is a feline amphibian in the neighbors' yard. Moreover, for Brian, *it is one and the same mental state that has these two contents*, the first socially determined and the second personally determined. So we end up having to say that Paul has a belief with two distinct, contradictory contents. Given the likelihood that the concepts individuals associate with terms in the language they speak are quite often out of sync with those terms' socially determined contents, we seem committed to a practice that to a large extent makes a mess of our fellows' mental lives. (Nor need the double contents we count an individual as having be contradictory. The very idea that a given belief typically has two distinct contents is suspect enough.)

With respect to his (less fanciful) Paul case, Brian argues that we should say that Paul's beliefs "are not inconsistent in their psychological contents" (1988, 2017, 158)—because they are, for Paul, inferentially isolated. Paul might have distinct beliefs univocally attributable to him by "Paul believes that cats have tails" and "Paul believes that cats do not have tails" (where "cat" has its social meaning in both), but his rationality is not impugned if these beliefs have different psychological roles for him. But what I am concerned with here is cases in which we accept a third-person attribution to a single occurrent belief state that has a different psychological (in Brian's sense) content. It seems that Brian is committed to saying that a belief can have two distinct, even contradictory, contents. From Aunt Lydia's (social) point of view, Paul believes there is a feline mammal in the yard. And her attribution of this belief to Paul is true. From Paul's (subjective) point of view, Paul believes that there is a feline amphibian in the yard. And his self-attribution of this belief (were he to make it) is true. This is not a case in which two distinct beliefs having *prima facie* contradictory content are assigned on the basis of distinct utterances, but of assigning a single, occurrent belief different (incompatible) contents. There is nothing for Paul to compartmentalize. The issue concerns what we ought to say Paul believes at the moment Aunt Lydia says that Paul believes there is a cat in the neighbors' yard. It is not at all plausible that Paul's belief has, simultaneously, the content *there is a feline mammal in the yard* and the content *there is an amphibian in the yard*. And we should be suspicious of a theory that implies that this is possible.

### *1.2. The Burgean Intuitions*[6]

Tyler Burge (1979, 1982, 1986) presents cases that are meant to elicit intuitions that, in combination with a plausible general principle about belief ascription, provide a strong reason to reject any individualist conception of mind. The intuitions (the "Intuitions") concern *what it is natural to say* about what the individuals described in the thought experiments believe, and the general principle (the "Principle") is that, *all things being equal*, belief ascriptions it is natural to make are literally true. The Intuitions are supposed to override any sense that the *ceteris paribus* clause of the Principle is sprung because of the conceptual idiosyncracies of Burge's imagined subjects: they believe what they say *in spite of* their deviance from the communal norms governing the usage of their words.

The Intuitions about what it is natural to say are powerful. Burge is surely right that in the situations he describes it is natural to attribute beliefs to his subjects using the very words they utter, even though their understanding of those words is at odds with their socially determined meanings. Nonetheless, I think the Intuitions are not sufficient to establish Burge's thesis. What it is natural to say in a given case need not be literally true; and there may be compelling reasons for thinking that it is not. I will argue that in *any* case of the kind required by a Burgean thought experiment there is a reason for not taking the homophonic ascriptions at face value, which is not neutralized by the intuitive naturalness of making them.

In the arthritis example, we have an individual (I will call her Anna) who, according to Burge, believes that she has arthritis in her thigh, in spite of the fact that her understanding of the term "arthritis" deviates from its meaning in the language she speaks ("arthritis" "as used in [her] linguistic community, does not apply to ailments outside joints. Indeed, it fails to do so by a standard, non-technical dictionary definition" (Burge 1979, 78)). Though she does not have a proper grasp of the concept *arthritis*, Anna nonetheless *has* this concept, and it partly constitutes the content of her belief. Counterfactual Anna, who has the same physical history as Anna up until the moment she expresses her worry about her thigh, is a member of a different linguistic community, in which "arthritis" applies by definition to rheumatoid diseases that can occur in muscle as well as joints. In this counterfactual context, none of Anna's "arthritis" utterances mean what they do in her actual context, and none of her beliefs have their actual content. Since by hypothesis the only difference between the actual and counterfactual situations is the practices of the linguistic communities Anna is a member of, we seem compelled to conclude that it is these factors, and not something internal to Anna, that determine the contents of her "arthritis" beliefs.

It is essential to Burge's argument that it be literally true in the actual context that, in spite of her confusion, Anna believes that she has arthritis in her thigh. If she does not believe this in the actual case, then the counterfactual case is irrelevant, and no conclusions about social content determination are established by the thought experiment. (In the counterfactual case, there is no discrepancy between what "arthritis" means and what Anna thinks it means.) It is only on the assumption that Anna believes she has arthritis in her thigh that the content-determining role of sociolinguistic context is made salient by a comparison with the counterfactual case.

One might be tempted to think that Anna's statement to her doctor is evidence that she does *not* have the concept *arthritis*, and, hence, that she cannot have the belief that she has arthritis in her thigh. After all, counterfactual Anna does not have the concept *arthritis because* "arthritis" in the counterfactual community applies by definition to a disease that can occur in muscle (or otherwise outside of joints). So why should actual Anna's belief that "arthritis" applies to (we may suppose) those very muscle ailments not preclude her from having the concept in the actual case? The reason is, Burge argues, that Anna is not, to our knowledge, an abnormal speaker of English, or obviously deceitful, dissembling or deranged; and there is nothing odd about any of her previous "arthritis" utterances. So we should take her utterances at face value: what she says is what she believes; and we should take our own ascriptions at face value as well: what she believes is what we say she believes. There is, as Burge says, "a methodological bias in favor of taking natural discourse literally, other things being equal. . . . Literal interpretation is *ceteris paribus* preferred" (Burge 1979, 88). And we should continue to do this even after we become aware of Anna's misconception, because there is a very strong intuition that the natural and correct way to describe her mistake is to say that she (falsely) believes that she has arthritis in her thigh.

These considerations show that comparison with the counterfactual case is not the crux of Burge's argument. The reasons for thinking that it is literally true that Anna believes that she has arthritis in her thigh, despite her confusion, are themselves reasons for thinking that psychological content can be (and typically is) socially determined. Given that literal interpretation is preferred even in cases of partial understanding, or misunderstanding like Anna's, and that literal meaning is determined socially, it follows that the contents of Anna's thoughts are determined socially. The counterfactual case is meant to reinforce this conclusion by showing that thought content can change with change of linguistic context, without any difference in intrinsic properties of thinkers. But the contrast depends upon having established that actual Anna's thought contents are sociolinguistically determined. The heart of the argument is the explanation of how this works.

A different kind of example is developed in "Intellectual Norms and Foundations of Mind" (Burge 1986). Here we have a subject (I will call him "Andy") who is the victim of neither partial understanding nor misunderstanding with respect to the specimen term ("sofa"). Andy knows the meaning of the word "sofa" in his language. He knows that sofas are by definition pieces of furniture, and he is fully competent in the use of the word. Nonetheless (according to Burge), he doubts that sofas are furniture. Andy has become convinced that they are not furniture, but some sort of artworks or religious artifacts. He expresses his suspicion by saying "Sofas are not pieces of furniture!" He is wrong, however. His belief that sofas are not furniture was formed on the basis of systematically misleading evidence.

In a counterfactual case, in contrast, we are to suppose that a physically identical Andy says something *true* when he utters the sentence "sofas are not pieces of furniture". In the counterfactual language community, the word "sofa" is applied by definition not to pieces of furniture, but to works of art or religious artifacts, just as Andy suspects. When counterfactual Andy says "Sofas are not pieces of furniture!" his utterance, and the belief it expresses, are both true. They do not, however, have the same content as Andy's actual utterances. He counterfactually neither says nor believes that sofas are not pieces of furniture, because "sofa" in the counterfactual community does not mean *sofa*.

The pattern of reasoning in the Andy case is the same as in Anna's: the difference between the contents of actual and counterfactual beliefs is due to the actual and counterfactual meanings of the words uttered, which are determined by factors extrinsic to the speaker. Moreover, the points made above with respect to the role of the intuition about what Anna believes in the actual case, and the comparison to the counterfactual case, apply to Andy's case as well. The comparison of actual Andy and counterfactual Andy is not what establishes the anti-individualist conclusion; it merely dramatizes it.

Further, in Andy's case it is not misunderstanding that is overridden by communal meaning, and which provides the essential contrast to the ordinary case. Andy understands perfectly well what his community takes "sofa" to mean. It is, rather, as Burge says, "nonstandard theory" (1986, 709). Nonetheless, there is an important parallel to Anna's case. Both Anna's and Andy's utterances are *prima facie* conceptually problematic: neither involves a merely empirical divergence from communal standards and belief. Anna's utterance indicates conceptual *confusion*, and Andy's indicates an attempt at conceptual *subversion*. I will characterize what the cases have in common as conceptual *dissonance*. In all of Burge's examples it is the fact that the individuals in question think what they say, in spite of the conceptual dissonance of their utterances, that provides the reason for thinking that the Principle has general application, and that communal linguistic meaning determines mental content.

The inclusion of the *ceteris paribus* clause in the Principle indicates that Burge thinks there *are* conditions under which literal interpretation is not preferred. This might mean that the individuals' words are themselves to be reinterpreted. If there can be cases of mismatch between thought content and linguistic content, then, it remains to be seen what sorts of criteria there are for identifying them. Burge (1978, 134, 1979, 90–91) mentions utterances involving slips of the tongue, spoonerisms, malaprops, and radical misunderstandings as appropriate candidates for reinterpretation. In a parenthetical remark (1979, 91), however, Burge indicates that he thinks utterances involving malaprops or radical misunderstandings are *not* exempt from the Principle. He says that he is "not convinced" that someone who believes that "orangutan" is a word for a fruit drink and says, "An orangutan is a fruit drink" should not therefore be taken to *mean that* an orangutan is a fruit drink and *believe that* an orangutan is a fruit drink.

But it seems that Burge could reject such radical cases and still have an important thesis about the determination of mental content. (He has in fact, in conversation, disavowed the intuition about the orangutan case.) He says (*id.*, 92): "The thought experiment depends only on there being some cases in which a person's incomplete understanding does not force reinterpretation of his expressions in describing his mental contents. Such cases appear to be legion". I take it that Burge means that his argument does not require commitment to the Principle for *every* utterance. Standard practice can call for reinterpretation in cases of linguistic incompetence or momentary lapses without derailing the anti-individualist argument. What the argument requires is cases in which the Principle overrides conceptual dissonance of one kind or another. Conceptual dissonance is a *prima facie* reason for thinking that all things are not equal. This is why Burge stresses that the deviance from community norms is not merely empirical. Mere empirical deviance would not raise the issue of non-literal interpretation, and would therefore not provide the resistance needed to reveal the determinative role of the Principle. Since homophonic interpretation is still preferable in these cases, they do show something interesting and important about psychological content.

But *why* should we think that homophonic interpretation is preferable in these cases? Why is the Principle's *ceteris paribus* clause not sprung by the conceptual oddity of the utterances? The answer constitutes, I think, the very heart of Burge's argument. We do not reinterpret in these cases because of the Intuition about the correct way to describe them is so powerful. Burge (*id.*, fn. 4) says "I used to believe that a fortnight is a period of ten days". He knows that what he used to believe cannot be true; he knows he made a conceptual error. But he describes what he used to think using the very word he did not understand. This is, Burge stresses, the natural and intuitively correct thing to say. But it shows that communal meaning trumps individual misconception in determining the contents of a generally competent speaker's thoughts.

The role of the Burgean Intuitions should now be clear. The Principle applies in these cases in spite of *prima facie* evidence that all things are not equal because of the clear and firm Intuition about the naturalness of our homophonic ascriptions.

The Intuition is undeniable. Nevertheless, I think it is misleading. It cannot be uncritically accepted as evidence that all things are equal in the situations Burge describes. I think there are features of our ordinary belief-ascribing practices that militate against Burge's anti-individualist conclusion. These practices are governed by a principle of charity enjoining ascription of contradictory or incoherent beliefs except, perhaps, in extraordinary circumstances, and also by the principle that utterances betraying linguistic incompetence should not be interpreted literally.

It has been objected to Burge (beginning with Fodor 1982) that all things are not equal in Anna's case because the sentence "she has arthritis in her thigh" is, *by hypothesis*, self-contradictory or conceptually incoherent, and there is a competing principle governing ordinary discourse that says that one's attributions ought to be charitable. The question whether or not Anna has such a belief should be distinguished from the question whether or not we attribute one to her in using a homophonic ascription. If Anna utters the sentence "my arthritis has spread to my thigh", it might be open to question what she actually meant (what she actually thought). But if *we* utter the sentence "Anna believes that she has arthritis in her thigh", then there is no question that the embedded sentence "she has arthritis in her thigh" is *for us* conceptually incoherent. For, again as Burge stresses, Anna's error is not an ordinary empirical one; it is a *conceptual* matter that arthritis cannot occur outside of joints. But given that the kinds of errors Burge describes are common, to suppose that individuals' words should be taken at face value in such cases is to turn a practice of intending to make sense of their behavior (attitude attribution) into a practice that routinely makes nonsense of their mental lives. If this is not our practice, then the kinds of cases Burge describes in "Individualism and the Mental" are ones in which literal interpretation is not preferable, and the conclusion he wants about the contents of thought does not follow from the naturalness of our attributions. The fact that we find it natural to make them in spite of their incoherence no doubt requires an explanation. But if the principle of charity is upheld, it cannot be maintained that we ought to take them to be literally true.[7] It can also be argued that the principle of charity prevents attribution of the belief that sofas are not furniture to Andy since, *by the ascriber's lights*, that belief is conceptually incoherent.

Nonetheless, as strong as the charity objection is, I think it does not really get to the bottom of Burge's argument for anti-individualism. Given the role the examples are supposed to play in the thought experiments, it really is not necessary that they involve the sort of *prima facie* conceptual incoherence Burge's actual examples exhibit. The examples are supposed to illustrate the domineering role of the Principle by presenting it with a serious obstacle to overcome. They are supposed to show that even when an individual's errors raise the specter of reinterpretation, homophonic attribution is completely natural and compelling, and therefore the Principle still applies. I have argued that the Anna and Andy cases run afoul of the principle of charity. But perhaps Burge can accept (because he can explain away) cases in which reinterpretation is forced, because there remain so many cases in which it is not. Giving up the original examples need not spoil the argument for anti-individualism, if there are others that can play the same role. Here is one.

Consider Marge. Marge fancies herself a sophisticate, and often opines upon the finer things in life. On one occasion, she declares "You can tell the quality of a diamond by how many faucets it has". (It is not a slip. When pressed ("*Faucets*?"), Marge does not retract her statement.) If we say that Marge *said that* the quality of a diamond depends on how many faucets it has, it seems clear that what we are saying is literally true. That *is* what she said—what the words she used mean in her language. Moreover, it seems entirely natural to *say that* Marge believes that the quality of a diamond depends on how many faucets it has. Marge is, of course, confused. But we describe her confusion using the very word she misuses, just as we do in the case of Anna. And after she has been corrected

Marge might describe her misstatement using the words she uttered (just as Burge did in the "fortnight" case).

Marge's utterance is sufficiently dissonant to raise suspicions about her competence with the term "faucet", and, hence, to present a *prima facie* obstacle to literal interpretation. But it does not run afoul of the principle of charity. It is certainly odd to say that diamonds have faucets; but it is not conceptually or logically impossible that it be true. (If you look closely and carefully enough, as at Albritton's pencil, you can see the tiny things.) So perhaps this is just the kind of example that Burge needs. It does not involve a contradiction, but neither is it an ordinary empirical error. It is a rather extraordinary one: faucets are bits of plumbing. It is bizarre to think that diamonds have plumbing. Anyone who seriously says so thereby provides *prima facie* evidence of not knowing what a faucet is—of not being competent with the concept *faucet*. However, since the Intuition applies in Marge's case, the Principle ought to apply as well, and Marge ought to have the (our) concept *faucet*, and think that diamonds have them, in spite of her confusion.

But there are strong counterintuitions in cases of this kind. If we reflect, and ask ourselves if Marge really was thinking that diamonds have *faucets*, I think the answer has to be "No". This really is not what she thought. She simply misexpressed herself. She had a false belief about which word to use to say what she was thinking, and that belief led to her anomalous utterance. (Cf. Bach 1988; Crane 1991.) In spite of the fact that the Intuition holds, the *ceteris paribus* clause of the Principle is sprung: all things are not equal in Marge's case, because she is not fully competent with the words she uses.

Since Burge accepts that malaprops are evidence of a lack of the minimal competence required for an individual to be subject to the Principle (1979, 90), he ought to agree that it is not literally true that Marge believes that diamonds have faucets. The crucial point here, however, is that *it is nonetheless intuitively completely natural* to say that this is what she believes. But it is clear that we do not think that our homophonic ascription to Marge is literally true. We know that she meant to say "facets", and that this is what she was actually thinking. So the presence of the Intuition provides no assurance that we should apply the Principle in spite of a speaker's errors. But Burge's argument for anti-individualism depends on this: naturalness of homophonic ascription is supposed to overpower any inclination to reinterpret. Cases of this type show that the Intuitions concern only what it is natural to *say*, since, on reflection, we do not take our ascriptions to be literally true. The Intuitions do not prevent the *ceteris paribus* clause of the Principle from being sprung.

Insofar, then, as Brian's case for a socially determined kind of belief content relies on Burgean Intuitions, his two-factor theory of content is unmotivated. An internalist need not (and should not) recognize two kinds of intentional content.

## 2. Phenomenal Intentionality

In "Phenomenal Intentionality as the Basis of Mental Content", Brian says that

> Internal intentionality is to be located primitively in perceptually based concepts. It will be derivatively located in nonperceptual concepts via their conceptual connections with perceptual concepts. The subjective intentional properties of nonperceptual concepts are always a matter of, as it were, looking sideways via their connections with perceptual concepts.
>
> (Loar 2003b, 2017, 310; page number references in this section are to this work)

These foundational, perceptually based concepts include *singular perceptual demonstratives*, which pick out individuals, *perceptual recognitional concepts*, which are "demonstrative concepts that purport to pick out, perceptually, kinds and properties" (*ibid.*), "certain general concepts of approximate spatial relations, shapes, and the like, and a certain conception of a three-dimensional object as it persists over time" (313). The intentional content of these concepts, their "directedness" toward particular objects, properties and relations (whether or not they refer), is derived from the directedness of perceptual experience—the experience *as of* objects, properties, and relations, which is itself determined by perceptual phenomenology. The intentional content of perceptual experience is an intrinsic feature of its phenomenology, and is determined entirely independently of relations to external objects and properties. Perceptual concepts inherit their intentional contents from perceptions, and nonperceptual ("systematic" or "theoretical") concepts acquire theirs in virtue of their inferential relations with them—their conceptual roles. All internal mental intentionality, therefore, is derived from the intentionality of perception.

I have two problems with Brian's view. The first is with the notion of a *perceptual concept*. I do not think this is workable. Perceptual concepts, as Brian understands them, *incorporate* perceptions:

> The feature [the directedness of visual demonstrative concepts] presumably belongs primarily to a visual perception, and derivatively to a visual demonstrative concept that incorporates the perception.
>
> (302)[8]

I do not think it is possible for concepts to incorporate percepts. Concepts and percepts are fundamentally distinct and incompatible kinds of mental entities, and cannot be combined in such a way that their amalgamation constitutes a *concept*. We can have concepts *of* (*referring to*) perceptual experiences; but the internal intentional contents of these concepts are not individuated with respect to the percepts they are of, by incorporation or otherwise.[9]

I also want to take issue with Brian's account of a particular kind of perceptual concept, *recognitional* concepts. I do not think these kinds of concepts exist either, and not just because concepts cannot contain perceptions. There are no, in my view, and cannot be, concepts of the kind that Brian places at the foundation of mental intentionality.

My second problem with Brian's view is that it is too conservative about what kinds of phenomenology there are. In recognizing only familiar sensory kinds of phenomenology, Brian limits the possibilities of his internalism, and its effectiveness in giving a general account of conceptual content. An experiential theory of conceptual content that restricts phenomenality to sensory experience inherits the notorious difficulties of the Empiricist program in coping with non-perceptual concepts.[10] It does not have the resources to explain non-sensory intentionality. I do not think the inclusion of conceptual roles can remedy the situation, unless non-sensory phenomenology is somehow thereby smuggled in.

I develop these objections in the next two sections.

### 2.1. Perceptual Concepts

It is traditional to make a sharp distinction between concepts and percepts, thought and perception, sapience and sentience. I think there are powerful intuitions supporting this distinction, and that these two kinds of mentality must always be kept strictly separated in theorizing about the mind. Though there may be total conscious occurrent states containing concepts and percepts, percepts cannot be parts of concepts, and concepts cannot be parts of percepts. The tendency to blur the distinction comes, it seems to me, from a commitment (tacit or explicit) to the idea that the content of a concept must determine what, in general or in particular, it purports to refer to. This is especially so in the case of indexicals and demonstratives.

Intuitively, my thoughts *this is an unpleasant sensation* directed at two different sensory experiences on two separate occasions, are different thoughts. They are about different sensations, differ in their truth conditions, and may differ in truth value; so, the standard argument goes, they must have different contents. And it seems the only way to explain this is to assign different contents to the two tokens of *this*. One way to do this is to incorporate sensations into the token demonstrative concepts. It is also often remarked that in order to understand an experiential concept, one must have had the relevant experience. For example, a congenitally blind person could not have the concept *red*. To understand red, to cognitively grasp the concept *red*, one must experience red. This suggests that the experience is somehow intimately involved with the concept—perhaps as a constituent of it.

Another source of this tendency, it seems to me, is a bias toward approaching the study of mentality from the third-person perspective—particularly from the point of view of our practices of attribution and communication. If you want to tell someone what I said when I said, "This is an unpleasant sensation"—if you want them to understand what I said—you cannot just leave it at repeating my words. Many have the intuition that if the third party has no idea what sort of sensation I was referring to, she will not really (or not completely) understand what I said. The attributor/communicator must supplement the content of the demonstrative "this sensation" in such a way as to direct the hearer's attention on the relevant kind of sensation.[11] But these practical requirements of third-person attribution and communication can be met without shoehorning identifying content into demonstrative concepts. The relevant information can be communicated separately.

Moreover, one need not accept that *grasping concepts of* phenomenal properties requires experiencing them. I once knew someone who was born without a sense of smell. After many conversations with her, I realized that her grasp of the *concept* of olfactory experience was no different from mine. We would say the same thing if we were asked to explain what it *is*: it is a kind of sensory experience, as different from others as they are from each other, involving the nose, often confused with taste (she did not fail to notice that other people enjoyed food a lot more than she did), etc., etc. In contrast, knowing *what smelling is like* in general (knowing *what it is like* to have olfactory experience), or what, in particular, *lavender* smells like—does require experience. However, I maintain that this kind of knowledge is not *conceptual* at all.[12]

But why (people keep asking me) can we not just say that perceptual (phenomenal) concepts are "hybrids", like (on some views) emotions, consisting of sensory and cognitive components? As I said above, nothing prevents the occurrence of complex occurrent states of consciousness comprising sensory and cognitive components; but I insist that there cannot be *cognitive* components that themselves incorporate perceptual ones, nor *perceptual* components that incorporate cognitive ones. This is not a quibble about how to use the word "concept". It is an insistence that we recognize the fundamental differences among different kinds of mental states, and the impossibility of their combining in such a way as to produce a state that is of one kind, but not the other.

It is clear that there cannot be cross-modal *sensory* incorporations. One's total conscious state may include simultaneous auditory and olfactory experiences; but there can be no sounds parts of which are smells, or smells parts of which are sounds. This is simply impossible. Phenomenologies do not mix *in this way*.[13]

I think this is true of cross-categorical (sensory/cognitive) incorporations as well.

My tendentious reason for believing this, which I will defend shortly, is that occurrent concepts (and thoughts) are themselves experiences, of a unique *sui generis*, cognitive kind, and that, therefore, the Principle of Phenomenal Immiscibility applies to them, with respect to any other kind of experience. Sounds cannot have smells in them, and neither can concepts—for the same reason.

But there are also good non-tendentious, intuitive reasons for resisting cross-categorical incorporation even if one denies that there is conceptual phenomenology. The traditional distinction between the two kinds of mind—sentient and sapient—is, I think, based on our own experience. It seems clear, from the subjective point of view, that thinking is different from sensing. We recognize that they are different kinds of mental activity, and that we can engage in one without engaging in the other. Further, we find it conceivable that there are creatures who can sense but cannot think, and creatures who can think but cannot sense. But if one can sense without thinking, and *vice versa*, it must be that percepts and concepts are, metaphysically, different kinds of things.

Another strong intuitive reason for resisting conceptual-sensory assimilation is this. Concepts (conceptual contents) must be *thinkable*; but percepts (and images) are not. It is nonsense, a category mistake, to say that what you were *thinking* (or part of what you were thinking) was, e.g., *the taste of cinnamon*, or *the sound of a piano*. It is true that you can think *about* these experiences, but only in the sense that you can have otherwise-content-individuated concepts that refer to them. Concepts must be capable of being *thought*, in the course of thinking a complete thought of which they are constituents. But sensory experiences cannot be thought. One can no more think the taste of cinnamon than one can hear it. (Nor, for that matter, can one think physical objects and properties—trendy Continentalisms like "How do you think Derrida?" notwithstanding. This is a reason for rejecting certain widespread accounts of the contents of singular thoughts.) If these intuitions are sound, then there can be no perceptual concepts, as Brian understands them.

I also think there are no recognitional concepts, as Brian understands them, though for different reasons. Recognition, in my view, essentially involves a particular kind of nonconceptual experience—a feeling of familiarity. The application of a demonstrative concept (*that feeling*) to a familiar experience is not what makes it familiar; nor is a demonstrative concept individuated by the experience it is applied to. A person with perfect pitch does not have a different concept of middle C from me. The fact that she instantly identifies the pitch when she hears it does not make her concept different from mine. What is different between us is her infallibly correct application of it on the basis of her experience of it. Her experience of middle C is like my experience of red: I recognize red on sight; she recognizes middle C on hearing. But I do not think I have a different concept of red from someone who is color blind, or totally blind.

Now, it might be wondered why it should matter to Brian if there are no perceptual concepts (as he understands them). Perhaps conceptual incorporation of percepts is not a necessary feature of his view: perceptual experience could be a foundation for conceptual intentionality without incorporation. I agree that incorporation is not necessary (for me, because impossible) for a phenomenal theory of intentionality. But I think it is essential to Brian's account, on which the intentionality of all concepts is derived from the intentionality of perceptual experience.

For Brian, content cannot arise from inferential relations among concepts, since, for him, thinking is "something lively—there is something it is like to engage in it", whereas conceptual roles on their own are "too *blank* to constitute internal mental content as we perceive it"—because they are "purely dispositional" (296). There is a phenomenology of thinking; but there is no phenomenology of dispositional states. Conceptual roles are "central in individuating thought contents" (*ibid.*), but they cannot be *sources* of contents, since they are not phenomenal.

Furthermore, a view on which non-intentional conceptual roles are "phenomenalized" by inclusion of pure, non-intentional perceptual states—which are, in their turn, thereby "conceptualized" (i.e., *intentionalized*)—is, according to Brian, not available. Sensory phenomenology is inseparable from its intentionality ("We can hardly peel the phenomenal aspects of [e.g.] vision away from its intentionality" (297)). The phenomenalization of conceptual roles would, necessarily, simultaneously be their intentionalization. And since (as it seems Brian assumes) there is only sensory phenomenology, sensory (perceptual) states are the only source of intentionality.

Finally, given that phenomenal properties are intrinsic, phenomenal concepts cannot get their content from extrinsic relations to sensory states, including reference. Brian thinks psychological contents are not individuated by external referential relations. But if he thinks this because he thinks that content is phenomenal, and phenomenology is intrinsic, then he ought to accept it for internal reference as well. Phenomenal concepts (including recognitional concepts) are not individuated by phenomenal states in virtue of referring to them. They must incorporate them. This is, on Brian's theory, the only way to *conceptualize* sensory phenomenal intentionality. The content of a concept is internally determined. This does not just mean that it is determined by features internal to thinkers: it is determined by features internal to concepts themselves.

To close this section, I want to identify what seems to me a significant tension between Brian's claims that conceptual roles are "too blank to constitute internal mental content", and that they are "central in individuating thought contents" (296). I think what Brian has in mind is that position in a conceptual network is not in itself sufficient to confer content: the interconnected concepts must have independently derived content. It cannot be that *every* concept derives its contents from its inferential connections to other concepts. There must be a foundation of *intrinsically* contentful concepts.

However, it is not clear that relatedness to other concepts can *constitute* the content of a concept if phenomenology is both intrinsic and conceptually foundational. In general, the phenomenal character of a state will not be altered by causal connections (dispositional or manifest) with other states. Nor, therefore, will its content. (Phenomenal context effects are not to the point here.) At best, then, it seems that tracing connections to other concepts will enable individuation only in an *epistemic* sense: the intrinsic content of a concept can be revealed, if it is not immediately available to introspection, in its inferential connections to other concepts.

## 2.2. Conceptual Phenomenology

My tendentious explanation for the intuitive facts appealed to above about what is thinkable and not, is that thinking is a distinctive kind of experience, and that different kinds of experience are individuated by their different kinds of phenomenology. Thinking is not the same kind of experience as seeing, hearing, smelling, tasting, and so on. So thinking must have its very own brand of phenomenology—a phenomenology which I have elsewhere (Pitt 2004) characterized as *proprietary*, *distinctive* and *individuative*. Experiential modes in general are distinguished phenomenally. Vision, audition, olfaction, gustation, etc. are modes of experiencing, and each is constituted by its own proprietary kind of determinable phenomenology (visual, auditory, olfactory, gustatory, . . .). Hence, there is a proprietary determinable phenomenology for thought—what I have called (Pitt 2004) "cognitive" phenomenology ("conceptual" and "propositional" phenomenology will do as well). And just as there are differences *within* each kind of sensory phenomenology that distinguish them from others of the same general kind (e.g., green percepts from yellow percepts), there are differences within conceptual phenomenology that distinguish conceptual contents from each other. There are cognitive, as well as sensory, determinables and determinates. Moreover, on this view, the various determinate cognitive phenomenologies *are* intentional contents (Pitt 2009).

So, for the same reason that there cannot be sounds with smells as constituents, there cannot be concepts with smells as constituents. Furthermore, just as sounds cannot be individuated with respect to smells, phenomenal concepts cannot be individuated with respect to their non-conceptual referents. The contents of my concept *that smell* do not change depending upon which smell I am attending (referring) to.[14]

I have both epistemic and metaphysical reasons for believing that there is a proprietary, distinctive, individuative phenomenology of thought content.[15] Briefly, the epistemic reason (developed in Pitt 2004, 2009) is that there is available to us a mode of access to the contents of our conscious occurrent thoughts—viz., introspective and non-inferential—that would not be available to us if occurrent conscious thought contents were not distinctively presented to us in conscious experience. In general, discriminatory non-inferential introspective awareness of occurrent conscious states requires that the states accessed be differentiated *in consciousness*—that is, they must be introspectively distinguishable and identifiable as the states they are. (This is analogous to the role that distinguishability and identifiability of objective properties plays in purely perceptual discrimination.) But differentiation in consciousness is entirely a matter of difference of phenomenology. Thus, we can be non-inferentially introspectively aware that we are experiencing a pain, and not a smell or a sound, that the pain is burning, and not achy or slashing, or that it has gotten worse, because pain experiences have proprietary, distinctive, individuative phenomenologies. And we can be non-inferentially introspectively aware *that* we are thinking, and not feeling pain or hearing a sound or smelling a smell, and that we are thinking about covalent bonding, and not about beer, or the end of American democracy. But if conscious thoughts can be thus discriminated from other conscious states (or events) and identified as the thoughts they are, introspectively and non-inferentially, they too must have proprietary, distinctive, individuative phenomenologies, which constitute their intentional contents.

This is a transcendental argument: a certain kind of access to conscious occurrent thought content is possible (which is not to say either that it is infallible or that it is the only kind of access we can have to our thoughts); but it would not be possible if there were no proprietary, distinctive, individuative phenomenology of thought; hence, there is such phenomenology.

The metaphysical reason (developed in Pitt 2011) focuses on the fact that conscious states in general are, *qua conscious*, phenomenally individuated. What distinguishes conscious smells from conscious sounds is their distinctive kinds of phenomenologies (olfactory and auditory). Hence, if conscious thoughts are not conscious sights, smells, sounds, . . ., then they must have their own kind of phenomenology that constitutes their determinable phenomenal kind. And if the thought that yttrium conducts electricity is a different thought than the thought that robots are stealing our luggage, then, like the taste of honey and the taste of ashes, they must have different determinate phenomenologies.

Now, Brian claims that not all contents of occurrent conscious concepts (hence, thoughts) are immediately accessible in introspection. This is, for example, true of what he calls "systematic" or "personal theoretical" concepts, such as *mother*, *female*, and *child*:

> We do not take in the intentional properties of a systematic concept all at once. . . . We do so rather by finding our way about among a systematic concept's lateral interconceptual connections. . . . The

> phenomenological world-directedness of a personal theoretical concept, I want to propose here, derives from its intimate conceptual connections with perceptual intentionality. . . . So the idea that every concept can be revealed in an introspective glance, or even in an introspective stare, is not essential to the defense of internal, phenomenological, intentionality.
>
> (Loar 2003b, 2017, 315)

But it cannot be the case that *all* concepts are systematic in this way. Some must wear their contents on their face. Otherwise, given Brian's rejection of the idea that sheer relatedness—blank conceptual roles—can confer content, the search for intentional properties would be viciously circular. And the question is whether these "facial" contents can all be sensory.

The history of failed attempts to construct an empiricist psychosemantics strongly suggests that they cannot. It is highly doubtful that a theory that relies on sensory phenomenology as the ultimate source of all intentional content can account for the contents of, for example, philosophical, mathematical and logical concepts and beliefs. The concept of objective causal necessity cannot (as Hume showed) be derived from experience, either introspective or extrospective, which only presents us with the way things are, and not how they must or cannot be. (This led Hume to deny that we have any such concept, redirecting the term "necessity" to experiences of constant conjunction and expectation.) Nor do concepts like *transfinite ordinal, least convergent series*, *infinitesimal*, *entailment*, *logical necessity,* and *possible world* have sensory contents. And it is not obvious that how the contents of such concepts can be generated by inferential connections to sensory concepts.

Moreover, even if sensory experience provides occasions for the formation of such concepts, it cannot confer their contents upon them. One might form a general geometrical concept like *triangle* in response to sensory experiences of a variety of physical representations; but, as has been long observed, general triangularity is not represented by any particular sensory experience (and not least because there are no experienceable triangles). The contents of concepts (the conceptual machinery) needed to form a general concept on the basis of sensory experiences are not themselves to be found in those experiences, all of which are particular. Nor do they arise from the connections particular concepts bear to each other. What is *understood* when we grasp abstract philosophical, logical and mathematical concepts is not sensory, and cannot be reduced to the sensory.

To accommodate these facts, a phenomenally-based theory of content must recognize a non-sensory cognitive phenomenology, in addition to sensory phenomenology. Moreover, given the impossibility of sensory incorporation, cognitive phenomenology must be taken to constitute *all* distinctively *conceptual* intentional content. (This is not to deny that sensory experiences have *nonconceptual* intentionality.) Insofar as Brian's theory does not recognize this kind of phenomenology, it is, in my view, compromised. It is not yet a theory that a Phenomenal Intentionalist should be satisfied with.

## Notes

1. Loar (1976, 1987, 1988, 1991, 1995, 1997, 2003a, 2003b).
2. Where a cited paper is reprinted in Loar 2017, page number references are to that volume.
3. I have not seen this remark in print. I heard Fodor make it, and Strawson reports it in his 2008.
4. I challenge the standard semantics of singular terms (proper names and indexicals), as applied to the theory of mental intentionality, in book *The Quality of Thought* (under contract with Oxford University Press).
5. I set aside here the complication that an ascriber's concept need not match the concept expressed in his language by the term he uses.
6. This section is adapted from a much longer and more detailed discussion of Burge in *The Quality of Thought.*
7. I discuss Burge's response to this objection, which I think is inadequate, in *The Quality of Thought.*
8. See also Loar 1997.
9. I have in mind here accounts on which phenomenal concepts are individuated referentially. Referential individuation is as problematic for internally directed concepts as it is for externally directed ones. Externalism is just one form of referentialism (extensionalism). (Cf. Farkas 2008, 77–79.)
10. I also believe that Brian's account of *reference* as an external, causal (as opposed to descriptive) relation will run into problems with (at least some) concepts of abstract objects. I develop this objection in *The Quality of Thought.*
11. Analogous considerations are often appealed to in the case of proper names (and indexicals). For example, I will not understand what you said when you said "Don is totally bogus" if I do not know who Don is—which Don you are referring to; and you must somehow supplement the name in such a way as to get me on to the right one. And neither will *you* understand what you said, or succeed in thinking a thought, if you cannot supply a referent (Evans 1982, 74).
12. I elaborate and defend this nonconceptual account of knowing what it is like, what Earl Conee (1994) calls "phenomenal knowledge" (I call it "acquaintance knowledge") in my forthcoming paper "Acquaintance and Phenomenal Concepts".
13. This is what I call the *Principle of Phenomenal Immiscibility.* To say that oil and water are immiscible is not to say that there cannot be a collection of water molecules and oil droplets in suspension. Oil and water can be mixed in *that* sense. But oil droplets cannot be partially composed of $H_2O$ molecules, and $H_2O$ molecules cannot have oil droplets as constituents.
14. I present and defend a cognitive-phenomenal account of the contents of indexical and demonstrative concepts in chapter four of *The Quality of Thought.*
15. This should be carefully distinguished from the thesis that there are proprietary phenomenologies for the various propositional *attitudes*, which may in fact be individuated by psychological roles. Cognitive phenomenology is the phenomenology of *content*—a *conceptual/propositional* phenomenology.

## References

Bach, K. 1988. "Burge's New Thought Experiment: Back to the Drawing Room," *Journal of Philosophy* 85, 88–97.

Burge, T. 1978. "Belief and Synonymy," *Journal of Philosophy* 75, 119–138.

Burge, T. 1979. "Individualism and the Mental," *Midwest Studies in Philosophy* 4, 73–121.

Burge, T. 1982. "Other Bodies," in A. Woodfield, ed., *Thought and Object*, Oxford University Press, 97–121.

Burge, T. 1986. "Intellectual Norms and Foundations of Mind," *Journal of Philosophy* 83, 697–720.

Conee, E. 1994. "Phenomenal Knowledge," *Australasian Journal of Philosophy* 72, 136–150.

Crane, T. 1991. "All the Difference in the World," *Philosophical Quarterly* 41, 1–25.

Evans, G. 1982. *The Varieties of Reference*, Oxford University Press.

Farkas, K. 2008. *The Subject's Point of View*, Oxford University Press.

Fodor, J. A. 1982. "Cognitive Science and the Twin-Earth Problem," *Notre Dame Journal of Formal Logic* 23, 98–118.

Horgan, T. and J. Tienson. 2002. "The Intentionality of Phenomenology and the Phenomenology of Intentionality," in D. J. Chalmers, ed., *Philosophy of Mind: Classical and Contemporary Readings* Oxford University Press, 520–533.

Loar, B. 1976. "The Semantics of Singular Terms," *Philosophical Studies* 30, 353–77.

Loar, B. 1987. "Subjective Intentionality," *Philosophical Topics* 1, 89–124.

Loar, B. 1988. "Social Content and Psychological Content," in R. H. Grimm and D. D. Merrill, eds., *Contents of Thought: Proceedings of the 1985 Oberlin Colloquium in Philosophy*, University of Arizona Press, 99–110.

Loar, B. 1991. "Can We Explain Intentionality?," in B. Loewer and G. Rey, eds., *Meaning in Mind: Fodor and His Critics*, Blackwell, 199–136.

Loar, B. 1995. "Reference from the First-Person Perspective," *Philosophical Issues: Content 6, Ridgeview Publishing Company*, 53–72.

Loar, B. 1997. "Phenomenal States: Second Version," in N. Block, O. Flanagan and G. Güzeldere, eds., *The Nature of Consciousness: Philosophical Debates*, MIT Press, 597–616.

Loar, B. 2003a. "Transparent Experience and the Availability of Qualia," in Q. Smith and A. Jokic, eds., *Consciousness: New Philosophical Perspectives*, Oxford University Press, 77–96.

Loar, B. 2003b. "Phenomenal Intentionality as the Basis of Mental Content," in M. Hahn and B. Ramberg, eds., *Reflections and Replies: Essays on the Philosophy of Tyler Burge*, MIT Press/Bradford Books, 229–257.

Loar, B. 2017. *Consciousness and Meaning: Selected Essays*, K. Balog and S. Beardman, eds., Oxford University Press.

Pitt, D. 2004. "The Phenomenology of Cognition, Or, *What Is It Like to Think That P?*," *Philosophy and Phenomenological Research* 1, 1–36.

Pitt, D. 2009. "Intentional Psychologism," *Philosophical Studies* 146, 117–138.

Pitt, D. 2011. "Introspection, Phenomenality, and the Availability of Intentional Content," in T. Bayne and M. Montague, eds., *Cognitive Phenomenology*, Oxford University Press, 141–73.

Pitt, D. Forthcoming. "Acquaintance and Phenomenal Concepts," in S. Coleman, ed., *Cambridge Classic Arguments Series: The Knowledge Argument*, Cambridge University Press.

# 10 Loar on Lemons

## The Particularity of Perception and Singular Perceptual Content

*Mark Sainsbury*

This paper advances two claims. The positive claim offers a correctness condition for perceptual experiences, one that does justice to the so-called "particularity of perception":

(T1) the perceptual content of a perceptual experience is correct iff there are perceived objects of which it is non-accidentally true.

The negative claim is that, subject to a qualification entered later (§7):

(T2) There is no singular perceptual content,

where singular content can be defined as follows:

> A representational vehicle has singular content iff there is a unique object it rigidly designates.[1]

The claims are connected by the idea that (T1) shows that we *do not need* to posit singular perceptual content in order to do justice to the particularity of perception, and (T2) shows that in any case we *could not* use singular content in that way.

I shall assume that to perceive is to represent, and that we perceive, track, and count individual objects. These premises do not entail that there are perceptual representational vehicles with singular content. The distinction between qualitative and numerical identity is available conceptually, but not perceptually. Perceptual representation is not sensitive to numerical identity, and this blocks it from having singular representational content. I reach this conclusion in the light of Brian Loar's rich and suggestive discussion in "Phenomenal intentionality as the basis of mental content".[2]

I'll begin by showing, in §1, how the issues to be discussed have been distorted by the implicit assumption that there are just two kinds of content: general content, corresponding conceptually to quantified content, and singular content, corresponding conceptually to the content possessed by singular demonstrative concepts or proper nominal concepts. By contrast, I'll suggest that there is at least one other kind of content, alluded to in (T1) above, which I call "feature-expressing". Although I will have to use linguistic predicates in order to point towards feature-expressing contents, this should not be taken as an endorsement of the view that perceptual representational vehicles are predicate-like, or indeed in any way language-like. In (§2), I'll show that measuring instruments are appropriately associated with feature-expressing correctness conditions on the lines of (T1). This will give those who see value in the comparison between perceptual systems and measuring instruments a reason to accept (T1).[3] In the remainder of the paper I offer direct arguments for (T1) and (T2), starting in §3 by recalling Loar's example of the shifting lemons. Subsequent sections amplify some related theoretical issues, and the final section offers a qualification of some earlier claims, and has something to say about the nature of feature-expressing contents.

## 1. Feature-Expressing Content

Perceptual experiences have representational content. I take this widely-held thesis for granted.[4] More controversial is the nature of this content. We experience particular things, trees, people, chairs. Representationalists about perception may well suppose that we have perceptual representational vehicles with singular content: their nature is to rigidly designate just one individual object and not anything else. Not only is this a natural view, there are arguments which apparently make it compulsory. Salient among these are mirror cases, which go back to Grice (1961); similar examples have been sympathetically discussed more recently by Soteriou (2000: 180) and Tye (2018) among others. In Grice's example, I am standing in front of one of several pillars. An angled mirror obscures the pillar straight ahead of me, reflecting the image of an indistinguishable pillar off to one side. Despite the correspondence between the qualitative aspects of my experience and a pillar straight ahead, it is intuitive that some kind of error has occurred. In some sense, I undergo misrepresentation: my perceptual content is inaccurate. The example shows that the content of my perception cannot only be purely general, for example expressible by "There's a pillar ahead", since this content is true. A frequently made suggestion is that there is singularity in the content. It is more like "That pillar is ahead" (as in Burge 1991; McDowell 1991: 266–267). We cannot understand "that pillar" as referring to the one in front of me, since I am visually isolated from it. If the content corresponding to "that pillar" is true of anything, it is true of the reflected pillar off to the side, rather than straight ahead, so the total content is not true, so my experience is mistaken; and this intuitively is the right result.

Arguments against existentially general content favor singular content only if these are the only alternatives.[5] But they are not. Examples like the pillar show beyond doubt that the content is not merely existentially quantified. But this does not establish that the content is singular, for there are forms of content that are neither existentially quantified nor singular. One example of such content is the feature-expressing content that figures in (T1). These contents can properly be said to be, or fail to be, true *of* objects, and they are linguistically expressed by predicates or open sentences. They are properties or features, and taken by themselves they are not evaluable as true or false. According to (T1), perceptual representations that express features as contents are central to perceiving. The work supposedly done by singular perceptual content is instead done by the causal relation between a perceiver and something perceived.[6]

The correctness condition stated by (T1) is, in a sense, object-involving: a perceptual experience is correct iff there are objects of which its content is correct. This might seem to lead right away to the conclusion that some perceptual content is singular, but the transition would be confused: (T1) makes no mention of any perceptual representational vehicles with singular content. According to (T1), the particularity of perception is ensured by perceiving particulars, not by deploying singular contents.

(T1) provides a starting point for the usual distinctions between veridical, illusory and hallucinatory experience. A veridical experience is one with perceived satisfiers of its content; an illusory experience is one with perceived objects which fail to satisfy the content; a fully hallucinatory experience involves no perceived objects.

Applied to the pillar case, (T1) gives the intuitively correct result. The pillar straight ahead is not perceived, so it cannot enter the correctness condition stated by (T1). The pillar to one side is perceived (at least, on many views), but it does not satisfy the feature-expressing perceptual content *is straight ahead*. (T1) correctly rules the perceptual experience to be mistaken, but does not attribute singular content.

## 2. Measuring Instruments

A car's gas gauge represents the level of gas in the tank.[7] It represents correctly just if the fuel in the connected tank is at the level represented. The gauge contains no proprietary representation of the tank itself, no representational vehicle whose reference is the tank. The needle does not specifically represent the tank, nor does its position on the dial do so, nor does the dial or its markings. The very same gauge, with its needle in the same position, would represent the level of the gas in a different tank were it properly connected to that tank rather than to the tank it is actually connected to. If the needle points to a position marked "1/2", we should view the gauge's proprietary content as something like *is half full*, correct iff true of the connected tank, that is, iff that tank is half full. A gas gauge not connected to a tank does not have a correct content (and perhaps not an incorrect one either). In summary:

(T3) A measuring instrument measures correctly, on an occasion, iff there is suitably causally related object of which the measurement is non-accidentally true.

Just as the gauge contains no representational vehicle that refers to the connected tank, perceptual experience contains no representational vehicle that refers to perceived objects. This does not prevent a state of the gauge from being evaluated as correct or incorrect relative to a properly connected gas tank; likewise, it does not prevent a perceptual state from being evaluated as correct or incorrect relative to perceived objects. In both cases, an object involved in the correctness condition is one related by a suitable causal and information-carrying link to the representational system.

A feature-expressing content like *is half full* lacks truth conditions, and so is neither true nor false. We can make sentential attributions of content to measuring instruments, saying for example that the gauge represents *that* the tank is half full. The attributed content is true or false, depending on whether the connected tank is or is not half full. Different elements of the attributed truth conditional content arise in different ways. The position of the needle is a representational *vehicle*; how the gauge is calibrated determines its representational *content*. Some gauges are calibrated so that having the needle in the vertical position means *full*, others so that the same position means *half full*. The gauge has no tank-specific representational vehicle; the tank enters the correctness condition by being suitably connected to the gauge. The gauge has no internal feature specific to that gas tank. The truth conditional content is hybrid, determined in part by a content for which the gauge has a specific vehicle, and in part by the gauge's relation to its surroundings. The separability of these elements of the hybrid is shown by what an intrinsically unchanged gauge would represent if connected to another tank.

The thermometer reads 85°. If its tip is in your coffee, it represents the temperature of your coffee. But it has no representational vehicle related to your coffee. It knows nothing of you or of coffee. Its representational vehicles are the positions of the indicator liquid and the associated markings. If the top of the liquid is alongside "85", and the calibration is for Fahrenheit, the content *is* 85° F. If the thermometer is correctly calibrated, that is, if its vehicles have contents that vary systematically with temperatures surrounding the tip, we can infer that the region surrounding the tip is at 85° F. The correctness condition does not require the content to contain an element dedicated to representing that region. Moving the thermometer elsewhere does not in itself change its specific representational contents. There is also a truth conditional attribution to be had: in the envisaged circumstances, the thermometer represents *that* your coffee is at 85° F. This propositional representation is achieved by the union of dissimilar means. The temperature is explicitly and internally represented by the level of the liquid. Its attribution to your coffee comes from a causal fact external to the thermometer itself: its tip is in your coffee.

If one of your perceptual states involves the content *is a green apple*, then intuitively, and by (T1), it is correct just if you are perceiving a green apple. There may also be sentential attributions to be had, for example: you see that the apple before you is green. This attributes a true or false content. But, as in the case of instruments, the content is hybrid. The *is a green apple* element is an intrinsic feature of the perceptual state, a content for which the state has a specific vehicle. Correctness is measured by whether this content is true of something perceived. This view of perception is encouraged by the analogs with instruments. Later, I provide a direct argument for it.

## 3. Loar's Lemons

Content is a theorist's notion, and its use must be justified by the role it plays in a theoretical account of the subject matter. Alleged intuitions about content stand in need of justification in terms of theoretical utility. If it is not theoretically useful to ascribe a content to something, we should not regard that thing as possessing content. In the case of perception, one would expect singular perceptual content, if there is such a thing, to make a difference either to phenomenology or to causal role. But in fact, it is hard to see how it could make a difference to either.

Many people (including myself) would be happy to accept the following principle connecting phenomenal character and content:

(T4) Experiences with subjectively the same phenomenal character have the same representational content.[8]

There is a straightforward argument from (T4) to (T2), the claim that there is no singular perceptual content. One experience might be subjectively indistinguishable from another, even if a perceived object in one is replaced by an indistinguishable perceived object in the other. This indistinguishability suggests identity of phenomenal character (or so many will assume—but see footnote 10 below). If there were singular perceptual content, it would differ in such cases, involving one of the indistinguishable objects in one case, the other in the other; and this is inconsistent with (T4).

However, (T4) is controversial, and so I cannot rely upon it. Indeed, the argumentative direction might be reversed: subjectively indistinguishable experiences intuitively have different correctness conditions if they involve different objects. It might seem that only by appeal to different singular contents can this fact be accommodated. And this would be inconsistent with (T4).

Another relevant principle connects causal role and content, and many theorists would find it appealing. This version is owed to Neander (2017: 192):

(T5) Differences in sensory-perceptual contents must be accompanied by differences in the internal causal roles of the relevant representations.

Perceptions of duplicates at different moments would not differ in their narrow causal role, and so (T5) would rule that they do not differ in content, which in turn means that these are not cases of singular perceptual content.

The conjunction of (T4) and (T5) makes a powerful package. Both exclude singular perceptual content, but if such content makes no difference either to phenomenology or to narrow functional role, serious doubt is cast on its explanatory value. Given the theoretical nature of content, to say that singular perceptual content has no explanatory value is to say that there is no such thing.

The remaining possibility is that singular perceptual content makes a difference to wide functional role. This might enable one to register in perception a specific member of one's own family or a specific location, and these would be valuable abilities. But (T1) shows that an explanation of them in terms of content is unnecessary: instead, an explanation based on which objects are perceived works fine. And the purely qualitative nature of the senses makes it impossible for them to register genuinely singular content, for they cannot register distinct duplicates in distinct ways.

These abstract reflections can be made vivid by considering Loar's notion of "singular visual directedness", which he illustrates with an example of successive lemon-experiences:

> Suppose some indistinguishable lemons are one after the other brought to my visual attention. The lighting, the position of my eyes and so on, are all held constant. I am asked to think something about each lemon in turn, say, "that's yellow". Afterwards I am told that some of the apparent lemons were hallucinations.
>
> ... Those visual demonstrative concepts, and the perceptions that underlie them, are all *singularly visually directed*.
>
> (2003: 302)

The example might be simplified and diagrammed as follows:

| *time* | t1 | t2 | t3 |
|---|---|---|---|
| *content*[9] | ℓ1 | ℓ2 | ℓ3 |
| *object* | lemon 1 | lemon 2 | |

The experience at t1 has content ℓ1 and lemon 1 is the object perceived; analogously for the experience at t2. The experience at t3 has content ℓ3, but no lemon is perceived: it is a hallucination of a lemon. In all three cases, the predicative element of the representational content is the same, namely *is yellow*. I will assume (I think in accordance with Loar's intention) that the subject is not aware, at the time, of the switch from one lemon to another, so there is no subjectively accessible difference of phenomenal character.[10]

Loar says that in all three experiences we have singular visual directedness, making plain that singular visual directedness does not require an object: it's enough that all the experiences "purport to pick out some object visually" (302).[11] Although experiences that differ in radical ways might share the property of singular directedness, it seems that for the lemon cases Loar has in mind something much more specific: the very same narrowest type of visual directedness is present in all three cases, in that the phenomenal character of all three both seems and is the same.

Loar clearly supposes that perceptual content will expressed by both singular and predicative elements. What should we say about the representational content of the envisaged singular element? I argue that there is no satisfying answer.

The two options worth discussing both treat it in a uniform way, either as in each case the same or as in each case different:

(a) the singular content is unchanged through t1 to t3.
(b) the singular content is different at each of the three times.

Option (a) cannot be correct: evidently the three cases have different correctness conditions, and if this is to be determined by content, there must be variation in singular content, since the predicative content is unchanged. Suppose that the singular content throughout is that of e1, and so is, or refers to, lemon 1, and that this remains unchanged through the experiences. Then e3 would refer to lemon 1 and would not be a case of hallucination. Similar absurdities result whichever choice one makes of supposedly unchanged singular content.

Option (b) is more promising. It can do justice to the intuition that in the first two cases, the subject's perceptual system is working correctly: ℓ1 and ℓ2 are different, the first having lemon 1 as its referent, the second lemon 2, and both lemons are correctly represented as yellow. And it can ensure that the experience at t3 is not correct, since ℓ3 has no referent. These results seem to me just what is wanted. But how could they be reflected in singular content? What mechanism explains the convenient but undetectable updating of the content of the supposed singular representational vehicle over the three cases?

External determination of content is, I shall assume, clearly possible in some cases. Oscar on earth refers to water by using "water", but

Twin-Oscar on Twin Earth refers to twin water by using a word that sounds just like the earth-word "water". Their phenomenology may be subjectively the same, even though their states involve different singular content. Is this a good model for the option (b) treatment of Loar's lemons?

The analogy is not exact. In Twin Earth cases the subjects are aware of a vehicle of content: a word, as I just presented the case, and there is a demand for determining what it means. The demand is met by providing a content that best explains subjects' relations to the world and their linguistic and cognitive activities. By contrast, in cases supposedly involving singular perceptual content there is no detectable vehicle of singular content, for such a vehicle would detectably change in the different cases; and the explanatory burden has already been discharged by the *perceiving* of the object, a causal-explanatory relation.

In the previous paragraph, I assumed that option (b) would register different contents by different vehicles. But there is a version of this option on which there is a single vehicle whose content changes over time, perhaps in the way that demonstrative *words* can be regarded as having changing content, changes which in special cases may escape the conscious awareness of the subject. It is unclear to me what general theoretical structure would recommend this way of describing the lemons case. The alleged changing content plays no role in shaping either phenomenology or action.

On either version of option (b), the subject's perceptual state undetectably changes across the three times. No physical mechanism can explain the change in the first two cases, since perception-relevant energy patterns falling on the subject are unchanged, as are any perception-relevant activities in the subject. It is part of the way the example is set up that there are changes in the objects of the subject's perceptual states, and that these changing objects do not affect the subjectively accessible character of the states. Singular perceptual content would add an undetectable internal reflection of the external changes. But this is entirely superfluous from the explanatory point of view. It is given that the objects of perception change while the phenomenology is unchanged. The changes in the objects mean that, in a sense, the subject is in different states on the three occasions. But all this sameness and difference is straightforwardly accommodated by the causal facts, without alluding to singular perceptual content. Such content is theoretically unnecessary, and so does not exist.

In §4, I'll stress that I have no objection to singular *conceptual* representation, and I'll contrast this with supposed singular *perceptual* representation. In §5, I'll suggest a direct reason for being suspicious of singular perceptual content, one that is not premised on its theoretical dispensability.

## 4. Differences Among Representational Systems

The broader picture I wish to paint is that whereas individual identity is readily available in the contents of thoughts, it is not available in the contents of perception. Hence there can be no singular perceptual content. In thought, we can readily make sense of the distinction between qualitative and numerical identity. This is not available in perception, whose representational format is nonconceptual.[12] The individuality or particularity of perception is fundamentally generated by causation and not by content.

Perceptual representational systems differ from conceptual ones in at least three ways:[13] they have different expressive resources, different structural constraints, and different possession conditions. As an example, from the first category: conceptually, but not in visual perception, we can represent the content *was born in Jerusalem*. This shows that there is conceptual content that cannot be expressed by a visual perceptual content. The converse also holds: visual perceptual content makes very fine grained color discriminations. Perhaps the content of a perceptual experience is expressible by $red_{22}$, where "$\text{red}_{22}$" is a dummy expression supposedly referring to some specific shade for which neither you nor I have a concept. This shows that there is perceptual content that is not expressed in the normal conceptual repertoire (though perhaps it is available to color experts). More generally, determinables (like *red*) rarely[14] feature in perceptual content unless some more determinate shade does, but there is no analogous connection for conceptual content; and many perceptually accessible determinates (like $\text{red}_{22}$) rarely or never feature in conceptual content. Perceptual content has an analog-based "richness" (amount of detail) that is hard or impossible to match in a more "digital" conceptual system. There are endless further differences: perhaps some logical words like "not" and abstract words like "justice" express conceptual content that cannot be literally expressed perceptually; perhaps contradictions, easy to express conceptually, cannot be represented perceptually;[15] and so on.

Differences of structural constraints were noted by Berkeley. You normally cannot visually perceive the color of an object without thereby having shape-related perceptual content,[16] but you can say or believe that something is a certain color, without saying or believing anything about its shape. You may refer conceptually to a color using a semantically complex demonstrative phrase like "that color", or "the color of those curtains", but a visual experience of a color may have no matching complexity.[17]

Perceptual content has a high degree of involuntariness: open your eyes when there is light in your environment and, if you are sighted, you will have visual experiences with content whether you want to or not. Conceptual content, by contrast, involves some degree of voluntary manipulability. Although concepts are sometimes exercised involuntarily, as when one cannot help understanding words spoken in a familiar language, or when thoughts arise unbidden, having a concept requires you to be able at least sometimes to exercise it at will in the formation of thoughts. A possibly over-demanding version of this feature of concept possession is marked by Evans's Generality Constraint: "if a subject can entertain those thoughts [that *a* is *F* and that *b* is *G*], then there is no conceptual barrier, at least, to his being able to entertain the thought that *a* is *G* or the thought that *b* is *F*" (1982: 102). Some degree of conceptual manipulability is an essential source of conceptual richness, making possible our most distinctive cognitive activities, like remembering, planning, premeditation, and fiction.

The differences between perceptual and conceptual systems show that we cannot simply project features of conceptual systems onto perceptual ones. In particular, we cannot use the existence of conceptual singularity, which I do not dispute, to infer that there is perceptual singularity. In the next section, I'll suggest that there could not be perceptual singularity: that is, there could not be perceptual representational vehicles with singular content.

## 5. Perceptual Discrimination and Content

There can be perceptually indistinguishable duplicates: two peas, two grains of sand, a genuine banknote and a brilliant forgery. To say that they are perceptually indistinguishable is to say that, under the same conditions, a perceptual system, regarded as a causal mechanism, will respond to perceiving the one in just the same way as it would respond to perceiving the other. If they are placed side by side, they can be seen to be two, but perception cannot reveal which is which. When just one is perceived, everything of which the subject can be aware in perception is just the same as if the other had been perceived. The senses cannot discriminate the perceptually indistinguishable. This is not a fault in the system. Were it a fault, we could at least imagine how it could be fixed, but we cannot imagine a fix. The conclusion I draw is that to attribute singular content to a perceptual state would go beyond anything the state is capable of representing.[18]

A non-empty singular concept refers to just one thing. If it is applied to something other than that thing, the application is erroneous, however great the similarity between the object to which the concept is applied and the object to which it refers. There is no analog for percepts. If there were singular percepts resembling singular concepts, then the perceptual system would be in error in responding to a duplicate in just the same way as to the genuine referent. But there would be no *perceptual* error in such a case, even if a false belief were formed. In the first two time intervals of the lemon examples, the qualitative identity of the lemons seen, together with the sameness of phenomenal character, makes it impossible to regard either case as one of incorrect perceptual functioning. True, the perceptual system failed to notice that lemon 1 had been replaced by lemon 2. But, according to the example, the switch was made undetectably, so there is no perceptual error. On the basis of the experiences, the subject may well form the false belief that the lemon she saw at t1 is numerically identical with the lemon she sees at t2.[19] The belief is a conceptual structure, and employs representational resources not available to perception.

Perceptual content reflects how things appear, and indistinguishable duplicates cannot appear different (when viewed under the same circumstances).[20] This informally reprises (T4), and (T1) shows how we can get individual objects into the story without appealing to singular perceptual content. (T1) implements singularity causally, rather than representationally.

The senses are essentially detectors of qualities. That is what they are tuned to do. Although they seem to yield individual-specific information, enabling us to recognize people and places, they achieve this thanks to the fortunate rareness of indistinguishable duplicates in these cases. (By contrast, we are familiar with our inability perceptually to identify grains of rice or machine-made artifacts.) In this, the senses are like any other "identifying mechanism" that we possess or even can imagine: fingerprints, passwords, passports, Vehicle Identification Numbers, DNA profiles, iris scans, etc. These are complex qualities, and the qualities alone are causally involved in the initial output of any detector. The mechanisms can only represent the qualities of the causally relevant stimulus, and they will, evidently, not distinguish indistinguishable stimuli. By contrast, genuine singular content can be correct of only one of a collection of duplicates. A singular term like the name "Jim" does not apply to Tim, Jim's identical twin, even if they share fingerprints and iris scans.

When we want to find out which individual object an iris scanner is scanning, we need to consider the scanned object, and not just the scanner itself, which would be in the same qualitative state even if it had scanned an indistinguishable object. Qualitatively identical states with different causes count as "different". So a scan of Tim's iris is in that respect different from a scan of Jim's, even if their irises are qualitatively indistinguishable. But it is a familiar fact about perception, equally true of scanners, bank note detectors, fingerprints, signatures, and so on, that the signal itself does not individuate its specific cause: causes are fixed qualitatively, not singularly, in that a duplicate of something with certain causal powers shares those powers.

The underlying idea can be expressed in the following principle:

(T6) A representational system includes only such representational vehicles as have contents that the system could in principle discriminate.

Since perceptual representational systems cannot even in principle discriminate qualitative duplicate individuals, they cannot include vehicles having such individuals as their content; that is, they cannot include singular contents. This contrasts with conceptual representational systems, which can in principle make a distinction in thought between an object and a duplicate of it. (Of course, this does not mean that the distinctions are correctly made in practice.) Enlarging the point, conceptual systems can allow for the possibility of fool's gold and twin water, perceptually indistinguishable duplicates of gold and water (according to the usual pretense). But this distinction is not available within a purely perceptual system.

Although this position seems to me straightforward and commonsensical, it may seem unable to do justice to various important features of perception: our ability to bind, to track, to "individuate", to recognize. A single object can seem to have distinct properties, like being red and being round. How can the properties be *bound* to a single individual without the exercise of singular content? A predator *tracks* its prey across minutes or hours, locked on to the same target. We *attend* to individual objects, and *individuate* our friends by sight or voice. Argos *recognizes* Ulysses. We see things as *to the left* or *ahead* or *heading my way*. Surely all these perceptual activities are made possible by singular perceptual content? We need to represent that it's the same individual that is red and round, the same individual that was there and is now here, that it's Tim, not Jim, that it's Ulysses; and egocentric properties seem to presuppose the singular identification of a self or other suitable origin.

In the next section, I'll show how those activities find a natural place within the picture I propose; and in §7 I'll enter a qualification.

## 6. Apparent Problems for the Feature-Expression Account

*(a)* *Binding*: One task set by "the binding problem" is to explain how different perceived features can be "bound together" as features of a single object. Psychology and neuroscience try to find explanations of this ability. A philosophical question that arises, and which is directly relevant to this paper, is: can a subject bind different perceived features as features of a single object without exploiting singular perceptual representational content? For example, suppose (to take a standard kind of philosophical example) a subject is confronted by a round red thing and a green square one. She registers the features round, red, square, and green. But how does her representational system allocate the first two features to one object and the second two to another? What makes for the difference between seeing something red and round together with another thing that's green and square, and seeing something green and round and another thing that's red and square?

A possible answer is that the subject's perceptual system exploits singular perceptual representational content. A linguistic analog is that the correct binding occurs by exploiting two perceptual analogs of singular terms, one suitably conjoined with the features red and round, the other with the features green and square. It can be doubted whether this is genuinely explanatory. In any case, the feature-expression account gives a different and more straightforward answer.[21]

If a perceived object triggers a feature representation, that feature is thereby "attributed" to the perceived object in the straightforward sense that the correctness of the representation depends on whether or not the represented feature is possessed by that object. This notion of attribution follows the relation of perceiving:

(T7) If a representation of feature *F* is caused by perceiving the *F*ness of *x*, then *F* is attributed to *x*.

This is all we need in order to resolve the binding problem without appeal to singular representational content. A cluster of features is "bound to" an object *x* just if the perceptual situation is one in which all those features are "attributed" to *x* in the sense of (T7) (compare Neander 2017: 235). In the example, red and round are attributed to one thing, green and square to another, since the former directly caused the representation of red and the representation of round (and neither the representation of green nor the representation of square), while the latter directly caused the representation of green and the representation of square (but neither the representation of red nor the representation of round). Some object can satisfy *is red* and *is round* and another can satisfy *is green* and *is square* without any object satisfying both *is red* and *is square* or any object satisfying both *is green* and *is round*.

*(b) Numerosity:* According to Pylyshyn (2007: 25–27), perceivers can

(i) perceive more than one object at a time, even if the different objects are qualitatively identical, and in a way that makes their distinctness apparent.[22]
(ii) accurately estimate the cardinality of small sets of things (maximum 5), if suitably arranged, using a faster and more automatic mechanism ("subitizing") than ordinary counting.

These abilities seem closely related, and might suggest the deployment of singular perceptual representations. For example, perhaps the twoness of simultaneously perceived qualitative duplicates is perceptually represented by two singular representational vehicles with distinct referents, and these representations are the constant elements deployed through tracking. And perhaps subitizing reveals just how many of these singular representations a perceptual mechanism can produce at one time (and this is the moral that Pylyshyn suggests in the discussion just referred to).

Explanations that appeal to singular representations are unnecessary. They may also be unsatisfying. For example, Pylyshyn suggests that one possible explanation for subitizing is that the subject may be "counting the number of indices deployed" (2007: 26), where indices are singular representations. But explaining the ability to count objects by the ability to count indices seems unhelpful, since the latter ability stands equally in need of explanation. My main point, however, is that although these experiments reveal psychological mechanisms of great interest, an explanation in terms of singular representations is not required.

Relational features can be represented in perception, for example *is taller than* or *is to the left of*. (The egocentric aspects of locational content are discussed shortly.) As in the examples, some relations obtain only between distinct things (they are irreflexive). Nothing more is required for a perceptual system to register distinctness (that is, the numerical feature of twoness) than to represent an irreflexive relation. Applying (T1), the perceptual content of a perceptual experience $x$ *is taller than* $y$ is correct iff there are perceived objects $x$ and $y$ of which it is non-accidentally true. The irreflexivity of the relevant content ensures that it obtains of $x$ and $y$ only if $x \neq y$. The relevant relation could simply be distinctness itself.

The system could also represent cardinality features directly, like *being three*, a possibility Pylyshyn considers as an alternative to the use of indices (2007: 24). The skill of subitizing would then be described as skill with the application of such cardinality features.

(c) *Tracking:* A predator engaged in tracking by sight needs to try to keep the prey in view. Or, if it loses sight momentarily, needs to try to regain sight. The lioness is tracking a specific antelope. She takes care to continue to perceive it, or to regain sight of it if continuity fails. Does not this involve a continual process of reidentification? And does not this in turn require a sequence of singular contents, perceptually connected by the equivalent in perceptual content of the identity relation? Should not tracking be modeled on the schema: $x$ is at location L, $y$ is at L*, and although L≠L*, $x=y$? This might be understood as involving singularity in the perceptual representation of $x$ and $y$.

A perceptual content could be, simply, *moves*. If the content is correct on an occasion, it is correct of a perceived object, one that moves, and so "remains the same" through change of place. This feature is integral to the feature *moves*, so movement as such need not introduce singular contents. (For motion, there are familiar questions, not to be addressed here, about the relation between the temporal extent of what is perceived and the temporal extent of the perceiving.) This gives the right result for illusions of movement. The seemingly moving scrolling messages seen on some public illuminated screens (e.g. in transit systems) are not really moving: it's just that different lights come on successively. This is properly regarded as an illusion of movement, since the perceived object does not possess the perceptual content *moves*, despite the fact that perception insists on attributing this content even in the clear presence of the belief that it does not apply. As in Müller-Lyer cases, the inconsistency of perceptual content with belief content does not make the former disappear.

Tracking requires more sustained attention than the minimum needed for a perception to count as of movement. Must not the tracker exploit a singular content for what he is tracking? This worry should already have been assuaged by the account of binding. Tracking consists in successive binding of successive features. In the favorable case, a single object is perceived across changes in place. This is a fact about perception, but is not reflected in singular perceptual content.

One of Pylyshyn's surprising results is that perceivers are good at tracking small numbers of similar objects through dissimilar paths of motion. A full account of tracking needs to apply to these special cases: MOTs (2007: 34ff). Although this is a skill calling for psychological explanation, it gives no special reason to suppose that tracking involves singular content.

*(d) Recognition*: According to Ruth Millikan, "the ability to reidentify things that are objectively the same when we encounter them in perception is the most central cognitive ability that we possess" (2000: 109). I do not dispute that this is an important ability, but I deny that it is a purely perceptual ability. Strictly speaking, recognizing an individual as such is not a perceptually available achievement. Instead, the most perception can offer is registration of qualitative as opposed to numerical identity, perhaps exploiting the notion of *familiarity* or some determinate of this (familiar parent, or whatever). As employed in perceptual systems, this is a purely qualitative notion, correctly attributed to objects that share qualities (to some contextually determined degree) with previously encountered objects. We are often right to believe in numerical identity on the basis of perceiving qualitative identity (in the case of people, though not in the case of grains of rice), but such beliefs are not elements in our perceptual system.

Perception can at best target qualitative identity, whereas recognition, properly speaking, targets numerical identity. Since qualitatively identical but numerically distinct pairs of large interesting objects are rare, qualitative identity is normally a perfectly adequate substitute for numerical identity, and the majority of the things we encounter daily are fungible in the sense that we would not care whether they were numerically the same (shirt, car, computer) or perfect duplicates. That is the basis of most real-life forms of "identification": it is rare for distinct people to have indiscriminable fingerprints or iris patterns, or for distinct cars to have the same VIN number. So, often, recognizing a qualitative pattern is as good as recognizing an individual as such. But not always, as shown by grains of rice and by mass produced paper clips.

What perception does offer, as a kind of substitute for genuine recognition, is a feeling of familiarity, qualitatively based. Ulysses strikes Argos as familiar: he exhibits familiar perceptible qualities. But Argos would have been fooled by a duplicate. His perceptual system could not be blamed, had he been fooled, for no amelioration of it that we could even conceive would have prevented the error.

Familiarity and genuine identification come apart in certain cases. One is the Capgras delusion, whose victims claim that their closest friends, even spouses and pets, are mere qualitative duplicates, and are not the real thing. Numerical identity is mistaken for merely qualitative identity. Another is dejà vu, in which what is in fact an unfamiliar scene induces a sense of familiarity, which may lead the subject falsely to believe in a numerical identity. In normal cases, when we recognize our spouse or a friend, though our perceptual basis is merely qualitative, our belief in numerical identity is well-founded.

The claim is not that perception may confuse qualitative with numerical identity. On the contrary, perceptual content cannot access numerical identity and so in a sense cannot confuse it with anything else. That's why the experience at t2 in the lemons case is correct: the perceived object is indeed yellow. The switch to a new lemon, distinct from the one seen at t1, was undetected, but perceptual experience does not claim otherwise, and hence cannot in itself be accused of anything incorrect on this basis. A false singular *belief* may arise, that lemon 2 is lemon 1, but this is made possible by additional representational resources at the conceptual level, which contains genuinely singular concepts.

(e) *Perceiver-dependent properties* A needed refinement relates to the representation of perceiver-dependent properties, like *being straight ahead* or *to the left* or *over there* or *heading my way*. Do these not make implicit reference to individual things: the perceiver herself, a direction, or a location she occupies? This is a hard question for all theorists,[23] since we regard a subject's capacities to self-refer or to refer to a specific location as relatively high level ones, but perceiver-relative contents seem to be required for the most primitive kind of perceiver, even magnetotactic bacteria.[24] The solution is that the perspectival coordinates, like the perceived objects, are not specifically represented in perceptual content, even though they shape its satisfaction conditions. They relate to perceptual content as gas tanks relate to gas gauge content.

Suppose a subject S is facing in direction D relative to S's position, P, and that under these circumstances, S veridically sees an apple off to the left. On one view, S's experience must contain singular contents for S, D, and P. But that seems too demanding, even when setting aside the difficulties we have already encountered in getting objects, as opposed to their duplicates, into perceptual content. Self-identification is a notorious problem, and it's hard to see how there could be any direct way of identifying locations, as opposed to exhibited qualities: the most direct perceptual identification of a location is in the first instance an identification of the qualities present at it. They can be specified less directly, in terms of relations to other locations or directions, like the perceiver's position or angle of gaze, but these specifications in turn appear to involve something singular.

Egocentric parameters can feature in the satisfaction conditions for S's experience, without featuring in its content, just as the gas tank enters into the satisfaction conditions for a reading of the gas gauge. Suppose someone, S, sees an apple off to the left. The feature-expressive content is *an apple off to the left*. The satisfaction condition could be expressed: S's content is correct iff true of *an apple off to the left* of S, relative to her position, P, and direction of gaze, D, at the time of the experience. Only the italicized portion of this correctness condition features in the perceptual content. There is obviously a lot more detail to be filled in. For example, if you rotate your head to the right, straight ahead is not your direction of gaze (which is to the right), but it is a projection of a line connecting your spine and your sternum (in that order). But as in the simpler example, these elements may appear in a correctness condition for a perceptual state without having proprietary representation in that state. This view enables us to accommodate the phenomenon for which "de se contents" were designed, without exaggerating what is involved in located perception. Located perception is available to simple organisms, as it should be. Once again, causation rather than content does the job.

If perception could reveal numerical as opposed to mere qualitative identity, it would involve singular content. But perception cannot do this any more than any of our specially engineered "identifying" mechanisms can. Perceptually based claims of numerical identity inevitably derive from perceptual registration of qualitative identity.

## 7. A Qualification

A basic iris scanner is connected to an electronically operated door latch. When someone approaches the door, their iris is scanned. The scanner checks the scan for a match with the scans in its database. If it finds a match, it opens the door. Otherwise, the door remains closed.

A more sophisticated iris scanner has an additional layer of data: the scans in its database are associated with names. This scanner can keep track of who is in the building at any time. It can maintain a display of everyone who's there. It doesn't merely open the door, it also keeps an individual tally.

Tim and Jim have qualitatively identical irises, ones that cannot be distinguished by any scanner. If Tim's iris has been authorized, the basic scanner will open the door for Jim. (For simplicity, let's suppose that Tim is not in the building.) As I was considering such a case earlier, this is a scanner that has not made a mistake: it has correctly identified an iris pattern. It would have made a mistake if it had contained singular content specific to Tim as opposed to Jim. The sophisticated scanner, by contrast, will respond to Jim not only by opening the door, but also by indicating that Tim is in the building even if he is not. The sophisticated scanner has made a mistake, by deploying an incorrect singular content. So some scanners do deploy singular contents.

Should we think of perceptual systems as like the basic scanner or like the sophisticated scanner?[25] A "basic" perceptual system would be purely qualitative, with no singular content. Its failure to discriminate duplicates is not a fault in the system, for we cannot even imagine how a system of this kind could be repaired in such a way as to enable it to make the discrimination. But a different kind of system, a "sophisticated" perceptual system, would couple the basic system with one that would output singular representations, and these outputs could be assessed for accuracy according to whether these representations are correct. Perhaps our actual perceptual systems are sophisticated, deploying singular content in recognizing one's spouse, one's friends, one's car. This process reliably delivers singular truth, even if the system could be fooled by a duplicate.

When thinking about individual objects, the question may seem unimportant. One might continue to say, with maximal conformity with what I have argued so far, that the "perceptual system", *strictly speaking*, is purely qualitative but may get coupled to a distinct system, perhaps a concept-deploying one, so that the resulting hybrid permits the deployment of content of both kinds. On one view, the sophisticated scanner is not strictly speaking just a scanner, but a scanner coupled with a distinct system which links the scanner's qualitative material to singular facts. Alternatively, one might say that although basic perceptual content is qualitative, sophisticated perceptual content may involve deployment of concepts, some of them singular. The source of the concepts is regarded as part of a unified system which also delivers the qualitative material. On this view, the sophisticated scanner is really a special kind of scanner, rather than a hybrid of a scanner and something else: some scanners can do more than respond merely to qualities. Perhaps there is no important difference between these descriptions.

When one considers other things that we expect from perceptual systems, we find ourselves on a familiar philosophical battleground. I have said nothing about the features whose expression plays the central role in defining correctness for perceptual states in (T1). But many of these features are themselves subject to the argument from duplication. There could be something that is perceptually indistinguishable from a lemon but which is not a lemon; for example, it is a botanically unrelated but superficially indistinguishable fruit. If the earlier argument about singular content was good, this would entail that a content corresponding to *is a lemon* cannot be a perceptual content. Visual perceptual content would be confined to non-twin-earthable qualities, perhaps just the "sensible qualities", colors, shapes and perhaps some others. On this view, the perceptible qualities would be those for which there could be no perceptually indistinguishable duplicates. But this is a controversial claim. Many theorists take a much broader view of the range of nonsingular content that can be deployed in perception (for example, Schellenberg 2011). The broad view may seem to undermine what I have said about singular content. Given that perceptual systems can deploy contents for natural kinds, even if they could not distinguish them from distinct natural kind duplicates (fools' kinds), why should not perceptual systems deploy singular contents?

The example of the basic and the sophisticated scanners may serve to moderate and somewhat refashion the debate. The analog of the broad view of the range of perceptual contents sees the sophisticated scanner as in some sense a single system with more than one kind of content. The analog of the narrow view, counting as perceptual content only cases that are insensitive to distinctions among qualitative duplicates, insists that only the basic scanner is a scanner, properly speaking, and that the sophisticated scanner is hybrid, a scanner bolted to a different kind of system.

Can this really be a matter of great philosophical debate? Everyone agrees that the perceptual systems of infants are much less discriminating than those of adults, that perceptual systems require the training of experience, and that this is a highly complex and long-running process during which the range of content output by the organism on the basis of its perceptual experiences is enormously enriched. Suppose an information processing system that begins with only non-singular content ends with singular content. Perhaps, for example, we want to say that Argos does genuinely recognize Odysseus, which entails that he must be in a state that deploys a singular content. On one view, we should say that this means he has coupled a nonperceptual system to his perceptual system. On another, it means his perceptual system has been trained to deliver this content, on a merely qualitative basis. I can imagine reasons for preferring one description to another coming from developmental psychology or neural anatomy, but not from philosophy.

Similarly, suppose a subject's overall information processing system begins with some qualitative input from a lemon and ends up with content true just of lemons, and not of lemon look-alikes. How much does it matter whether the output is allocated to the perceptual system as such, or rather to a hybrid system part of which is genuinely perceptual and part of which is not? On the former option, it has to be allowed that it is not a content that belongs to the basic or most primitive part of the perceptual system, for reasons given in this paper. There has to be a distinction of levels. But it is unclear to me how there could be philosophical reasons to prefer one as opposed to the other of the competing views: that the different levels demarcate a distinction *within* the perceptual system, or that they mark a distinction *between* the perceptual system and a system of some other kind. I am therefore happy to regard the thesis of this paper as that there is no basic singular perceptual content. This can be expressed, using the narrower view of content, as the thesis that there is no singular perceptual content at all, or, using the broader view, as the thesis that there is singular perceptual content but that none of it is basic.[26]

## Notes

1. This could be nuanced in at least two ways. One might wish to expand it to allow for empty cases, ones in which the contents count as singular in virtue of "purporting" to rigidly designate, even though they in fact designate nothing. And one might wish to narrow it to apply only to simple representational vehicles.
2. Loar (2003), though he does not draw the same conclusion.
3. "[P]erceptual systems are thus brought under the umbrella of measuring instruments generally (which is surely where they belong . . .)" (Churchland 2013: 90). Although there's value in the comparison with instruments, it requires care: the representational features of instruments are derivative from the use to which they are put. Aside from their use by us, instruments are mere lumps of matter, lacking representational capacities.
4. The paper assumes only a version of representationalism that, according to Pautz, "is compatible with nearly every view on experience", according to which experiences "merely *have* contents in some sense", leaving open whether they are "*identical with* relations to contents" (2010: 254).
5. Schellenberg is a recent example of someone who seems to make this assumption (2018: 24).
6. Some motivations for singular content are satisfied by (T1). For example, Soteriou writes "When a subject perceives an object, the veridicality of the experience is dependent on how things are with the object being perceived" (2000: 184). This is (approximately) entailed by (T1). But Soteriou also goes further than this premise: "The particularity of a successful visual experience should be reflected in the intentional content of the experience" (2000: 175).
7. My discussion is influenced by Dretske's writing, e.g. his (1995).
8. Chalmers (2006: 50) defines phenomenal content as content that meets the condition specified in (T4).
9. Strictly, the topic on this row is the representational *vehicle* at the relevant time. Content is a semantic property of a vehicle. Since in this case the candidates for content are lemons, it would be more accurate to regard the third row as specifying content. This way of putting it will sound strange to some ears, so at this point I adopt the more common idiom.

10. The formulation is intended to make room for the possibility that some experiences with subjectively indistinguishable phenomenal character in fact differ in their phenomenal character (think of phenomenal sorites).
11. Loar's "all" is implicitly qualified by "concepts", whereas in my presentation I make it sound as if it is qualified by "experiences". This adjusts for my emphasis on the distinction between perceptual and conceptual systems of representation, detailed in §4 below. For language, the notion of purporting to refer can be explicated in a partially syntactic way: an expression purports to refer if it may properly occupy the kind of position in a sentence occupied by expressions that really refer. This explanation is not available if (as I believe) perceptual content lacks sentential structure. A functional role explanation is required.
12. Compare Pylyshyn (2007: 46): "true individuation requires concepts and conditions of identity".
13. These and similar differences are noted in the psychological literature, e.g.: "perception and conception differ in content, representational format, and methods of processing" (Mandler 2004: 45).
14. The unusual cases are those in the visual periphery.
15. Unless examples like the waterfall illusion do really provide contradictory perceptual content, which is open to doubt.
16. In abnormal cases one might perceive the color of a Ganzfeld without perceiving an object or a shape; or one might be so close to a large object that it filled one's visual field, thus depriving one of shape information but not of chromatic information. Berkeley connected color not to shape but to extension, and so his thesis does not require the restriction to normal cases.
17. "I can say that A and B are of different size without saying how much they differ in size or which is larger, but I cannot picture A and B as being of different size without picturing one of them as larger and indicating, roughly, how much larger it is. Similarly, if a yellow ball is situated between a red ball and a blue ball, I can state that this is so without revealing where (on the left or on the right) the blue ball is. But if this information is to be communicated pictorially . . . [e]ither the blue or the red ball must be pictured on the left." (Dretske 1981: 137–138)
18. Compare Churchland's description of a perceptual processing network: "The network itself draws no such distinction, between a reappearing individual on the one hand and sundry instantiations of an abstract universal on the other" (2013: 74).
19. The converse mismatch is familiar from the Müller-Lyer illusion: false perceptual content but true belief content.
20. Something like this view has been in the literature for some time. For example, McGinn (1982: 51) writes: "the content of experience is not to be specified by using any terms that refer to the object of experience on pain of denying that distinct objects can seem precisely the same". And Davies: "where there is no phenomenological difference for a subject, then there is no difference in content" (1992: 26). This thought has often been taken to favor an existentially general view of perceptual content, but that argumentative strategy depends on the false presupposition that singular and existentially general are the only options for perceptual content.
21. Compare Pylyshyn (2007: 47): "we may need to distinguish the process of feature-clustering and individuating from the process of picking out and referring to objects." Many observations in Pylyshyn's book seem sympathetic to the picture I offer, but a central ingredient of his theory, indices or FINGSTs, which are, apparently, singular perceptual representations, run counter to it.

22. As mentioned in the previous note, Pylyshyn's indices (FINGSTs) may be singular contents, or vehicles of singular contents, posited to underlie this achievement: "a central function of indexes is to select and refer to (or bind arguments to) several visual elements at once" (2007: 28).
23. The puzzle is well expressed by Peacocke: "An animal without language can see something as moving away from it, can hear something as coming towards it. These perceptions have a de se content, and it is very implausible that their occurrence in any way presupposes the possession of concepts . . ." (2015: 177). My solution to the puzzle associates such experiences with subject-involving correctness conditions, but without requiring the subject to deploy a representational vehicle designating the subject. This is much less demanding than the capacity to think of oneself as oneself. Peacocke's attributions implicitly have sentential complements, e.g. "that something is moving away", and in my view these entail concept-possession on the part of the subject of the attribution.
24. These contain linear chains of magnetosomes which act like compasses, enabling bacteria containing these structures to orient relative to bodies of magnetic rock.
25. Thanks to Martin Montminy for pressing this question.
26. A version of the paper was presented to a philosophy department colloquium at the University of Oklahoma. My thanks to the participants for their helpful comments.

## References


Burge, T. (1991). "Vision and intentional content". In E. Lepore & R. Van Gulik (Eds.), *John Searle and His Critics* (pp. 195–213). Cambridge, MA: Basil Blackwell.

Chalmers, D. (2006). "Perception and the fall from Eden". In T. S. Gendler & J. Hawthorne (Eds.), *Perceptual Experience* (pp. 49–125), Oxford: Clarendon Press.

Churchland, P. M. (2013). *Plato's Camera: How the Physical Brain Captures a Landscape of Abstract Universals*. Cambridge, MA: MIT Press.

Davies, M. (1992). "Perceptual content and local supervenience". *Proceedings of the Aristotelian Society*, *92*, 21–45.

Dretske, F. (1981). *Knowledge and the Flow of Information*. Cambridge, MA: MIT Press.

———. (1995). *Naturalizing the Mind*. Cambridge, MA: MIT Press.

Evans, G. (1982). *The Varieties of Reference*. Oxford: Clarendon Press.

Grice, H. P. (1961). "The causal theory of perception". *Proceedings of the Aristotelian Society, Supplementary*, *35*, 121–152.

Loar, B. (2003). "Phenomenal intentionality as the basis of mental content". In M. Hahn & B. Ramberg (Eds.), *Reflections and Replies: Essays on the Philosophy of Tyler Burge* (pp. 229–257). Cambridge, MA: MIT Press/Bradford Books. Reprinted in *Consciousness and Meaning: Selected Essays by Brian Loar*, Katalin Balog and Stephanie Beardman (Eds.), Oxford: Oxford University Press (2017: 291–317).

Mandler, J. M. (2004). *The Foundations of Mind: Origins of Conceptual Thought*. Oxford: Oxford University Press.

McDowell, J. (1991). "Intentionality de re". In E. Lepore & R. Van Gulik (Eds.), *John Searle and His Critics* (pp. 215–225). Cambridge, MA: Basil Blackwell.

Reprinted in his: *Meaning, Knowledge, and Reality*, Cambridge, MA: Harvard University Press (1998: 260–274).

McGinn, C. (1982). *The Character of Mind*. Oxford: Oxford University Press.

Millikan, R. (2000). *On Clear and Confused Ideas*. Cambridge: Cambridge University Press.

Neander, K. (2017). *A Mark of the Mental*. Cambridge, MA: MIT Press.

Pautz, A. (2010). "Why explain visual experience in terms of content?". In B. Nanay (Ed.), *Perceiving the World* (pp. 254–309). Oxford: Oxford University Press.

Peacocke, C. (2015). "Perception and the first person". In M. Matthen (Ed.), *The Oxford Handbook of the Philosophy of Perception* (pp. 168–180). Oxford: Oxford University Press.

Pylyshyn, Z. (2007). *Things and Places: How the Mind Connects with the World*. Cambridge, MA: MIT Press.

Schellenberg, S. (2011). "Perceptual content defended". *Noûs*, *45*(4), 714–750.

Schellenberg, S. (2018). *The Unity of Perception*. Oxford: Oxford University Press.

Soteriou, M. (2000). "The particularity of visual perception". *European Journal of Analytic Philosophy*, *8*, 173–189.

Tye, M. (2018). "How to think about the representational content of visual experience". In C. Limbeck (Ed.), *The Philosophy of Perception, Proceedings of the Austrian Ludwig Wittgenstein Society*. Berlin: De Gruyter.

# 11 The Sense of "Looks"

*Michael Tye*

Brian Loar was a great philosopher, careful and original in his writings. Interestingly, although he had much to say about physicalism and the nature of phenomenal states (and he uses the term "appearances" on any number of occasions), so far as I am aware, he had nothing to say in any of his writings about how the term "looks" is to be understood. The present essay is an attempt to fill this gap and to do so in a way of which, I hope, Loar would have approved.

I begin with some distinctions made with respect to "looks" by another philosopher Loar himself admired, Frank Jackson. In his *Perception* (1977), Jackson distinguished between three senses of the term "looks": the epistemic sense, the comparative sense and the phenomenal sense. In drawing this tri-partite distinction, Jackson was following the lead of Roderick Chisholm (1957) with one difference. Where Chisholm held that there is a non-comparative sense of "looks", Jackson held that there is a distinctively phenomenal one. More recently, some philosophers have sided with Chisholm, e.g., Alex Byrne (2009) and Mike Thau (2002). Others have claimed that there are just comparative and epistemic senses, e.g., Charles Travis (2004), while still others have argued that there is only a single sense, the comparative one, e.g., Wylie Breckenridge (2007).[1]

In my view, all these claims are mistaken. There is indeed just a single sense attaching to the word "looks", but this sense is neither epistemic nor comparative; nor is it phenomenal, as Jackson elaborates the phenomenal sense. Nonetheless, there *is* a phenomenal sense that attaches to certain modified expressions of the type "looks *F*", and there is also a comparative one that attaches to others. A correct understanding of "looks" and "looks *F*" has consequences, I maintain, both for the thesis that visual experiences have a representational nature and for how we think of visual illusions.

The essay is divided into four sections. I begin by laying out the three-part distinction that Jackson drew. I then present Chisholm's position and explain why Jackson, in opposition to Chisholm, denies that there is a non-comparative sense of "looks" that is not phenomenal. The third section argues, against Jackson and Chisholm, that there is a single sense of "looks". It is shown that this sense is not the comparative sense recently proposed by Breckenridge; nor does it fit Jackson's characterization of the phenomenal sense of "looks". There is also a discussion of expressions of the type "looks *F*" and how the sort of sense that attaches to 'looks *F*' varies with different substitution instances for "*F*". The final section discusses visual illusions, and it links the view developed for "looks" and "looks *F*" with the claim that visual experiences are representational.

## 1. Jackson's Tri-Partite Distinction

Jackson claims (1977, p. 30) that in a sentence such as "It looks as if the neighbors have gone away", "looks" is used epistemically. What is meant is that there is visually acquired evidence, for example, the fact that the windows all have curtains drawn at mid-day, that supports the proposition that the neighbors have gone away. According to Jackson, not all uses of "looks as if" reflect this visual, epistemic sense. If I remark, "It looks as if the stock market is getting ready for a decline", I am using the term "looks" epistemically, but I need not be basing my remark on *visually* acquired evidence. In such a case, what is meant is simply that there is evidence that supports the proposition that the stock market will go down.

One reaction to this last claim is to question whether it is literally true that it *looks* as if the stock market will go down. I shall not pursue this point further here. Instead, I shall put to one side possible non-visual uses of "looks" and concentrate on visual uses.

In addition to the epistemic use, Jackson claims further (p. 31) that in sentences of the form "*X* looks like an *F*", the term "looks" is used comparatively. Here what is meant is that *X* looks the way *F*s normally look when seen in conditions *C* by observer *S* (for some appropriate *C* and *S*). Thus, if I say "That looks like a duck', I mean that looks the way ducks normally look in daylight to humans. If I say "That looks like a dot", with respect to a house on the horizon, I mean that the house looks the way a dot looks on a page close to me (or to other normally sighted humans similarly situated). I do not mean that the house looks the way a dot looks at a distance.

The third sense of "looks" according to Jackson (p. 77), is to be found in sentences of the form "*X* looks *F* to *P*" or "There looks to be an *F*" where the term "*F*" is a term for color, shape or distance. This sense is the phenomenal one, Jackson claims (pp. 35–48), and it is distinct from the previous two, since sentences of these sorts cannot be analyzed either epistemically or comparatively.

Why not? Well, consider first the comparative option. As Jackson notes, there might be a disparity between the colors that objects actually have and the colors they look to have. Further, objects might look red on occasion even though in reality there are no red objects at all. This shows that

(1) *X* looks red to me

does not mean either

(1a) *X* looks the way red things normally look to me in normal circumstances

or

(1b) *X* looks to me the way red things normally look to normal observers.

It does not help to replace these putative analyses of (1) with the following conditional comparative proposal:

(1c) If there were any red things, X would look the way red things normally look to normal observers.

As Jackson points out, there might be a world created by a Cartesian evil demon who hates red things but tolerates non-red things looking red from time to time. Such a demon might decide to destroy the world if any red things come into existence. In this scenario, if something looks red to me on a given occasion, (1) would be true but (1c) would be false since if there were any red things, "nothing would look any way to anyone" (Jackson, p. 35).

Counter-examples can also be adduced that go the other way around. There might be someone who sees the world in shades of grey and who makes as many total color discriminations as we do. Such a person might see red objects as a unique shade of grey. For this person, a red object would look to him the way red objects normally look to him in normal circumstances, but they would not look red to him. So, (1) can false while (1a) is true. Alternatively, suppose that I have eyes that are incredibly sensitive to red so that red things dazzle me when I see them in normal light and thus they do not look red then. Nonetheless in certain circumstances, objects might look red to me. In this scenario, (1b) and (1c) are both false but (1) may be true.

Turning now to the epistemic option, something might look red to me even though I have visually acquired evidence that supports the proposition that the thing is blue. For example, I might notice that the thing is under unusual lighting conditions and I might know a thing's looking red under those conditions is an indication that it is really blue (just as in Jackson's example, I might know that the curtains being drawn at mid-day is an indication that the neighbors are away). So, (1) cannot be analyzed as "*X* looks as if it is red".

## 2. Chisholm on "Looks"

Like Jackson, Chisholm claims that 'looks' has epistemic and comparative senses. According to Chisholm (1957), the epistemic sense is in play whenever it is meant that the speaker believes, or is inclined to believe, that something is the case on the basis of adequate, visually acquired evidence. This may be expressed in a sentence using the "looks as if" construction. But it can also be expressed simply by saying that so-and-so looks to be *F* to someone. Thus, according to Chisholm, if I say that the ship looks to be moving to me, I likely mean that my visual evidence, as I view the ship, supports my belief or my inclination to believe that the ship is moving.

Notice that Chisholm's elucidation of the epistemic sense of "looks" is somewhat different from that of Jackson. For Jackson, what matters is what proposition the visual evidence supports. For Chisholm, what matters is what the speaker believes, or is inclined to believe, on the basis of that evidence. On the face of it, Jackson's elucidation is preferable; for something might look to me as if it is bent even though I have no inclination to believe that it is bent. Suppose, for example, that, being of a very skeptical frame of mind, I am unusually reluctant to trust the evidence of my senses. Seeing an object that looks to me as if it is bent, I do not immediately believe that it is bent nor am I even *inclined* to believe this without further investigation. Still, the visual evidence does support the proposition that the thing is bent.

The comparative sense of "looks" is operative, according to Chisholm, when the speaker is comparing the look of something to the way certain other things ordinarily look, or might be expected to look. This may be expressed using the "looks like" construction but it need not be. For example, if I say "The stick looks to be bent", in Chisholm's view, I may be using the term "looks" comparatively, and I will be if what is meant is that the stick looks the way bent sticks ordinarily look or might ordinarily be expected to look. In such a case, I need not believe or have any inclination to believe that the stick really is bent.

The third sense of "looks", according to Chisholm is the non-comparative one. This is standardly expressed in sentences of the form "*X* looks to be *F* to *P*", when it is not supposed (1) that *P* believes that *X* is *F* or (2) that *P* has any inclination to believe that *X* is *F* or (3) that *X* looks the way certain other things look in the appropriate conditions. So, for example, if I say that the ball looks to be red to John, I am using the term "looks" non-comparatively so long as it does not *follow* from what I say that John believes that the ball is red or that John is inclined to believe that the ball is red, or that the ball looks to be the way red things look in so-and-so conditions.

Chisholm claims that this non-comparative sense extends to cases in which there are no *F*s (p. 116). I may say, "That looks centaurian", for example, without having any inclination to believe that centaurians look the way that does, there being no centaurians. Nor need it follow that that looks the way centaurs look for the same reason.

Jackson's response to Chisholm (p. 89) with respect to the above non-comparative, non-phenomenal example is to insist that "looks centaurian" *is* comparative. What is meant when we say that that looks centaurian is that that looks the way centaurs would look, if there were any. This cannot be quite right, as it stands, at least if we follow Kripke in supposing that mythical beasts are necessary non-existents. But a plausible alternative comparative gloss is that that looks the way creatures with the visible features usually associated with being a centaur would look, if there were any such creatures, or perhaps that that looks the way centaur pictures normally look. To see that the latter alternative is indeed plausible, suppose that the given creature doesn't look at all like centaurian pictures but looks very like armadillo pictures, say. Then patently "That looks centaurian" is false. Conversely, suppose that the given creature *does* look just like centaur pictures. Then surely "That looks centaurian" is true. Corresponding points can be made with respect to the first alternative.

Still, on the face of it, Chisholm was right to claim that there is a non-comparative sense of "looks" that extends to cases in which there are no *F*s. Consider a possible world in which people believe that there is an evil demon who is tricking them in all sorts of ways and in particular for present purposes that he is making certain things look red to them even though in reality nothing is red. People in this world do not believe that anything really is red nor are they inclined to do so. Nor further is it the case that things that look red look the ways red things usually look; for there are no red things. Moreover, in the given world, it is not the case that things that look red look the way red pictures look; for if there are no red things, there are no pictures that are red. Nor finally is it the case that things that look red look the way things with the visible feature typically associated with red things look; for that feature is just the color, red, and again there are no red things. Accordingly, given Chisholm's understanding of epistemic and comparative uses of "looks", this use of "looks red" is non-comparative.

## 3. The Single Sense of "Looks"

Wylie Breckenridge (2007) has claimed that the following is true:

> (*S*) There is a sense of "look" such that: if "*X*" means *O*, an object, and *Pred* means *F*, a property, then "*X* looks *Pred*" means that *O* looks the way *F* things look.

Breckenridge has claimed further that the comparative sense presented here is the *only* sense of "looks". In his view, the definite description in (*S*), "the way *F* things look", is not to be qualified in the manner of Jackson or Chisholm. It is not a rough and ready formulation, to be completed as "the way *F* things are ordinarily expected to look" or "the way an *F* normally looks in C to *S*". It is complete, as it stands.

Let us take first the claim that there is a univocal sense of "looks". This seems to me very plausible. No one thinks that in the following sentences:

(1) John runs quickly
(2) John runs like an ostrich
(3) John runs as if every step hurts,

the term "runs" changes its meaning. Why think that the term "looks" is any different in these sentences:

(4) Spot looks red
(5) Spot looks like an ostrich
(6) Spot looks as if in pain?

To be sure, the complements of "looks" are different just as the complements of "runs" in (1)-(3) are different. But to suppose that there is a comparative sense for the term "runs" in (2) and a non-comparative sense for "runs" in (1), for example, would be mad. Why isn't it equally mad to say the same sort of thing about "looks"?

These reflections suggest that the naïve view that there is no lexical ambiguity in the term "looks" is the right view to take. Jackson and Chisholm (among others) were just wrong. This also explains nicely why the following inference is valid:

*X* looks red and old

Therefore,

*X* looks red.

If, as Jackson, supposes, "looks" in "looks red" has a phenomenal sense and "looks" in "looks old" has a comparative one, then (a) the sentence "*X* looks red and old" would be zeugmatic, as is the sentence 'He caught a cold and a fish', but patently "*X* looks red and old" is not zeugmatic (Thau, p. 230), and (b) the inference from "*X* looks red and old" to "*X* looks red" would be invalid, when patently it is valid.

But if the term "looks" has a single sense (at least in visual contexts), what is that sense? Breckenridge claims it is the comparative sense, suitably elucidated. According to Breckenridge,

*X* looks red to me,

is to be analyzed as

*X* looks to me the way red things look (the way things look if red), where the latter sentence is to be understood as asserting that *X* looks a certain way *W* such that the property of looking that way *W* is generically connected to the property of looking the way red things look. The properties generically connected here need not be instantiated, Breckenridge tells us, so there need be no red things for something, *X*, to look red to me. Rather they are non-extensionally related by a law-like relation of the sort that connects the property of being a turtle and the property of being long-lived, given that it is a law that turtles are long-lived. Breckenridge claims that if we understand the comparative claim in this way then there is no need to qualify it further or to relativize it to specific conditions or specific perceivers.[2]

Unfortunately, this still won't work. Consider first a world in which there are objects of varying hues and certain creatures that have evolved to see things in various shades of grey.[3] It is a law of nature for these creatures that red things look shade of grey *G*. Where C is one such creature,

> *X* looks red to C,

said of a red object, is false. But

> *X* looks to C the way red objects look

is true, since *X* does look the way red objects look to creatures of C's type and there is a lawful connection between that property and the property of looking way *W*, where W is the way *X* looks to C.

Perhaps it will be replied that ceteris paribus red things look *red*, so the analysans is really false here. But this would be too hasty. The properties supposedly generically connected are looking way *W* and looking the way red objects look. But while it is true that ceteris paribus red things look red *to us*, it is also true that ceteris paribus red things look shades of gray *to creatures of C's type*. So, there isn't really any such property as *the* property of looking the way red things look. In one context, when we speak of looking the way red things look, we pick out one property; in a different context, we pick out another.

One possible response to this is to insist that there *is* such a property as the property of looking the way red things look while allowing that the context of evaluation for the possession of that property varies. This is true for the property of weighing 170 pounds. Relative to a context of evaluation of earth, the claim that I weigh 170 pounds is true; relative to a context of evaluation of the moon, it is false. As applied to "looks" statements, the suggestion is that if we are saying how *X* looks to C, we take the context of evaluation for "*X* looks red" to be creatures of C's type. Unfortunately, this does not help; for in the example above, "*X* looks red to C" is false but "*X* looks to C the way red things look" is still true.

Furthermore, the suggestion offered by Breckenridge that generic truths are to be understood as being made true by certain non-extensional relations obtaining between properties seems very dubious. It is a generic truth that mosquitoes carry malaria. But there is no context-independent law-like relation connecting the property of being a mosquito and the property of carrying malaria. Rather what is true is that the *relevant* mosquitoes in the *relevant* conditions carry malaria.

What, then, is the sense of "looks"? Answer: the term "looks" picks out the property of looking, just as the term "mass" picks out mass, the term "water" picks out water and the term "runs" picks out the property of running. This is fixed. It does not vary with its complement. There is no lexical ambiguity in "looks" any more than there is with "mass" or "water" or "runs".

Where the complement of "looks" is "as if . . . ", the complement is to be spelled out epistemically. Where the complement is "like . . . .", the complement is to spelled out comparatively. Where the complement is just a simple predicate, the situation is more complicated. Consider the case of "talks". When "talks" is followed by a simple modifier, for example, "angry" or less awkwardly "angrily', often that modifier functions as a comparative definite description. It implicitly describes a way of talking as the way that angry people usually/often talk. In many cases, where "looks" is followed by a simple predicate, for example, "old", the predicate functions in just this way. So, "old" in "looks old" is short for "the way that old people normally look". But predicates following 'looks' do not always function in this manner. This is what is shown by the counterexamples adduced above in the case of "looks red" against Breckenridge. It is also shown by the following thought experiment.

Imagine that on age-inverted earth, people are born looking the way old people look on earth and that as they get older they look more and more the way young people look on earth. This is a variant on the movie *The Curious Case of Benjamin Button*. John, on age-inverted earth is only 14 years of age, and that is a young age there just as it is on earth for humans. So, on age-inverted earth, "John looks old", as uttered by the locals there, is false. It is false since John does not look the way old people look on age-inverted earth. On the contrary, John looks young. On earth, there is a person, serendipitously called "John", who has just the same visual appearance as John does on age-inverted earth but who is actually very old. So, on earth "John looks old", as uttered by us, is true. How can this be? John and age-inverted John look different; for one looks old and the other looks young, yet they have exactly the same visual appearance. If age-inverted John is magically instantaneously transported to earth and is standing next to earth John (or vice-versa), side by side, they cannot be told apart on the basis of their appearance alone. *In and of themselves*, they look exactly the same.

This story does not seem obviously contradictory. But why not? The answer, I suggest, is that, as noted above, when we say that an individual looks old (young), we are comparing the look, or the visual appearance of the person, to other relevant individuals in certain relevant conditions.

We are saying that the individual looks a certain way *W* and then we are describing that way *W* comparatively. In the story above, John and age-inverted John, in and of themselves, look exactly the same, even though one looks old and the other looks young, because intrinsically the way John looks is the same as the way age-inverted John looks. These intrinsic ways are properties John and age-inverted John both have.[4] And these ways can be picked out by predicates that function noncomparatively.

If the sense of "looks" is not itself comparative, and it is also not epistemic, is it phenomenal? The answer pretty obviously is "no". "Looks" has a single sense, and since it occurs in such contexts as "looks old" or "looks valuable" or "looks angry", patently that sense cannot be a phenomenal one. As already noted, the term "looks" picks out the property of looking, and that is all there is to it. As for looking *F*, when we characterize something as looking *F*, we characterize it as looking a certain way, which is specified by '*F*' either directly or indirectly. Where '*F*' refers directly, 'looks *F*' gets at what we might call 'the intrinsic look' of the thing to which it applies. The phenomenology of the visual experience of the viewer then supervenes on the property of looking *F*. 'Looks *F*' thus may reasonably be taken to have a *phenomenal* sense, where '*F*' refers directly to a way of looking; for the ways things intrinsically look fix the phenomenal characters of the experiences of the individuals to whom things look those ways.

As for which predicates are substitution instances for '*F*' in 'looks *F*', when 'looks *F*' has a phenomenal sense, the answer, I suggest, is predicates for which thought experiments like the one involving John and age-inverted John cannot be constructed. And these include predicates for color and shape, as Jackson originally proposed. Here is an illustration of why the thought experiment for 'old' does not work for 'red'.

Imagine that on color-inverted earth, objects that are red are made to look green by the act of an interfering demon and that objects that are green are made to look red. On earth, the statement, 'That looks red', said of a ripe tomato, is true. On color-inverted earth, the statement 'That looks red', said of a ripe tomato *after* the demon's act, is false. Under this scenario, it is obviously a mistake to claim that the two ripe tomatoes, one on earth and one on demon-affected color-inverted earth, have the same intrinsic appearance. Patently, they do not. The thought experiment for 'old' cannot get off the ground.

It might be replied that it is a mistake to suppose that 'That looks red', said of a ripe tomato on color-inverted earth after the demon's act, is false. After all, the tomato does look the way red things then look on color-inverted earth, and so, on one reading, 'That looks red' is true there. This reply is unconvincing. By hypothesis, on color-inverted earth, after the action taken by the mischievous demon, red things no longer look red. They look green. To be sure, ripe tomatoes look *like* other red things there (both before and after). But only initially do they look red;

later they look green. This description of the scenario is a perfectly intelligible one, and it is lost on the proposed comparative reading of 'That looks red'.

What about for shape? Consider the case of looking bent.[5] On earth, straight sticks usually look straight. On bendy earth, due to the activity of another interfering demon, straight sticks usually look bent. Of course, each of these sticks also looks the way straight sticks usually look. But that doesn't make it look straight. If you asked anyone on bendy earth to trace out the shape of one of these sticks, they would trace out a bent shape. So, while '*X* looks bent', said of a straight stick on earth is (usually) false, '*X* looks bent', said of a particular straight stick on bendy earth, is true. Given these facts, can it still be true that the two sticks share the same intrinsic appearance? Surely not. Being bent is not like being old.

Some philosophers (most notably Susanna Siegel 2006) have claimed that pine trees look different to tree experts and to novices. If this is true, it suggests that the property of being a pine is phenomenologically relevant and thus that '*F*' in 'looks *F*' can take as an instance a predicate that refers directly to the property of being a pine. Similarly, for a range of other natural kind and artefact terms.

I reject this view. A given tree can certainly look *like* a pine to the expert and not to the novice. The same tree can certainly look *as if* it is a pine to the expert and not to the novice. But can the tree *intrinsically* look different to the two people? The pine tree expert, upon looking at a pine tree or a group of pine trees may well fixate her eyes differently from the novice. Furthermore, and relatedly, she may well experience different shapes from the novice with respect to salient parts of the tree, somewhat as a chess expert, viewing a chessboard in the middle of a game; she may pick out various patterns of pieces the novice may miss. But if we fix all the apparent colors, all the apparent shapes of the parts, both small and large, including gestalt shapes, and all other uncontroversially visual properties for the two individuals, can the pine tree really look intrinsically different to the expert and the novice? It is very hard to see how it can.

The phenomenological irrelevance of the property of being a pine tree is also shown by a thought experiment broadly like the one laid out above for being old. Imagine that on pine-inverted earth, there are no cedar trees but there are pine trees which generally look the way cedar trees look on earth. These trees are classified as pines by novices and experts alike. So, the statement "That looks to be a pine", said by the locals of one such tree, is true on pine-inverted earth. On earth, there is a cedar tree that intrinsically looks just like this one tree. Now, the statement, "That looks to be a pine tree," said of the earth cedar, is false. How can this be?

The two trees look different; for one looks to be a pine and the other does not. Yet, side by side, they cannot be told apart on the basis of their appearance alone. *In and of themselves*, they look exactly the same. This is possible, I suggest, because the intrinsic way the two trees look does not include the property of being a pine tree. That property is irrelevant to the intrinsic look of a thing.

## 4. Consequences

The question that now arises is this: how are we to account for the fact that sometimes in the context "looks *F*", the predicate directly refers to a property? One possible answer is that when something, *X*, looks *F*, and "*F*" refers directly, as in the case that "*F*" is a color or shape predicate, there is an event of looking and that event is *F*. Leaving to one side the oddity of supposing that there is an event of looking, how *could* such an event be red or round? These predications seem unintelligible.

An alternative is that when something, *X*, looks *F*, where "*F*" refers directly, it instantiates the property of looking *F*-ly. But what is it for something to look redly or look squarely, if redly and squarely are not to be spelled out in comparative terms (as ways red/square things look)? Again, these predications seem unintelligible.

A third possibility is that when something, *X*, looks *F*, it presents an *F* appearance, where "*F*" names a feature of the appearance. Now we must allow that if a tomato looks red and round, there is an appearance that is literally red and literally round. Once again, it is very hard to make sense of this view for familiar reasons.

What, then, is the right answer? I suggest it is that looking has a representational nature. Sometimes, when we use the modifier "*F*" with "looks" we directly get at properties in the content of the relevant representational property. What it is for something to look red to person, *P*, for example, is for *P* to undergo a visual experience that represents it as red. In other cases, we describe the relevant representational property indirectly in a comparative way. This is what is going on when we say that something looks old.

This gets at a crucial difference between, for example, dancing (or running or eating) and looking. While one can dance a certain way and not be that way—for example, one can dance charmingly and not be charming—no one supposes that in such a case there is an *illusion*. Likewise, for running and eating. But when something looks a certain way, bent, say, and it isn't that way, we all agree that there is an illusion. Why? What's the difference that makes a difference? The answer, I suggest, is that in the case of an illusion, something is *represented* as being a certain way and it isn't that way. Nothing is represented any way in dancing (or running or eating).

This is not the only possible answer. Travis (2004, p. 65) says that in the case of an illusion, the error lies at the level of the epistemic look. In the case of the Muller-Lyer, for example, the lines epistemically look unequal to me. That is, the lines present an appearance from which it would be reasonable to conclude that the lines are unequal in length. Since they are the same length, there is an illusion. But what is the feature of the appearance on the basis of which it would be reasonable to draw the above conclusion? Travis' view seems to be that the lines look *objectively* unequal. Since such a look could easily go with two lines being of different lengths, the look *indicates* that the lines are of different lengths and thus "someone may be misled by the Muller-Lyer" (p. 68). The mistake that results for the viewer, according to Travis, does not require that in the illusion, one line is visually represented as being longer than the other.

As for what counts as an *objective* look, Travis has in mind the sort of thing to which J.L. Austin was drawing our attention when he remarked in *Sense and Sensibilia* (1962, p. 43) that petrol and water have the same objective look. Petrol just objectively looks like water (since both objectively look clear). The difficulty here is that if I reasonably conclude that a surface I am seeing is red, say, then, on Travis' view, if I am subject to an illusion, the surface must look objectively red. But this need not be the case. Suppose, unknown to me, I have been given a drug that makes things look to me other colors than they are. It may well be reasonable for me to conclude that the object ahead is red, on the basis of how it looks, and thereby I may be subject to an illusion, even though it does not *objectively* look red. In reality, the thing is green, let us suppose, and green things *objectively* look green.[6]

Perhaps it will be replied that the red surface looks red *to me*, not green *to me*, in the above circumstances, and this is the root of my epistemic mistake. I agree. But this reply is not available to Travis; for if the surface looks red to me, and it isn't really red, then the surface looks a certain way to me and it isn't that way. Intuitively, that fact *alone* surely suffices for there to be an illusion.[7] No further appeal to objective looks is necessary (or relevant).

There is one further account of illusions worth mentioning here. According to Michael Martin (2006), in the case of the illusion above, the green surface is what I actually see, but I cannot tell by introspection alone that I am not veridically perceiving a red surface.[8] Likewise, with the Muller-Lyer, I am seeing two lines of the same length, but I cannot tell by introspection alone that I am not veridically perceiving two lines of different lengths. If this is what a visual illusion consists in, there is no need to suppose that visual experience in such cases is misrepresenting or indeed representing at all.

This account faces several difficulties. First, simpler creatures (including very small children), lacking any psychological concepts, may not be able to introspect their mental states. Such a creature, in seeing a green surface, cannot tell by introspection alone that it is not veridically perceiving a red surface. But it does not follow from this that the creature is subject to an illusion. It could be that the creature sees the green surface veridically. Secondly, even if a child can introspect a range of her mental states, she may not be able to tell by introspection that she is not seeing five objects, say, since she may not yet be able to count to five. On Martin's account, if she is actually seeing four objects, she is subject to a visual illusion. But this need not be so. She could be seeing four objects veridically. A third problem is presented by the case of Marianna (a cousin of Mary's). Marianna has spent her life in a black and white room and she is then released into another room in which there is a green patch of paint on a white wall. Marianna sees the patch but she does not know its color, and so she cannot tell by introspection that she is not experiencing red. Marianna here meets Martin's conditions for undergoing an illusion with respect to the color of the patch, but intuitively there is no reason to classify her case in this way.

There is a final point to be made on behalf of the representational view of illusions. Take the Muller-Lyer again. Here two lines of equal lengths look to be of different lengths. Going *only* on how things look, we find ourselves under pressure to think that the two lines really are of different lengths. The "voice" of experience commands us to believe that the lines are of different lengths and while we can resist that "voice", having other reasons to doubt that the lines differ in length (or being unusually hard to persuade), it is there pressuring us to go along with it. What explains this? There is nothing like it in the case of dancing or running or eating. Mary may dance charmingly or run awkwardly or eat slowly, but we feel no pressure to believe that she really is charming or awkward or slow.

The answer, it seems to me, is that when an object looks a certain way, *F*, our visual experience not only has an indicative content but also an *imperative* content. It commands us to believe that the object is F. We can decide to ignore the command, of course, but the authoritative "voice" of experience is presently pushing us to obey it. These observations are straightforwardly accommodated by a representational approach to looking *F*, along with a suitable account of the tone of the relevant representation.[9] But they do not fit well at all with other theories. That is further reason to take the representational view very seriously.[10]

## Notes

1. The claim that "looks" is ambiguous has been very widely accepted. See, e.g., Ayer (1956), Vesey (1956), Price (1964), Quinton (1973), Leeds (1975), Dretske (1995), and Martin (1997).
2. With one exception. Something might look red in a world in which all red objects are square. In looking red, this item does not look the way red objects look, since (let us suppose) it does not look square and red objects look red and square. As Breckenridge notes, this sort of case can be handled by stipulating the the relevant way red objects look is the maximally specific way they look.
3. This is a (minor) variant on the case on page 250 above.

4. By "intrinsic way of looking" here (and later), I mean simply "way of looking independent of the ways other things look".
5. I earlier noted that Chisholm claims that "looks *to be* bent" has a comparative connotation, on one acceptable reading of "looks to be bent".
6. For another example of this sort, see Byrne (2009).
7. If I I have the information that things are not as they look color-wise in my current environment, it will not be reasonable for me to conclude that something that looks red to me is red. Even so, if the thing ahead looks red to me, then, given that it isn't red, I am subject to an illusion. It is just that I am not deceived by the illusion.
8. This oversimplifies minimally, but the oversimplification does not matter for present purposes.
9. For the full story here, including what to say about the case of hallucinations, see my forthcoming.
10. I am indebted to Mark Sainsbury for helpful conversation.

## References


Austin, J.L. (1962), *Sense and Sensibilia*, Oxford: Oxford University Press.

Ayer, A.J. (1956), *The Problem of Knowledge*, London: MacMillan.

Breckenridge, W. (2007), *The Meaning of 'Look'*, doctoral dissertation, Oxford University.

Byrne, A. (2009), "Experience and Content," *Philosophical Quarterly*, 59, pp. 429–451.

Chisholm, R. (1957), *Perceiving: A Philosophical Study*, Ithaca: Cornell University Press.

Dretske, F. (1995), *Naturalizing the Mind*, Cambridge, MA: MIT Press.

Jackson, F. (1977), *Perception: A Representative Theory*, Cambridge: Cambridge University Press.

Leeds, S. (1975), "Two Senses of 'Appears Red'", *Philosophical Studies*, 28 pp. 199–205.

Martin, M.G.F. (1997), 'The Reality of Appearances,' in *Thought and Ontology*, M. Sainsbury (ed.), Milan: Franco Angeli, pp. 81–106.

Martin, M.G.F. (2006), "On Being Alienated," in *Perceptual Experience*, T. Gendler Szabo and J. Hawthorne (eds.), Oxford: Oxford University Press, pp. 354–410.

Price, H.H. (1964), "Appearing and Appearances," *American Philosophical Quarterly*, 1, pp. 3–19.

Quinton, A.M. (1973), *The Nature of Things*, Boston: Routledge & Kegan Paul.

Siegel, S. (2006), "Which Properties Are Represented in Experience?," in *Perceptual Experience*, T. Gendler Szabo and J. Hawthorne (eds.), Oxford: Oxford University Press, pp. 481–503.

Thau, M. (2002), *Consciousness and Cognition*, Oxford: Oxford University Press.

Travis, C. (2004), "The Silence of the Senses," *Mind*, 113, pp. 57–94.

Tye, M. (forthcoming), "How to Think about the Representational Content of Visual Experience."

Vesey, G. (1956), "Seeing and Seeing As," *Proceedings of the Aristotelian Society*, 56, pp. 109–124.

# Part III

# The Metaphysics of Intentionality and Consciousness

# 12 Hard, Harder, Hardest

*Katalin Balog*

In this paper, I will discuss three problems concerning phenomenality.[1] The first two problems have been dubbed "The Hard Problem"[2] and "The Harder Problem".[3] The third problem has received less attention and I will call it "The Hardest Problem". However, I do not really mean to indicate a competition among these problems as to which is the most difficult. They are all hard (perhaps equally so) and I think that they cannot really be solved separately. Their solution has to come in a piece, and that's part of what makes all of them so hard.

Together the three problems present, I suggest, a particularly difficult challenge to those philosophers who are both physicalists[4] and phenomenal realists,[5] and agree with dualists that there is an explanatory gap involving phenomenality.[6] This is not to say that dualists and Russellian monists[7] don't have their own problems—it is just that these problems don't arise in the same form for them. The problems concerning phenomenality that beset dualism and Russellian monism are at least as hard as these but I confine myself here to the problems that arise within a physicalist metaphysics.[8] My aim here is to spell out the relations between these three problems and then to explore how they appear from the perspective of an approach originally championed by Brian Loar (1990, 1997) that has been quite fruitful in so far as the first two problems are concerned.[9]

Loar's approach—dubbed "the phenomenal concept strategy" by Stoljar (2005)[10]—attempts to explain the various special and puzzling features of phenomenal states in terms of their relationship to the concepts we apply to them. It is useful here to invoke the distinction between first person and third person concepts; while third person concepts, such as TABLE[11] or ELECTRON do not depend on how the subject is situated or related to the referent, first person concepts do. Some examples of first person concepts are indexicals, such as HERE or NOW or I. Phenomenal concepts are special, subjective, first person concepts whose canonical applications are based on introspection of the subject's own mental states as in the thought I HAVE ALREADY HAD THIS FEELING IN

MY KNEE where the notation "THIS FEELING" indicates a phenomenal concept that I formed on the basis of introspecting current sensations in my knee.

Phenomenal concepts are widely thought to be special and unique among concepts in that they refer—in some further specifiable way—directly yet substantially to phenomenal experience. Later, in Section 2, I will have more to say about their exact nature. Of course, not all applications of phenomenal concepts are introspective applications. Clearly, one can token a concept that refers to pain without literally experiencing pain—these can be called "indirect phenomenal concepts"—as when I reply to my dentist's question by "I am not in pain" or when I see someone stub their toe and think THAT HURTS. Because only phenomenal concepts applied in introspection pertain to the arguments in this paper, for the rest I will ignore these indirect phenomenal concepts.

The basic idea of the phenomenal concept strategy is that dualism seems plausible not because it is true but merely because of structural features of phenomenal concepts. Recently some philosophers who advocate a physicalist approach to both the Hard and the Harder problem (e.g., Papineau 2002, 2003) have called into question whether what I call the Hardest Problem—the problem of explaining, within the bounds of physicalism, how phenomenal concepts can refer determinately to physical or functional states of the brain—can be solved. I propose that the phenomenal concept strategy is capable of handling not just the first two problems but the Hardest Problem as well.

Here is a first pass at stating the three problems.

The *Hard Problem* is a *metaphysical*, and *explanatory problem* concerning the nature of phenomenal states. There is an expectation that if physicalism is true then there ought to be an account of how physical states (most likely, brain states) give rise to phenomenality. Failing that, there ought to be a physicalistically acceptable explanation of why it is *not* possible to give such an explanation.

The *Harder Problem* is *epistemological*. The problem is that if physicalism is true then all facts supervene on physical facts, including facts about phenomenality, and so it is natural to expect that, given enough physical information, one can know whether another being has phenomenal states and, if he/she/it does, the character of her phenomenal states. But it seems that one cannot know this. The concern is especially acute with respect to beings that are physically not much like humans. It seems one couldn't really know if a physically different creature, say, a dog, a fish, a Martian, or very sophisticated robot, with which humans share certain functional similarities, overlaps with humans phenomenally one way rather than another way or not at all.[12] If physicalism is true then one ought to be able to explain in physical terms why our knowledge of others' phenomenal states seems limited in this way even though they involve perfectly objective physical facts. This problem is closely connected with the Hard

Problem, and I will propose an account of phenomenal concepts that goes some distance in handling both.

The *Hardest Problem* is a problem about *reference*. Both the Hard and the Harder Problems presuppose that one's subjective phenomenal concepts refer determinately—modulo vagueness—to real, objective states that can be instantiated in minds other than one's own. This assumption is equivalent to the plausible idea that there is a matter of fact—even if it is not possible to know—about whether a phenomenal concept that applies to me also applies to another creature; whether we share our phenomenology. The Hardest Problem is the problem of explaining how this could be so in a physicalist framework. It has proven very hard to provide an account of how a phenomenal concept can refer to a determinate physical or functional state.

The problem is especially difficult given two facts about phenomenal concepts. One is that they are not physically or functionally defined; they have a special direct way of referring. And the other is that it is quite plausible that there will be *several distinct* physical and/or functional states that are correlated with any given phenomenal state. What would determine that a phenomenal concept refers to one of these to the exclusion of others?

The difference between these alternatives is vast. Take a phenomenal state P that is correlated with the neurophysiological state N and functional state $F_1$ and $F_2$.[13] N might be only instantiated by humans, whereas $F_1$ might be instantiated by fish as well and $F_2$ might be instantiated by humans, fish *and* robots. On the assumption of determinacy, there are three distinct scenarios corresponding to different metaphysical and semantic facts. If our phenomenal concept C of P refers to N (N then being identical to P) that means P only occurs in humans but not in fish or robots. If C refers to $F_1$ then P occurs in both humans and fish but not in robots. And finally, if C refers to $F_2$ then P occurs in humans, fish *and* robots. It seems to be a perfectly factual matter which one of these scenarios obtains. But it is hard to give a physicalist account that corresponds to one or another of these alternatives as it is hard to think of a physical way in which reference could be established to one of N, $F_1$, and $F_2$ to the exclusion of the others.

This was a first, rough pass at formulating these three interlocking problems for physicalism. I will now proceed as follows. In Section 1, I go into more detail about them. In Section 2, I take a look at them in the light of the phenomenal concept strategy. This approach is promising for physicalism in that it provides a plausible account of how phenomenal states can be physical even though there is an irremediable explanatory gap (Hard Problem), why it might be impossible to find out whether other creatures have phenomenal states even if phenomenality is purely physical (Harder Problem); and it can also deal with many other philosophically perplexing features of phenomenality, like privileged access, infallibility, etc. Given this promise, I want to see whether, from a physicalist point of view, we are at the point where all of the pieces of the puzzle fall into place. In Section 3, I tackle the Hardest Problem for the physicalist project. I propose that the supposed referential indeterminacy of phenomenal concepts is a misconception and that the phenomenal concept strategy is capable of handling the Hardest Problem as well.

## 1. Three Problems

### *1.1. The Hard Problem*

The Hard Problem is a metaphysical and explanatory problem for physicalists concerning the nature of phenomenal states. On the physicalist assumption, the question arises how physical states of the brain give rise to phenomenality. Block (2002, p. 423) puts it like this: "Why is the scientific basis of a phenomenal state the scientific basis for that state rather than another or rather than a nonphenomenal state?" Since this question seems to lack a perspicuous answer, the physicalists have a "hard problem" on their hands.

The consequence is various challenges to physicalism. One is the Zombie[14] Argument. David Chalmers[15] has argued that if phenomenality were physical, phenomenal propositions (that is, propositions involving phenomenal concepts) would have to be *a priori derivable* from the complete physical truth about the world.[16] However, he argues that phenomenal propositions are not so derivable. This is made evident by the fact that zombies are conceivable. The conclusion is that physicalism is false. In my opinion, this argument is not sound,[17] but it challenges physicalists to explain why zombies are conceivable.

Another argument against physicalism is based on explanatory considerations. As Levine observes,[18] there is an explanatory gap between neuro-physiological (or functional) and phenomenal descriptions. Discovering which neuro-physiological (or functional) states are correlated with a given kind of phenomenal state (say, experiencing red) doesn't explain why or how phenomenal states arise at all. Once there was also an explanatory gap between, for example, ordinary talk of transmission of traits of parents to their offspring, and physical and biochemical descriptions. But that gap has mostly been bridged by genetic theory and molecular genetics. We, or at least molecular geneticists, have a pretty good understanding of how biochemical processes can provide the mechanisms that underlie the transmission of traits from parents to children. Once we understood the molecular biology of genes, we would understand why a particular gene codes for such and such proteins and, given further knowledge about the organism, we would understand why that in an organism codes for eye color. The case of phenomenality is different. Those scientific theories that might come forth seem utterly unexplanatory.

Take the simpler example of $H_2O$ and water. Even if you deny (*pace* advocates of the conceivability arguments) that the statement "$H_2O$=water" is a priori derivable from the full physical description of the world, the hypothesis that, for example, $H_2O$ is not water is hard to make sense of.[19] Once we have all the micro-physical information about $H_2O$ and understood and gathered all relevant macroscopic information about water, we can close the explanatory gap between water and $H_2O$, no matter whether this is construed as a priori derivation or as posteriori theorizing.

The case of phenomenality is different. Though the search is still ongoing, it is not impossible that one day the neural correlate of phenomenality will be found. Neurophysiological state N or functional state F is the neural correlate of phenomenal state P if there is at least a nomological connection between them: if N or F is coextensive with P in all creatures natural and artificial in (at least) all nomologically possible worlds.[20] The physicalist claims that the relationship between P and N or F is actually metaphysical rather than nomological; that P is identical to either N or F. However, the hypothesis that neurophysiological state N, or functional state F is not identical to phenomenal state P is clearly intelligible, and an open question, for *any* N or F, no matter how much we know about the actual neurophysiology. And so, if physicalism is true, we will never be able to understand why.

We will talk more about the explanatory gap in Section 2. Let's now focus on the search for the neural correlate of phenomenality. There is an underlying assumption that guides the scientific study of the mind, namely that phenomenal states will turn out to be—or to be nomologically connected to—genuine, unitary physical (neurophysiological) or functional states.[21] I have been presupposing, along with most philosophers who address these issues, that it is clear exactly what a physical state is and that not every predicate that is physically definable—e.g., by disjoining physical predicates—denotes a genuine unitary physical state. Similarly, I have been presupposing that not every specification of a causal role or disjunction of causal roles characterizes a genuine functional state. The usual thought is that genuine states (functional, physical or otherwise) in some way "cut nature at the joints"; that they are the states that figure in laws of nature.

Though at the moment it is still an open question if this assumption will turn out to be correct, the alternative, i.e., that phenomenal states are not correlated with any unitary neurophysiological or functional states in all creatures that share the state but rather with a disjunction of physical or functional states, seems to physicalist phenomenal realists like Loar (1997) tantamount to eliminativism unless one posits a genuine non-physical state that unifies all these instances. It is an interesting question whether this is correct, but, to simplify matters, I would like to put the whole issue aside and I will assume that the search for a neural correlate of phenomenalityness is a viable project.

### 1.2. *The Harder Problem*[22]

There is a further issue that complicates the physicalist position which goes beyond the Hard Problem. At first, it seems that once the neural correlates of phenomenality are found, physicalism will be in a good position to identify phenomenally conscious organisms and the kinds of phenomenal state they have—since if physicalism is true then phenomenal facts are objective physical or functional facts and so we should be able to tell whether they obtain (and whether our usual methods of attributing them on the basis of behavioral evidence are accurate). But even if we assume, as I will for the moment, that this can be done with respect to other humans, the physicalist may still not be in a position to determine whether other beings—dogs, fish, Martians, robots, etc.—are phenomenally conscious or what the character of their phenomenal states are. The trouble is that even if the neural correlates of phenomenal state P are identified in humans, there are systematic reasons why there would be more than one candidate state—N, $F_1$, $F_2$, etc.—to play this role and so why we would still not be in a position to tell whether P is instantiated in other beings.

Here is why. Canonical evidence for the neural correlates of phenomenality comes from the human case. But quite plausibly, for every neurophysiological state that is nomologically correlated with a phenomenal state in humans, there are one or more functional states that are also nomologically correlated with that phenomenal state in humans. And since phenomenal concepts refer to phenomenal states directly—and not through a neurophysiological or functional definition—reflection on them is not sufficient to identify which of these is the actual referent. This fact is related to the Hard Problem: because there is no explanatory metaphysics of phenomenality in physical or functional terms, even if neural correlates for every single phenomenal state in humans are found, phenomenal states still cannot be identified with their correlated neuro-physiological states, as opposed to any of a number of equally correlated functional states. That means that physicalists also won't know which phenomenal states are to be projected beyond ourselves, to animals, Martians, robots, and so on. If the search for the neural correlate of phenomenality in humans proves fruitful, brain research can narrow down the range of states that might be identified with phenomenality considerably. But in all likelihood, it won't be narrowed down enough to settle on a single candidate. Though this epistemic handicap is not unique to physicalists—dualists are also not in a position to know the distribution of phenomenal states over other species—this ignorance is especially problematic for physicalists who claim that the distribution of physical properties fixes the distribution of all properties.

You might wonder why it should be the case that phenomenal states are nomologically correlated in humans with a range of neurophysiological and functional states. It may turn out that we have inductive evidence to the claim that P is nomologically correlated in humans with N. The problem is this: it follows *with logical necessity* if N (and so P) is instantiated, that there are multiple functional states $F_1$, $F_2$ . . . $F_n$ (one of whose realization is N) that are also instantiated. And while it is possible in principle that some (or all) of these functional states are *not* nomologically correlated with P in humans—that, e.g., $F_i$ can be instantiated in the absence of N (and so P)—it seems very plausible that, as a matter of fact, *at least some* of these functional states *are* nomologically correlated with N (and so P), i.e., that they don't have nomologically possible realizations in humans other than N. If that is the case, P has *multiple correlates* in humans. Though this is ultimately an empirical matter, I find the thesis of multiple correlates very plausible. I also find it plausible that some of these functional states are shared by other species even when these species don't share with us their neurophysiological realization.

This means that as far as we know—assuming physicalism, and the existence of these correlations—phenomenal states might be neurophysiological, or they might be functional. Because of the explanatory gap, N and F always seem compatible with the presence or absence of the relevant phenomenal state. If this is correct, then it is impossible to know what (if any) phenomenal states might be realized in other creatures that share with us the relevant functional organization but not the particular neurobiology or physical makeup.

This is not quite the skeptical problem of Other Minds (though it is related to it). Even if you dismiss skepticism about whether other humans are phenomenally conscious—after all, they share with you all of the possible candidates for neural correlates of phenomenality—you are still in no position to know about the phenomenal states of other creatures, and you don't even have a conception of how to remedy this situation. Even if you knew, on the basis of inductive evidence, all the neural correlates of phenomenality, you still wouldn't know what it's like for a cat, a fish, a Martian, or robot to taste a lemon. There is a sinking feeling that this is wrong. That if physicalism is true then someone knowledgeable about the physical facts should be knowledgeable about all the facts. A satisfactory physicalist account, at a minimum, should explain why this is not so.

### 1.3. *The Hardest Problem*

The previous discussion presupposed that phenomenal concepts, such as the concept REDISH[23] refer determinately to objective states—modulo the vagueness exhibited by most general concepts. It is presupposed in our understanding of the Harder Problem that, though there are indeterminate cases due to vagueness, e.g., it might be indeterminate whether a chimpanzee on a given occasion is having a reddish experience or a bluish experience, often there *is* a determinate fact of the matter about experience; in other words, it very well *might be* a determinate fact on some other occasion that they are undergoing a reddish experience. We hold it as a central piece of folk wisdom, and I have presupposed it in my discussion of the Hard and Harder Problems, that there is *generally* a matter of fact—even if, as the Harder Problem indicates, we are incurably ignorant about it—about whether this or that creature has this or that phenomenal state. But further reflection on the Harder Problem casts this assumption into doubt. This is the Hardest Problem. The Hardest Problem for physicalism is a problem of reference: how do phenomenal concepts that, in their canonical, first person, introspective applications, refer directly to a thinker's own phenomenal states succeed in referring *determinately* to objective states of this thinker?

The worry arises from the same issue we have discussed before: it is plausible that there are multiple distinct—neurophysiological and/or functional—correlates of phenomenality in humans. The epistemological consequence of this is the Harder Problem, that is, the problem that we cannot know if other species or even sophisticated robots share our phenomenal states. But the Harder Problem was predicated on the assumption that, modulo vagueness, there generally *is* a matter of fact about these questions. In the usual case, a member of another species, or a sophisticated robot, either does or doesn't share our phenomenal states. The Hardest Problem is that it is hard to see how this can be true, given physicalism. In other words, it is hard to see how phenomenal concepts can refer determinately to one of these co-instantiated brain states to the exclusion of others.[24] What, if anything, determines which of these neurophysiological or functional states are the referents of phenomenal concepts?[25]

The "phenomenal concept strategy", first deployed by Loar (1990, 1997) has been shown to provide a plausible physicalist solution of the Hard and Harder Problems.[26] I propose that it also holds the key to the Hardest Problem. Let us now look at the general account of phenomenal concepts that underlies the phenomenal concept strategy.

## 2. Three Problems in Light of an Account of Phenomenal Concepts

One of the ways physicalists have tried to deal with the Hard and Harder Problem is to deny the special status of phenomenality. This route is predicated on the belief that the conceivability of zombies and the existence of the explanatory gap are not compatible with physicalism. It has been proposed that phenomenal concepts can be analyzed in non-phenomenal terms, e.g., in terms of functional role[27] or representation.[28] If these analyses were successful, the explanatory gap could be bridged, and the conceivability of zombies denied. All we would need to do is find the neurophysiological states that realize the functional or representational states figuring in the analysis of phenomenal concepts.[29] I find this position very unintuitive. I think that phenomenal concepts refer to phenomenal states directly and they are not functionally analyzable.

Others have tried to close the gap by proposing scientific accounts of phenomenality that are explanatory in the way that the genetic theory of the transmission of traits is explanatory. It has been suggested, e.g., that being a phenomenal state is being processed in a global workspace;[30] that phenomenal states are representational;[31] that they involve higher order thought;[32] that there are "dynamic sensory-motor contingencies" associated with each sensory modality and these sensory-motor contingencies are somehow explanatory of the qualitative character of the particular sensory modality;[33] and that a state is phenomenal if it encodes highly integrated information.[34] In my view these suggestions, too, miss the mark. These theories are no more explanatory than neuro-physiological accounts. The question still remains unanswered: why couldn't it be that different (or no) phenomenal states arise, for example, from those particular sensory motor contingencies? None of these theories can give an explanatorily satisfying answer for this question.

There are also those who, having lost hope in a physicalist solution to the Hard Problem, deny that phenomenality is real.[35] On the other hand, those physicalist phenomenal realists who think that physicalism is compatible with the conceivability of zombies and the explanatory gap (Hard Problem), and the lack of epistemic access to the phenomenal states of creatures with different neurophysiology (Harder Problem) have to come up with a convincing story about why this is so—how it is that phenomenalityness is physical yet it is impossible to produce an explanatorily satisfying theory about its scientific nature that would enable us to detect if snails, or any other creatures, are phenomenally conscious, and that would reveal the illusoriness of the zombie-scenarios right from the start. This story cannot evoke the idea that phenomenality is metaphysically special. After all, a phenomenal state, on this view, is just another physical or functional state, 40 Hz oscillations, or being processed in a global workspace or what have you. The most promising story—the only promising story, in my view—has to do with the special way phenomenal concepts operate. I suggest that there already exist the broad outlines of such an account.

It can be shown that this account not only provides a physicalist resolution to the Hard and the Harder Problem but also explains the other perplexing epistemic features of phenomenality as well.[36] Here, however, I am going to focus exclusively on those three problems.

### *2.1. The Constitutional Account of Phenomenal Concepts*[37]

The key idea underlying the phenomenal concept strategy is to give a physicalistic account of how phenomenal concepts can refer to phenomenal states *directly* and yet in a *substantive* manner. To spell this out I need to cover some background on the nature of concepts in general.

I take concepts to be constituents of thoughts, and I take concepts and thoughts to be mental representations. I will also assume that concepts and thoughts are language like[38]—concepts are the words of *Mentalese*.[39] The important point for the following is that since tokening concepts and having experiences are occurrent entities (events, processes), they can be constituents of one another or bear causal relations to one another.[40]

Tokens of a concept, e.g., DOG possess a number of different properties and relations that are relevant to this discussion: i) realization properties, ii) conceptual role and iii) semantic properties.

i) When one tokens an instance of DOG, say in thinking the thought DOGS BARK, that token is realized by some neural property. The neural properties that are relevant to the token's being a token of DOG are its *realization properties*. A concept's realization properties are analogous to the physical properties that realize a spoken, written. or electronic token of "dog".
ii) A concept's *conceptual role* is the totality of causal relations (and dispositions) that tokens of thoughts containing the concept bear to each other and to perceptual inputs and behavioral outputs. Certain aspects of a concept's conceptual role may be essential to or even individuative of that concept while others are merely accidental; e.g., it is essential to the concept OR that one be inclined to make certain inferences, such as the inference from *P* to *PvQ*. It might also be essential to perceptual concepts, e.g., RED, that they be caused by certain perceptual inputs. Presumably, however, it is not essential to RED that one be caused to believe RED IS MY FAVORITE COLOR by the same perceptual inputs. How exactly to draw the distinction (which may be vague) between a concept's essential and non-essential roles is controversial.[41]
iii) A concept's *semantic properties* concern what, if anything, the concept refers to. For example, the concept DOG, refers to the property of being a dog. Exactly what determines the reference of a Mentalese word (with particular realization and role states) is a difficult and controversial matter.[42] It is widely (though not universally) held that a concept's role (or the part of it that is essential to the concept) at least plays a part in determining the concept's reference. This part is the concept's *mode of presentation*. It often, but not always, has the form of a description—i.e., the thinker is disposed to infer the description from the tokening of the concept—i.e., from ARISTOTLE one

> is disposed to infer THE TEACHER OF ALEXANDER, etc. One can think of these descriptions as contents of a file attached to the concept. It is also widely accepted that reference is determined at least partly by external—causal, informational or teleosemantic—relations of the concept to its environment.

A thinker typically has only partial epistemic access to features i-iii by introspection. When I attend to my thoughts, I typically can obtain introspective knowledge of their semantic contents, e.g., that I am thinking about dogs. It is also plausible, though controversial, that one can obtain information about the conceptual roles of one's concepts—and which of these are essential—by intuitions based on thought experiments, e.g., by asking oneself questions like "could one know p if p were false?". But the realization properties of one's Mentalese words—the "shapes", or "mental ink" they are written in, so to speak—are almost always completely opaque. Almost always, with the exception—I propose—of *phenomenal concepts*.

I propose an approach to phenomenal concepts that fits into this general framework but that also showcases the special nature of phenomenal concepts. An examination of phenomenal concepts suggests that a successful account of them will posit an intimate connection between phenomenal states and the concepts we form of them. Loar (1990, 1997) suggested the idea that phenomenal concepts are *direct recognitional* concepts. Abstracting from some of the details, the core idea that I take him to express is that when a person is having a particular experience, they can deploy a concept that refers directly to the experience in that the referent is somehow present in the concept's *mode of presentation*. How is one to understand this idea?

There is an ambiguity in Loar's account that points the way toward an answer. Loar sometimes describes phenomenal concepts as in some way "tracking" their referents. This indicates that—despite his suggestion that the mode of presentation in some way involves the referent itself—he is thinking of a phenomenal concept and its referent as distinct entities related by causation. But such an account leaves too much of a distance between a phenomenal concept and its referent; it allows, for example, for the seemingly absurd possibility that when the causal mechanism connecting phenomenal states and phenomenal concepts breaks down you might introspect having a certain kind of phenomenal experience when in reality you are having none of the sort. Causation seems to be the wrong model for how the reference of phenomenal concepts is determined.

The solution is to posit a relationship between phenomenal concepts and phenomenal states that is more intimate than causation: to hold that each canonical (first person, introspective) tokening of a phenomenal concept is constituted by a phenomenal experience whose phenomenal properties the concept refers to.[43] Imagine seeing a red flower and wondering whether others have the same kind of phenomenology as you do. You think to yourself: I WONDER IF OTHERS' EXPERIENCE IS ALSO REDDISH WHEN SEEING THIS FLOWER. Your tokening of the concept REDDISH here is constituted by the particular instance of reddish phenomenology that the flower occasions. That is the "mental ink" in which this instance of REDDISH is written. In other words, according to this view, phenomenal concepts (in their canonical applications) have very special *realization properties*: the neural properties realizing them are instances of the very same neural properties they refer to. But what is so special about phenomenal concepts, on this account, is not only that their *realization properties* are instances of their *referents*, but that this very fact is crucially involved in determining their *semantic properties*. Not only are these concepts realized by instances of their referents, but they refer to what they do at least in part *in virtue* of this fact. Their realization properties and conceptual role together determines their referent. This is, of course, very different from any other concept. Most concepts are not realized by tokens of their referents at all; but even those, like the concept ATOM, that are realized, mean what they do completely independently of this fact about their realization.

There are many details about this account that need to be worked out.[44] What I propose here is to see what light this account can shed—assuming all those details can be hammered out—on the three problems of phenomenality we have been talking about.

a) *The conceivability of zombies* is explained by the *directness* of our phenomenal concepts. Phenomenal concepts are supposed to be different in this way from concepts like WATER and even name concepts like CICERO. Chalmers and Jackson (2001) claim that these concepts are associated *a priori* with descriptions (e.g. "the transparent potable liquid . . .", "the Roman orator who is at the origin of a causal chain culminating in this token") and these connections are *sufficient* to rule out a priori a scenario where, e.g., everything is physically the same but yet there is no water. One doesn't have to commit to this to see that zombies are conceivable; however, the conceivability of zombies is only significant if this is the case. So the point is that even if one allows this to be true with respect to WATER, or CICERO, it is clearly not so with respect to phenomenal concepts; and *that* is the reason why the existence of zombies cannot be ruled out a priori.[45] The directness of phenomenal concepts, on the constitutional account, is explained by the fact that their reference is determined by how they are constituted—and *not* by any description that is associated *a priori* with them—and, importantly, this fact is perfectly compatible with physicalism. One can hold the constitutional account, and therefore be comfortable with the conceivability of zombies, whether one is a physicalist or a dualist.[46] The conceivability of zombies is explained solely by the special cognitive architecture involved in phenomenal concepts which is orthogonal to the issue of the metaphysical nature of phenomenality.

b) *The explanatory gap*. Recall that the problem of the explanatory gap is that no amount of knowledge about the physical facts (brain functioning and so on) is able to explain why a particular brain state has a particular feel, e.g., feels giddy. This contrasts with the way the fact that water is composed of $H_2O$ molecules together with physical and chemical laws explains why water is potable, transparent and so on. Once we have an explanation of why $H_2O$ behaves in watery ways (and that it is the only substance that does so), we have an explanation of identity statement. The hypothesis that water=$H_2O$ is quite natural in the light of all the above information[47]—indeed, the opposite hypothesis strikes one as borderline incomprehensible. The idea that the processes involving $H_2O$ molecules are only nomologically correlated to the non-physical and non-chemical processes involving water is a non-starter.

On the other hand, the hypothesis that a phenomenal state is *not identical* with some neurophysiological/functional state of the brain is quite compatible with the evidence. Since we can't explain why a brain state feels giddy in neuro-physiological terms, the dualist hypothesis that phenomenal states and brain states are merely nomologically correlated makes perfect sense.

The reason the explanatory gap cannot be closed in the case of phenomenality is that, while we do not have any special access to the nature of water that is not based on physical or functional information, we do have *substantial* insight into the nature of phenomenal experience that is not mediated by such information. As far as we know, the nature of phenomenality might elude any physical or functional understanding; it might be something over and above the physical.

However, the constitutional account can explain our *direct* and *substantial* grasp of phenomenal states—and so the explanatory gap—in a way that is perfectly compatible with physicalism. It explains it in terms of the constitution relation between concept and referent. When I form a phenomenal concept, I grasp its referent in terms of the shared phenomenality of concept and experience—*what it's like* to be in that state is the same as what it's like to entertain the concept. When, e.g., I focus on the reddishness of my experience of a flower—not on what it represents but on its qualitative character—"holding" the experience up for inspection in my mind, my conception of it contains that very experience. Having the experience and thinking about it then shares something very substantial, very significant: the phenomenal character of the experience. It is this shared phenomenality that produces the sense that one has a direct insight into the nature of the experience.

However, as is clear from what we have said, this kind of direct insight into the nature of phenomenal experience does not reveal anything about the metaphysical nature of phenomenality. It is very different from the kind of insight that a scientific analysis of the brain would provide into the nature of a brain state. The one involves *having* the state, the other, *analyzing* it into its components. Those are very different activities. On the constitutional account, the existence of the explanatory gap—a product of our substantial grasp of phenomenal states—does not preclude the possibility that phenomenality is purely physical.

c) *The Harder Problem*. Physicalists need to provide an account of why it is impossible to know if creatures physically different from us share phenomenal states with us. This problem is connected to the Hard Problem. If we understood how phenomenality arises from brain processes in the way we understand how water arises from a collection of $H_2O$ molecules, or digestion arises from chemical processes in the digestive system—that is, if we could close the explanatory gap for phenomenality—we would be able to tell, for any physical or functional state, whether it is a phenomenal state. We would also be in a position to know—in principle at least—what phenomenal states, if any, other creatures have in common with us. But we can't.

How does the constitutional account help reconcile us to such ignorance? It does by giving an account why the explanatory gap arises that is still compatible with physicalism. Given the constitutional account of phenomenal concepts, such ignorance is what we should *expect*, even on a materialist assumption. We do not know what phenomenal states if any non-human individuals have because we know our own phenomenal states *qua* phenomenal in a very special way. It is the nature of these concepts, i.e., the fact that we directly apply them to phenomenal states that explains why no perspicuous physical explanation of phenomenal states can be found, and why, consequently, we can't know if creatures different from us share phenomenal states with us. There is no need to suppose that physicalism is false in order to explain why the explanatory gap arises. Physicalism has the resources to settle the questions posed by the Hard and Harder Problem.

### 2.2. *The Hardest Problem*

The constitutional account of phenomenal concepts promises to resolve the conceptual and epistemic puzzles raised by the Hard and the Harder Problem—even if it doesn't quite dispel the illusion of mystery. The Hard and Harder Problem, in this telling of the story, persists as an illusion, a metaphysical version of the Müller-Lyer illusion. The constitutional account, however, runs into difficulty with the Hardest Problem.

In the previous discussion, I have tacitly assumed phenomenal realism—according to which there is a matter of fact about what phenomenal qualities are instantiated, e.g., whether chimpanzees have the same phenomenology when looking at red objects as we do. There is a further, related intuition that it is a determinate matter of fact whether our phenomenal concepts apply to other creatures as well—modulo the familiar issue of vagueness and borderline cases—even if we can never find out. The Hardest Problem is that it is very hard to see, on a physicalist account, how this could be the case.

In what follows, I will argue for two claims. The first is that the Hardest problem, by presenting a serious challenge to the determinacy of phenomenal concepts, also threatens phenomenal realism, and with that, our solution to the Hard and Harder Problems. The second is that, luckily for the physicalist, one needn't hold the indeterminacy of phenomenal concepts to uphold physicalism. In the end, the constitutional account of phenomenal concept can answer the questions raised by the Hardest Problem without resorting to indeterminism.

The problem when it comes to phenomenal concepts is that there is good reason to suppose that there are multiple neural and functional states that are nomologically coextensive with any given phenomenal state in humans. If this is the case, then it is very hard to see how there could be a matter of fact about which of these states our phenomenal concepts refer to, *especially* given the theory of phenomenal concepts that we discussed above. To explain why, we will have to go into a little more detail about the constitutional account.

Direct phenomenal concepts pick out their referent from the subject's point of view. In this way, phenomenal concepts are like the indexicals "I", "now", "here". But while we understand perfectly well how "here" picks out an objective, determinate spatial location (since the thinker has an objective spatial location at any time and "here" picks it out), things are much less straightforward for phenomenal concepts. The constitutional account claims that, e.g., REDDISH picks out its referent via an instance of *that very property*, reddishness. We conceptualize reddishness via introspectively attending to an instance of it in our experience and thereby incorporating it in a phenomenal concept. But how does this cognitive machinery determine the proper reference of the concept thus based in an instance of the referent?

On the constitutional account, REDDISH can be understood as the concept *this attended reddish experience* where "* *" stands for whatever concept forming mental mechanism is involved in turning an experience currently attended by the subject into a concept that represents the very property it instantiates; and "this attended reddish experience" simply stands for a particular experience that the subject is attending. There is a further complication which I have to put to the side for now, involving the conceptual machinery that determines which exact phenomenal property is being referred to, given that a phenomenal concept's constitutive experience is an instance of many different properties, e.g., reddish, dark reddish, crimsonish, etc.[48]

The question is, how could a phenomenal concept C of a phenomenal property P (e.g., reddish) pick out a neural property N, to the exclusion of some functional property F that is equally nomologically coextensive with P in humans (though perhaps not in other organisms)? Suppose P is identical with F, but *not* with N. How could phenomenal concepts track *that* fact? It is hard to see how; phenomenal concepts do not seem to have the right kind of built in complexity to disambiguate between these different but coextensive properties.[49]

David Papineau (2003) argues, on the basis of these considerations, that phenomenal concepts refer indeterminately; and that consequently, there is no matter of fact of whether other species, or certain kinds of mere functional replicas, share our phenomenal states.

Attempting to make it sound like this is not a problem for physicalism, he summarizes the situation in the following way:

> But I do not want to argue that there is something less than definite in the doppelganger's [a functional but not physical duplicate of a human being] experience itself. The doppelganger definitely feels as it does, however that is. My thesis is only that it is indeterminate whether it is *pain*, where I take this indeterminacy to arise from vagueness in our human term "pain". The indeterminacy doesn't lie in the doppelganger's experience itself, but in whether that experience is similar enough to cases of human pain to fall under our term "pain", a term whose content derives from exemplars provided by human pain.
>
> (2003, p. 218)

There are a number of problems with this view.

First, the supposed indeterminacy of phenomenal concepts is peculiar and is different from other familiar cases of referential indeterminacy. Take the case of the concept HEAT which was once used for both temperature (the average kinetic energy of the molecules in an object) and amount of heat (the total amount of kinetic energy of the molecules in an object). But while in this case progress in science pointed to an ambiguity in the concept which resulted in the formation of two distinct concepts replacing the old unitary concept HEAT (i.e., TEMPERATURE and AMOUNT OF HEAT), no such possibility exists for the phenomenal concept PAIN. On Papineau's account of how phenomenal concepts work, one could only refine the concept PAIN to refer determinately to either $N_{pain}$ or $F_{pain}$ (the neuro-physiological and functional states that are each nomologically coextensive with pain in humans) in non-phenomenal ways, employing physical and functional descriptions to pick out their respective referents. By his own admission, no *phenomenal concept* could achieve such disambiguation.

The supposed indeterminacy of phenomenal concepts also differs from the indeterminacy of vagueness. There are colors that fall somewhere between, say, red and orange, so it is indeterminate which concept applies, but there are also colors that fall under RED determinately. Though phenomenal concepts do have this kind of indeterminacy, the indeterminacy Papineau talks about is not of this sort. According to him, there are no instances of REDDISH that apply determinately to $N_{red}$ or $F_{red}$.

The indeterminacy that Papineau has in mind is also different from the referential indeterminacy that concepts such as RABBIT possess, according to Quine. RABBIT, he suggests, refers indeterminately to rabbits, undetached rabbit-parts, momentary rabbit stages, etc. This referential indeterminacy, however, doesn't extend to propositions in that, e.g., THERE IS A RABBIT is true or false for all permissible assignments of reference. On the other hand, if REDDISH refers indeterminately to $N_{red}$ and $F_{red}$ then THIS MONKEY HAS A REDDISH EXPERIENCE might come out true under one interpretation ($F_{red}$) but false under the other ($N_{red}$).

More importantly, though, if there isn't something "less than definite in the doppelganger's experience itself" then, it seems, there is something definite about my experience and its phenomenal character as well. As far as I can see, this is an affirmation of qualia realism—the view that there is a determinate matter of fact about the phenomenal character of the experience of conscious subjects. However, Papineau is not entitled to hold both that our concept PAIN refers indeterminately to $N_{pain}$ and $F_{pain}$ and also that pain itself is a "definite" state about whose phenomenal character there is a matter of fact.

On the natural assumption that PAIN refers to pain, which is a "definite" state of the subject, PAIN cannot also refer to both $N_{pain}$ and $F_{pain}$ indeterminately since, unless they are themselves identical, only one of them can be identical with the "definite" property pain. It follows then that accepting the indeterminacy of phenomenal concepts is incompatible with phenomenal realism and so it leads to eliminativism about phenomenal states.

But it is hard to be an eliminativist about phenomenal states. The Hard and Harder Problem, the explanatory gap, and all the other mysteries of phenomenality stem from the fact that we not only refer to phenomenal states directly—without phenomenal or functional modes of presentation—but we refer to them in a *substantive* way. We are *acquainted* with the referent of phenomenal concepts and from the first person point of view of that acquaintance—as opposed to the third person point of view from which we try to understand how phenomenality fits into a "scientific image" of the world—it makes little sense to suppose that there are no "definite" phenomenal states.

A physicalist qualia realist then is committed to the view that PAIN *does* refer unambiguously to either $N_{pain}$ or $F_{pain}$. I think such a position is actually quite plausible for the physicalist. To see why, we need to remind ourselves of how the Hard, Harder, and Hardest Problem arises. They arise because we try—and fail—to understand phenomenality and its place in the physical world from the third person point of view. In the case of the Hardest Problem, we are led to the view of referential indeterminacy via our failed effort to understand how reference gets disambiguated from the third person point of view. Since nothing from that point of view reveals how $N_{pain}$ but not $F_{pain}$ could be constitutive of a phenomenal concept, indeterminacy seems to follow.

I now propose that the resolution of all three problems is the same as well. In each case, the constitutional account of phenomenal concepts helps us recognize the problem as an illusion created by the special cognitive architecture of the first-person concepts we apply in introspection and their isolation from third person conceptions. To put it another way, the constitutional account helps us see how we can be led astray by our predilection to assimilate the first person to the third person.

When we focus on the role of introspection in phenomenal concepts, we can see how, *on the assumption* that pain is either identical to $N_{pain}$ or $F_{pain}$, phenomenal concepts could manage to pick out the correct referent, without that being discernible from the third person point of view. Since *only phenomenal states can be attended*, and therefore quoted in the mind in introspection—whereas non-phenomenal brain states cannot—it is evident how PAIN, a concept that works by quoting an instance of the referent, picks out whichever of $N_{pain}$ and $F_{pain}$ is identical to pain. If, for example, pain is $N_{pain}$ then that is what is being mentally quoted—since non-phenomenal states such as $F_{pain}$, could not be present in the mind for introspection. The way phenomenal concepts single out they referent cannot be understood from the third person point of view for the same reason that the phenomenality of pain cannot be understood from the third person point of view; because of the radically different cognitive machinery involved in first person phenomenal and third person physical/functional concepts.

Of course, if physicalism is true, facts about the reference of phenomenal concepts, like everything else, is grounded in physical facts, in this case physical facts about the brain. However, considered from the third person, scientific perspective, these facts cannot explain either the identity of pain with, say $N_{pain}$ rather than $F_{pain}$, nor the subjective nature of attention to phenomenal states, nor the nature of phenomenal concepts; nor, for that matter, why non-mental, non-phenomenal states cannot be attended. This is just a manifestation of the Explanatory Gap, which we have dealt with in the discussion of the Hard and Harder Problem. The Hardest Problem, exactly like the Hard and Harder Problem, turns out to be another artifact of an irreducible conceptual dualism with regard to phenomenal experience.

This account of referential determinacy in the face of the Hardest Problem invokes the spirit of Loar's (1995) attempt to account for referential determinacy in the face of Quinean considerations to the contrary. Loar argues that our first-person concept of reference tracks which of various external relations qualify as reference for our concepts (so, that the concept THAT RABBIT indeed refers to that rabbit and not, say, that rabbit surface), even while it is not possible to understand how this can be from the objective, third person perspective. He argues for the radical thesis that the reason we cannot disambiguate reference from the third person point of view is that, understood properly, reference is essentially a subjective concept with a phenomenal component that—just like phenomenal experience itself—is not explicable from the objective perspective.

While my view doesn't presuppose Loar's controversial thesis about the concept of reference, my solution to the Hardest Problem is in the spirit of his crucial insight: that it is compatible with physicalism that phenomenal experience make sense—in a certain way—only from the subject's point of view.

## Notes

1. Throughout the paper, when I talk about phenomenal states, I mean states for which there is, in Thomas Nagel's expression (1974), "something it is like" to have them. "Phenomenality" is the feature of such states that constitutes what it is like to have them. In the literature "consciousness" is often used interchangeably with "phenomenality"; but since the term "consciousness" is used in a number of different senses as well, I will stick to "phenomenality".
2. See Chalmers (1996, pp. xii–xiii).
3. See Block (2002).
4. By physicalism I mean the metaphysical view that the world's fundamental ontology is physical and the best account of that ontology is provided by fundamental physics. According to contemporary physics, this ontology consists of particles, strings and fields of various types that occupy space-time (or bear spatio-temporal relations to one another) and possess a limited number of quantitative states (mass, charge, electromagnetic potential and so on). Everything else, whatever other entities and states there are, is composed out of and realized by configurations of this fundamental physical ontology. Physics also claims that there are only a few fundamental dynamical and perhaps non-dynamical laws that govern the structure of space-time and evolution of its occupants. All macroscopic or special science laws, causal relations, probabilities are ultimately derived from the laws of fundamental physics and the arrangement of fundamental physical entities.
5. By "phenomenal realism" I mean that there are phenomenal states. Our concepts of these—phenomenal concepts—possess both first person and third person applications. First person applications have a cognitive immediacy while third person applications are mediated by perception (typically of behavior). I take it for granted that I know in my own case that

phenomenality (and various phenomenal states) exists but for other people and creatures there is room for various degrees of skepticism.

6. Levine (2001) observes that there is an explanatory gap between phenomenally and physically characterized facts. I explain the gap in Section 1. Those who think there is a gap reject (as I do) analytic functionalist accounts of phenomenal concepts and hold that zombies are conceivable.
7. A version of Russellian monism that has recently been revived (Chalmers 1996, 2002, 2017; Lockwood 1998; Stoljar 2001; Strawson 2003, 2006) is the view that the most fundamental states are both mental (or "protomental") and physical in that they possess a physical dispositional nature and a mental categorical nature. It is an interesting issue how this view fares with regard to the three problems but that is a topic for another paper.
8. For a discussion of the problems for dualism see Balog (2005).
9. Balog (2012a, 2012b) and Block (2002).
10. A similar proposal by Scott Sturgeon (1994) appeals to the special epistemology of phenomenal states.
11. I will indicate concepts and thoughts with capitalization.
12. Block 2002 uses the label "Harder Problem" for a whole cluster of issues concerning the epistemology of phenomenal states that goes beyond the scope of this paper. I am going to use the label only for the issue outlined above; consequently, my usage is slightly different from Block's.
13. N, of course, realizes both $F_1$ and $F_2$.
14. Zombies are (conceivable) creatures that are physically exactly like us but have no phenomenal states at all.
15. See Chalmers (1996, 2009).
16. The claim is a little more complicated. It is that every non-indexical truth is derivable *a priori* from the full physical description of the world and the laws and a proposition to the effect that this is the full physical description and laws.
17. See Balog (1999), especially with regard to Chalmers (1996). His 2009 formulation of the argument is harder to refute, but, as I will show later, can be equally defused using the phenomenal concept strategy.
18. Levine (2001, pp. 76–80).
19. Block and Stalnaker (1999) discuss the possibility of "ghost water"—a nonphysical kind that exists side by side with being composed of hydrogen and oxygen atoms and has all the same causal roles as the latter. Even if that is a coherent possibility, it would be the case that "water" refers to both $H_2O$ and ghost water and *not* that water refers to ghost water alone. So even in that possibility it wouldn't be the case that $H_2O$ is merely nomologically connected to water.
20. If the phenomenal state and the correlated physical state are the same then the correlation holds in all metaphysically possible worlds but if dualism is true the correlation may hold only in worlds in which there are laws linking the distinct phenomenal and physical states. The term "correlation" is neutral between metaphysical and nomological connection. If a correlation is found, i.e., if we have inductive evidence that N or F is coextensive with P in humans, the physicalist will posit the relationship to be metaphysical, while the dualist will posit a nomological connection. In either case, these correlations are supposed to be exceptionless, i.e., non-statistical in nature.
21. It is usually (but not universally) thought that the functional states that are candidates for identification with phenomenal states lie somewhere between the neurophysiological correlates of phenomenal states and the superficial functional roles associated with them cashed out in terms of stimuli and

behavior associated; i.e., they are thought to be some "deep" functional roles that our brain states have in terms of information processing.

22. I am not following very closely Block's exposition of the Harder Problem in Block 2002. Rather, I set up the Harder Problem in a way that helps connect it to what I call the Hardest Problem.
23. The concept REDISH refers to a *kind of phenomenology*—as opposed to the color red itself—normally had by looking at red colored objects.
24. See Papineau 2003 for a discussion of all three problems. Papineau in the end embraces the view—which he thinks is a consequence of physicalism—that phenomenal concepts don't have determinate reference and consequently that there is no matter of fact about application of phenomenal concepts to creatures physically different but functionally similar to us. In Section 3, I will take up whether this view entails eliminativism about phenomenality.
25. The Hardest Problem doesn't arise for dualism—on that view, phenomenal states are unitary non-physical states, and they are the unique referents of phenomenal concepts.
26. For further developments of the strategy, see, for example, Papineau (2002), Block (2002, 2006), McLaughlin (2006), and Balog (2012b).
27. Lewis (1966), e.g., is a clear example.
28. See, e.g., Jackson (2003).
29. This latter is predicated on the assumption that representational states can in turn be analyzed in terms of functional/causal relations.
30. Baars (1988).
31. See, e.g., Harman (1990) and Tye (2000).
32. See Rosenthal (2002).
33. See, e.g., Hurley and Noë (2003).
34. Tononi et al. (2016).
35. See, e.g., Rey (1988), Dennett (1991), and Frankish (2016).
36. For a discussion see Balog (2012a).
37. This section loosely follows my discussion of the same topic in Balog (2012a).
38. There are non-language-like, nonconceptual mental representations—image-like, map-like representations—as well. It is plausible that states with phenomenal properties, such as perceptions and sensations, are such representations.
39. This account of thought was originally proposed by Fodor (1975).
40. There are philosophers who would like to avoid Mentalese or avoid positing representations altogether. It may be that my account can be made compatible with their ontologies but that is not something that I can do here.
41. This is as difficult a problem as the others I am discussing but there is no space here to discuss it.
42. Another hard problem not to be addressed here.
43. Similar ideas are proposed in Papineau (2002), David Chalmers (2003), Block (2006), and Balog (2012a).
44. I have done some of this in Balog (2012a).
45. As I pointed out earlier there are dissenters who think phenomenal concepts have descriptive analyses; see e.g., Lewis (1966) and Jackson (2003). I will ignore this possibility and proceed on the assumption that, as Chalmers suggests, zombies are conceivable.
46. Chalmers (2003), e.g., proposes a dualist version of the account.
47. This is true even if one doesn't believe that the identity statement can be a priori derived from information about $H_2O$ and conceptual truths involving "$H_2O$" and "water".
48. Plausibly, this has to do with *phenomenal similarity*. One idea is that, however phenomenal similarity itself is constituted, a phenomenal concept's extension is determined by an associated disposition to make the relevant

similarity judgments, based on a comparator that, for example, uses a stored template or the like. So, my concept REDDISH refers to reddish in virtue of my disposition to deem reddish—as opposed to crimsonish—experiences as falling under it based on my recognition of their similarity to a stored template of a reddish experience. For more discussion of this, see Balog (2012a).

49. Notice that dualism, whatever other unattractive consequences it might have, does not face the Hardest Problem in the same way. A dualist can merely posit phenomenal states to be the unambiguous referent of phenomenal concepts.

## References

Baars, Bernard J., 1988. *A Cognitive Theory of Consciousness*. Cambridge University Press, New York.

Balog, Katalin, 1999. "Conceivability, Possibility, and the Mind-Body Problem", *The Philosophical Review*, *108*(4) (October). Reprinted in Volume XXIII of *The Philosopher's Annual*.

Balog, Katalin, 2005. "Ontological Novelty, Emergence, and the Mind-Body Problem". In Günter Abel (Ed.), *Kreativität*. Hamburg: Meiner Verlag.

Balog, Katalin, 2012a. "Acquaintance and the Mind-Body Problem". In Christopher Hill and Simone Gozzano (Eds.), *The Mental, the Physical* (pp. 16–43). Cambridge: Cambridge University Press.

Balog, Katalin, 2012b. "In Defense of the Phenomenal Concept Strategy". *Philosophy and Phenomenological Research*, *84*(1), 1–23.

Block, Ned, 2002. "The Harder Problem of Consciousness". *The Journal of Philosophy*, *99*(8), 391–425.

Block, Ned, 2006. "Max Black's Objection to Mind-Body Identity". In Dean Zimmerman (Ed.), *Oxford Studies in Metaphysics* (vol. 2, pp. 3–78). Oxford: Oxford University Press.

Block, Ned & Stalnaker, Robert 1999. "Conceptual Analysis, Dualism, and the Explanatory Gap", *Philosophical Review*, 108, 1–46.

Chalmers, David, 1996. *The Conscious Mind*, Oxford: Oxford University Press.

Chalmers, David, 2002. "Consciousness and Its Place in Nature". In S. Stich and F. Warfield, (Eds.), *Blackwell Guide to the Philosophy of Mind*. Malden, MA, USA: Blackwell.

Chalmers, David, 2003. "The Content and Epistemology of Phenomenal Belief". In Q. Smith and A. Jokic (Eds.), *Consciousness: New Philosophical Perspectives*. Oxford: Oxford University Press.

Chalmers, David, 2009. "The Two-Dimensional Argument against Materialism". In B. McLaughlin (Ed.), *The Oxford Handbook of the Philosophy of Mind*. Oxford: Oxford University Press.

Chalmers, David, 2017. "Panpsychism and Panprotopsychism". In *Panpsychism: Contemporary Perspectives*. Oxford: Oxford University Press.

Dennett, Daniel, 1991. *Consciousness Explained*. New York: Back Bay Books: Little, Brown and Company.

Fodor, Jerry A., 1975. *The Language of Thought*. Cambridge, MA: Harvard University Press.

Frankish, Keith, 2016. "Illusionism as a Theory of Consciousness". *Journal of Consciousness Studies*, *23*(11–12).

Harman, Gilbert, 1990. "The Intrinsic Quality of Experience". In *Phil Perspectives4, Action Theory and Philosophy of Mind* (pp. 31–52). Atascadero, CA: Ridgeview Publisher.

Hurley, Susan and Alva Noë, 2003. "Neural Plasticity and Conscoiusness". *Biology and Philosophy*, *18*, 131–168.

Jackson, Frank, 2003. "Mind and Illusion". In A. O'Hear (Ed.), *Minds and Persons*. Cambridge: Cambridge University Press.

Jackson, Frank and Chalmers, David, 2001. "Conceptual Analysis and Reductive Explanation". *The Philosophical Review*, *110*, 315–361.

Levine, Joseph, 2001. *Purple Haze*. Oxford: Oxford University Press.

Lewis, David, 1966. "An Argument for the Identity Theory". *Journal of Philosophy*, *63*(1) (January 6), 17–25.

Loar, Brian, 1990. "Phenomenal States". In *Philosophical Perspectives4, Action Theory and Philosophy of Mind* (pp. 81–108). Atascadero, CA: Ridgeview Publisher.

Loar, Brian, 1995. "Reference from the First-Person Perspective'. *Philosophical Issues: Content*, 6, 53–72. Reprinted in *Consciousness and Meaning: Selected Essays by Brian Loar* (eds. Katalin Balog and Stephanie Beardman). Oxford: Oxford University Press, 2017.

Loar, Brian, 1997. "Phenomenal States". In N. Block, O. Flanagan and G. Güzeldere (Eds.), *The Nature of Consciousness* (pp. 597–616). Cambridge, MA: MIT Press (revised version of Loar 1990). Reprinted in *Consciousness and Meaning: Selected Essays by Brian Loar* (eds. Katalin Balog and Stephanie Beardman). Oxford: Oxford University Press, 2017.

Lockwood, Michael, 1998. "The Enigma of Sentience". In S.R. Hameroff, et al. (Eds.), *Toward a Science of Consciousness II*. Cambridge, MA: MIT Press.

McLaughlin, Brian, 2006. "Identity, Explanation, and Consciousness: A Reply to Kim". forthcoming.

Nagel, Thomas, 1974. "What Is It Like to Be a Bat?". *Philosophical Review*, *83*, 435–450.

Papineau, David, 2002. *Thinking about Consciousness*. Oxford: Oxford University Press.

Papineau, David, 2003. "Could There Be a Science of Consciousness?". *Philosophical Issues*, *13*(1), 205–220.

Rey, Georges, 1988. "A Question about Consciousness". In H. Otto and J. Tueidio (Eds.), *Perspectives on Mind*. Dordrecht: Kluwer.

Rosenthal, David, 2002. "Explaining Consciousness". In Chalmers (Ed.), *Philosophy of Mind*. Oxford: Oxford University Press.

Stoljar, Daniel, 2001. "Two Conceptions of the Physical". *Philosophy and Phenomenological Research*, *62*, 253–281.

Stoljar, Daniel, 2005. "Physicalism and Phenomenal Concepts". *Mind and Language*, *20*(5), 469–495.

Strawson, Galen, 2003. "Realistic Materialism". In Louise M. Antony & Norbert Hornstein (Eds.), *Chomsky and His Critics*. Malden, MA, USA: Blackwell.

Strawson, Galen, 2006. "Realistic Monism: Why Physicalism Entails Panpsychism". In Anthony Freeman (Ed.), *Consciousness and Its Place in Nature: Does Physicalism Entail Panpsychism?* Exeter: Imprint Academic.

Sturgeon, Scott, 1994. "The Epistemic View of Subjectivity", *Journal of Philosophy*, *91*, 221–236.

Tononi, Giulio, Boly, Melanie, Massimini, Marcello and Koch, Christopher, 2016. "Integrated Information Theory: From Consciousness to Its Physical Substrate". *Nature Reviews Neuroscience*, 17, 450–461.

Tye, Michael, 2000. *Consciousness, Color and Content*, ch. 3., Cambridge, MA: MIT Press.

# 13 "Phenomenal States" and the Scope of the Phenomenal Concepts Strategy

*Janet Levin*

## 1. The Promise and Prescience of 'Phenomenal States'

Brian Loar's "Phenomenal States" has had extraordinary impact on the discussion of whether "what it's like" to have pains, color experiences, and other phenomenal states can be identified with physical (or psychofunctional) properties. The view that Loar advances is a progenitor of what is now called "a posteriori physicalism", "type-B materialism", "New Wave materialism", or the "Phenomenal Concepts Strategy",[1] an approach thought by many physicalists to provide the best account of how the phenomenal could be reduced to the physical, while explaining why dualism would nonetheless continue to exert an intuitive pull.

Loar begins by conceding that the best-known contemporary arguments against physicalism "take off from a sound intuition about concepts" which even the best efforts of analytic functionalists cannot dispel, namely, that "phenomenal concepts [that is, our 'subjective', introspection-derived, concepts of the qualitative character of our experiences] . . . neither a priori imply, nor are implied by, physical-functional concepts" (2017c, p. 196). It is this intuition, he argues, that supports Jackson's (1982) claim that Mary, the omniscient scientist raised from birth in a black-and-white environment, cannot know what it's like to see red, Kripke's (1972) claim that we can conceive of the existence of pain in the absence of any sort of brain activity, and Chalmers's (1996) claim that we can conceive of a creature (a "zombie") that is exactly like us physically, but has no conscious experiences whatsoever.

Loar notes, however, that these claims about what can be known or conceived—which derive from the *conceptual independence* of phenomenal and physical-functional concepts—do not by themselves yield the antiphysicalist conclusions of these arguments. What is needed, in addition, is a reason for thinking that the conceptual independence of these concepts implies that conscious experiences cannot be identical to physical-functional states or properties. And he argues that there is a common assumption that provides such reasons—which he calls the *Semantic Premise*:

> (SP) A statement of property identity that links conceptually independent concepts is true only if at least one concept picks out the property it refers to by connoting[2] a contingent property of that property.
> (2017c, p. 199)

Phenomenal-physical identity statements (such as "pain = C-fiber stimulation") fail to meet this condition, since neither term in these identity statements picks out its referent by "connoting" a contingent property of it: "pain" picks out its referent as the experience that *feels* a certain way—and anything that feels that way is pain (and vice versa); "C-fiber stimulation" picks out its referent as a certain type of neural activation—and anything that exhibits that type of activation is C-fiber stimulation (and vice versa). And thus, according to SP, given that these statements link conceptually independent concepts, we must conclude that they are false.

But why accept SP? One argument for the premise, as Loar notes (p. 199), is that it is a natural extension of Kripke's explanation of what it is that permits us to explain away the "appearance of contingency" of familiar *a posteriori* identity statements such as "water = H2O" or "heat = molecular motion".[3] A related argument, deriving from Max Black's well-known objection to J.J.C. Smart's (1959) argument for the identity theory, is that SP is required to explain how property identity statements can be both a posteriori and necessarily true.[4] However, if there is another way to explain, or explain away, these phenomena in the case of phenomenal-physical identity statements, then these identity statements may be regarded as (principled) exceptions to a generally plausible rule.

Loar's goal in "Phenomenal States" is to present an account of how phenomenal concepts pick out their referents that does just this. On Loar's account, phenomenal concepts are special sorts of self-directed type-demonstrative concepts of experience (which he often calls "recognitional" or "recognitional-demonstrative" concepts). They are mental designators acquired (at least standardly) by introspectively attending to one's current experience (against the "further conceptual background" that specifies that we're attempting to pick out a *property of an internal state* [p. 200]), and backed by dispositions to identify further experiences as "another one of those" or "more of the same".[5]

A subject's demonstrative focus on the experience-token that she is currently having ("internal state of *that* kind") is enough to single out that experience-token, but because a type-demonstrative must be backed by a disposition to reidentify further tokens as another of that type, it denotes not a particular, but whatever *property* is common to the instances that prompt (or would prompt) these reidentifications. And this, as Loar stresses, could well be a physical or psychofunctional property.[6] If so, then contrary to SP, a property identity statement (e.g. "pain = C-fiber stimulation") that links a phenomenal concept (which denotes rigidly and directly) and a "theoretical" rigid designator of that property (which denotes by "connoting" an *essential* property of its denotation) could be both a posteriori and true.

If Loar's semantics for phenomenal concepts is plausible, then physicalists have a response to both the conceivability and the knowledge arguments against physicalism. They can argue that even if the denials of phenomenal-physical identity statements can be conceived or imagined, those identity statements may nonetheless be (necessarily) true. And although what Mary gains upon leaving her black-and-white room is a panoply of new color concepts, they may well (directly) denote the neural properties involved in color vision that she had known about all along.[7] In addition, physicalists can argue that the way that phenomenal concepts pick out their referents is not shared by any other concepts invoked by the special sciences—which explains why there is an "explanatory gap" (Levine, 1983) between physical and phenomenal characterizations of our mental states that shows up nowhere else in our attempts at theoretical identification.

As I noted earlier, many physicalists have embraced this account as the most promising way to rebut these anti-physicalist arguments. But worries about it persist, among them that the identification of phenomenal concepts with self-directed type-demonstratives derived from introspection does not sufficiently distinguish them from non-phenomenal demonstrative concepts, or capture the richness of the knowledge provided by their acquisition, or sufficiently account for our special epistemic relation to phenomenal properties, or truly close the explanatory gap.[8] There have been many attempts by physicalists to address these questions, however, and I will not repeat them here.[9]

Instead—in the first part of the paper—I'll try to rebut some explicit objections to Loar's challenge to SP. I'll focus first on an objection by Stephen White, who (in his 2006, 2007, 2010) provides a long and intricate defense of SP based on Max Black's objection to Smart.[10] I'll then discuss an objection by David Papineau, who (in his 2007) argues that it's mistaken to think that the acceptance of SP is the primary source of doubts about physicalism, and gives an alternative explanation of what that source may be. In focusing on these objections I hope to highlight certain distinctive features of Loar's version of (what I'll from now on call) the Phenomenal Concepts Strategy, and show how it is uniquely equipped to deal with these objections, and also with the other worries, mentioned above, about whether such a "strategy" can succeed.

In later sections of the paper, I'll discuss Loar's attempt to expand the Phenomenal Concepts Strategy to explain what it is for a concept to have "narrow content", or "subjective intentionality" that is distinct from its externally determined referential content, and to do the same for our concept of reference itself. These projects, too, are prescient and promising—but in the end, as I'll argue, I am less sure that they can succeed.

## 2. White's Defense of SP

White defends SP by arguing that an a posteriori identity statement can be true only if there is an adequate explanation of how it can be *rationally denied or doubted*—and that this, in turn, requires that at least one of its constituent concepts pick out its referent by connoting a contingent property of it.[11] In developing his argument, White focuses not on Loar's SP, but on a slightly weakened and modified variation of it designed to avoid certain counterexamples,[12] which he calls the W(eakened) M(odified) SP:

> WMSP: A statement of identity that links conceptually independent concepts is true only if the expressions flanking the identity sign pick out their references by connoting contingently coextensive properties of that referent, or contingently coextensive properties of a property of that referent, or . . . and so on.
>
> (2007, p. 224)

White's argument for WMSP is rich and complex, and brings up many issues that deserve discussion,[13] but its primary structure is a "four stage argument" (2007, pp. 222–225) that comprises a sequence of requirements for an adequate explanation of how necessary identity statements could be subject to rational doubt or disbelief (and thus be a posteriori).

Requirement (1) is that "we must say how the world presents itself to the subject who believes incompatible and contradictory things about the same object by providing a set of possible worlds that are the way that subject takes the actual world to be"—which in turn requires that (2) "we must . . . provid[e] two distinct properties of the object in question which correspond to the subject's [distinct concepts of that object][14] and which are such that there is a possible world at which those properties are instantiated by different objects". And since the goal is to explain how any subjects, no matter what they know about the world, could be rational in doubting a posteriori identities, it follows that (3) the properties . . . that explain how a rational subject could fail to believe or disbelieve an a posteriori identity must be connected to the subject's [concepts of those properties] a priori".

In addition, to forestall a further objection,[15] White argues (p. 223) that, (4) the properties that satisfy (3) must be *thin*, that is, such that "there is nothing to [such a property] over and above what is understood by the subject who understands the predicate that expresses it" (p. 223).[16] It follows that, as WMSP demands, the concepts linked by a true a posteriori identity statement must "connote contingently coextensive properties of that referent, or contingently coextensive properties of a property of that referent . . . or (and so on)" to meet Requirements (1)-(4).

White provides interesting arguments for all these requirements, but I'll focus here on his argument for (1), the basis for all the others, which is—to repeat—that to explain how a rational subject could doubt or deny a true identity statement "we must say how the world presents itself to the subject who believes incompatible and contradictory things about the same object by providing a set of possible worlds that are the way that subject takes the actual world to be".[17]

But why must this be so? On Loar's view (a) the concepts linked in a phenomenal-physical identity statement acquire their common referent by, respectively, introspection and (theoretical) description, and (b) introspecting phenomenal properties—that is, accessing them "from the inside"—produces nothing but phenomenal concepts of them, and is the only method that can do so, and (c) phenomenal concepts have no a priori ties to any physical-functional concepts, and (d) the only general background information that directs their application is the (anodyne) assumption that phenomenal concepts denote properties of a subject's internal states.

If (a)-(d) are true, then it's clear why no amount of reflection upon a complete physical-functional description of the world can determine whether phenomenal concepts apply to the properties in it: the only way in which we can (standardly) acquire phenomenal concepts of those properties is by introspecting our own mental states. And this seems to provide sufficient explanation of how an empirically informed rational subject could doubt or disbelieve such identity statements. That is, if Loar's account of phenomenal concepts is correct, then there can be an explanation of the rationality of such doubting subjects that does not meet the condition expressed in Premise (1).

White objects, however, that to offer such an explanation would be to embrace "local eliminativism", a view that explains how someone could doubt or disbelieve a posteriori necessities in terms of differences in the *causal routes* from the different concepts to the referent, instead of differences in their (Fregean) *contents*. And local eliminativism, White continues, is untenable—because there is no principled way of explaining why these cases should be exceptions, and no principled way of explaining what the difference is between a phenomenal and a physical-functional concept "that would justify the claim that the a posteriori character of the identity had been adequately explained" (p. 221). However, the central argument of "Phenomenal States" is that treating phenomenal concepts as recognitional-demonstratives that pick out their referents directly via introspection both allows us to make a principled distinction between phenomenal and non-phenomenal concepts, and to explain why phenomenal-physical identity statements are the only "theoretical" identity statements that rational subjects could doubt or deny, no matter how much they know about the world.[18]

Still, it may be that even if "local eliminativism" need not go global, there may be other worries about phenomenal-physical identities that Loar's account of phenomenal concepts does not put to rest. After all, I've presented Loar's considered view as the contention that phenomenal concepts pick out their referents directly, without mediation by *any* "mode of presentation" whatsoever. This way of putting things, however, prompts the objection that these concepts, when used to reidentify instances of some particular phenomenal property in introspection as *another one of those*, do not seem "bare" or "naked", but rather seem to be accompanied by our awareness of *the way these states feel*. We have something in mind, that is, when we identify, and reidentify, a phenomenal property in introspection; thus it seems that phenomenal concepts do indeed pick out their referents by connoting higher-level *phenomenal* properties—and if they do, then phenomenal-physical identity statements remain vulnerable to SP.

Now Loar often explains this phenomenon by noting simply that when phenomenal concepts (but not, say, blindsight concepts) are deployed in introspection, they are used to identify instances of *phenomenal properties*, that is, the properties of mental states that (necessarily) *feel a certain way* to the (attentive) subjects who are introspecting them—so (although he puts it more politely) whaddaya expect!?[19] I think that this sufficiently explains why it is incorrect to think of phenomenal concepts as mere "pointers". But sometimes Loar characterizes phenomenal concepts in a somewhat different way, namely, that "a phenomenal concept has as its mode of presentation the very phenomenal quality that it picks out" (p. 205). A phenomenal concept, that is, picks out its referent by connoting an *essential* feature of it: that property itself.

This way of putting things may seem to make it clearer why it's incorrect to think of phenomenal concepts as bare pointers. But it also suggests another way of deploying WMSP against Loar's view, given that the theoretical-physical concept in a phenomenal-physical identity statement will *also* pick out its referent by connoting an essential property of it. The problem, as Loar puts it early on in "Phenomenal States"), is that many maintain that:

> if two concepts conceive a given property essentially, neither mediated by contingent modes of presentation, one ought to be able to see a priori—at least after optimal reflection—that they pick out the same property. Such concepts' connections cannot be a posteriori; that they pick out the same property would have to be transparent. (p. 199)[20]

This principle, like SP, has a track record, since there are many familiar cases in which identity statements linking concepts each of which "conceives a given property essentially" can be seen a priori (after optimal reflection) to be true, for example, mathematical and geometrical statements such as "being a square = being an equilateral rectangle" and "2 + 3 = 5"—as well as various philosophical theses about the nature of such things as free action, knowledge, or the good. Loar, however, argues that this principle is false, and in particular, that the phenomenal recognitional-demonstrative and the physical-functional concept in an identity statement (e.g. *pain* and *C-fiber* stimulation) can both be regarded as conceiving the same property—in this case, C-fiber stimulation—essentially, but doing so in distinct, irreducible *ways*. As he puts it (p. 211),

> [w]hat generates the problem is not appreciating that there can be two conceptually independent "direct grasps" of a single essence, that is, grasping it demonstratively by experiencing it, and grasping it in theoretical terms. The illusion is of *expected transparency*: a direct grasp of a property ought to reveal how it is internally constituted, and if it is not revealed as physically constituted, then it is not so. The mistake is the thought that a direct grasp of essence ought to be a transparent grasp.

White embraces this requirement of transparency, and argues that the only way a property denoted by a concept can be its own mode of presentation is if the property is "thin"—that is, has no "intrinsic features besides those of which the subject is immediately aware" (2007, p. 215).[21] And thus, he continues, phenomenal concepts "cannot figure in true, *a posteriori* mental-physical identities of the kind with which we are concerned." It is not clear, however, what the argument for this claim is, beyond White's contention (for example, in his argument for Requirement [4]) that the restriction to "thin" properties is necessary to avoid local eliminativism. But as I've already argued, Loar can endorse what White calls local eliminativism—and keep it in the neighborhood—by making a principled distinction between phenomenal and non-phenomenal concepts, and providing an explanation, based on the unique features of phenomenal concepts, of why rational subjects could doubt or deny phenomenal-physical identity statements no matter how much they know about the world. Finally, Loar can say what it is for concepts not linked a priori to "present" the same essence, namely, that (p. 203) they "directly rigidly denote" the same property, where this means that they denote the same property in all metaphysically and epistemically possible worlds.[22]

However, even if my challenge to White's defense of SP (and WMSP) is successful, it may ultimately be irrelevant to a proper defense of physicalism. As mentioned earlier, David Papineau (2007) has argued that the real source of opposition to physicalism lies elsewhere. I will discuss his argument in the next section.

## 3. Papineau on Phenomenal-Physical Identity Statements and Loar's SP

In his (2007) Papineau argues that Kripke's challenge to the physicalist is best understood as a demand not merely to explain how phenomenal-physical identity statements can seem false to people with no views about the matter, but rather "to explain why they *still* appear possibly false, even to people who *do* believe them" (p. 479). According to Papineau, the crucial premise in Kripke's antiphysicalist argument is not

(I) If a necessary true claim is a posteriori, then at least one of its terms must be associated with a descriptive content (p. 476), but rather,
(II) If a necessary truth still seems contingent after it is believed, then it must have some descriptive content (p. 480).

Papineau supports this contention by contrasting the epistemic position of a "committed physicalist" who comes to believe that "pain is C-fiber stimulation" is true with the epistemic position of a person who comes to believe, after initially being doubtful, that "Cicero is Tully" is true. Once someone comes to believe the truth of "Cicero is Tully", Papineau suggests, it no longer appears "possibly false"; that is, one is not tempted in the least to doubt or deny that identity statement, even while acknowledging that it is possible to do so, since its denial is conceptually coherent (p. 488). But, he contends, phenomenal-physical identity claims will seem possibly false, in the relevant sense, even to a committed physicalist.[23] And thus if (II) is true, and neither the physical nor the phenomenal term in the identity statement has any descriptive content, there are grounds to doubt the necessity of the identity, and thus its truth.

However, Papineau argues that although (II) may be true, it does not accurately represent the epistemic position of committed physicalists. It's not that they believe phenomenal physical identity statements, but find that they still seem contingent, but rather that they don't "fully believe" these identities: while they have the *theoretical* conviction that these identities are true, they don't really believe them at an "*intuitive* level" (p. 483). And thus (II) is false. As he puts it (p. 483), ". . . at neither level do we get an appearance of *contingency*—an appearance combining actual truth and possible falsity. That I take to be ruled out by Kripke's argument. Rather we get an impression of actual falsity—a fortiori possible falsity—at the intuitive level, and an impression of actual truth—and so no possible falsity—at the theoretical level". Nonetheless, Papineau contends, since these intuitive and theoretical beliefs are held on different "levels", one's intuitive belief in dualism and theoretical belief in physicalism are not really in conflict. And since one's theoretical beliefs are one's considered beliefs, physicalists need not take their intuitive beliefs to pose problems for their metaphysics.

In my view Papineau's distinction between two "levels" of belief gives too much credence to Premise II.[24] It is also, in my view, unnecessary, since there is sufficient material in "Phenomenal States" to challenge Premise II itself. Attention to the fact that phenomenal concepts have no conceptual links to physical-functional concepts or reference-fixing conceptions makes it clear why a phenomenal-physical identity statement still seems contingent—or at least can be conceived to be false—even after it is believed.[25]

In short, the fact that our phenomenal concepts give us no conception of anything beyond the phenomenal seems to explain sufficiently why even "committed physicalists"—those who "fully believe" phenomenal-physical identities to be true—feel an intuitive pull away from physicalism when they think about the nature of phenomenal states. Moreover—and this is something that Papineau does not consider—this isolation can explain why rational subjects would have the same intuitions about *dualism* if they were to think of it as a substantive metaphysical thesis rather than merely as the denial of physicalism.[26] Nonetheless, Papineau's discussion is useful in prompting us to focus, once again, on what's distinctive about Loar's view.

To sum up: Loar's characterization of phenomenal concepts in "Phenomenal States" provides a particularly effective defense of physicalist theories of experiential states against arguments such as Kripke's, Chalmers's, Jackson's, and any others that rely, even implicitly, on SP and its consequences. It characterizes our phenomenal concepts of experiential states as (type) recognitional-demonstratives, and explains how such concepts can refer to physical (or physical-functional) states of the brain both rigidly and directly; that is, without introducing, or connoting, any irreducibly non-physical modes of presentation of those states. In addition, unlike any recognitional-demonstrative concepts we may have of kinds such as water, Saguaro cactus, or gold, there are no background presuppositions that guide the use of phenomenal recognitional-demonstratives that put constraints *on the metaphysical type* of the items they denote.[27] In short, the view of phenomenal concepts that Loar presents in "Phenomenal States" has more resources than most to counter these well-known anti-physicalist arguments.[28]

However, Loar also appeals to phenomenal concepts to solve other difficult problems in the philosophy of mind and language. In his (2017b,d,e,f) he invokes type-demonstrative phenomenal concepts of certain features of our perceptual experiences and thoughts about objects and properties to characterize the "psychological content" of our concepts of (external) objects and properties, and, even more ambitiously, he invokes type-demonstrative phenomenal concepts to characterize our concept of *reference* in a way that seeks to minimize Quine's worries about "inscrutability"—and here, at least arguably, the terrain gets rougher, or at least more complicated, for the Phenomenal Concepts Strategy. I will discuss these proposals in the next two sections.

## 4. Phenomenal Concepts and Phenomenal Intentionality

In an important—and again pioneering—series of articles (2017a, 2017b, 2017d, 2017e, 2017f), Loar maintains that externalists such as Putnam and Burge are correct to claim that the references of concepts such as *water* and *arthritis* (among many others) depend in part upon facts about a subject's environment or the usage of these concepts by her linguistic community—and therefore are not determined solely by what's in the subject's head. He calls this "social" content. Loar argues, however, that there is another type of content, "psychological" content, that *is* determined solely by what's in the head, and can thus be shared by ourselves, by our counterparts both on Twin Earth and in communities with different linguistic practices, and even by isolated brains in vats—and in these articles he sets out to characterize the nature of this special sort of content.[29] As Loar acknowledges, this is not so easy to do, and it seems that his views on the matter have evolved. Thus, although he discusses this question in a number of places, I will focus on "Transparent Experience and the Availability of Qualia" (2017e) and especially "Phenomenal Intentionality as the Basis of Mental Content" (2017f) since these represent his most recent work on the topic.

After considering and rejecting the idea that the psychological content of a concept can be identified with the subject's object-directed dispositions (2017e, p. 281), or more generally, with the concept's conceptual role (2017f, p. 296)—on the grounds that conceptual role is "too *blank* to constitute internal mental content as we conceive it"—Loar suggests that there is a *phenomenological* commonality among (at least) the perceptual concepts of all those whose psychological profiles are the same, a kind of *intrinsic outer-directedness* (or *phenomenal intentionality*) that is salient upon reflection, but hard to define. As he puts it in his (2017e, p. 281),

> We cannot define [our concept of directedness], for it is a phenomenological concept. We have a feel for what seeing a lemon shares with an indistinguishable hallucination. We can reflect on the two experiences in imagination and see what they have in common . . . [and] discern a non-relational phenomenal quality of visual experience . . . From this oblique perspective we . . . can identify similar object-directedness throughout all normal visual experiences and in hallucinations phenomenally identical to them. We thereby grasp the general concept of object-directedness. Such higher-order phenomenological concepts are, I want to say, recognitional concepts, type-demonstratives that pick out repeatable phenomena, in this case, intentional features of experience.

Here he calls the shared phenomenal object-directedness of these experiences "intentional qualia". Similarly, in his (2017f, p. 302), Loar invites us to

> Suppose some indistinguishable lemons are one after the other brought to my visual attention . . . I am asked to think something about each lemon in turn, say "that's yellow". Afterwards I am told that some of the apparent lemons were hallucinations. . . . I am asked whether, despite this, my successive visual demonstrative thoughts all visually presented their objects in the same way. Surely, a natural reply is "yes", in a rather intuitive sense.

There he calls this distinctive feature of experience "phenomenal intentionality" (or p. 314, "the paint that points"), and adds that we can discern it in our perceptual concepts of kinds and spatial properties as well. He contends, moreover, (p. 317), that "We are, it seems to me, as entitled to speak of phenomenal intentionality as we are of the felt qualities of a sensation".

And so, perhaps, we are. But there are some important differences between these concepts and the type-demonstratives we use to pick out the felt qualities of sensation, *what it's like* to see red or feel pain, in introspection. First—if we indeed acquire these recognitional concepts from the "oblique perspective"—we can only discern the phenomenal property of directedness "obliquely", by comparing imagined or remembered perceptual experiences with one another, or with an experience one is having at the time. Moreover, and unlike the fairly specific phenomenal concepts of properties such as what it's like to feel pain or see red, the phenomenal type-demonstrative concept of *directedness* is supposed to be highly general, applicable to many different kinds of perceptual experiences and phenomenally identical hallucinations.

And thus the phenomenon in question seems harder to pin down—and this, in turn, makes it harder to determine whether there is in fact a common neural (or otherwise physical-functional) property that the concept *directedness* denotes.[30] Second, it's not completely clear why the property denoted should be considered to be a kind of *content*, parallel (at least in certain ways) to the referential (social) content that both Loar and the externalists agree that our concepts of objects, kinds, and properties possess. Why not regard it as just another phenomenologically salient property of our perceptual experiences that may be useful for psychological explanation?

Now there may be acceptable answers to both questions. As for the first, it may just be a matter of psychological fact that there's a phenomenologically compelling commonality among our perceptual experiences of objects, natural kinds, and various perceivable properties that, although strictly undefinable, seems well enough described as the presentation of various phenomena as external to oneself.[31] Indeed, it's (at least arguably) plausible that there are bio-evolutionary reasons for perceptual experience's exhibiting this commonality, since we are, after all, creatures whose survival depends on our ability to interact with objects and other individuals like ourselves in the world outside the mind.[32] And therefore, there may be just as good grounds for thinking that these commonalities can be identified with physical (or physical-functional) properties as there are for the "felt qualities of sensation".

As for the second question, Loar asks it himself (p. 305): "Why call directedness intentional if it is non-relational, if it is about the how rather than the what of perception?", and he immediately answers, "What else to call it? It seems to be the primitive basis of our intuitions of the phenomenal 'aboutness' of perception." But he doesn't seem satisfied to leave things there. He goes on to say, in attempting to depict the relation between phenomenal directedness and genuine (external) referential content (pp. 316–17), that "[d]irectedness is an object-independent property. But it is intimately involved in what is often called the diaphanousness of perception. Directedness is diaphanousness without an actual object . . . [or] diaphanousness toward intentional objects, whether 'mere' or real". He continues (p. 317), with reference, once again, to a succession of experiences as of seeing a lemon:

> Now imagine having one of the lemon experiences without knowing whether it is veridical. You are strongly tempted to say "that object". Your perceptual processing presses mightily on your belief inclinations, so strongly that you seem to commit yourself, by using a demonstrative, and to take it back at the same time: "that object may or may not exist". . . . Suppose you then discover that it is real. At this point the question arises of the object's actual nonphenomenological relation to your perception. It turns out that a certain optical-causal relation holds in all such cases. The ghostly internal relation gets embodied in something nonmental and out there.

And thus, even if we're merely hallucinating a lemon, the phenomenal similarity of that experience to (what we recognize to be) the veridical experience permits us to regard it as having a distinctive kind of internal "directedness"—without requiring that we be related to any object, either merely intentional or real.[33]

Now Loar warns (p. 316) that this answer may not be "fully digestible". But in my view this indigestibility, whatever it amounts to, could be avoided. First, if we understand Loar's claim that phenomenal intentionality or directedness is indefinable as the claim that (just as for our phenomenal concepts of "felt sensations") this salient feature of experience must be picked out purely demonstratively, then all we need to do is point at an instance of directedness, and have the disposition to identify further instances of this property as *another one of those*. It does not seem necessary to characterize this salient though undefinable "directedness" as any sort of diaphanousness, or ghostly relation at all, especially since Loar takes pains to maintain that phenomenal intentionality is intrinsic and non-relational. And if there is a common physical-functional property possessed by all (or most) of the instances reidentified, then directedness—like felt sensations—can be identified with a physical-functional property.

Could it be that there is a *presupposition* that guides the use of the demonstrative that requires that what is demonstrated be some or other sort of *relation*? This would be unfortunate, since as Loar points out, the only possible items to which subjects hallucinating lemons could be related are intentional objects—and he makes clear that this is a problematic view. And, as he suggests, it would get the phenomenology wrong: insofar as we take there to be a kind of directedness that is common to both veridical experiences and hallucinations, we require only that the directedness that we're demonstrating be a particularly distinctive sort of non-relational property. As Loar puts it, p. 317, "The lemon demonstratives had this property in common: They purport-to-pick-out-an-object".[34]

Still, the paragraph quoted above may reflect the worry that something more needs to be said about what's distinctive about phenomenal directedness. It seems that Loar wants to avoid characterizing it as just some purely sensory feature of the state I'm in when seeing or hallucinating a lemon; there has to be something about this feature of experience that can explain why we naturally take it to purport-to-pick-out-an-object, even if we think that the experience is not, or may not be, veridical. But there is a reasonable, if perhaps boring, explanation available to Loar of what makes these experiences phenomenally outer-directed, even in the face of skepticism about whether any such objects exist, namely, that we have the *inclination to believe* that we're perceiving a lemon, and to form other relevant beliefs, given our desires and other mental states. In short, what contributes to the distinctive and common phenomenal character of our experiences that purport to point is that they share a distinctive conceptual role.

Granted, Loar argues that one cannot characterize the outer-directedness of a perceptual concept (or perceptual experience) *solely* as a matter of its having a distinctive conceptual role. As noted earlier, he maintains (p. 296) that conceptual roles are "too *blank* to constitute internal mental content as we conceive it . . . phenomenological reflection on thinking hardly conceives its properties in purely dispositional terms".[35] Moreover, he continues, we can't just add "pure" phenomenology to conceptual role to get psychological content. As he puts it (p. 297), "we can hardly peel the phenomenal aspects of vision away from its intentionality; we just do not have nonintentional conceptions of visual fields or the like".

Now I'm not quite on board with Loar's final claim, but no matter. The suggestion I've made does not require that conceptual role alone account for the "liveliness'" of what it's like to have an experience that purports to point to a lemon that exists outside the mind, nor that we be able to isolate some non-intentional phenomenal feature to add to an otherwise purely dispositional characterization of an experience. All that's required—or so it seems—is that the inclination to believe that there's a lemon before me, or to reach out as if to touch a lemon, is a feature of the experience that *contributes to* its distinctive "outer-directed" phenomenology. And this would be so if an experience without this dispositional feature just wouldn't feel *that way* (and also that analogous dispositions are present in other experiences of outer-directedness, whether veridical or not).[36] We may not be able to read off the phenomenal character of these experiences from a description of their conceptual role plus qualitative "remainder", but Loar's point, in "Phenomenal States", is that this is not required for that description to pick out a phenomenal property of a mental state.

That is, it seems that, given the right combination of phenomenology and conceptual role, backed by bio-evolutionary contingencies that make it likely that we have physical-functional states that seem natural to characterize, from a first-person point of view, as purporting-to-pick-out-an-object—we may be able to make lemonade. I'm not so sure, however, that this is true for Loar's attempt, in his (2017d), to use phenomenal type-demonstratives to solve the problem of the inscrutability of reference. I will discuss this question in the next, and final, section.

## 5. Phenomenal Concepts and the Determinacy of Reference[37]

In his "Reference from the First-Person Perspective" (2017d), Loar suggests yet another role for phenomenal concepts, namely, to specify the relation of *reference* from the first person, and thereby respond to Quine's argument that there is no objective (causal-relational) "fact of the matter" whether a term or concept such as "rabbit" refers to rabbits rather than temporal stages of rabbits or undetached rabbit parts.[38] Unlike some philosophers who argue that there are indeed such objective facts of the matter, Loar concedes Quine's point. He also denies that appeal to disquotation can single out an objective referential relation that holds between "rabbit" and rabbits, but not "rabbit" and rabbit stages.[39]

Nonetheless, Loar argues that we can identify, from the *first-person perspective*—once again by employing a phenomenal type-demonstrative concept—a commonality that holds between our *concepts* of concept-object pairs such as ("rabbit", rabbit) and ("tree", tree) but not between pairs such as ("rabbit", rabbit-stage) and ("tree", tree surface), namely, that they are *related in that characteristic way*; that is (p. 264), as "appear[ing] to have a characteristic configuration, a distinctive feel, as if the object is peculiarly salient in the company of that concept". He continues (p. 267–8):

> it is as if there is a rule that generates, open-endedly, the concept-object pairs themselves—even though we know reflectively that the rule governs not the pairs themselves but our conceptions of them. This merely subjective perspective on concept-object pairs is phenomenologically

> stable, and from it we are able to conceive that objective external relation (as we judge it), which holds of this pair and that pair etc. It is in this sense that we may count our conception of the visual-demonstrative relation as a recognitional concept that is formed from an essentially first-person perspective.[40]

Loar's initial examples involve visual-demonstrative concepts, but he maintains that this phenomenologically stable type-demonstrative will also pick out that distinctive feature of (our conceptions of) other concept-object pairs (such as ("Cary Grant", Cary Grant) and ("copper", copper)) that have, as he puts it, a similar "mention-use" structure. And, as he argues, once we have put these concept-object pairs "on the table" (via our first-person phenomenal concepts of the distinctive "feel" they have in common), we can consider those pairs objectively, from the third-person point of view.

Now one might expect Loar's conclusion to be that, upon consideration, we will indeed find that these concept-object pairs have an objective commonality. This, after all, was his conclusion about the referents of our recognitional-demonstrative phenomenal concepts of what it's like to feel pain or see red and also of the "outer-directedness" of our perceptual concepts of objects, kinds, and properties in the world. But this is not the case. Loar acknowledges that, even when we've managed to get all those "mention-use" pairs "on the table", we will find no objective causal-relational facts that can distinguish them from sequences of non-standard pairs such as ("rabbit", rabbit stage).[41]

Nonetheless, he argues (p. 271), "the objective indeterminacy of semantic properties does not have the eliminative, subversive consequences it is usually seen to have. For, our ordinary conceptions of semantic relations are in part subjective; that is, it is essential to those conceptions that they conceive the relations they pick from the mention-use configuration." And, he suggests, if this conception is phenomenologically robust, then we have vindicated our intuition that our *concept* of reference cannot be regarded as stipulative or deflationary, or otherwise an eliminable or inconsequential feature of our thoughts about the relation between our concepts and the world. Granted, this conclusion may be disappointing to those who seek an objective feature exclusive to all and only the concept-object pairs such as ("rabbit", rabbit) that we "put on the table" from a subjective point of view. But this of course isn't Loar's objective; his goal is only to show that we have a substantive phenomenal type-demonstrative *concept* of a special relation that holds of just these "mention-use" pairs.

However, there is some cause for worry as to whether even this is so. First, there's a question (raised initially by D. Sosa, 1995) about why it is that only pairs such as ("rabbit", rabbit) get "put on the table" for further scrutiny. After all, recall how Loar characterizes the "phenomenologically stable" type-demonstrative in question, namely, being related *in that characteristic way*; as "appear[ing] to have a characteristic configuration, a distinctive feel, as if the object is peculiarly salient in the company of that concept." Recall, too, that Loar notes that "it is as if there is a rule that generates, open-endedly, the concept-object pairs themselves".

Now it may well be that "mention-use" pairs such as ("rabbit", rabbit) meet both these conditions. But so may pairs such as ("rabbit", rabbit stage)—and therefore we cannot distinguish the former from the latter set of concept-object pairs in this way. Indeed, there are other open-ended sequences of concept-object pairs that may also appear to have a distinctive and salient relation, e.g., ("one", two), ("two", three). To be sure, Sosa notes, Loar could argue that for sequences of pairs like the former—and only those—there is a phenomenologically distinctive, albeit ineffable, *way* in which the object is "salient in the company of the concept". However, he argues, Loar needs to say more about what makes *that* salient relation between concept and object the relation of *reference*—even from the first-person perspective.

It seems, however, that Loar may be able to answer that question, given that his goal is merely to show that there is *some* phenomenologically distinctive relation between concept and object in pairs such as ("rabbit", rabbit)—but nowhere else[42]—that we can identify from the first person: if this relation *seems* from the first person to be reference, that's enough for it to be reference-from-the-first person. And this, for Loar, would be enough to show that even if there is no objective relation that holds between pairs like ("rabbit", rabbit) that doesn't hold equally between pairs like ("rabbit", rabbit stage), and even if the disquotational schema provides at best a deflationary account of objective reference, our first-person conception of that schema is a substantive feature of our *concept* of the reference relation.[43]

However, this raises yet another question, namely, whether the sort of distinctive salience that we recognize, from the first person, in a concept-object pair such as ("rabbit", rabbit) is to be found in all and only instances of pairs that exhibit the mention-use configuration. Presumably, in considering the pairs ("rabbit", rabbit) and ("rabbit", rabbit-stage) *at one time*, we may find that (our concept of) the former, but not the latter, relation has a special sort of phenomenological salience. But this does not guarantee that we won't at some point find other sorts of concept-object pairs to be related *in that characteristic way*. In addition, we may find that certain instances of the mention-use configuration strike us *in that way* more than others.

This (quasi-Wittgensteinian) worry is often raised for *all* accounts of phenomenal concepts that treat them as type-demonstratives backed by dispositions to identify other particulars as *that again*, or *another one of those*; that is, that we have no right to assume that successive uses of the demonstratives are picking out instances of the same type of thing.[44]

But (at least arguably) there is a reasonable response to this worry when directed to our phenomenal concepts of *what it's like* to see red or feel pain. First, the contingencies of what goes on when one focuses on one's own mental states in introspection narrow the possibilities for *which* property of those states one may be picking out when inclined to judge "that again". Second, there seem to be good bio-evolutionary reasons for thinking that one's dispositions to reidentify the "felt" features of one's own sensations and perceptual experiences are reasonably accurate, and thereby (by and large) pick out instances of the same phenomenal (and thus, for physicalists, the same physical-functional) property. Moreover, although one cannot acquire the phenomenal concept of *directedness* so directly, there may be good bio-evolutionary reasons for thinking that we can (by and large) successfully reidentify instances of *that* phenomenal (and thus, for physicalists, physical-functional) property as well.[45]

However, unlike for phenomenal concepts such as *what it's like to see red* or *what it's like to feel pain*, and for the phenomenal concept of *directedness*, it's harder to argue that there are bio-evolutionary reasons that make it likely that, in the case of (subjective) reference, we're reidentifying instances of the same phenomenal (and for physicalists, the same physical-functional) type. We can understand why it's important to be able to identify instances of our sensations and perceptual experiences, and why it's important to have a phenomenologically distinctive conception of *directedness*, but why should there be bio-evolutionary reasons to ensure that use-mention pairs have a substantive and common phenomenology that distinguishes them from non-standard pairs such as ("rabbit", rabbit-stage)—even when conceived from the first-person—especially if there's no objective causal-relational difference between the two.

Loar may well have an answer to this question, but even if not, it may not matter: having a substantive phenomenal concept of *directedness* seems enough to ensure that we have a substantive grip on how we conceptualize our relation to objects and properties in the world—even if it's only a "purported" relation that can be shared by an isolated brain in a vat. As I've argued in previous sections, Loar's introduction of the "Phenomenal Concept Strategy" has successfully shown that there is no logical bar to thinking of the phenomenal properties of our sensations and experiences as physical-functional properties, and it seems reasonable to suggest that this strategy can be extended to naturalize the intrinsic phenomenal outer-directedness of our perceptual experiences and thoughts about the world. And this, in my view, is accomplishment enough.[46]

## Notes

1. So-called, respectively, by McLaughlin, Chalmers, Horgan, Stoljar. See Horgan (1984) for a similar view.

2. Loar does not explicitly say what it is for a concept to "connote" a contingent property, but he gives a number of examples: first, by being associated with a *description* that specifies a higher-level property (or "mode of presentation") possessed by its denotation in this, but not all possible, worlds; second, by being associated with a *non-linguistic conception* that demonstratively specifies such a property, for example, the "visual conception" or "perceptual mode of presentation" (p. 198) one might associate with the concept *gold* when specifying gold as the stuff that *looks like that*. Nor does Loar explicitly say what sort of relation there must be between a concept and what it connotes, but it must have some sort of special epistemic status; e.g. it must be *a priori* (Kripke, 1972, pp. 135–6), or (perhaps equivalently) regarded as true in every "world considered as actual".
3. It may seem, for example, that there could be worlds in which H2O exists in the absence of water, or molecular motion exists in the absence of heat—and thus worlds that stand as counterexamples to those identity statements. But if, after further thought, we recognize that we take 'water' and 'heat' to have their references fixed by descriptions that pick out contingent properties of their denotations (for example, *the stuff that fills Earth's lakes and oceans* and *the phenomenon that produces heat sensations in humans*), we can redescribe those putative counterexamples as worlds in which H2O exists in the absence of (not water, but) *the stuff that fills Earth's lakes and oceans*, or a world in which molecular motion exists in the absence of (not heat, but) *the phenomenon that produces heat sensations in humans*. And since those properties of water and heat are merely contingent, the existence of *those* worlds is compatible with the truth of the identity statements in question. This is how Kripke presents the situation in his argument against phenomenal-physical identities (1972, Lecture 3), where he gives many similar examples—and then points out that no such contingent reference-fixing descriptions are available to explain away the apparent contingency of statements such as 'pain = C-fiber stimulation'. However, although Kripke gives many examples of necessary a posteriori statements for which this condition holds, he never gives an explicit argument for why it must hold for all.
4. To be sure, Smart, Black, etc. say that statements such as 'water = H2O' express "contingent identities", but their debate is now understood as directed toward identity statements that are necessary a posteriori.
5. In a later discussion (2003, pp. 117, 120), Loar suggests that one is typically *confident* that one can reidentify the property in question, but this does not seem essential to the view.
6. This view does not rule out mistake: the concept can denote a property even if the re-identifications are occasionally prompted by instances of other properties. And if no physical property (or benign disjunction of them) consistently prompts one's disposition to reidentify one's internal state as "another one of those", then one must embrace an error theory—or dualism. There is the further question of what it means to say that an instance of a property "prompts" one to classify it as "another one of those". If the property in question is a physical property, then this can be taken to mean "causes". If it's *not* a physical property, then . . . well, beats me! (But see Chalmers on "pure phenomenal concepts".)
7. And it is because there are no conceptual links between Mary's newly acquired phenomenal concepts and the physical-functional ones she already possesses that, if she were to forget all information about those phenomenal-physical identities and the typical causes of various kinds of experiences, but retained the newly acquired phenomenal concepts, she still wouldn't be able to apply those concepts to an individual on the basis of a full objective description of the world. See Stoljar (2005), Nida-Rumelin (1996).

8. See, for example, Chalmers (2007), Levine (2007), and more recently, Goff (2017).
9. For more detail, see my (2007), (2008), and (2018). Also see Papineau (2002), Balog (1999, 2012), Hill and McLaughlin (1999), Diaz-Leon (2014).
10. To be sure, it seems that much of the skepticism about phenomenal-physical identity statements, including Kripke's, can ultimately be traced to this objection. Nonetheless, White's worries have been discussed less frequently in the literature than most others—but see Block (2007) for some trenchant criticisms of the view.
11. See White (2007), p. 212. Chalmers (2006), in arguing that any statement with a necessary epistemic intension must be a priori, seems to have similar concerns.
12. An example of a case that is a counterexample to SP, but not WMSP, is described in Note 15.
13. For some of them, see Block (2007).
14. White calls these concepts "Representational Modes of Presentation" or RMP's.
15. For example, consider the a posteriori statement 'the diameter of the Earth = n meters'. Suppose we take both concepts to rigidly denote the same number—the first by means of the associated description 'the *actual* diameter of the Earth', and the second by means of 'n times the length of the *actual* meter stick'. Each description will be connected *a priori* with the property it uniquely designates, but there will be no worlds in which their designations come apart—and thus there is no possible world that is the way a doubting subject takes our world to be. This is why (4) must be added.
16. White suggests that there are three equivalent ways of characterizing thinness:

    (1) A property is thin iff it confers no empirically discoverable essence on the things in which it is instantiated.
    (2) A property is thin iff the predicate that expresses it has an intension that is invariant wrt contexts of acquisition and/or utterance.
    (3) A property is thin iff the predicate that expresses it is fully intentionalized—that is, we do not have to determine the reference of this expression at the actual world to determine its extension at a possible world.

    Similar criteria, it seems, are that the concepts must be semantically stable or not "Twin Earthable" (Bealer), or semantically neutral (Chalmers). I won't discuss the question of whether these notions are equivalent, but see Byrne and Pryor (2006) for a related discussion.
17. Such a principle seems to be what Kripke relies on when he attempts to differentiate identity statements such as 'water is H2O' from phenomenal-physical identity statements on the grounds that, for the former but not the latter, there are epistemically indistinguishable (but metaphysically different) worlds at which those statement would be false.
18. White's argument is much more nuanced and complex, and this sketch does not do it justice, but I think I have presented its conclusion in a way consistent with White's text.
19. What he *does* say is that "if phenomenal concepts reflect basic recognitions of internal physical-functional states, they *should* be conceptually independent of theoretical physical-functional descriptions. That is what you expect quite apart from issues concerning physicalism". (p. 202) This observation also provides an answer to White's worry that an explanation of the cognitive difference between phenomenal and physical concepts that appeals merely to differences in their causal roles is not acceptable, since it is not an explanation that permits subjects to justify their doubt or disbelief in some phenomenal-physical identity statement at the "personal level". If the

cognitive difference lies in the fact that one has access to a phenomenal property—a *feeling*—by means, respectively, of introspection and some non-introspective route (e.g. identifying it via MRI scan), this seems to provide sufficient "personal level" justification.

20. See Goff (2017) for a recent version of this (seemingly evergreen) worry, and see Diaz-Leon (2014) and my (forthcoming) for a response.
21. Compare Goff (2017).
22. I myself would say instead that there's no reason to deny that phenomenal and physical-functional concepts pick out their (physical) referents transparently, since the only characterization of this notion that does not beg the question against the physicalist is that these concepts pick out the same property in all metaphysically and epistemically possible worlds (or, Chalmers puts it, in worlds considered as counterfactual *and* actual.) See my (2018) for further elaboration.
23. Papineau here is contrasting attitudes toward a property identity claim with attitudes toward a singular identity claim, but he could make the same point about the difference in property identity statements as well.
24. Papineau compares it to "the Muller-Lyer illusion [which, while] at a theoretical level we know that the lines are the same length . . . at a more intuitive level of judgment, they strike us as of different lengths" (p. 483). But Papineau's citing of "doxastic split personality" doesn't seem to capture what's going on in these cases either: it's unclear that anyone who knows about the Muller-Lyer illusion *believes*, at any level, that the lines are of different lengths; they think they just *look* that way.
25. Thus one cannot get to the point of being able to say, as Papineau does in describing what happens when someone comes to believe that 'Cicero = Tully' is true, "Can you still think that 'they' might have been different people? What would you be thinking? That *this* person might not have been himself? Surely you will no longer have any room for the thought that Cicero and Tully might have been different people" (p. 479).
26. This view has been expressed most forcefully by another (albeit grudging, and now even less enthusiastic) defender of physicalism, Thomas Nagel, who in his (1965/2001) explanation of why it is that "physicalism repels me, though I am persuaded of its truth" (p. 110), suggests that there is an unbridgeable gap between our subjective and objective conceptions of our mental states that impels us to believe that they could not be conceptions of the same thing. Even more important, Nagel goes on to suggest that if this is

> the source of my uneasiness about physicalism . . . it is no more an argument against physicalism than against most other theories of mind, including dualism. . . . A non-corporeal substance seems safe only because in retreating from a physical substance as a candidate for the self, we are so much occupied with finding a subject whose states are originally and not derivatively mine—one to which the physical body can be related in a way which explains how *it* can be mine—that we simply postulate such a subject without asking ourselves whether the same objections will not apply to it as well.
>
> (p. 110)

It is hard to see how even the most committed physicalist could be more persuasive.

This explanation also does justice to Papineau's contention that even if scientists "have now uncovered overwhelming evidence that in the actual world pain always goes hand-in-hand with some brain-process K . . . [it would] still strike them that there could be a possible being with process K but no pain" (p. 492).

27. This is not to say that, on Loar's view, phenomenal type-demonstratives are *completely* isolated—and recognizing this can help to address another criticism of the "Phenomenal Concept Strategy". In his (2005), Daniel Stoljar argues that if the apparent contingency of phenomenal-physical identity statements such as "pain = C-fiber stimulation" is due to the special features of phenomenal concepts, then *all* statements linking phenomenal and non-phenomenal concepts should seem contingent. But there are statements of this sort that do not appear contingent at all, e.g. "If n is a number, n is not a red sensation", and thus this strategy is ineffective. Now Stoljar may be correct that some versions of the Phenomenal Concept Strategy are stuck with this overgeneralization, but Loar's view, it seems, can avoid the problem. As noted earlier, Loar acknowledges (p. 601) that "recognitional concepts are generally formed against a further conceptual background" that constrains their reference, and thus if, as he suggests, phenomenal concepts have the form "internal state of that kind", one can know a priori that whatever red sensations are, they are properties of internal states, and thus not numbers. And this sufficiently explains why "If n is a number, n is not a red sensation" does not seem contingent.
28. Treating phenomenal concepts as (type-) recognitional-demonstratives does not close all the important questions. The fact that phenomenal concepts *can* refer to physical (or physical-functional) states does not guarantee that they *do*—and as we've seen, Loar acknowledges the possibility that our successive (actual and counterfactual) identifications of instances of our internal states as *that again* may not pick out instances of the same physical (or physical-functional) type. But it seems that there are bio-evolutionary reasons to make this plausible. Nonetheless, there are problems that remain; among them Block's (2002) "harder" problem of whether we can know whether type-demonstratives pick out neural states or functional states, and Balog's (this volume) "hardest" problem of whether there is a fact of the matter as to which. I will not discuss these questions here.
29. In my discussion I'm ignoring some important subtleties of Loar's argument in which he (i) maintains that non-perceptual concepts also possess phenomenal intentionality and (ii) explains how this is possible. See his (2017d, Sections 11–14) for details. See also Horgan and Tienson (2002) for another early discussion of "phenomenal intentionality".
30. See Balog (2017, p. 152) for an expression of the worry about whether such a property could be naturalized—and what would count as success.
31. It's another question whether these phenomena are perceived as in space. For example, sounds can be perceived as outside the mind, but there's controversy about whether they are perceived as having a spatial location.
32. Many (e.g. Burge, 2010) have argued for this evolutionary hypothesis, on the grounds that it's needed to insure the kind of objectivity that enables us to survive in the world we live in. Burge, however (along with others) argues that these considerations support a purely externalist account of intentionality.
33. As he puts it (p. 317), ". . [This] explanation is phenomenological-psychological; it is from a combined first-person/third-person perspective that directedness is intimately connected with reference".
34. As David Chalmers put it in his talk at the memorial conference for Loar (October 9, 2014), it's best to think of the phenomenon in question not as the "paint that points", but the "paint that *purports* to point".
35. Presumably, he's understanding the characterization of conceptual role to provide a (person-level) *analysis* of directedness. Otherwise he could simply

invoke the phenomenal concept strategy to explain why the "blankness" of conceptual role does not imply that it's not the referent of our phenomenal concept of directedness.

36. There is a lot more that needs to be said about how exactly the reference of these partially demonstrative, partially discursive, concepts is to be determined, but I will not make any suggestions here. (But see my 2002 for an attempt.)
37. This section is a revision of my (2001, Section 5). That paper addresses the problem in more detail and criticizes other attempts (Blackburn's and Searle's) to characterize reference from a first-person point of view. In neither place, however, do I even purport to point to all the interesting features of Loar's suggestions in this paper.
38. As Quine makes clear, we have to think of our terms for kinds and other objects and properties as referring all together—and making "compensatory adjustments" for our other terms—but I won't go into details.
39. As he puts it, (p. 262): "No disquotational pattern is to be found among pairs of terms and objects. You do not produce the woman George Sand by peeling away quotes from "George Sand". No disquotational principle unifies any set of concept-object pairs, or explain what later pairs have in common with earlier pairs. I cannot then point to a relation between terms and objects by virtue of its holding of certain disquotational term-object pairs, it seems; for there are no such pairs."
40. Moreover, he notes: (p. 68): ". . . our conception from the mention-use perspective of 'that relation' is a concept of a function, and given that function has in its extension 'that tree', that tree), the pair ('that tree', that tree-surface) in not in its extension. In other words: if the apparent rule picks out (c, a) and one judges that a is not identical with b, then the rule rejects (c, b)". However, as he stresses, this does not provide *objective* grounds for taking the former relation to be reference.
41. As he puts it (p. 265):

    > When we shift from the phenomenological perspective, the pairs that we have placed on the table are not special, from the new objective perspective. Our objective investigation can be seen as having a significant semantic upshot only from the subjective perspective. And so, success in advancing this present proposal requires the reader's phenomenological cooperation. The apparent concept-object linkages are (I venture to suggest) something recognized in one's own experience, when one exercises the corresponding concept-concept pair.

42. Although this provides a general idea of the view, it is not quite right. Loar states (pp. 267–8) that there may be other pairs that generate this special phenomenology, presumably those that link our concepts of visual and other perceptual demonstratives with our concepts of the objects that produce them.
43. As he puts it (p. 268):

    > This merely subjective perspective on concept-object pairs is phenomenologically stable, and from it we are able to conceive that objective external relation (as we judge it), which holds of this pair and that pair etc . . . . even though the instances I have in mind change. This parallels the fact that I retain the same recognitional concept of a certain unnamed kind of flower that I see around town, despite the change in its instances.

    He continues, however (p. 271), "From the subjective perspective, reference is determinate, while realized by external objective relations that are themselves, as Quine points out, not unique in their objective roles".

44. For one among many examples, see Tye (2009) for an objection to the suggestion that phenomenal type-demonstratives can refer successfully to the phenomenal (*what it's like*) properties of our sensations and perceptual experiences. And, for one among many responses to such objections, see my (2012).
45. Again, see Burge (2010).
46. I am grateful to Georges Rey, Kati Balog, and Arthur Sullivan for their helpful comments on a draft of this paper—and also to Christopher Hill for his comments on a much earlier version. And I am indebted to Brian Loar for his friendship, colleagueship, intellectual inspiration, and intellectual guidance, over many, many years.

## References

Balog, K. (1999). "Conceivability, Possibility, and the Mind-Body Problem". *Philosophical Review* 108: 497–528.
Balog, K. (2017). "Introduction to Part II". In Balog, K. and Beardman, S. (eds.), *Consciousness and Meaning: Selected Essays*. New York: Oxford University Press.
Balog, K. (this volume). "Hard, Harder, Hardest".
Block, N. (2002). "The Harder Problem of Consciousness". *Journal of Philosophy* 99 (8): 391–425.
Block, N. (2007). "Max Black's Objection to Mind-Body Identity". In Alter, T. and Walter, S. (eds.), *Phenomenal Concepts and Phenomenal Knowledge*. New York: Oxford University Press.
Burge, T. (2010). *The Origins of Objectivity*. New York: Oxford University Press.
Byrne, A. and Pryor, J. (2006). "Bad Intensions". In Garcia-Carpintero, Manuel and Maci (eds.), *Two-Dimensional Semantics: Foundations and Applications*. Oxford: Oxford University Press: 38–54.
Chalmers, D. (1996). *The Conscious Mind*. Oxford: Oxford University Press.
Chalmers, D. (2006). "The Foundations of Two-Dimensional Semantics". In Garcia-Carpintero, M. and Macia, J. (eds.), *Two-Dimensional Semantics*. Oxford: Oxford University Press.
Chalmers, D. (2007). "Phenomenal Concepts and the Explanatory Gap". In Alter, T. and Walter, S. (eds.), *Phenomenal Concepts and Phenomenal Knowledge*. New York: Oxford University Press.
Diaz-Leon, E. (2014). "Do a Posteriori Physicalists Get Our Phenomenal Concepts Wrong?". *Ratio* 27, 1 March.
Goff, P. (2017). *Consciousness and Fundamental Reality*. Oxford: Oxford University Press.
Jackson, F. (1982). "Epiphenomenal Qualia". *Philosophical Quarterly* 32: 127–136.
Hill, C. and McLaughlin, B. (1999). "There Are Fewer Things in Reality Than Are Dreamt of in Chalmers' Philosophy". *Philosophy and Phenomenological Research* 59: 445–454.
Horgan, T. (1984). "Functionalism, Qualia, and the Inverted Spectrum". *Philosophy and Phenomenological Research* 44: 453–469.
Horgan, T. and Tienson, J. (2002). "The Intentionality of Phenomenology and the Phenomenology of Intentionality". In Chalmers, D. (ed.), *Philosophy of Mind: Classical and Contemporary Readings*. Oxford: Oxford University Press: 520–533.
Kripke, S. (1972). *Naming and Necessity*. Cambridge, MA: Harvard University Press.

Levin, J. (2001). "The Myth of Jones and the Return of Subjectivity". *Mind and Language* 16 (2).

Levin, J. (2002). "Is Conceptual Analysis Needed for the Reduction of Qualitative States?". *Philosophy and Phenomenological Research* 64 (3).

Levin, J. (2007). "What Is a Phenomenal Concept?". In Alter, T. and Walter, S. (eds.), *Phenomenal Concepts and Phenomenal Knowledge*. New York: Oxford University Press.

Levin, J. (2008). "Taking Type-B Materialism Seriously". *Mind and Language* 23 (4).

Levin, J. (2012). "Tye's Ptolemaic Revolution, Critical Notice of M. Tye's *Consciousness Revisited*". *Analytic Philosophy* 53 (1).

Levin, J. (2018). "Once More Unto the Breach: Type B Physicalism, Phenomenal Concepts, and the Epistemic Gap". *Australasian Journal of Philosophy* 97 (1): 57–71.

Levine, J. (1983). "Materialism and Qualia: The Explanatory Gap". *Pacific Philosophical Quarterly* 64: 354–361.

Levine, J. (2007). "Phenomenal Concepts and the Materialist Constraint". In Alter, T. and Walter, S. (eds.), *Phenomenal Concepts and Phenomenal Knowledge*. New York: Oxford University Press.

Loar, B. (2003). "Qualia, Properties, Modality". In Sosa, E. and Villanueva, E. (eds.), *Philosophical Issues* 13.

Loar, B. (2017a). "Social Content and Psychological Content". In Balog, K. and Beardman, S. (eds.), *Consciousness and Meaning: Selected Essays*. New York: Oxford University Press.

Loar, B. (2017b). "Subjective Intentionality". In Balog, K. and Beardman, S. (eds.), *Consciousness and Meaning: Selected Essays*. New York: Oxford University Press.

Loar, B. (2017c). "Phenomenal States". In Balog, K. and Beardman, S. (eds.), *Consciousness and Meaning: Selected Essays*. New York: Oxford University Press.

Loar, B. (2017d). "Reference from the First-Person Perspective". In Balog, K. and Beardman, S. (eds.), *Consciousness and Meaning: Selected Essays*. New York: Oxford University Press.

Loar, B. (2017e). "Transparent Experience and the Availability of Qualia". In Balog, K. and Beardman, S. (eds.), *Consciousness and Meaning: Selected Essays*. New York: Oxford University Press.

Loar, B. (2017f). "Phenomenal Intentionality as the Basis for Mental Content". In Balog, K. and Beardman, S. (eds.), *Consciousness and Meaning: Selected Essays*. New York: Oxford University Press.

Nagel. T. (1965/2001). "Physicalism". In Rosenthal, D. (ed.), *Materialism and the Mind-Body Problem*, 2nd Edition. Indianapolis, IN: Hackett Publishing.

Nida-Rumelin, M. (1996). "What Mary Couldn't Know: Belief about Phenomenal States". In Metzinger, T. (ed.), *Conscious Experience*. Paderborn, Germany: Schoningh/Imprint Academic.

Papineau, D. (2002). *Thinking about Consciousness*. Oxford: Oxford University Press.

Papineau, D. (2007). "Kripke's Proof Is Ad Hominem Not Two-Dimensional". *Philosophical Perspectives* 21: 475–492.

Smart, J.J.C. (1959). "Sensations and Brain Processes". *Philosophical Review* 68: 141–156.

Sosa, D. (1995) "Reference from a Perspective vs. Reference". *Philosophical Issues* 6: 79–89.

Stoljar, D. (2005). "Physicalism and Phenomenal Concepts". *Mind and Language* 20 (5).

Tye, M. (2009). *Consciousness Revisited: Materialism without Phenomenal Concepts*. Cambridge, MA: MIT Press.

White, S. (2006). "A Posteriori Identities and the Requirements of Rationality". In Zimmerman, D. (ed.), *Oxford Studies in Metaphysics*, vol. 2. New York: Oxford University Press.

White, S. (2007). "Property Dualism, Phenomenal Concepts and the Semantic Premise". In Alter, T. and Walter, S. (eds.), *Phenomenal Concepts and Phenomenal Knowledge*. New York: Oxford University Press.

White, S. (2010). "The Property Dualism Argument". In Bealer, G. and Koons, R. (eds.), *The Waning of Materialism*. New York: Oxford: Oxford University Press.

# 14 Phenomenal Concepts and the First-Person Perspective

*Joseph Levine*

Loar (Balog & Beardman 2017, chapter 10) introduces the notion of a "phenomenal concept" in order to respond to the Conceivability Argument against materialism, as well as the closely-related Explanatory Gap argument. Briefly, the idea is that conceivability and explanatory questions don't have the metaphysical (or epistemological) implications that the advocates of those arguments claim for them because of the peculiar nature of the concepts we form of phenomenal states from the first-person perspective; these peculiar concepts he dubs "phenomenal concepts". I have criticized this approach in print before—specifically in Levine (2018, chapter 1). While I will draw on some of that discussion in this paper, what I want to do here is broaden the discussion so as to include certain of Loar's fundamental views regarding the nature of intentionality. Charting the interaction of his views on intentionality and phenomenality yields insights about both topics, and puts my original critique of his doctrine of phenomenal concepts in a different light.

I will begin my critical evaluation of Loar's overall position on both phenomenal consciousness and intentionality listing what I take to be his fundamental commitments. As he was painfully aware, these commitments don't all fit easily together, and the subtlety and intricacy of his position arises from his attempt to reconcile them with each other.

The first commitment is physicalism, or "naturalism", in Loar's words. Since I think "naturalism" can mean a number of different things, I'll use "physicalism".[1] Loar is definitely committed to physicalism as it is understood in philosophy of mind; indeed, his position is the paradigm of what Chalmers (1996) calls "Type-B Physicalism". The main idea is that all phenomena supervene on, or are "grounded" in, fundamental physical processes and states. Operationally, physicalism entails the metaphysical impossibility of zombies—creatures that are physically identical to normal human beings but that have no conscious experience.

Another of Loar's commitments—and this is what makes his physicalism of "Type B"—is that there is no conceptual connection between physicalist-functionalist concepts and phenomenal concepts. So, even though phenomenal properties supervene on physical properties, it is not the case that there is any *a priori* entailment from even the most comprehensive physical-functional description to phenomenal descriptions. While physicalism mandates that there is a metaphysical entailment between the two descriptions, Loar maintains there is no conceptual entailment.

The term "non-reductive physicalism" is sometimes used to characterize this position, but Loar eschews it explicitly. In fact, Loar (Balog & Beardman, chapter 12) argues against what he calls "non-reductive physicalism". So what distinguishes his "Type B" physicalism from the "non-reductive" variety? To be physicalist, for Loar, is to subscribe to supervenience: no difference in mental properties without a difference in physical properties. What then distinguishes non-reductive from Type B physicalism is that on the latter there is an explanation of the supervenience and on the former there isn't. (This isn't quite how Loar puts it, it's my own formulation, but I believe it captures what he had in mind.). For all versions of Type B physicalism that I know of the idea is that while phenomenal properties may not be identified with straightforwardly physical properties—like neurological properties—they can at least be identified with functional properties. We can then get an explanation—indeed a derivation (in principle)—of the supervenience of the mental on the physical by first identifying the mental with the functional, which would be done on empirical grounds, and then deriving the relevant functional description from the physical one. The fact that the identification of the mental with the functional is *a posteriori*, not *a priori*, is what makes his physicalism of the Type B variety. The problem that Loar sees with non-reductive physicalism—and I agree wholeheartedly with him here—is that it leaves the metaphysical supervenience relation brute and unexplained.

Recent versions of the anti-materialist Conceivability Argument, as in Chalmers (1996), depend upon certain semantic assumptions that render the two defining features of Type B physicalism, that there is a metaphysical entailment of the mental from the physical but not a conceptual one, incompatible. I have argued (in Levine 2001 and 2018, chapter 9) that semantic considerations alone do not entail that these two defining features of Type B physicalism are incompatible. The point is that if one adopts a Russellian, as opposed to a Fregean conception of meaning the alleged incompatibility doesn't arise. However, another of Loar's basic commitments is to a broadly Fregean conception of meaning, hence the tension between the two features of Type B physicalism becomes quite pressing for him.

What I mean by this is that the Fregean is committed to the idea that meaning, intentionality generally, is a matter of how the subject herself "conceives" the world. To use Frege's term, it's constituted by the "mode of presentation" of the world to the subject. If we want to understand what someone means by her use of language—or just the contents of her thoughts—then we have to see how she is conceiving the world. This way of understanding meaning and the intentionality of thought is contrasted with the broadly Russellian view that language—whether public or mental—is directly about objects and properties in the world. To know how a subject conceives of things is just to know the referents of her public and mental symbols.

A number of Loar's papers involve his attempts to work out how to maintain the basic Fregean idea in the face of the arguments of Kripke (1980), Putnam (1975), and especially Burge (1979), which seem to support the Russellian approach. The view that names and natural kind terms rigidly designate is not itself that hard to accommodate. One can allow that the modal behavior of such terms is governed by external world conditions and still maintain that there is a level of meaning that captures the internal, narrow content determined by how the subject conceives of the world.

Usually it is claimed by those who believe in narrow content that this aspect of meaning is captured by the "that-clause" involved in de dicto attributions of propositional attitudes. But given Burge's arguments about the meaning of "arthritis"—arguments that Loar endorses—one can't retreat to this position. In particular, in response to the challenge to produce a sentence that precisely captures narrow content, Loar admits that Burge's arguments seem to show that this is impossible. The problem is, Loar says, that public language is irremediably infected with external, particularly social deferential, meaning. But he challenges the assumption made in most discussions of content that that-clauses are supposed to capture subjective meaning, or narrow content. Indeed, he argues that this assumption is responsible for the failure to accurately characterize the subject's point of view on her own thoughts and statements. In particular, he argues (Balog & Beardman, chapter 5) that abandoning this assumption is the key to solving Kripke's (1979) puzzle about Pierre.

So what does capture narrow content, or subjective meaning, as he often terms it? Loar began as basically a conceptual-role theorist when it comes to narrow meaning. The idea is that wide content is determined by causal and social deferential conditions while narrow content is determined by the roles that concepts and terms play within one's overall theory of the world. However, while never abandoning the idea that subjective (or narrow) meaning centrally involves conceptual role, he came to the view that subjective meaning is also determined by what he, along with others following him, called "phenomenal intentionality". This is where his views about phenomenal consciousness and intentionality become intertwined. Let me describe the dialectic that brought him to this view.

There are two problems that confront the conceptual role theorist. First, holism. It's notoriously hard to see how to cordon off just those conceptual connections that are meaning-constituting from the rest that result from the acquisition of knowledge about the world. This is a problem so long as one wants to generalize over many individuals when attributing meanings and thought contents. If you want to say that one has to believe that all bachelors are unmarried in order to properly be claimed to have a belief in which the concept of a bachelor figures, that doesn't seem hard to accommodate. But if you have to also share beliefs about the living habits of bachelors with someone else in order to be said to have the same concept as they do, then it seems hopeless. To this challenge Loar responds with what seems to me just a hope that the appropriate cordoning off can be accomplished. Nowhere, at least in the papers of his that I've read, does he really tackle the problem.

There is another challenge that Loar does address though, and to my mind it's the more interesting one. (I don't mean to imply that the problem of holism isn't important. It's just that, for my purposes here, the problem to be described plays a greater role.) As he puts it, conceptual role seems too "formal", too "syntactic", to adequately capture how a subject *conceives* of the world. The idea of a conception of the world seems to be a semantic, intentional notion that has "aboutness", or "directedness", as he often puts it, built into it. After all, what we're trying to characterize with this notion of subjective, or narrow meaning is the way the world is according to the conception of the subject: how do you do that with a system of relations among representations? Don't we need a notion of truth conditions—how the world would be if it conformed to one's subjective conception—to capture narrow meaning?

Notice how the Two-Dimensional theory of meaning, at least as understood by Chalmers (2006) on his "epistemic" conception of 2D semantics, does seem to capture this aspect of subjective, or narrow meaning. On this view, there are two intensions—two meanings—associated with a statement or term. The primary intension is a function from possible worlds to truth values/extensions where the worlds are considered "as actual", whereas the secondary intension is a function from possible worlds to truth values/extensions where the worlds are considered "as counterfactual". So, for instance, one's primary intension of the term (or concept) "water" determines extensions for the term in every possible world in a way that picks out $H_2O$ in this world but XYZ in Twin Earth world, whereas the secondary intension picks out $H_2O$ in every possible world. The primary intension thus does determine how the world is in a certain sense, and it involves semantic notions like truth conditions and extensions.

Loar didn't take this route. (For one thing, it leads pretty straightforwardly to the Conceivability Argument.) Loar presents the problem of how to understand subjective, or narrow content in greatest detail in (Balog & Beardman, chapter 9). The paper begins with the following:

> To say that mental content or intentionality is in the head is to say this: internal properties of the mind constitute how a person represents the world to himself. Not "they constitute the *means* by which

> he represents the world to himself", but "they constitute *the way the world is according to* how he represents it to himself, how he conceives the facts, how he conceives the world as being".
>
> (165)

Crucial to Loar's notion of subjective intentionality is the idea that "knowledge of the references of my own thoughts is privileged in a certain way, and that perspective involves no apparent conceptions of external reference relations". (172–3) To use his example, when I think to myself that Freud lived in Vienna, "I register what the thought is about" (173), and this doesn't seem open to doubt or require descriptive knowledge of the causal/historical/social conditions that led to this thought. So one's internal, private content is imbued with "aboutness", intentionality, of a sort that is distinct from the kind of external, socially conditioned reference described by Kripke-Putnam-Burge. Immediately after presenting this thesis, Loar launches into a discussion of its two principal challenges: the "Argument from That-Clauses" and the "Argument from Unmotivation".

We have already talked about the issue of that-clauses, so I'll skip that here. The more interesting problem is "Unmotivation". Here is how he puts it: "Internal properties—whether biochemical, neurophysiological, psychofunctional, or common-sense functional—cannot motivate the ascription of, or explain, or imply, externally directed truth conditions".[2] Yet, we experience ourselves as thinking genuine thoughts that determine a conception of the world apparently independently of our external causal-historical-social relations. Putting Unmotivation together with subjective intentionality, Loar asks: "If I wish to accommodate both intuitive perspectives—the subjective/projective perspective and the naturalistic third-person perspective—must I lapse into dualism?" (175)

His way out here is to apply to the feature of mental "directedness", or subjective intentionality, the same move he applies to the problem of identifying phenomenal and physical/functional states: the "phenomenal concept strategy".[3] Allegiance to the idea that mental content is about how the subject herself conceives the world is the core of Loar's Fregeanism. In a sense, the anti-naturalistic challenge which seems to be problematic for the Fregean conception is now aimed at that very conception itself: how can it be that the internal conditions that objectively, from the third-person perspective, obtain when one is entertaining a thought—i.e. purely physical/functional conditions—are also the very same conditions that we recognize subjectively as involving reference to objects and properties in a privileged, "transparent" manner? Loar's reply is that this question cannot be answered, for the same reason that we can't explain why the relevant physical-functional properties constitute phenomenal experiences. That is, our experience of subjective intentionality gives rise to a kind of "phenomenal concept" of thought—a first-person perspective concept that is triggered in the very having of a thought, and there is no way to infer descriptions involving such concepts from those couched in purely third-person, naturalistic terms. I will explore this proposal a little more below, but first we need to introduce the final element, "phenomenal intentionality".

Above I described Loar's treatment of the two problems of that-clauses and Unmotivation. But there is still the third problem mentioned earlier, about the merely formal character of conceptual role and how that seems to conflict with its ability to ground a notion of a subject's conception of the world. This is where phenomenal intentionality enters the scene, and with this doctrine Loar simultaneously addresses this problem for his position on subjective intentionality along with the raging debate over representationalism about phenomenal properties.

A three-sided debate concerning the intentionality of phenomenal properties has been going on for the last two decades or so. Many materialists about phenomenal consciousness have argued that phenomenal properties are essentially representational properties (Byrne 2001; Dretske 1995; Harman 1990; and Tye 1995). To visually experience red is for one's visual system to represent the surface reflectance property of being red (or something of the sort). What's crucial for these philosophers is that representation be understood in a naturalistic—usually causal/nomic—manner. The idea is to reduce the mind-body problem from two problems—phenomenality and intentionality—to only one, intentionality, with the further idea that this is the more tractable problem. Opponents claim that while phenomenal properties might represent certain external (naturalistic) properties, like surface reflectances, their representational features are not essential and intrinsic to them (Block 1990). Thus, inversion scenarios are possible, where my reddish experience represents red but my inverted twin's experience—qualitatively identical—represents green.

The third side in the debate is the phenomenal intentionality position, adopted by Loar. (I believe he coined the term. See Kriegel (2013) for the current state of play on this topic.) This position shares with the representationalists the claim that phenomenal properties (at least those involved in normal perception) are inherently intentional, so that experiencing red is a matter of having redness presented to the subject. However, unlike the representationalists, they do not share the view that intentionality can be given a naturalistic analysis, so therefore this is not a reductionist view in the way that representationalism is. While Loar is a naturalist/physicalist, as emphasized above, he does not sign on to the standard naturalization views of intentionality. His reductivism, as described earlier, comes via the phenomenal concept move of synthetically identifying both phenomenal and intentional properties with physical-functional ones.

But phenomenal intentionality is not for Loar merely a thesis about phenomenal character, it also, as I mentioned, plays an important role for him in addressing the "it's merely syntactic" challenge to his appeal to conceptual role as the basis of internal meaning. We have this first-person perspective on our thought and experience which seems to involve a way the world seems to us, and mere relations among ideas don't seem to get at the apparent "aboutness" of it. But if we start with the intentionality inherent in phenomenal experience—that phenomenal experience is itself a way of being presented with a way the world is, at least regarding its perceptible properties, then we have the basis for building a genuine notion of how the subject conceives the world. Conceptual role still plays a fundamental role, as the conceptual connections that obtain among phenomenal experiences and thoughts involving many different kinds of concepts (natural kind, social deferential, etc.) will be the determiner of the latter's subjective intentional properties. But the idea is that the "directedness" of phenomenal intentionality provides the basis for the claim that subjective intentionality constitutively involves a way of conceiving of the world.

There is a significant way in which Loar's understanding of subjective and phenomenal intentionality diverges from both the standard Fregean conception of meaning and from the way others employ the notion of phenomenal intentionality. What Loar and others share is this idea that subjective meaning is supposed to capture how the world is according to the subject, from the first-person perspective; this is given extra substance by adding in the component of phenomenal intentionality. However, it is also important to the general Fregean perspective that in some way—although not necessarily all on its own—subjective meaning is a determinant of objective reference. After all, subjective meaning is supposed to be the mode of presentation of the external world of mind-independent objects and properties to us. Similarly, for those involved in what Kriegel (2013) calls the "phenomenal intentionality program", at least as he presents the principal theses in his introduction to that volume, phenomenal intentionality isn't only supposed to capture how the world is presented within the first-person perspective, but it is also supposed to be the basis for all intentionality.

Loar's views on the relation between subjective and objective intentionality are difficult to interpret, and they clearly changed over time. But given both his physicalism and his acceptance of causal determinants of reference, I think a case can be made that his overall view is compatible with a fairly radical bifurcation between the two. I don't intend this as a criticism, since I myself am inclined to such a view. Let me briefly present the case.

For one thing, contrast again Loar's conception of subjective meaning with that of the Two-Dimensional theory. As described above, on the 2D theory the primary intension—that feature of meaning that represents its subjective aspect—determines a function from worlds to extensions. It's this function that is doing the primary work of reference-determination.

All that's left to be done for the actual referents to be fixed is to fix which among all the possible worlds is the one we occupy. But the determination work itself is really being done by the subjective aspect. Then, of course, once we have the referent, we take it around to other possible worlds for the purpose of counterfactual assessment, which is embodied in the secondary intension. But this isn't really a matter of reference determination in the way that the primary intension is.

On the other hand, when it comes to Loar's notion of subjective meaning, it's much less clear what role the subject's conception is supposed to play in determining objective reference. Perhaps when it comes to social deferential concepts one can say it's the subject's intention to use her words the way others do that's doing the determination work. But when it comes to terms whose reference is determined causally, or through nomic covariation, it's harder to see what the subjective conception is doing. Loar does not think that what we have in mind are the causal theories themselves and then reference is determined by applying these causal descriptions to the world we inhabit. Rather, like many a Russellian, he's happy to let the causal work go on behind the subject's back.

Now add to the mix his "phenomenal concept strategy" with regard to subjective meaning. From the first-person perspective, we confront a world of objects and properties that we transparently pick out in thought and experience. But that very phenomenon itself, with all its apparent directionality and relational structure, turns out to be brutely identical to our occupying certain physical-functional states. These states, objectively characterizable from the third-person point of view, have nothing directed or relational (at least not in the relevant sense) about them. The cognitive scientist can go about assigning representational content to these internal states on a basis that is independent of the apparent world inhabited by the first-person perspective.

The overall view, then, seems to be (or is at least compatible with) a view of two somewhat independent kinds of reference determination. On the one hand, a world is presented to the subject within the first-person perspective and its objects and properties are a function of the primitive intentional objects/properties of the phenomenal states along with the conceptual connections that link the non-phenomenal concepts with each other and, ultimately, with the phenomenal ones.

On the other hand, from the third-person, scientific perspective, the subject's brain embodies a functional system with input-output connections to the world, and through a combination of causal contact with the world and internal connections among the functional states, it is hoped that a unique assignment of intentional contents to the internal states can be determined. I don't think Loar really thought of these as independent assignments—nor have I made the case that they are totally independent, as both perspectives do employ the same set of internal causal/functional connections—but it seems to me that there is nothing in the view that enforces a unique, or even nearly unique mapping between the two.

In fact, you can't even really talk of there being a mapping "between the two" because the directional intentionality, the apparent relation to objects/properties determined by phenomenal intentionality, are just that—"apparent". Given the brute identity that holds between phenomenal states and physical-functional states on Loar's view, along with the lack of any relational-referential structure inherent in the physical-functional states themselves, the most you get from the intentional nature of phenomenal states is "purported" reference to merely intentional objects. While many philosophers claim to understand what is meant by a "merely intentional object", I confess to puzzlement about what this is supposed to be. What seems to push Loar into this commitment to merely intentional objects for phenomenal states, or their merely "purported reference", is his commitment to the identity of phenomenal states with physical-functional states. His defense of that thesis, as already mentioned, relies on his account of phenomenal concepts. So, in the rest of the paper I want to do three things. First, review briefly my original objection to his phenomenal concept strategy. Second, show that his account of phenomenal intentionality only strengthens my objections. Finally, I want to sketch an alternative conception of subjective intentionality that naturally coheres with much of what Loar had in mind but without the physicalism, and instead embraces an explicit commitment to a bifurcated account of intentionality overall: one for the world of the first-person perspective and the other for the world of the third-person perspective.

In Levine (2018, chapter 1) I presented an argument against the phenomenal concepts strategy that went as follows. Leave aside for the moment the question whether the requirement that the phenomenal facts, along with all other higher-level facts, be a priori derivable from the physical facts, the basic facts, is a reasonable one to place on physicalism. As mentioned above, many physicalists seem to acknowledge the burden as one they must either meet or provide an argument for why they may escape it in this case. I believe a thoroughgoing Russellian semantics can avoid this general requirement. But still, as Loar recognized, there does seem to be a difference between the cases where we might not have strict bottom-up derivability but still find no explanatory gap and the phenomenal-physical case where an explanatory gap persists.

An example of this "core contrast", as I called it, is the case of water and the case of pain. Whereas on a Russellian view of natural kind terms it won't be possible to derive statements containing the term "water" from basic physical-chemical descriptions, there is no doubt in anyone's mind that the physical-chemical facts provide a complete explanation for the water facts. But the qualitative character of pain does not seem to be explained by appeal to the underlying physical-functional facts. What explains this core contrast? Loar thought that appeal to the special nature of phenomenal concepts, the very concepts we employ to represent to ourselves pain experiences (along with all other phenomenal states), does the job.

The idea then, is that our inability to see how physical-functional facts explain phenomenal, or qualitative character, is a matter of the special way this feature of mental life is represented by the subject from the first-person perspective. Assuming this is the strategy, I argued that even if it's right that there is something special about phenomenal concepts that explains the core contrast, the physicalist is not automatically out of the woods. For a constraint on a legitimate physicalist explanation of the explanatory gap is that one's account of this special nature attributed to phenomenal concepts not invoke any property or relation that is not itself physically explicable.

So what is supposed to be so special about phenomenal concepts? Loar describes them as "recognitional" concepts, and also sometimes as "type-demonstrative" concepts. I argued that when you wade a bit into the weeds of such accounts, it seems what's doing the work to insulate phenomenal concepts from any explanatory connections with their third-person, physical-functional correlates, is their lack of any descriptive content. This lack explains why there is no "hook" as it were for an explanation in physical-functional terms of the phenomenon they represent to grab onto. My argument was that this didn't accomplish more than putting phenomenal concepts in the same category as regular demonstratives and names and natural kind terms on the Russellian theory. Therefore, it doesn't really explain the core contrast at issue: why we find it explanatory to identify water with $H_2O$ but not pain with c-fiber firing?

On the contrary, I argued, the problem of the explanatory gap arises precisely because of the richness of our first-person representation of experienced qualitative character. We have what I called a "substantive and determinate" conception of phenomenal character that appears not to provide those explanatory hooks for the attempted physicalist-functionalist explanations to grab onto. What can explain this? I argued that it seems we need to appeal to a *sui generis* relation of "acquaintance" to account for this special means of representing experience from the first-person perspective. But this relation doesn't seem to admit itself of a physicalist-functionalist explanation, hence the phenomenal concept strategy does not succeed in defending physicalism from the explanatory gap. It does not explain the core contrast without appealing to a relation that itself seems to open its own explanatory gap.[4]

The argument above proceeded on the assumption that phenomenal character itself was simply an experiential property, "mental paint" to use Harman's (1990) phrase. The idea was that given our substantive and determinate conception of this property, revealed to us through some acquaintance-like relation, the kind of brute identity posited by the phenomenal concept strategy left an explanatory gap. However, now we are supposing that phenomenal states possess an intentional structure. Phenomenal states themselves involve not just the instantiation of a property but the *experience* of a property, which makes the state itself intentional. If it's intentional then it seems it must be about something—it seems to be a relation to something—and so the question arises, a relation to what? If phenomenal intentionality involves an inner directedness, as Loar wants to say, what is it directed on?

As we noted earlier, Loar thought we could avoid answering that question by characterizing phenomenal intentionality in terms of a mere purported aboutness, or directedness. This was crucial to his phenomenal concept strategy since the physicalist-functionalist states with which he wanted to identify phenomenally intentional states had no such relational/directional structure. There is no way of characterizing the supposed objects of phenomenally intentional states in physicalist-functionalist terms. Indeed, he seemed to acknowledge that if he is forced to find real intentional objects for phenomenal states then he would be pushed into some version of dualism.

I want to argue, however, that adding in intentional structure to phenomenal states makes the claim that they are brutely identical to physical-functional states even more implausible than it was when we considered them a form of mental paint. The extra implausibility stems from the need to think of phenomenal intentionality as non-relational; or, if one thinks of it as relational, then as a relation to mere "intentional objects". Let me try to make the case by contrasting phenomenal states with purely cognitive states.

Among the phenomena that have traditionally motivated the representational theory of mind—what historians of early modern philosophy call "the new way of ideas"—is the fact that we can patently think about what doesn't exist. Ponce de Leon can search for the non-existent fountain of youth; kids can believe in the non-existent Santa Claus; and according to atheists billions of people believe in a non-existent God.

Since these states clearly have differential effects on our behavior, one can't just assimilate them all together as states about nothing. Believing in the non-existent God gets you to church or synagogue, believing in the non-existent Santa Claus gets you to put milk and cookies out on Christmas Eve, and Ponce de Leon hacked his way through jungles to find the non-existent fountain of youth. So, given that these "relations" all relate the subject to the same thing—i.e. nothing—how do we explain their differential effects?

This is where the representational theory of mind comes to the rescue. While all three beliefs mentioned above fail to have genuinely existing objects outside the mind, they do have a kind of object—different in each case—within the mind that explains their differential influence on behavior. Each belief is a relation to a mental representation that purports to refer to something different. True, they don't refer to anything, so therefore not something different. Still, the representations themselves are distinct from each other, and it's the representations—not their referents—that explain the subsequent behavior.

The representational theory also removes the whiff of backward causation that haunts teleological explanations. If I behave so as to bring about a situation that does not yet obtain—say a carpenter building a piece of furniture—we want to say that the goal, though not yet fulfilled, somehow played a causal role in bringing itself about. How is that possible? Well, it isn't really the piece of furniture that played a causal role in its own construction, but rather a pre-existing representation in the mind of the carpenter that played that role. Any hint of paradox or backward causation thus immediately disappears.

As mentioned above, philosophers have often used the expression "intentional object", or better, "mere intentional object", to refer to these purported but non-existent objects that nevertheless seem to play a role in causal explanations of behavior. But in fact, we really don't need to talk about these objects at all; it suffices to refer instead to the representations that purport to refer to them, since they really do exist. We can also explain how they play their distinctive psychological roles by characterizing both the specific psychological roles that, say, the Santa-Claus-representation and the fountain-of-youth-representation play, and also their common psychological role by virtue of playing the singular-term role in the mental representational system. So I think talk of intentional objects need not entail anything we'd want to quantify over. We can both say that "Santa Claus" and "Pegasus" have the same reference—i.e. nothing—and also explain their distinctive roles in psychological explanation by appeal to the syntactic and conceptual roles of their mental analogues, which do exist.

Notice how the intentionality of propositional attitude states can fit easily into Loar's naturalism. Assuming a physicalist-functionalist account of the semantics of mental representations can be formulated—a big "if", though most presume some sort of causal, or nomic, covariation account must be right—then there is no problem with any empirically established identity between intentional states like belief and physical-functional states. As just argued, there is no problem about non-referring mental representations either, since their explanatory function can be fulfilled without appealing to their referents. There might be some other notion of "content" that we want to appeal to, but it needn't involve any actual relation to a referent.

But now, can we make the same story work for phenomenal intentionality? One of the first attempts to eliminate any reference to phenomenal objects was Smart's (1959) reply to a Leibniz Law objection to the Identity Theory. His paradigm case of a mental state was having a yellowy-orange after-image, and he considered the claim that it was identical to the having of a certain brain state. The objection went like this: The after-image is yellowy-orange but the brain state isn't, so therefore they can't be the same thing. His response was that the identity isn't supposed to hold between the after-image itself and the brain state, but rather between the experience-of-having-the-after-image and the brain state. The experience, as opposed to the after-image, was never thought to be yellowy-orange, therefore there is no Leibniz Law objection to the alleged identity claim.

While this is certainly a fine answer to the specific Leibniz Law objection, it does leave one wondering, as in the old Pepsodent commercial, "... where the yellow went". This issue emerged within Smart's discussion in a different way when he worried, in the famous "Max Black" objection, that the anti-materialist could sneak "irreducibly psychic" properties back into the picture by arguing as follows. Even if the experience is in fact identical to the brain state, still, in order to explain why this identity claim is *a posteriori* don't we need to appeal to the yellowy-orange qualitative character (not his term, but it's what the irreducibly psychic property would be) in order to explain the contingency (as he thought of it, but we would say the *a posteriori* character) of the identity claim? It was in response to this worry that he introduced his well-known "topic neutral" analysis of our concept of qualitative character. But, as we've seen in the literature since then, very few philosophers, even materialists, accept this topic neutral, or functional, characterization as a genuine *analysis* of what we have in mind by the qualitative character. This is the source of Type-B materialism, after all, and it's something Loar clearly signed onto.

One way to put the problem with Smart's topic-neutral analysis was pointed out by Cornman (1962) at the time. Smart thought he could say that what we have in mind when claiming to be having an experience of this kind is that we're in a state that is like the state we're in when really seeing something yellowy-orange, like an orange, and that, of course, could turn out to be a brain state. But Cornman pointed out that there are too many dimensions of similarity along which states could be alike, and to pin it down it seemed like you needed to specify the yellowy-orange qualitative character, which brings back the irreducibly psychic property. Agreeing with this, Loar's move is, as we discussed above, to allow that we have a special non-analyzable phenomenal concept of this qualitative character, but then claim it can just be brutely identical to the physical-functional state in question.

But the problem of where the yellow went bites back, I contend, once we analyze the phenomenal state in terms of phenomenal intentionality. Take that yellowy-orange after-image again. In the physical world, there is no object that's yellowy-orange, only, say a white wall on which our visual system projects the colored shape. It surely seems like we're looking at something, standing in an intentional relation to something that really has a certain quality to it. It's not an orange, so the quality can't be claimed to be a quality of the physical object, as Representationalists would have it. So where is it? Well, the only answer seems to be that it's a mere intentional object, like Santa Claus.

But it clearly isn't like that at all, at least as I see it. When I think about Santa Claus—or a yellowy-orange after-image, for that matter—there is nothing of any quality that is experienced as an object of my consciousness, other than perhaps an accompanying visual image of a fat guy with a white beard in a red suit (or the yellowy-orange patch), or an auditory image of the words themselves. But those images are themselves the objects of phenomenal intentionality and so they are precisely what's at issue here; they are not themselves the intentional objects of the thoughts in question. The intentional objects are in no way present to me in the experience of having the thought.[5] Therefore it makes perfect sense to assert that the thought relates me to nothing at all, but still plays an important psychological role qua representational state.

Phenomenal intentionality, unlike the kind that applies to non-phenomenal states, characterizes experience, and it is hard to see how to adequately capture an experience without somehow committing oneself to what is experienced. The qualities revealed to the subject of experience have no source in the structural-dynamic world of physical causation and seem to be creatures of the experienced world only. Mere intentional existence, to the extent it's just a sophisticated way of speaking of nothing, is easy to swallow as an account of thoughts without objects they are about, despite their purporting to be about something. We can ultimately make functional-computational sense of the purporting. But I don't see how that begins to make sense of the yellowy-orange after-image, which, dare I say, may not be fully a something, but it's not a nothing either.

I want to emphasize here something I just said in passing, namely, that the qualities we experience have *no source* in the world of physics. In Levine (2001, chapter 4) I argued against eliminativists about qualia that they had no account of our ability to form our substantive and determinate conceptions of the various qualitative characters we experience. It's not just that we form representations that play certain inferential roles involving similarity judgments and the like. There is something quite specific, determinate, and substantive in our experiential encounters with each quality itself.[6]

I quoted Loar above asking, after presenting his view of phenomenal intentionality, whether he's forced into dualism. I claim that some form of anti-materialism is the only way to adequately encompass phenomenal experience, with its specific form of intentional structure, in one's overall metaphysical framework. How do I propose to do that? Actually, I don't think that's easy, and I don't have a worked-out view. I will just allude to a view I speculatively developed in a couple of papers (Levine 2018, chapters 11 and 12), one of which is subtitled, "A Cartesian Theater Revival", to give the flavor of it.

I think somehow our minds create a virtual world out of the representational states that are physically-functionally realized in the brain. Somehow what is described there, in the systems studied by cognitive science and accessible from the third-person perspective, is portrayed in this virtual world for which the subject of experience is the lone audience member. I draw an analogy between the script of a movie and the movie itself. To go back to the Wittgensteinian phrase mentioned above—"not a something but not a nothing either"—this is the realm of this virtual world, the world of conscious experience. Materialists have often battered qualia realists with all sorts of evidence that the fine-tuned relational structure of phenomenal experience—the precise character, dimensionality, etc. of the various phenomenal quality spaces of vision, audition, and the like—can be explained by appeal to physically realized functional-computational structures. So what more do you want, they ask? I respond, yes, on my story, where the computational machinery provides the script, it's to be expected that the fine-tuned relational structure is determined by the detailed computational structure. Yes, for example, the opponent-process theory of color vision does explain why we can't see, or even imagine, a reddish green. (Assuming that's right.) But you want to know what more I want? I want an account of what fills these nodes in the quality space, and that seems always out of the materialist's reach. Or so it seems to me.

Of course I'm being extremely speculative and liberal in my interpretive stance here in saying that the view I just outlined so sketchily can find a source in Loar's work. But I do believe that Loar struggled mightily with his dual commitments to naturalism and the significance of the first-person perspective. I also think he rightly saw that the two defining features of mental life—intentionality and phenomenality—were intertwined in a manner much more complicated than is appreciated by most representationalists and advocates of phenomenal intentionality. He thought his notion of the phenomenal concept could resolve the conflict between the two commitments. I think he was wrong, but we learn so much from his work on the way to reaching that conclusion.

## Notes

1. For how I understand this term, see Levine (2016).
2. So one might wonder whether this is any different from the relation that generally holds between physical and functional properties. The difference is this. We do think, given how functional properties are characterized as causal roles, that there is a derivation—hence explanation—from the physical to the functional. The problem here is that there is no derivational route from the functional to the subjectively intentional. While there may be a derivation from the functional to conceptual role—as this can be cashed out in terms of causal role—for aboutness, or directedness, this doesn't hold.
3. So named in Stoljar (2005).
4. Obviously this brief presentation of the argument is not meant to be convincing on its own. For the details please see Levine (2018, ch. 1).

5. There is a question about so-called "cognitive phenomenology" that one might press against this last claim. (See Bayne & Montague, 2011). But that's not directly relevant to this point and certainly not something my opponent here—particularly Loar—would press.
6. One might wonder here about hallucinations. Surely they are cases of straightforwardly representing what's not there and they are perceptual experiences, not just thoughts. So one might think the contrast I'm making between perceptual experience and thought doesn't hold up. However, hallucinations are not a problem for this argument. True, when I "see" pink elephants on parade while under the influence of a hallucinogenic drug, the objects I seem to see aren't actually there. We can explain what's going on as my representing something out there as instantiating the qualities of pinkness and being elephant-shaped though nothing in fact does. But where did these representations get that meaning in the first place if the qualities allegedly instantiated in the hallucinatory object themselves don't exist? If the quality of pinkness itself doesn't ever get instantiated, how did it get into my representational repertoire in the first place?

## References


Balog, K. & Beardman, S. eds. (2017). *Consciousness and Meaning: Selected Essays, Brian Loar*. Oxford: Oxford University Press.

Bayne, T. & Montague, M. eds. (2011). *Cognitive Phenomenology*. New York and Oxford: Oxford University Press.

Block, N. (1990). "Inverted Earth", in J. Tomberlin, ed., *Philosophical Perspectives, 4: Action Theory and Philosophy of Mind*. Atascadero, CA: Ridgeview Publishing Co.

Burge, T. (1979). "Individualism and the Mental", in P.A. French, T.E. Uehling, & H.K. Wettstein, eds., *Midwest Studies in Philosophy*, 4. Minneapolis: University of Minnesota Press.

Byrne, A. (2001). "Intentionalism Defended", *The Philosophical Review*, 110, 199–240.

Chalmers, D. (1996). *The Conscious Mind*. Oxford: Oxford University Press.

Chalmers, D. (2006). The Foundations of Two-Dimensional Semantics. In M. Garcia-Carpintero & J. Macia, eds., *Two-Dimensional Semantics: Foundations and Applications*. Oxford: Oxford University Press.

Cornman, J. (1962). "The Identity of Mind and Body", *The Journal of Philosophy*, 59 (18), 486–492.

Dretske, F. (1995). *Naturalizing the Mind*. Cambridge, MA: Bradford Books/MIT Press.

Kriegel, U. ed. (2013). *Phenomenal Intentionality*. Oxford: Oxford University Press.

Kripke, S. (1979). "A puzzle about belief", in A. Margalit, ed., *Meaning and Use*. Dordrecht: Reidel.

Kripke, S. (1980). *Naming and Necessity*. Cambridge, MA: Harvard University Press.

Harman, G. (1990). "The Intrinsic Quality of Experience", in J. Tomberlin, ed., *Philosophical Perspectives, 4: Action Theory and Philosophy of Mind*. Atascadero, CA: Ridgeview Publishing Co.

Levine, J. (2001). *Purple Haze: The Puzzle of Consciousness*. New York: Oxford University Press.

Levine, J. (2016). "Naturalism and Dualism", in K. Clark, ed., *The Blackwell Companion to Naturalism*. Oxford: Wiley-Blackwell.

Levine, J. (2018). *Quality and Content: Essays on Consciousness, Representation, and Modality*. Oxford: Oxford University Press.

Putnam, H. (1975). "The Meaning of Meaning", in K. Gunderson ed., *Language, Mind, and Knowledge*. Minneapolis: University of Minnesota Press.

Smart, J.J.C. (1959). "Sensations and Brain Processes", *The Philosophical Review*, 68, 141–156.

Stoljar, D. (2005). "Physicalism and Phenomenal Concepts", *Mind and Language*, 20 (5), 469–494.

Tye, M. (1995). *Ten Problems of Consciousness: A Representational Theory of the Phenomenal Mind*. Cambridge, MA: Bradford Books/MIT Press.

# 15 The Non-Primacy of Subjective Intentionality[1]

*Georges Rey*

## 1. Introduction

Although we were very good friends for many years, Brian and I differed pretty fundamentally about our approach to the philosophy of mind. He was a practitioner of the kind of often highly nuanced reflection on ordinary thought and talk that flourished in post-WWII Oxford during his student years there in the 60s. I was a little younger, stayed on this side of the Atlantic, and, though I was and remain impressed by the *apperçu* of the likes of Wittgenstein, Austin, and Brian, I was lured by the prospect of the more systematic, empirically informed work in linguistics and psychology that was being pursued at MIT by Chomsky and Fodor. So long as it looked as though psychology seemed to offer little improvement on ordinary thought (as I think it looked to those post-war Oxonian philosophers), the merely reflective methodology seemed right; but as soon as the science took off, as I believe it did and has continued to do, it seemed to me that we should adjust our philosophy of mind accordingly. I remember Brian often shaking his head at this what I think he regarded as so much naive scientism that he feared had me in its thrall.[2]

These differences affected how we understood both the phenomenal and the intentional. I will address only the latter here, leaving phenomenality of at least the usual sensory sort (regarding, e.g., color and pain) to another day. One reason for doing so is that intentionality seems to me to play an essential role in scientific explanations that seems to go far beyond subjective, introspectible, or phenomenal states. It is crucially involved in the explanation of a vast array of both human and likely many animal unconscious cognitive states and processes, whether or not they involve phenomenality or (as I shall argue below) any other introspectible state. Indeed, whether phenomenal states as they are understood by many philosophers actually play any explanatory role at all in psychology—and, indeed, precisely what those states are and whether they are real—is much less obvious, and, indeed, might not be true.[3] And so I won't be focusing here on Brian's (1997/2017: 200ff) influential discussions of "demonstrative recognitional" concepts, and how they might account for the usual phenomenal qualitative "paint" with which may people take themselves to be peculiarly acquainted. I shall be concerned here only with his recruitment of those concepts on behalf of intentionality, or what he regards as the specific "paint that points" (2003/2017: 314). My main claim will be that, at least in the case of intentionality, its subjective, perhaps phenomenal aspects are significantly less qualitative than they are in the usual cases of sensations, and so provide less reason to be confident that we're picking out a stable property across occasions. In any event, such subjective aspects are quite inessential to the important explanatory role of intentionality in psychology. *Pace* Quine and other recent skeptics on whose discussions Brain seems to rely, it should be studied as objectively as any other part of nature.

## 2. Brian's Primary Subjective Intentionalism ("PSI")

Brian set out PSI most explicitly in his (1987/2017), "Subjective Intentionality":

> I will now sketch a strategy that takes the subjective as primary: an objective relation or property is *semantic* by virtue of its direct or indirect connections with subjective intentionality. . . . Our primitive notion of aboutness is subjective, and this is the foundation of the semantic.
>
> (1987/2017:190)[4]

There and in a later essay (1997/2017) he advanced his now well-known proposal about such subjective notions, that they involve what he calls "recognitional" concepts. These are concepts that

> have the form "x is of *that* kind"; they are type-demonstratives. These type-demonstratives are grounded in dispositions to classify, by way of perceptual discriminations, certain objects, events, situations.
>
> (1997/2017: 200)

They are not mere abbreviations of other notions we may be define or understand independently, which might be consciously unavailable to us, or dependent upon experts to define (pp. 200–201). They are "recognitional at [their] core; the original concept is recognitional" (pp. 200–1); and, crucially, they are "perspectival", "in part individuated by [the] constitutive perspective" of the mind that entertains them (p. 201).

As Brian (ibid., p. 200) notes, recognitional-demonstratives can be deployed about non-mental phenomena, e.g., plants, animals, stars. But they can also be deployed introspectively to recognize certain internal properties which science, but not introspection, might show to be physical chemical ones (pp 201–2). Recognitional concepts are in this way "conceptually independent" of the scientific ones that might be recruited to explain their deployment (p 202). And Brian thinks this goes a little way towards explaining the "explanatory gap" that Levine (1983) and others have noted between the physical and the phenomenal, but without metaphysical commitments to any sort of dualism.

But Brian (ibid., p. 210) recognizes that it really doesn't go very far, since there doesn't seem to be an explanatory gap between the physical and, say, a style of art that one might recognize demonstratively. Brian goes to try to explain the irreducibility of our concepts of our usual *phenomenal* states as due to a kind of modal "transparency" people seem to expect of the phenomenal, whereby

> It is natural to regard our conceptions of phenomenal qualities as conceiving of them as they are in themselves, that is, to suppose we have a direct grasp of their essence.
>
> (p. 211)

It seems to us, Brian suggests, that we know introspectively all there is to know about the nature of pain, and so we are averse to the suggestion that it may have some (further?) essentially physical properties.

I'm not sure that even this suggestion captures what is troubling about our conception of the phenomenal—even if there were further essential properties of it that were opaque to me, I still might be perplexed about how the properties that do seem evident could possibly be physical—but I'll suppose for the sake of argument that it does. The issue I want to pursue here is whether the strategy is plausible for the intentional and the apparent explanatory gap that many, following Brentano, have thought also lies between it and the physical.

I think it may help to understand Brian's strategy—both some of its appeal, but also, we'll see, some of its limitations—to compare recognitional-demonstratives to the striking case of essentially first-person indexical thought, which arguably involves a symbol constrained in one's system of internal representation in ways analogous to the constraints on the first-person pronoun, "I".[5] Thus, it might be a symbol that can be betokened *only* by individual thinkers themselves as a result of either sensory stimulation, self-attribution of a mental state, or in causing oneself to act. In such a case, there is of course a sense in which the concept expressed by such a symbol would be hopelessly subjective and perspectival. A person's "I" thoughts could only be thought by the person himself, and they wouldn't be psychologically equivalent to a thought expressed without that indexical: *I am ill* is not the same thought as *GR is ill* or *the present thinker is ill*, since I could have the *I* thought while being totally amnesiac about my identity, and even about my status as a thinker.

I would expect that a demonstrative-recognitional thought would be subject to analogous conditions surrounding the use of a mental first-person indexical, although spelling them in detail might be difficult. For starters, we'd need to explain how a recognitional demonstrative picks out a *kind* of state, unlike "I" which picks out the specific individual who uses it (so far as I know, Brian nowhere attempts to do so). Moreover, as with the phenomenal, it can certainly *seem* as though our own "I" thoughts are "transparent" to us: it's my use of (the mental equivalent of) "I" that seems to put me in touch with something that seems "essentially me." And one can feel something of an explanatory gap between it and the physical—witness the extensive literature on a personal identity that seems to go beyond the usual objective, e.g., bodily criteria that are standardly provided for it.[6]

Different people can, of course, each have thoughts, each about themselves, since they each have a symbol in their brain that also respects the same constraints. Similarly, for Brian, "a recognitional concept can be ascribed outside its constitutive perspective" (1997/2017:201): the very kinds of states I discriminate in my own case could be discriminated using the same recognitional concepts by others in their own cases, and all of the states so discriminated, at least in the case of sensations, could plausibly turn out to be the very same kinds of physio-chemical states. Thus, do we have concepts of other people's phenomenal states, and, we might add, as we do of their first-person indexical ones? Again, this is not the place to consider whether this strategy succeeds for the phenomenal. The question for us whether it can be extended to account for the intentional.

Brian explicitly intended to extend the strategy to the intentional:

> I will now sketch a strategy that takes the subjective as primary: an objective relation is *semantic* by virtue of its direct or indirect connections with subjective intentionality.
>
> (1987/2017:190)

> The intentional notions . . . of specific guiding conceptions, of conceiving a reference as an external object, and so on, should be taken as reflexive or subjective notions, arising not within an objective or impersonal framework of descriptions and explanation, but from subjective reflection on how our own thoughts appear to us. The third-person use of such intentional notions can be regarded as sort of projection.
>
> (1991/2017:236)

He provided a "display" account of how our own thought appears to us whereby we at least sometimes deploy it with immediate authority each in our own case:

> My thoughts appear *self-interpreting*. . . . [W[hen I display a thought in order to think to think about it, my conception incorporates certain aspects of the displayed thought.
>
> (1987/2017:175–178)

For example:

> My thought that Freud lived in Vienna appears transparent or intrinsically directed at objects because from my subjective perspective nothing would count as bringing it in to the scene without also bringing on Freud and Vienna. Thus, what makes certain thoughts *about Freud*, from my perspective, is simply that they have this in common: if the thought heaves into sight, so does inevitably does Freud.
>
> (1987/2017: 176)[7]

As he puts it in his (1995):

> A certain primitive idea of what thought is *about*, it is natural to say, derives from concepts' appearing to bring objects onto the subjective scene.
>
> (1995/2017: 264)

Interestingly, he claims that this displaying of a concept has a specific introspectible, phenomenal character like the sort we find in the case of sensations. This is such an (at least for me) unusual idea, it's worth quoting it in full:

> It seems quite natural that when a concept-object pair is thus displayed—without explicit semantic commentary—it will appear to have a characteristic configuration, a distinctive feel, as if the object is peculiarly *salient* in the company of the concept.
>
> (ibid: 264)
>
> A [visual demonstrative reference relation] O* is a reference relation because it holds of pairs linked *in that way*. Here we have to suppose that "in that way" applies across concept categories. This means that pairs such as the following have an intuitive phenomenological similarity: <the next occurrence of "that tree", that tree>, <"Plato", Plato>, <"copper", copper>, and so on. Evidently this makes sense only when one exercises those concepts for oneself. Given that the similarity among the pairs is not objective—is merely subjective—then so is what makes a relation a reference relation. But we have a reasonable understanding of what that is.
>
> (p266)

That is, Brian actually seems to think of these features as "intentional qualia" (ibid.:p281), or, again, as he picturesquely puts it, "the paint that points" (2003/2017:314).

As in the case of sensations, being able to think about my own thoughts by displaying them in this way provides a basis for thinking about the thoughts of others:

> [C]onceiving how another person conceives things is *projective* and not *descriptive*. I understand your thought by thinking (i.e., entertaining) a thought so as to be in a position to judge that you have a thought like that one. . . . I try out a thought. I project it onto you, and if in fact you have a thought like that one, I understand how you think.
> (1987/2017: 180)

That is, I "display" the thought to myself and then suppose that it's similarly displayed for others.

Brian thought that intentional ascription in general is rooted in such idiosyncratic first-person attribution, analogously to the way he thought we have a general concept of others' phenomenal experience. He argued that such an approach has the advantage of explaining how *the properties or relations* picked out by intentional *concepts* are in fact physical properties and relations, despite these latter concepts not being "reducible" to physical terms:

> A complete objective description leaves out subjective conceptions, not because it cannot fully characterize the properties they discriminate or fully account for the concepts themselves as psychological states, but simply because it does not employ them.
> (1997/2017: 212–213)

This is, or course, precisely the situation with "I" thoughts, there being a perfectly plain objective explanation of the specially restricted processes that give rise to a non-objective first-person conception of oneself that couldn't itself be expressed objectively.

Intentionality, of course. involves a lot more than mere indexical and demonstrative thoughts, and Brian recognizes the need of a "theory theory":

> both reference and truth are concepts in some large theory relating thoughts to the world, a theory that explains objective individual and social properties distinctively enough that a special category results—the semantic.
> (1987/2017:190)

But, since he thinks that the property can't be entirely objective, he advocated "a theory-theory strongly anchored to a subjective element" (p. 190), i.e., to the display feature of how a person thinks about their own thoughts, and presumably that this display feature and its essential nature are "transparent" to the thinker.

## 2.1. *What Brian Was Not Claiming*

### 2.1.1. *Not Metaphysical?*

On the whole, Brian seems to think of subjective intentionality as a feature of our *conceptions* of our thoughts, not as a metaphysical property of the thought states themselves. Indeed, he is seen as being one of the pioneers of the "phenomenal concept strategy", characterized by Katalin Balog (2017)[8] as:

> The idea that [the relevant] conceptual, epistemic, and explanatory gaps can be explained by the nature of phenomenal *concepts* rather than [by] the nature of non-physical phenomenal properties.
>
> Balog (2017:138)

This, at any rate, is how Balog understands at least Brian's (1995/2017) view, which she thinks:

> should not be taken as a denial that reference consist[s] in perfectly *naturalistic, physical-functional relations between concepts and their referents*. It is rather an instance of Brian's general outlook—labeled by Chalmers (2002) in the context of the metaphysics of consciousness "type B materialism"—according to which one should take subjective phenomena and the subjective perspective fully seriously and then explain *the failure of various third-person strategies to understand the phenomenon via appealing to the conceptual isolation of first-person subjective understanding*.
>
> (ibid., p. 149, emphasis mine)

However, Brian sometimes does express the view more metaphysically:

> a relation's (property's) *being semantic is not an objective feature of it*, even though *such a relation (property) is itself objective*, and connects us in real enough ways to the real world.
>
> Loar (1987/2017):190, emphasis mine)

That is: there are objective relations that connect us to the world, but their *being semantic* is not an objective property of those relations.

This is also how, in a recent review of Loar (2017a), Joe Levine seems to understand Brian's project.

> Our experience of subjective intentionality gives rise to a kind of "phenomenal concept" of thought—a first-person perspective concept that is triggered in the very having of a thought, and *there is no*

> *way to infer* descriptions involving such concepts from those couched in purely third-person, naturalistic terms.
>
> Levine (2018, emphasis mine)

But precisely to what extent Brian thinks *there is no way to "infer"* the subjective from the objectively is actually not entirely clear. On the one hand he insisted that "there is no question of an objective explanation of why the [objective and subjective referential] relations should coincide, given that one of them arises only from the subjective perspective" (1987/2017: 190), but on the other, as in the passage just quoted above (1997/2017: 212–213), he seemed to allow that an "objective description . . . could fully account for the concepts themselves as psychological states", perhaps along the lines of a first-person indexical analogy that I have suggested. I find the latter plausible. After all, there's nothing explanatorily mysterious about a first-person indexical explained as involving constraints on the role of a certain symbol in one's thought, even if the specific perspectival content it expresses may not be enjoyed by anyone but the person entertaining it. Why shouldn't we able to make analogous inferences in the case of people's use of recognitional-demonstratives? Just as I can have a sense of myself by reflecting on the role in my mind of a first-person indexical, so can I have a sense of my phenomenal states by reflecting on the role in my mind of recognitional-demonstratives, even though the specific concepts I deploy couldn't be conveyed in physical terms.

Since Brian did carefully distinguish concepts from "qualities" at his (1997/2017:195–196), and my concerns don't really turn on the metaphysical issue, I shall simply assume he was speaking in the loose way whereby "features" can be mere conceptions, not real properties. So I will understand his view to be that, apart from our subjective conceptions, there are no objective facts about semantics, but that there are if we include those subjective conceptions. The view seems to me rather like a dispositional view of color properties: the intentionality of a state, like the supposed color of a rose, is inherently based upon how human beings react and think of certain objective phenomena, and cannot be characterized in isolation from those reactions. So construed, Brian's appeal to recognitional concepts tries to explain the explanatory gap, but without any extravagant metaphysics.

#### *2.1.2. Not Genetic or Epistemic*

One sort of data that might be thought to cast doubt on SPI is the fact that much intentional ascription doesn't *appear* to involve a projection from the first-person, indeed, may not be available to those who deploy it. Particularly striking in this regard is a recent study by Hamlin and Wynn (2011) which tested the reactions of mere four-month-old infants to "Heider-Simmel"-style cartoons: the infants seem to understand the motions of various simple geometric figures in cartoons as animate movements directed towards the satisfaction of certain goals: e.g., as a circle trying to ascend a slope to a ledge, a triangle helping it by pushing from below, and a square as hindering it by pushing down from above.[9] That is, they seem to be ascribing states to these figures intentional content that "refers", e.g., to the ledge and to the other figures, and, moreover, to be presuming that the figures, themselves, have thoughts about the other figures' intentions! It's hard to believe that the four-month-olds are projecting an experience they *introspectively* recognize as referring to these figures—indeed, that they have at that point much introspective thoughts about themselves or reference at all. Of course, perhaps they do. But showing this would certainly require some ingenious experimentation that to my knowledge, has not yet been done.[10]

Brian, however, stresses that he's not making a "genetic" claim:

> Perhaps despite appearances, I shall not be suggesting a genetic account of how a person's semantic conceptions arise; rather, the idea will be, one's thoughts on these matters naturally cohere in certain ways, and that coherence explains what is distinctive of semantical relations and properties.
>
> (1987/2017:190)

Thus, the "theory-theory" of intentionality might be a (we can suppose) innate network of ideas that is triggered by the appearance of a certain animate-looking motion.

Nor is Brian's claim epistemic:

> A subjective account of semantic properties has nothing to do with epistemological foundationalism. We are not inside battling our way out; rather we have a vast array of beliefs, indeed, knowledge of the external world, and a question has arisen about the relation of subjective intentionality to the external world as we know it.
>
> (1987/2017:192)

So it may well be that people might be justified in ascribing intentional states to someone even though some premises about their own referential states didn't figure in the justification.

So what sort of claim is Brian making? I take his "theory-theory" that we set out above to be this: there is a complex network of ideas involving mental states which is rooted in an essential way in a person's subjective experience of their mental episodes of reference, in the way, perhaps, that a concept of person might be rooted in their use of a first-person indexical. A triggered idea need not evoke the justifications to which some might appeal if pressed.

### *§2.2. Brian's Reasons*

Speaking for myself, I must confess that I find Brian's view intuitively implausible. Since I first encountered them, I must say I've always been doubtful of the traditional "arguments from analogy", whereby people are supposed to know about the mental states of others by analogy with themselves. I know full well that other people and certainly many animals perceive and think about all manner of different things and in very different ways than I do, e.g., that some people and animals can sense and remember pitches and odors and echolocate in ways that I can't, and seem often to have experiences, desires, thoughts, and beliefs that I find quite alien. Even when I think other creatures may have thoughts with roughly the same intentional content as mine, I'd be very reluctant to think that they think them in *the same way* that I might display my own thoughts to myself (for starters, I expect foreigners often display thoughts in their own language which I likely don't know—intentional content is so much more *abstract* than what can plausibly be "displayed"). Nevertheless, I often find their behavior far more intelligible than I do my own—I think I know better why bees dance as they do than I know why I do (which is not to say I know "what it's like" to be a bee, or an echolocating bat). Charles Gallistel (1990) has provided us substantial understanding of how a great many animals navigate, and Clayton *et al.* (2007) plausible insights into the surprisingly complex psychology of corvids, all without the slightest commitment to the character of their own or the animals' subjective experiences, or even whether they have any at all, much less whether they are all alike. Moreover, *pace* Sydney Shoemaker (1996), I see nothing incoherent in the possibility of there being people who are "self-blind": they may be incapable of introspection, thinking of themselves in the same "objective" way that they think of others, quite along the lines Peter Carruthers (2011) has claimed is in fact true of us all (which is not to say I think it very likely), and which, of course, I suspect is true of the above four-month olds (at least for a while). So I wonder what drove Brian to his views.

From what I can tell, Brian provides two main motivations for PSI:

(i) a Quinean pessimism about the reduciblity of intentional talk/properties objective, to naturalistic (physical) terms.

and

(ii) a Cartesian insistence that one has special knowledge of one's own, subjective introspectible states that is not capturable from an objective third-person point of view, but that serves to render intentional states determinate (1987/2017: 173, 2003/2017: 303).

In what follows, I shall first raise reasons to be less anxious about (i) than Brian and too many other philosophers have been (§3), and then point to specific recent research on introspection that undermines Brian's recourse to (ii) as a solution to what he regards as the problems of (i) (§4).

## §3. Irreducibility and "Unmotivation"

I think one of Brian's reasons for PSI is his pessimism about the explanation of intentionality, and specifically of what he takes to be the lack of a sufficient connection between intentional states and the objective conditions of a brain (what he calls the "Argument from Non-Motivation" (1987/2017:166).

> Internal properties—whether biochemical, neurophysiological, psychofunctional, or common-sense functional—cannot motivate the ascription of, or explain, or imply, externally directed truth conditions.

I fear he thinks this because of standard "irreducibility" arguments, according to which necessary and sufficient conditions for intentional ascription cannot be provided in physicalistically acceptable terms:

> [T]o assert that there are properties that are internal, objectively intentional, and compatible with physicalism, presumably just means that their intentionality is expressible in—cognitively equivalent to something in—physicalist terms. How else could one construe "objectively intentional"?
>
> (1987/2017:187)

Now, to be sure, this linking of objectivity to reduction has been a widely held view since at least Quine (1953, 1960). I, myself, have been as mesmerized by it as any, but the more I've thought about it the more I'm become puzzled about exactly what the issue is that is so very pressing. For two reasons:

(i) Understood as a scientific question about integrating an intentionalist psychology into a general naturalistic (presumably ultimately physical) theory of the world, the requirement seems oddly premature. Psychology may not be still in its infancy, but it's pretty obviously going through a turbulent adolescence in which there is still not widespread agreement about its status and appropriate methodology: is it a mere instrument for making "rational" sense of people, or a theory that attempts to spell out the underlying mental structures that are responsible for behavior and various cognitive competencies? And if it is the latter (as I follow Chomsky and Fodor in thinking it is), surely no one yet has a seriously good idea about precisely what those structures are, what the significant functional parts (e.g., different "modules" for different domains and processes, different forms of memory and attention), and what sorts of (different?) data-structures are deployed in those different parts. Lacking any serious psychology of this sort, no one is in any position to specify the character of the (different?) intentional properties and relations it may require, much less show how those properties and relations might be integrated into lower level (e.g., neural, biological, chemical or physical) theories.[11]

Even if one thought—as I mentioned at the start Brian differed from me in thinking—that a theory of intentionality was only responsible to "common-sense" psychology, what reason is there to think that anyone really has a sufficient understanding of *it*? Is it one unified conception, or a motley of fragments of views of different aspects of human and animal mental processes? Are some of its dubious views (say, in free will and immortal souls) essential to it? Or can one flexibly defer to science as one does in other domains? Can even its general character really be ascertained by armchair reflection alone?[12]

(ii) A particular suggestion that surprisingly was not taken up by "functionalists" like Brian in the 1960s and later is that the ultimate account of intentionality, like accounts of mental states such as belief and desire, might be parts of a rich, Ramsified "functionalist" theory, no one term of which is "reducible" to expressions outside of the theory independently of a great many of the others.[13] Brian was, of course, hardly a stranger to such Ramsified reductions. His (1981) is a rich discussion of them. But, for all its richness, there seems to be a peculiar constraint that runs throughout it:

> A propositional attitude-ascription describes person's state in two dimensions: it places the state within a certain *system*—it captures the functional role, and it ascribes truth conditions. *These are distinct matters*: for functional role involves state's lateral connection with other states, input and output, while truth conditions involve vertical relations with extra-mental things, properties, and states of affairs.
>
> (1981: 57–8; see also p. 145,153)

Brian's (1981) book is more complex than can possibly be examined here, and perhaps I have missed a crucial argument in it, but I don't see why a functionalist should insist upon this ultimate division of labor between the internal "laterally" characterized attitude states of a thinker, and their "vertical" meanings, especially if the lateral functional states are "long armed", extending into the environment, in ways that Ned Block (1990) has urged they well might be. To be sure, one can set out the project of a computational theory of mind by distinguishing the two parts of the theory:

For any agent x, time t, and propositional attitude, *A that p*, there exists some computationally definable relation $C_A$ such that:

x A's that p at t iff $(\exists\sigma)(xC_A\sigma,t \ \& \ \sigma$ means that p$)$[14]

(where σ is presumably a sentence in x's system of internal representation). But while this is a valuable methodological distinction in how one proceeds theoretically, dividing the work on the purely computational aspects of psychology from the intentional aspects, it doesn't preclude at the end of the day Ramsifying over *both* clauses and ultimately defining mental states in terms of them both taken together as (to use a nice phrase of Shoemaker, 2000), an explanatory "package deal".

Brian (1987/2017) does briefly explore this possibility:

> Make the content of "observational" thoughts depend upon local or proximal input ("There goes a cat-like object", "This one is larger than that one"), and make the contents of the rest depend on their cognitive relations to observational thoughts. [Any] indeterminacy, it might be held, can be eliminated by Ramsifying: non-observational mental terms are cognitively tied to each other and to observational terms so that collectively they constitute a Theory, which then spreads satisfaction conditions from observational to non-observational terms.
>
> (1987/2017:167; see also p. 190)

He thinks, however, that this strategy faces the following problem:

> On the Ramseyan model truth conditions can spread from observational thoughts to the rest only if mental logical connectives and forms have suitable truth conditional properties. . . . Whence such semantic properties? You cannot just say: these features *behave* like disjunction, negation, existential quantification, predication. It would still be a substantive question what the *point* would be of assigning semantic interpretation on that basis. . . . What in the "inferential" relations among observational and non-observational would warrant assigning truth conditions to the latter *collectively*?

He concludes:

> Given only the internal facts, there seems to be no objective reason not to count the "non-observational thoughts" as some among myriad contentless states with causal relations to the observational thoughts. If such internal states play a role in psychological explanation, then would that not show merely that psychological explanation can, to that extent, abstract from truth conditions in favor of functional properties?
>
> (1987/2017: 167)

The worry seems to be that there's no intrinsic reason to ascribe content to material that merely causally interacts with the observation sentences.

But this overlooks the "package deal" and potentially "long arm" character of psychological explanation. Intentional explanation is invoked when no other explanation captures significant facts and regularities in an animal's states and behavior. The best explanations we have of navigational abilities, sensitivity to many perceptual stimuli, acquisition of language, elementary and sometimes quite sophisticated problem solving, and complex social interactions are ones in which intentional states are attributed not only to observational states, but to the logically complex internal states that are responsible for them and their relations to external phenomena. Surely there is explanatory "point" enough here for assigning quite subtle semantic interpretations to all manner of internal state, precisely along the lines that (non-behaviorist) psychologists increasingly do. That we could, if we chose, "abstract" to mere functional (or even merely syntactic) roles doesn't show that those roles aren't in fact precisely the roles identified by their relations to the world and which might play the roles of intentional states in a full psychology. Just how to spell out the ultimate theories of such diverse and complex functional roles of mental items, modules, processes, and abilities is substantial work that no one should expect to be finished soon, much less the project of integrating the resulting theories into the rest of our theories of the world.

In any case, the two issues I've raised here seem to me to provide strong reasons to resist the urgency of the requirement people have for a "reduction" of the intentional that seemed to be part of what was motivating Brian in his insistence on PSI in its stead.

## §4. Cartesian Privileges

But Brian was not motivated merely by pessimism about reduction. He was likely even more concerned to capture what he thought was right in a traditional Cartesian conception of first-person authority:

> From a pre-critical perspective, knowledge of my own thoughts is privileged in a certain way, and that perspective involves no apparent conceptions of external reference relations. This is a basic conception of mental representation, and, understood correctly, it makes sense of "representational content in the head" in a way compatible with the Argument from Unmotivation.
>
> (1987/2017: 172–173)

To my mind, however, even if there were a serious problem about the reduction of the intentional, it seems to me highly unlikely that an appeal to subjectivity would solve it. Despite Brian's imaginative efforts to show otherwise, subjectivity just doesn't seem to have the right sorts of resources, at least not in the case of semantic properties such as reference.

Brian's "demonstrative recognitional" concepts are a welcome addition to the understanding of people's conceptions of many sorts of phenomena, phenomenal states perhaps among them. But while the content of the usual phenomenal states involving colors and sensations may be somehow sufficiently clear and "immediate", and plausibly involves recognizing the same physical-functional state on different occasions, this seems to me far less likely in the case of intentionality.[15] As we noted above, Brian seems to think that the "directedness" of thought, and the related notions of "refer" and "about" are transparent notions that we can demonstratively "recognize" by noticing that when *we think that we have a thought that p* we do so by "displaying" the content [p] itself.

Perhaps Brian is capturing a feature of his introspections that I'm missing in mine, but, again, speaking for myself, I don't find there to be remotely an identifiable sensation or "quale" associated with the ascription of intentional states. The experience seems more like something more purely conceptual, rather in the way I might see an object as a car, or a writhing thing as a worm, as a result of conceptualizing certain genuinely sensory material regarding, e.g., shapes and movement in terms of my on-going theory of the world. I certainly would be less confident about applying one of Brian's recognitional-demonstratives in such cases as a way of identifying such an abstract property as *intentionality* (or purported referentiality or directedness). The abstractness and familiar difficulties in understanding this odd property seems to me to undermine any confidence that at least *I*, pre-theoretically, might have in thinking I am thereby "recognizing" the same underlying physical-functional state from occasion to occasion in myself, much less in others, as I plausibly might be doing in the case of genuinely sensory states. I'd be very surprised if others found themselves in a different position.

In any case, it seems to me that the most that can be had from Brian's "display" conception of self-knowledge is what Wittgenstein (1953/2016:§279) nicely parodied, as someone claiming they know how tall they are by placing their hand on their head to prove it ("displaying" their height?). Just as such a person could be picking out in fact different lengths on different such occasions, so might someone who is thinking about thinking some thought by "displaying" it be in fact thinking about a different relation in every case. There are, after all, so many different candidates: Frege's peculiar notion of "bedeutung", often translated as "reference", is a quite technical notion wedded to his specific theory of his formal language, and other logicians have other notions (e.g., of "assignments" and "satisfaction") for theirs; Russell famously argued that, despite appearances, neither "the present king of France" nor "the author of Waverly" are actually referring expressions at all—and, along those lines, one might well wonder what ordinary people are doing when they take themselves to be "referring" to non-existent entities, such as angels or gods. And, of course, Quine (1960:chap 2) famously argued that there was "no fact of the matter" about whether one was referring to, e.g., a rabbit or its undetached parts. But even when we take ourselves to succeed in "referring" to "actual things", do we really bear *the same relation* to all the enormously wide variety of them that we routinely take ourselves to be ordinarily referring to (or "thinking about"): not only the usual tables and chairs, trees and flowers, but *numbers, plays, contracts, pains, the sky, ocean waves, rainbows*; or (to take some now standard examples from Chomsky 2000:135) *flaws in arguments, "Joe Six Pack", a person's health*, and "*the inner track that Raytheon has on the latest missile contract*"?

Perhaps for many people the experience *seems* to them to be of the same relation, and perhaps even that it is "transparent" to them in a way that Brian thought gave rise to the explanatory gap. But surely whether it *is* the same relation and is "transparent" to us—or, really, whether it even *appears* to be; even this seems to me far from certain—is not an issue we can decide merely on the basis of their deploying a conception rooted in first-person displays and demonstratives. Why think that folk notions of "reference", "aboutness", "representation", are any clearer or determined subjectively than are folk notions of life, matter, motion, force, space, time—or, to take a case whose transparency we noted is notoriously problematic, personal identity? Indeed, one can well wonder with Wittgenstein whether in thinking we are detecting a relation of reference across the board in the way that Brian proposes, we aren't simply naively insisting on an essential unity that underlies what are actually quite diverse relations between our thoughts and the world.[16]

It is worth bearing in mind in this connection a possibility that Nisbett and Wilson (1977) raised in light of experiments on people's demonstrable tendencies to confabulate their "introspections". They propose that when people take themselves to be introspecting about mental processes:

> they do so not by consulting a memory of the mediating process, but by applying or generating causal theories about the effects of that type of stimulus on that type of response. . . . [T]hey may resort in the first instance to a pool of culturally supplied explanations for behavior of the sort in question or, failing in that, to search through a network of conative relations until they find an explanation that may be adduced as psychologically implying that behavior.
>
> (1977: 248–249)

Peter Carruthers (2011) cites further experiments on behalf of such skepticism about introspection of propositional attitudes, and, of course, Wittgenstein (1953/2016) and Ryle (1949) were highly skeptical of the conception of an inner "private world" of thoughts and sensations that many people take themselves to be introspecting. Whether or not any of these claims are correct about some of the specific cases they discuss,[17] there seem to me no question that they've undermined the right to the kind of *uncritical confidence* Cartesians like Brian seem to have had about introspective subjectivity generally, particularly about notions as fraught as *reference* and *intentionality*—or their essential conditions![18] It seems to me that, even here, *appearances of appearances* can be deceptive: it can appear to us that we couldn't be wrong about how things appear to us, but why couldn't we be misunderstanding how things appear to us? Why suppose there even *appears* to be "phenomenal paint", or, if there is, that *it* appears to be pointing? Maybe we're just in the grip of a traditional Cartesian picture. Consequently, I don't think Brian was entitled to claim without a more detailed theory of self-knowledge that we have a serious grasp of our own subjective intentionality.

In any case, it is simply not true of *me* that I regard my subjective "first-person *perspective* on the reference of my own thoughts as somehow essential or constitutive of my conception of reference, intentionality, or 'aboutness'" (1995/2017:272). As I indicated earlier, I find that my own experience of intentionality is based more on explanations of a very wide assortment of people, many of them foreign or otherwise quite different from myself, as well as on the behavior of birds, bees, and babies, none which really seems to depend upon my subjective conceptions, much less my always projecting my own thoughts into them.

## §5. Conclusion

I have no doubt that Brian's category of "recognitional concepts" and his "display" notions of self-conscious thought may have a role to play in an account of our ordinary conceptions of intentionality, of some of the privileges we think we each enjoy about our introspectible lives, and why those conceptions seem resistant to objective explanation. My quarrel with Brian's views is over whether they are in any way *foundational* to a theory of intentionality, in a way that would solve the problems he thought attached to its apparent irreducibility. They seem either not sufficiently substantive or, if substantive, not sufficiently reliable for the purpose. And, in any case, given the lack yet of any sufficiently articulated psychological theories of propositional attitude states in humans and animals, it's hard to see why the problems about the irreducibility of the intentional shouldn't be postponed until we have them, and are then in a position to set about the (likely tedious) task of Ramsification. But I guess this latter point is a fundamental methodological issue over which an Oxonian like Brian and an MIT enthusiast like myself never quite agreed, despite the richness of our friendship and conversations.

## Notes

1. This paper is a continuation of long exchanges between Brian and myself over many years, and in many different places: conferences, cafes, museums, train stations. I, of course, wish he were still here to make what would inevitably be imaginative replies. This all remains so vividly a personal dialogue that I find I can't refer to him other than by "Brian." I do trust that, like many

philosophers, Brian would take my efforts here to clarify our disagreements to be a perfectly fine way to honor him, as I and the present volume intend.

I'm grateful to Janet Levin for perceptive comments on an earlier draft, and for allowing me to see a draft of her contribution to this volume.

2. It's clear from many passages that Brian takes himself to be in general concerned with "common-sense psychological explanation", as contrasted with explanations in a scientific psychology (see, e.g., 1988/2017:153–154n3). A passage revealing of the difference between Brian's and my attitudes in this regard is his passing treatment of Chomskyan linguistics:

> There may be a Chomskyan sense of knowledge—having an internal representation—in which a speaker knows the rules of his language, but that is a psychological hypothesis and, however reasonable it is, we do not want to build into it an *explication* of what it is for *L* to be the language of [a population] *P*. Better that it be offered at a later stage, as an *explanation* of how it is possible for a complex entity like English to be the language of the population of English speakers.
>
> Loar (2017b:45)

But, as Chomsky (1986:20–22) has reasonably insisted, the notion of what is ordinarily taken to be the *external* language of a population is not particularly well-defined, and in any case has far less place in a serious linguistic theory than the notion on an internal computational system underling individual linguistic competence. I see no reason to think that, here, as in the familiar cases of other natural kinds (such as chemical elements or diseases; see Putnam 1962/1975a, 1975b), the underling scientific *explanation* of a phenomenon (or our concept of it) may be precisely what provides its best *explication* (or serious definition). Brian would likely have disagreed.

3. This would depend in part on whether phenomenal states involve problematic "qualia" over and above representations of them in people's minds/brains. I doubt that they do (see my 1996, 1997, 2018), but, to put it mildly, the issue is much disputed, and I have no need to discuss it here.
4. Versions of SPI are also defended by Bealer (1984) and Searle (1991). Bealer essentially deploys Quinean arguments in the context of a common-sense rather than behavioristic psychology (about which, more below). Searle's main argument is that no objective account of mental states could capture what he calls "aspectual shape", or the different ways a mind may construe the world, as in the case of thinking of water as "$H_2O$" or as merely "water." But, as his own nomenclature shows, this is patently false: it could surely be an objective feature of a brain that it represented water with a complex chemical formula or with a simple primitive (see Rey, 1991 for discussion). Uriah Kriegel (2014), inspired by Brian, defends SPI as a rich research strategy with many followers. I shan't address here what further reasons for SPI these authors may advance.
5. Cf. Frege (1918/1984), Castañeda (1966), Perry (1979). I imagine a specific way in which such a symbol might be incorporated into a language of thought in my (1997:chap 11). For simplicity in the present discussion I shall assume that people's systems of internal representation involve a "language of thought", a view to which Brian was not entirely inhospitable; see his (1987/2017:83).
6. Cf. Roderick Chisholm's (1976) interesting insistence that there is a fact about who someone is even after a perfectly symmetrical "split-brain" case. See Peacocke (1992:215ff) for discussion.

7. Of course, Brian couldn't have meant that Freud, *himself*, *literally* heaves into view. In his (1995/2017) he seems to recognize this and indicates what I think he has in mind by talking about "concept-concept pairs: (" "George Sand" ", "George Sand"), (" "Lisbon" ", "Lisbon")" (1995/2017:262), raising it all, as it were, one semantic level (of course, in the case of *thought* it perhaps need not be the pairing of *natural language* expressions). In this way, Brian's view can be regarded as a kind of "disquotational" theory of self-knowledge, only applied to thoughts, not words (unless, of course, thoughts just *are* words). Similar views were proposed by Davidson (1987). I think it may be how Quine (1969) thought of knowledge of our own thought content, when "we acquiesce in our mother tongue and take our words at face value" (p49).
8. Readers who know Brian's work only from the original journal articles should consult Balog's (2017) introduction to his philosophy of mind papers for a useful perspective on them as a whole. She also discusses another issue that SPI by itself doesn't decide, that of "narrow content", or whether the content of thought depends only upon facts about the thinker's body, or also upon "wide" relations of the thinker to the external world. As she rightly points out, "the concept of intentionality could be essentially subjective even if there is no narrow content" (p145). Consequently I won't address the issue of narrow content here.
9. The cartoons were first created by Fritz Heider and Marianne Simmel (1944), and variants of them have been used in many experiments since. In the Hamlin and Wynn (2011) study, after exposure to the cartoons, the infants showed a preference to keep company with the "helpers" rather than the "hinderers", suggesting that they must have internally represented the motions of the figures in something like these terms. The stimulus material can be viewed at http://cic.psych.ubc.ca/research-materials-videos/example-stimuli and is amusing to watch by way of noting our own irresistible inclination to interpret the figures in precisely the same intentionalistic way.
10. It's hard enough to experiment on 4-month olds; seriously daunting to dream up an experiment to test their self-awareness of their own referential states.
11. Tyler Burge (1993) has expressed even stronger reservations about the requirement for reduction:

    > The flood of projects over the last two decades that attempt to fit mental causation or mental ontology into a "naturalistic picture of the world" strike me as having more in common with political or religious ideology than with a philosophy that maintains perspective on the difference between what is known and what is speculated. Materialism is not established, or even deeply supported, by science.
    >
    > (1993:117)

    This seems to me quite excessive in the opposite direction. As I argue in my (2001), materialism, broadly construed, is one of the most successful research programs ever undertaken. I just don't think its success is quite as pressing a matter as so many recent philosophers have supposed.
12. It's worth noting the degree to which intentional indeterminacy arguments like Quine's (1960) or Bealer's (1984) presume that somehow our position with respect to intentionality is like the position of Einstein reflecting on the indeterminacy of motion. But surely the comparison is embarrassing. Neither folk psychology, much less (of all things!) Skinnerian behaviorism are remotely comparable to the highly developed physics that concerned Einstein.

13. Thus, it is ironic that the very authors who noted that there was no way of defining, e.g., belief and desire independently of each other, are often ones who worry that characterizing intentionality of one state might involve mentioning that of another, as in Fodor (1987), in Brian's (1991/2017) critique of Fodor's proposal, as well as in Brian's (1995) worries about

    > a circle of interpretation. . . . The determinacy of singular demonstrative reference depends on the determinacy of the reference of the kind concepts that serve as qualifiers of the singular demonstratives, and *vice versa*. (1995:257)

    The uncertainty of Brian's views here is brought out by Balog (2017), who, on the one hand, writes that, for Brian, "semantic concepts have to be *functionally* explicated so as to fit intentionality into the natural physical order" (p145), but then two pages later notes that "according to Brian, on demonstrative reference, there is no way out of a vicious circle of interpretation" (p147). But what needs to be shown is that the circles here are in fact *vicious*. Especially for an advocate of Ramsified functionalism, the viciousness of a circle is inversely proportional to the size of the circle and its explanatory powers, and, as I'm stressing, there is no way to determine this absent serious psychological theory.
14. I develop this suggestion at length in my (1997:chaps 8–11). See Field (1978) for essentially the same formulation.
15. Katalin Balog (2017:152) and Janet Levin (this volume: §V) also express doubts about the extension (Levin also cites Sosa, 1995).
16. Perhaps surprisingly, recent advocates of something close to Wittgenstein's skepticism in this regard are Chomsky (2000) and Pietroski (2005).
17. I raise doubts about what seem to me Carruthers' needlessly extreme views in my 2013.
18. A further semi-skeptical remark about (*de re*) essentialist intuitions in this area. The view that phenomenal states are (*de re*) necessarily the kinds of states they are, e.g., pains necessarily pains, is false if, as many believe, such states are *functional* states, since it's clearly *contingent* whether some physical state plays a certain, e.g., "pain" role. Just as a weed might not (*de re*) be a weed, or a king a king, so might a pain not be a pain. "Pain", like "weed" and "king", may rigidly designate *a functional role*, not *the particular physical state* that realizes that role. Whether or not this is true, I see no reason to think the issue can be settled by introspection (see Feldman, 1974, and my 1997:§11.6 for discussion). None of which is to say there aren't *other* problems with functionalism, as with most views in this domain.

## References


Balog, K. (2017). Introduction to Loar (2017), Part II, pp. 137–152. In Loar.

Bealer, G. (1984). Mind and anti-mind: Thinking has no functional definition. *Midwest Studies in Philosophy*, 9:283–328.

Block, N. (1990). Inverted earth. In Tomberlin, J. (ed.), *Philosophical Perspectives 4*. Atascadero: Ridgeview Press.

Burge, T. (1993). Mind-body causation and explanatory practice. In Heil, J. and Mele, A. (eds.), *Mental Causation*. Oxford: Oxford University Press, pp. 97–120.

Carruthers, P. (2011). *The Opacity of Mind*. Oxford: Oxford University Press

Castañeda, H. (1966). 'He': A study in the logic of self-consciousness. *Ratio* (Misc.), 8:130–157.

Chalmers, D. (2002). Consciousness and its place in ature. In D. Chalmers (ed.), *Philosophy of Mind: Classical and Contemporary Readings*. Oxford: Oxford University Press.

Chisholm, R. (1976). *Person and Object: A Metaphysical Study*. La Salle, IL: Open Court.

Chomsky, N. (1986). *Knowledge of Language: Its Nature, Origin and Use*. New York: Praeger.

——— (2000). *New Horizons in the Study of Language*. Cambridge: Cambridge University Press.

Clayton, N., Dally, J. & Emery, N. (2007). Social cognition by food-caching corvids: The western scrub-jay as a natural psychologist. *Philos Transactions of the Royal Society, B: Biol Sciences* (1480):507–522. Published online 2007 Feb 19. doi: 10.1098/rstb.2006.1992

Davidson, D. (1987). Knowing one's own mind. *Proceedings and Addresses of the American Philosophical Association*, 60:441–458.

Feldman, F. (1974/1980). Kripke on the identity theory. *Journal of Philosophy*, 71:665–676.

Field, H. (1978). Mental representation. *Erkenntnis*, 13:9–61.

Fodor, J. (1987). *Psychosemantics*. Cambridge: MIT Press

Frege, G. (1918/1984). Translated as 'Thoughts' by P. Geach and R. Stoothoff. In McGuinness, B. (ed.), *Collected Papers on Mathematics, Logic, and Philosophy*. Oxford: Blackwell, pp. 351–372.

Gallistel, C. (1990). *The Organization of Learning*. Cambridge, MA: Bradford Books/MIT Press.

Hamlin, J.K. & Wynn, K. (2011). Young infants prefer prosocial to antisocial others. *Cognitive Development*, 26(1):30–39. https://psycnet.apa.org/record/2011-03172-003

Heider, F. & Simmel, M. (1944). An experimental study of apparent behavior. *The American Journal of Psychology*, 57: 243–259. http://dx.doi.org/10.2307

Kriegel, U. (2014). Two notions of mental representation. In Kriegel, U. (ed.), *Current Controversies in Philosophy of Mind*. New York: Routledge.

Levin, J. (this volume). "Phenomenal concepts" and the scope of the phenomenal concepts strategy.

Levine, J. (1983). Materialism and qualia: The explanatory gap. *Pacific Philosophical Quarterly*, 34:354–361.

——— (2018). Review of Loar (2017). *Notre Dame Philosophical Reviews*, September 24.

Loar, B. (1981). *Mind and Meaning*. Cambridge: Cambridge University Press.

——— (1987/2017). Subjective intentionality. In Loar (2017a), pp. 165–194.

——— (1988/2017). Social content and psychological content. In Loar (2017a), pp. 153–164.

——— (1991/2017:236). Can we explain intentionality. In Loar (2017a), pp. 220–237.

——— (1995/2017). Reference from a first-person perspective. In Loar (2017a), pp. 256–272.

——— (1997/2017). Phenomenal states: Second version. In Loar (2017a), pp. 195–219.

——— (2003/2017). Phenomenal intentionality as the basis for mental content. *In Loar*, 2017a: 291–317.
——— (2017a). *Consciousness and Meaning*. Oxford: Oxford University Press.
——— (2017b). Two theories of meaning. In Loar (2017a), pp. 29–47.
Nisbett, R.E. & Wilson, T.D. (1977). Telling more than we can know: Verbal reports on mental processes. *Psychological Review*, 84(3):231.
Peacocke, C. (1992). *A Study of Concepts*. Cambridge: MIT Press.
Perry, J. (1979). The problem of the essential indexical. *Noûs*, 13:3–21.
Pietroski, P. (2005). Meaning before truth. In Preyer, G. & Peters, G. (eds.), *Contextualism in Philosophy*. Oxford: Oxford University Press.
Putnam, H. (1962/1975a). Dreaming and depth grammar. In *Mind, Language and Reality: Collected Philosophical Papers*, vol II. Cambridge: Cambridge University Press, pp. 304–324.
——— (1975b). The meaning of 'meaning'. In *Mind, Language and Reality: Collected Philosophical Papers*, vol II. Cambridge: Cambridge University Press., pp. 215–271.
Quine, W. (1953/1961b). Two dogmas of empiricism. In *From a Logical Point of View*, 2nd revised edition. New York: Harper & Row, pp. 20–47.
——— (1960). *Word and Object*. Cambridge: MIT Press.
——— (1969). Ontological relativity. In *Ontological Relativity and Other Essays*. New York: Columbia University Press.
Rey, G. (1991). Constitutive causation and the reality of mind: Commentary on John Searle, consciousness, explanatory inversion, and cognitive science. *Behavioral and Brain Sciences*, 13(4):620–621.
——— (1996). Towards a projectivist account of conscious experience. In Metzinger, T. (ed.), *Conscious Experience*. Paderhorn: Ferdinand-Schoeningh-Verlag, pp. 123–142.
——— (1997). *Contemporary Philosophy of Mind: A Contentiously Classical Approach*. Oxford: Blackwell.
——— (2001). Physicalism and psychology: A plea for a more substantive philosophy of mind. In Gillet, C. & Lower, B. (eds.), *Physicalism and Its Discontents*. Cambridge: Cambridge University Press.
——— (2013). We aren't all self-blind: A defense of a modest introspectionism. *Mind and Language*, 28(3):259–285.
——— (2018). Taking consciousness seriously: As an illusion: Commentary on keith frankish, illusionism as a theory of consciousness. *Journal of Consciousness Studies*:197–214.
Ryle, G. (1949). *The Concept of Mind*. London: Hutcheson.
Searle, J. (1991). Consciousness, explanatory inversion, and cognitive science. *Behavioral and Brain Sciences*, 13(4):585–596.
Shoemaker, S. (1988/1996). On knowing one's own mind. In Shoemaker (1996), *The First-Person Perspective and Other Essays*. New York: Cambridge University Press, pp. 25–49.
———. (2000). Introspection and phenomenal character. *Philosophical Topics*, 28(2):247–273.
Sosa, D. (1995). Reference from a perspective versus reference. *Philosophical Issues*, 6:79–89.
Wittgenstein, L. (1953/2016). *Philosophical Investigations*, 4th revised edition, edited and trans by G.E.M Anscombe, P. M. S. Hacker & J. Schulte. Chichester, UK: John Wiley and Sons Ltd.

# Contributors

**Katalin Balog** (Rutgers University—Newark) wrote a PhD dissertation on "Conceivability and Consciousness" supervised by Brian Loar. Her primary areas of research remain the philosophy of mind and metaphysics—especially problems which lie at their intersection, such as subjectivity, the self, and free will.

**David Bourget** (University of Western Ontario) is a philosopher of mind whose research specializes on consciousness, representation, and intentionality. He is also well known for computing projects that support research in Philosophy—David is the Director of the Center for Digital Philosophy at Western, which maintains and develops the unparalleled PhilPapers.

**Daniel W. Harris** (Hunter College) works primarily in the philosophy of language and the philosophy of psychology, and is doing innovative work at the intersection of those two fields—on the cognitive underpinnings of humans' capacity for communication.

**Uriah Kriegel** (Jean Nicod Institute) works primarily in the philosophy of mind and metaphysics. Much of his recent work has focused on the structure of conscious phenomena beyond perceptual consciousness, involving some relatively neglected modes of conscious experience, such as agentive, emotional, and moral consciousness.

**Janet Levin** (University of Southern California) was a colleague of Brian Loar's at USC. Her research is focused on the philosophy of mind, philosophy of psychology, and epistemology. She has done a lot of influential work on qualia, phenomenal concepts, functionalist approaches to the mind, and the varieties of materialism.

**Joseph Levine** (University of Massachusetts—Amherst) is widely known for his explorations of the explanatory gap between the subjective experience of consciousness and the objective characterization provided by science. He has published extensively on relations between conceivability and possibility, and other modal aspects of the mind-body problem.

**Michelle Montague** (University of Texas at Austin) researches in the philosophy of mind, metaphysics, the philosophy of language, and the history of analytic philosophy. Her recent projects have been focused on the nature of mental content, and have involved original explorations into the intersection of intentionality and phenomenology.

**John Perry** (Stanford University and University of California, Riverside) has been a leading figure at the forefront of the philosophy of language and the philosophy of mind since the 1970s. Among a long list of important contributions, his work on indexicality, reference, and content is an essential part of the canon.

**David Pitt** (California State University, Los Angeles) is primarily a philosopher of mind, who has also published wide-ranging work in metaphysics, philosophy of psychology, and the philosophy of language. David's recent research has focused on consciousness, indexicality, and phenomenal content.

**François Recanati** (Collège de France) is one of the most widely-read and influential contemporary philosophers of language. From speech acts to the theory of reference, from contexts to contents to cognitive files, it is hard to think of an important topic in the field to which François has not made a significant important contribution.

**Georges Rey** (University of Maryland, College Park) works primarily in the philosophy of mind and cognitive science. Stretching over decades, Georges has published numerous articles on rationality, conscious experience, mental content, and linguistic competence. He is perhaps best known for his thorough-going computationalism.

**Mark Sainsbury** (University of Texas at Austin) overlapped with Brian Loar at Magdalen College, Oxford, from 1968–1970. Mark has a very impressive array of achievements, spanning the history of analytic philosophy, philosophical logic, and multiple sub-areas within the philosophy of language and mind.

**Stephen Schiffer** (New York University) is also one of the most influential contemporary philosophers of language. Beginning with his first major publication *Meaning* (Clarendon Press, 1972) and continuing on into this present paper, no one has contributed more seminal work on the notion of meaning.

**Arthur Sullivan** (Memorial University of Newfoundland) is a philosopher of language whose research is focused primarily on the theory of reference, semantic externalism, and the semantics/pragmatics interface.

**Michael Tye** (University of Texas at Austin) is an accomplished philosopher of mind, known for his defence of a representationalist view of consciousness. Recent areas of research include perceptual states, phenomenal concepts, and animal minds.

# Index

9781032337906